D1562038

Parties and Elections in Corporate America

Parties and Elections in Corporate America

Howard L. Reiter

The University of Connecticut

St. Martin's Press   New York

Library of Congress Catalog Card Number: 86–60654
Copyright © 1987 by St. Martin's Press, Inc.
All Rights Reserved.
Manufactured in the United States of America.
10987
fedcba
For information, write St. Martin's Press, Inc.
175 Fifth Avenue, New York, NY 10010
cover design: Darby Downey
cover illustration: Eldon Doty
ISBN: 0–312–59758–4

Acknowledgments

Excerpts from *American National Election Studies Data Sourcebook 1952–1978,*
Warren E. Miller, Arthur H. Miller, and Edward J. Schneider. Cambridge: Harvard University Press, 1980. Data from pp. 81, 257–258, 261, 262, 385, 387.
Reprinted by permission of Harvard University Press.

From *Plunkitt of Tammany Hall* by William L. Riordan. First published 1963 by
E.P. Dutton. All rights reserved. Reprinted by permission of the publisher, E.P.
Dutton, a division of New American Library.

For Laura

Preface

This is an unusual textbook. If you compare it with others that are used at other colleges and universities, you will discover that this is very—even *radically*—different from them. Before reading it, you should know how it is different, and why.

First, this is an opinionated presentation of the realities of party politics in the United States. This in itself is not unique. Most parties texts deliberately present a point of view, usually on the question of what kinds of parties would be best for America. Some prefer highly centralized parties that stress issues; others want parties that seek only to win elections and not to promote issues. Both approaches (and there are others) accept the fundamentals of the American political system—corporate capitalism and fragmented government—and merely try to make the best of it. This book begins with the premise that the American system is fundamentally flawed, that other systems would better serve the needs of the American people, and that the kind of party system we have is a major element of that flawed system. It is a radical approach, and I make no apologies for it.

Some of you are thinking, Why did I write a book that is so opinionated? Why couldn't I have written an "objective" text? The answer is that there is no such thing as an objective text. Some of them, as I have noted, take viewpoints different from mine and argue them. Others do try to be neutral, but with these there are two problems. One is that neutrality is painfully boring. I could have written a text that would say uncontroversial things like, "There are two major parties in the United States. One is the Democratic party, the other the Republican. The Democrats controlled both houses of Congress from 1955 until 1981, and the House of Representatives since. The Republicans have won six of the past nine Presidential elections. Whether this is a good thing or a bad thing is up to you." Had I written this, I would have fallen asleep at the typewriter before the first chapter was completed, and you would have fallen asleep reading the first page.

Even if an especially gifted writer could write an exciting text that strove for neutrality, the second problem with "objective texts" is more serious—they are impossible. Every author has biases, beginning with the decision of what to write. The author of a parties text is implicitly saying, "I think that political parties are important, important enough to write a book about." *That* is a value judgment. Next comes what to put in the book. Do we include (as some texts do not) a chapter on the Presidency? How many pages will be devoted to national party conventions? How many to local organization? *These* are value judgments. The relative amounts of space given to different subjects are an expression of their importance to the author. But most important of all, a "neutral" text has an implicit bias. *If it is not criticizing the system, it is tacitly accepting it.* Merely to *describe* the Democratic party organization in Congress without passing judgment on it is to imply, "The system works fine, and here's what it looks like."

Now some of you are thinking, Why is he trying to brainwash me with his radical opinions? First of all, I do not delude myself into thinking that a couple of hundred pages read over a few weeks will overturn two decades of socialization into dominant American values. Some of you will be convinced, others (perhaps most) not. But bear in mind that all education is a kind of brainwashing, and texts which argue for the existing political system, or claim neutrality, are brainwashing you in the other direction. And that direction, after all, has a lot more support in society than mine. So relax and try to keep an open mind.

There is a second way in which this book is different from all other parties texts, and it comes from the artificial and misleading way we teach about human life in our educational system. I teach political science; the folks upstairs in my building teach economics; next door they teach psychology; across the street in one direction they teach sociology, and in another direction they teach literature. The student is left to conclude that these are easily separable entities, that politics can be meaningfully studied without understanding economics, society, and so forth. And if you look at other texts on political parties or almost any other area of American politics and government, you will see a lot about narrowly political institutions (Congress, the Presidency, the courts) and behavior (voting, running for office, writing to the mayor), but little or nothing about non-governmental power structures or about how closely entwined the political system is with the rest of American life. To be sure, authors will give lip service to how the diversity of the American people produces a multiplicity of interest groups and voting blocs with various claims on government, and how the government tries to balance their claims, but there is usually little or nothing about how the political system as a whole serves the needs of those who wield power in the private realm. One great advantage of a radical approach is that it pays close attention to this relationship, although you do not have to be a radical to see it. Scholars of various viewpoints have argued it, but political scientists who write parties textbooks seldom seem to do so.

This book represents a departure for me in several ways, and many people provided the encouragement that enabled me to forge on. I am indebted to John Hibbing of the University of Nebraska, Karsten Jensen of the Aalborg Universitetscenter in Denmark, Sidney Milkis of Brandeis University, and Bruce Stave of the University of Connecticut for reading and criticizing various chapters. The staff of the Institute for Social Inquiry at the University of Connecticut was most helpful in assisting me in quantitative analysis, Stephen Sacks of the University of Connecticut generously guided me past many word processing snafus, Kathleen Frankovic and her capable staff at CBS News provided data quickly and graciously, and the Department of Government at the University of Essex in England provided a congenial setting during part of the preparation of this book. At St. Martin's Press my tag team of editors, Michael Weber, Peter Dougherty, and Larry Swanson, as well as Sarah Rosenthal, Richard Steins, Denise Quirk, and Vivian McLaughlin provided much good shepherding, and at their behest Alan Fisher of the California State University at Dominguez Hills, Marion Just of Wellesley College, Charles Longley of Bucknell University, and Edward Sidlow of Northwestern University demonstrated that pertinent and helpful criticism need not be conditioned on ideological agreement. My wife Laura not only read and criticized each chapter but also gave me her usual full measure of love and support.

Howard L. Reiter

Contents

Parties and Elections
in Corporate America

1

The Fallacy of Voting

On November 6, 1984, ninety-three million Americans trooped to the polls and cast their votes for president and numerous other offices. It was really a remarkable exercise—ninety-three million people, each convinced that going to a polling place and marking a ballot was a sensible thing to do. Indeed, most Americans consider voting to be the most important single element of American democracy; in the words of the man who won the American presidency that day, voting is "the crown jewel of American liberties."[1] The right to vote is considered so central that it is cited as the reason that Americans die in wars. Voting is the least controversial of the demands that oppressed groups make, and the right that Americans expect foreign nations like South Vietnam and El Salvador to guarantee if they expect our support.

Why has voting always been so venerated by Americans? The answer we usually think of is that voting is the way in which the political beliefs of the American people are translated into government policy. By being given a choice of leaders, we supposedly can select the one whose views are closest to our own and therefore get those views carried out; of course, the stipulation is that a majority of the voters agree with us. In this way, the majority rules in our political system. It is a pleasant view of how American democracy works, but it is one with a number of problems.

ISSUES AND VOTING

Let us imagine, for example, several voters faced, on that November day in 1984, with a choice for president among Ronald Reagan, Walter Mondale, and several other candidates. (No doubt there really were voters who had the following thoughts.)

Joan: "I'd really like to vote for someone I agree with, but the problem is that the candidates are so vague about their views. And they say different things to different audiences. How can a voter decide? I'll just have to make a guess as to who will do what I want."

Bill: "I don't like any of them. Why do we always have to choose the lesser evil, instead of the greater good?"

Mary: "I guess I like Reagan more than Mondale on several issues, like cutting Federal spending, abortion, and stopping the Russians; but I like Mondale more on the Equal Rights Amendment, peace, and gun control. No matter who I vote for, I'm only going to get some of the policies I want."

Bob: "I like practically all of Reagan's policies, but I'm afraid he'll get us into a nuclear war. I may have to vote for Mondale for that reason alone, but I'd hate for anyone to think that I like his record."

Laura: "To me, there is no more important issue than national health insurance. Yet neither of the candidates wants it."

Sam: "I prefer Mondale's policies to Reagan's, but he has been such an inept candidate that I am going to vote for Reagan anyway. We need a strong leader in the White House."

Leslie: "I don't have a lot of time to devote to reading about the campaign or watching it on TV, but I know that Republicans generally favor the issues I like, so I guess I'll vote for Reagan for that reason."

Notice how each of these intelligent, issue-oriented voters makes it hard for us to interpret the presidential vote in 1984 as an expression of public opinion. Joan has a hard time telling where the candidates stand, and whatever choice she ends up making will hardly be an expression of which one represents her views best. Bill's vote for the "lesser evil" is hardly an endorsement of his chosen candidate's views. Mary's vote is only an endorsement of *some* of her candidate's positions, and a rejection of others. Bob's vote for Mondale is only an expression of his fear of Reagan, not a ratification of Mondale's views. Whoever gets Laura's vote does not express her view on the most important issue to her. Reagan does not express Sam's views on issues; he only got Sam's vote because of his personal qualities. And Reagan only represents Leslie's views if he fits Leslie's notion of a typical Republican candidate.

What all this means is that to interpret the fact that the millions of people who voted for Reagan were actually endorsing his policy views is seriously to misinterpret their motives, if indeed there were many Joans, Bills, Marys, Bobs, Lauras, Sams, and Leslies in his coalition. The same goes for Mondale or any other candidate. This realization makes a mockery of a winning candidate's claim that he or she has a "mandate" from the voters, having received instructions as to how to behave in office. Only those voters who know all of a candidate's major positions and agree with all of them can be said to have contributed to such a mandate. Even then, the winner has no mandate for carrying out less-publicized positions.

Indeed, it is possible for a candidate to win a majority of the vote while the voters reject most of his or her stands on issues. Imagine that Reagan and Mondale are running against each other in a three-person electorate; we'll call those voters John, Cathy and Lee. There are five issues important to the voters: ERA, budget cuts, disarmament, abortion, and busing. In the following table, we can see which candidate each voter agrees with on each issue:

	John	Cathy	Lee
ERA	Reagan	Reagan	Mondale
Budget cuts	Reagan	Mondale	Mondale
Disarmament	Mondale	Reagan	Mondale
Abortion	Reagan	Mondale	Mondale
Busing	Mondale	Reagan	Mondale

If you read *across* each issue in the table, you will see that two out of three voters agreed with Mondale on every issue except ERA. If you read *down* each voter's column, you will see that John and Cathy voted for Reagan—assuming that each voter chose the candidate whom he or she agreed with the most—and Lee voted for Mondale. Therefore Reagan won two-thirds of the voters, who agreed with him on only one out of five issues! I'm not suggesting that this kind of outcome ordinarily happens, but it is a good illustration of the problems of expecting elections to serve as an expression of public opinion.

Another variation of this problem is the possibility that a candidate may win by amassing a coalition of small groups of voters, each of which favors a policy that is highly unpopular with all other voters. By making selective appeals, a candidate can win the votes of people who want to bring back slavery, people who want to outlaw the eating of meat, people who want to expel New England from the union, and so forth, until that candidate has a majority—but on a platform that nobody supports.

In fact, most of the major issues in American history have been re-solved not by elections but by other historical forces. Take slavery, for example. The American people never elected a president who promised to abolish slavery. Abraham Lincoln was elected in 1860 on a platform not of abolition, but of simply limiting slavery to the states in which it was then located. When a civil war ensued and Lincoln saw abolition as a useful military tactic, he signed the Emancipation Proclamation, which limited emancipation only to the areas still controlled by the Confederacy. In other words it was the war, and not the vote of the American people, that abolished slavery. Similarly, the New Deal's program of social welfare in the 1930s was not brought to power by popular mandate. Franklin D. Roosevelt was elected in 1932 promising to balance the budget, and the New Deal was only a slogan. The only mandate Roosevelt received was one to experiment, and it was over the next several years that his program took shape. Indeed, the only issue referred to in the headline in the *New York Times* the morning after he was elected was the repeal of Prohibi-tion—one of the few issues on which Roosevelt took a clear stand.

The electoral politics of the Vietnam War is especially enlightening as an illustration of how limited the electorate's influence is on policy. In 1964, Lyndon Johnson overwhelmingly defeated the hawkish Barry Goldwater, who had talked of using nuclear weapons to defoliate trees in Vietnam. Many who voted for Johnson did so expecting him to avoid military adventures, and were dismayed when, soon after the election, our involvement in Vietnam swiftly escalated. By 1968 there was widespread dissatisfaction with the war, and yet the electoral choice that year was between Johnson's vice president, Hubert Humphrey, who loyally supported the conduct of the war, and Richard Nixon, who was vague about his intentions. The millions of voters who wanted an end to the war had no choice in November 1968. For the next four years, Nixon continued and in certain respects expanded the war, while reducing the number of American troops. By 1972, advocates of American withdrawal had their champion in Democratic nominee George McGovern, who lost in a landslide to Nixon. Yet within weeks of the election, American forces were withdrawn from Vietnam. So the Vietnam era produced an electoral rejection of a hawk, followed by escalation; little choice in 1968; and an electoral rejection of a dove, followed by American withdrawal!

Even in 1984, public opinion surveys show that there was hardly a "mandate" for many of the policies of the man who won the presidential election by such a resounding margin. One reputable academic poll found no more than a quarter of the voters favoring such Reagan policies as greater involvement in Central America, greater spending on the military, and cuts in spending on the environment, education, jobs for the unemployed, science and technology, and programs to benefit blacks.[2]

Of course, everything that I have argued up to this point is aimed at suggesting that elections are not very good ways of expressing the policy views of the people who actually vote. Elections are even less effective as a means of carrying out the policy views of all citizens. At a time when nearly half the population over age eighteen doesn't even bother to vote in presidential elections, the victorious candidate is likely to win the votes of only slightly more than a quarter of the eligible voters. In 1984, for example, Reagan won about 59 percent of the votes of the 55 percent of the electorate who showed up at the polls—which means that he received the support of the 31 percent of the electorate, in an election commonly referred to as a landslide.

Some people argue that all these problems would be eliminated if citizens voted directly on issues, in referenda and initiatives. But given the low voter turnout, and the fact that the way the question is drafted can influence the outcome, it is unlikely that such practices will ever give a complete picture of public opinion on a particular subject. Furthermore, referendum and initiative elections share some of the same shortcomings as elections for candidates, and the rest of this chapter will enumerate them.

VOTING AS COST-INEFFICIENT

Economists suggest that much of human behavior can be explained by means of a cost-benefit analysis. We weigh the costs of our actions against the possible benefits, and if the benefits seem to outweigh the costs, we take the action. Why are you reading this book? The costs are the price of the book, and the fact that there are more exciting books to read, or even more exciting things to do than reading—seeing a movie, playing ball, making love, or whatever. On the other hand, the benefits include gaining knowledge (we both hope), satisfying course requirements, increasing your chances for a high grade, receiving parental approval. Implicitly, you regard these benefits as greater than those costs, and so here you are.

Economists also try to put a value on these costs and benefits, usually expressed in monetary terms. The price of this book is easy to put such a value on. The value of raising your academic average might be thought of in terms of how much more money you will earn by admission to graduate school or qualifying for another job. Even values of things like playing ball or winning parental approval can be expressed as how much you would be willing to pay for them. Economists acknowledge that people don't actually cost out all of their choices, but they do believe that people implicitly make rough cost-benefit determinations all the time. If the value of the benefits is greater than the value of the costs, then people will take the action.

What about voting? What are its costs? Well, it costs money for you to go to the polls—gasoline, car depreciation, taxi or bus fare. Let's say that you pay two dollars for transportation. Voting takes time, too, and time is valuable. Maybe you could have earned five dollars in that time. And don't forget the transportation and time costs of registering to vote—also two plus five dollars. There is also the cost of obtaining information about the campaign, such as newspapers or magazines bought for the main purpose of deciding your vote, or television or radio programs turned on? (Electricity costs money; but we should only count the print and electronic media that would not have been used if a campaign were not going on.) And there is also the time it took to read, watch or listen. Let's call those costs fifteen dollars.

Have we forgotten anything? Babysitters? (We won't count friendships lost during the campaign; arguments over candidates are not a necessary part of voting.) Let's throw in another ten dollars for miscellaneous expenses. This adds up to thirty-nine dollars as the cost of voting.

Now let's look at the benefits. There are two kinds: those that are contingent on your candidate's winning, and those that are not. In the first category are the benefits that you expect to derive from your candidate's victory. Maybe you think that your presidential candidate will be a much better manager of the economy than his or her opponent, which will enable you to earn ten thousand dollars more in four years than you otherwise would have. Or, in some cases, maybe you expect the winner to appoint you to a government job, and in four years you can earn fifty thousand dollars more than on the job you will have to take if your candidate loses. (If you're not sure you'll get the government job, you have to multiply that salary by the probability of your landing the job.) There are also non-economic benefits that may be of value to you, such as your candidate's foreign policy, social policies, and so forth. All of these can be assigned a value.

So far, voting looks like a great bargain: thirty-nine dollars for costs, thousands of dollars for benefits. But wait a moment. Your chances of getting all those benefits do not depend on *your* vote, but on the votes of everyone. In other words, you can stay home, pocket the thirty-nine dollars, and let everyone else's votes determine whether the candidate of your choice wins. Because if he or she does win, you will get those marvelous benefits whether or not you voted (unless you are only eligible for your government job if you can prove that you voted that day). Indeed, given the fact that your lone vote is extremely unlikely to affect the outcome, especially when the electorate is large, you would be foolish to spend that thirty-nine dollars. And if we are talking about a presidential election, your single vote must make the difference as to which candidate carries your state's electoral votes, and your state's electoral votes must make the difference in the electoral college.[3] This is exceedingly improbable.

You are probably thinking, But what if everybody thought that way? Then nobody would vote, and the system would collapse! My answer is whether or not *you* vote will not affect how most other people vote. You can pocket your thirty-nine dollars and practically nobody else will know about it one way or the other. Or, you might respond by asking, Won't my vote help to increase my candidate's showing and make a statement about the popularity of his or her views? First, recall my earlier arguments that elections are a very ineffective way of representing voters' views. But more to the point here, your one vote will not significantly affect the showing of a candidate in a major race; in a presidential contest, it will only affect whether your favorite gets 45,196,547 votes rather than 45,196,548—not enough to affect anybody's interpretation of the election.

This may strike you as very cynical or unpatriotic. I am not urging you not to vote, but only suggesting that voting is a cost-inefficient act, aside from its other shortcomings. Indeed, the only rationale for voting is the benefit to be derived whether or not your candidate wins. This can be thought of as civic pride—the satisfaction you get in voting, regardless of the outcome. You can put a value on this by thinking of how much it would cost someone to pay you not to vote. For some people, a dollar or two would be enough. For others, it would be hundreds of dollars, or even millions. And some people would never sell their participation in the electoral process. All of the people whose "price" is more than thirty-nine dollars (or whatever it costs them individually) will vote—and that is a bare majority of the eligible population.

So we conclude that if people behave the way economists think they do, then the only motive they have for voting is sentimental—we are taught that it is the patriotic, public-spirited thing to do. Otherwise it would not be worth the effort.

THE LESSONS OF VOTING

If voting is not all that it's cracked up to be, then why do we Americans depend on it so heavily to select important public officials? Perhaps part of the answer lies in the latent lessons it teaches us.

Many social activities really perform a complex set of functions.[4] Take schooling. It has an ostensible goal, the education of young people, which it more or less achieves. But public schools also teach people other things—obedience to authority, segregation of college-bound middle-class children from vocation-bound working-class and poor children, a competitive reward structure. Authority, social segregation, and competition are all features that we confront in American society all our lives. These and other concepts are the "hidden lessons" of American education.

What about voting? It has an overt purpose, the selection of candidates to hold public office, and except in the rare case of deadlocks this purpose is met. But elections have hidden lessons, too. Elections tell people that politics is most appropriately conducted in certain ways, such as:

Politics is individualistic

At various times and places in history, people have conducted politics by bringing the community together in one place to determine the outcome of political issues collectively. The best-known examples include the ancient Greek city-states, Israeli kibbutzim, New England town meetings, and communes of various kinds. This is a concept that is based on the argument that if politics is a society's way of deciding its collective future, then what better way is there of doing so than to have people resolve the issues through face-to-face argumentation and brainstorming? In contrast, voting is an isolated, individualized act. People do not share their ideas or persuade each other. Each person is like an unconnected atom; it is in this manner that Americans tend to see social life in general.[5] And yet we know that some of the most important social changes have been fostered by collective movements—by abolitionists, labor organizers, civil rights workers, and antiwar protesters. Indeed, we might well ask ourselves which nation underwent more profound political change in 1980—the United States, which chose a new administration through the ballot, or Poland, which without free elections established a mass movement that brought a new era in politics. Despite the crackdown in 1981, Solidarity has redefined the parameters of Polish life.

Politics is private

Which question is a greater invasion of privacy, What deodorant do you use, or Whom did you vote for in the last election? There is no obvious answer. People whose only political activity is voting are left to infer that politics is intensely personal and private, almost shameful. We vote not only individually, but often in booths with curtains, like Roman Catholics confiding their sins in the confessional. Again, instead of treating politics as the most *public* of activities, because it is concerned with the future of all of us, we treat it as something to be hidden. This is not to suggest that there is no virtue in the secret ballot, only that a nation whose most important political act is conducted in private is one that does not take politics seriously as the highest endeavor of the community.

Politics is episodic

Politics, we are encouraged to believe, occurs once a year in November, and for most adults it occurs only once every four years. We are able to discharge our highest civic function by taking a few minutes to go into a booth and flip a few levers once every four years. Although we are all free to engage in other political activities, such as collective action, writing to officials or working on campaigns, most adults are quite content to limit their political activity to that once-in-a-quadrennium lever flip. And if we think of voting as the crown jewel of our liberties, we will not think that citizenship requires anything else.

All in all, the message that elections sends us is to be passive about politics. Don't take action that involves any effort, don't unite with other citizens to achieve political goals, just respond to the choice that the ballot box gives us. In a strange way, then, elections condition us *away* from politics. A nation which defines its precious heritage in terms of political rights discourages its citizens from all but the *least* active, *least* social, *least* public, and *least* political form of activity. This should raise the most profound questions for us. Why should we as a society discourage political activism? What is the real role that voting plays in our politics?

Further Reading

In a chapter of his *Nixon Agonistes* (Boston: Houghton Mifflin, 1970) entitled "A Good Election," Gary Wills reviews some of the limitations of voting, and follows it up in his *Confessions of a Conservative* (Garden City, N.Y.: Doubleday, 1979), chapters 8–10. A review of the argument that voting is cost-inefficient, written in a lively style unusual for an academic journal, can be found in Paul E. Meehl, "The Selfish Voter and the Throw-Away Vote Argument," *American Political Science Review* LXXI (March 1977), 11–30. An especially systematic presentation of the case for and against voting is that of Anthony Downs, in chapter 14 of *An Economic Theory of Democracy* (New York: Harper & Row, 1957). Other arguments similar to mine can be found in Robert A. Dahl, *A Preface to Democratic Theory* (Chicago: Univ. of Chicago Press, 1956).

Chapter 8 of Kenneth Prewitt and Alan Stone's *The Ruling Elites* (New York: Harper & Row, 1973) discusses some problems with elections in American society that I have not covered. For a series of arguments for elections as meaningful expressions of the public will, contrary to my position in this chapter, see Gerald M. Pomper with Susan S. Lederman, *Elections in America,* 2nd edition: (New York: Longman, 1980).

Notes

1. "Voting Rights Act Signed by Reagan," *New York Times,* 30 June, 1982, p. A16.
2. National survey of the Center for Political Studies of the University of Michigan, distributed by the Inter-University Consortium for Political Research.
3. For the workings of the electoral college, see chapter 10.
4. The distinction between manifest and latent functions is developed in Robert K. Merton, *Social Theory and Social Structure* (Glencoe, Ill.: Free Press, 1949), 21–82.
5. Individualism in American culture will be discussed in the next chapter.

2

The Corporate Capitalist Setting

Books about politics often understate a critically important fact, that politics in any society does not exist in a vacuum. Rather, it coexists with an economic system which is responsible for the production and distribution of material goods and services, a social system in which the status of groups and individuals is determined, and a cultural system in which various principles are deemed worthy of honor or dishonor. This book is based on a simple premise, that in any society that is not in the throes of revolution or chaos there must be a fundamental compatibility among these various systems, and each must in the broadest sense support the others. If each does not actively support the others, then at least it must not undermine them.

Because this is a premise, it will not be proven. However, logic suggests that it would be extremely difficult for any regime to survive if there are serious discrepancies among its social systems. What if the government's policies were undermining the economy? What if the cultural values taught in schools were subversive of the political system? What if the economy were creating a new class of people who wanted to replace the form of government with one that would suit its needs better?[1]

Let us take this premise one step further. Government is normally not an end in itself; it is established for specific purposes. The most fundamental of human activities, those which involve people in their daily lives, tend to be what we ordinarily call social and economic. In most modern societies, then, the role of the political system is to buttress the social and economic order. In particular, the political regime tends to work in the interests of the groups and individuals who play a dominant role in society as a whole, the actors we call elites. (In some systems the socioeconomic elites are allied with religious or ideological elites.) This buttressing can take many forms, from overt and positive policies to help elites, to indirect forms of assistance, to refraining from taking actions that are opposed by those elites. Sometimes such political policies may appear at first glance to be opposed to the interests of elites, but a more sophisticated understanding may show otherwise. The highest task of political analysis is to understand these actions and non-actions and their effects.

If these assumptions are correct, then American political parties, and indeed the entire American political system, can only be understood fully if we take into account how they affect and are affected by the other social systems in the United States. Therefore the political parties courses and books that are concerned only with narrowly defined *politics*—that is, with government and the people, groups, and institutions that seek to influence it directly—are seeing only a very restricted part of the role that parties play in the American system. My task in this book is to demonstrate that some of those systems are linked together. So at the outset let me define the broader social context so that when reference is made to the social systems you will know exactly what I mean.

LIBERAL CAPITALISM

For as long as it has been a nation, the United States has adhered to a set of political principles that are known to students of political philosophy as classical liberalism. This is not to be confused with the twentieth century liberalism of the sort associated with Franklin D. Roosevelt or more recently with Edward Kennedy and Walter Mondale. Classical liberalism is a broader philosophy that *includes* not only Kennedy-Mondale liberalism, but Ronald Reagan conservatism as well. Its tenets, discussed below, are so familiar to Americans that the argument that they are not necessarily true may seem strange.

Individualism

This is the assumption that people can best be understood as individuals, not as members of social classes or other groups, and that one's life is determined by factors within one's control and not by greater social forces. Perhaps no value is so central to the way in which Americans view the world. Indeed, one of the first things that foreign observers notice about Americans is their virtual inability to perceive the world in collective terms.[2] To most Americans, "individualism" has such positive connotations, and the assumption of individualism seems so natural, that it is difficult to understand that there is something rather unusual in this nation's stress upon it. It is as though the sky above the United States were a different shade of blue from what it is everywhere else, and only those Americans who had been abroad would know that there was anything remarkable about that shade of blue.

Equality and natural rights

This is the assumption that all people have certain human rights, regardless of whatever legal rights they may or may not have in a particular system. All people have such rights, so in that sense liberalism is an equalitarian doctrine. The rights that are generally included in the liberal pantheon are within the political and legal realm: freedom of speech, freedom of religion, trial by jury, and so forth. They include one important economic "right," the right to own property, but not other economic and social rights, such as the right to a decent livelihood or adequate medical care. Also, these rights protect individuals from abuse by government, not by powerful interests outside government.

Limited government

A further tenet of liberalism is that government is at best a necessary evil. Its purpose, according to the Declaration of Independence, is to protect people's rights, not to achieve justice more actively by redistributing power or wealth in society. No American politician ever ruined his or her career by overstating the dangers of government power or by understating the dangers of power in the private sector. Ronald Reagan rode to power by promising to get the government, not corporations, off the backs of the American people.

Capitalism

Since the premise of this book is that politics, economics and other social systems must be compatible, it is necessary to point out that liberalism has an economic system which it fits best: capitalism. This is the system in which the means of production are primarily in private hands, as opposed to socialism, in which the means of production are jointly held by the people through the state or through collective enterprises. Capitalism is intensely individualistic, based as it is on the assumption that the people share no fundamental interests and that the economic system functions best as "every person for himself." It assumes private property rights, and it is based on the further assumption that the role of government in the economy will be relatively limited.

One other characteristic of capitalism has major implications for liberalism, and that is the fact that capitalism is profoundly *anti*-equalitarian. Capitalism assumes that people will compete for scarce resources, and that the fittest will survive. Such a system only works if people end up with unequal shares. This is supposed to give people the incentive to work hard and strike it rich, and achieve what is often called the "American dream." At the base of capitalism, therefore, is a social system in which inequalities are not only tolerated, but essential. As we shall see in a moment, this is one of the most important contradictions between American capitalism and democracy.

Because the values of liberalism are intertwined with those of capitalism, and in order to avoid any possible confusion between classical liberalism and Kennedy-Mondale liberalism, throughout this book I shall refer to this broader kind of liberalism as "liberal capitalism."

For the couple of centuries in which liberal capitalism has existed, critics have pointed out some of its shortcomings. While most of these criticisms have come from the Left, from philosophers such as Jean-Jacques Rousseau and Karl Marx and their followers, some conservative critics like Edmund Burke have leveled similar charges. Among the most telling have been:

Inequality.   As discussed above, for all of its equalitarianism in *political* rights, liberal capitalism assumes that *economic* inequality is right and proper. This may come as a shock, for Americans pride themselves on their devotion to equality, from the Declaration of Independence's famous assertion that "all men are created equal," to the Fourteenth Amendment's enshrinement of the goal of "equal protection," to Americans' oft-proclaimed adherence to the norms of "equal opportunity" and "one person, one vote." Despite such statements of national purpose, the United States and all other capitalist systems are predicated on the assumption that in the social and economic realm, inequalities will prevail. In principle, the system desires only that such inequalities be determined by inequalities of talent and hard work. But even if that were the case—and remember that there are plenty of people whose wealth was acquired by inheritance, luck, and nefarious means[3]—it would still be true that social and economic inequality is the basis of the American system.

The faith of liberal capitalism is that a social and economic system based upon inequality can coexist with a political system that promises everyone equal legal and political rights. The problem is that the social, economic, and political realms are so intertwined. The person who is struggling to make ends meet is going to have a harder time finding the time, energy and motivation to exercise his or her political rights than his or her well-off counterpart. The poor person accused of a crime may be less effectively defended than the wealthy person who can afford to hire the most expensive lawyer. The person who makes a hefty campaign contribution to a successful politician will find his or her constitutional right to express his or her views to officialdom better exercised than the person who cannot afford to contribute. And so forth.[4]

Indeed, some marvelous aphorisms have expressed this contradiction in liberal capitalist thought. The French novelist Anatole France wrote of "the majestic equality of the laws, which forbid rich and poor alike to sleep under the bridges, to beg in the streets, and to steal their bread."[5] Then there is the comment attributed to the American journalist A. J. Liebling, that "freedom of the press belongs to those who own one."[6]

Materialism.   While socialism is often alleged to be too "materialistic," stemming from Marx's use of the term in a philosophical sense, it is capitalism that has made the "bottom line" the chief criterion of social value. Capitalism is governed by the profit motive, and that which is profitable crowds out that which is not. For example, business firms are known to give short shrift to product safety, safety in the workplace, honesty in advertising, or the social value of products (for example, fuel efficiency in automobiles) if any of those goals reduce profits. Book publishers and film producers are more likely to fund best-sellers than works of cultural merit; broadcasters seek high ratings at the expense of artistic value; and even colleges and universities are increasingly basing decisions on which academic subjects to establish and augment and which to retrench or eliminate not on their value to the curriculum, but on the basis of how many tuition-paying students want to take those courses, and which courses serve the needs of private industry.

Egoism.   The individualism that is so central to liberal capitalism is a form of egoism, the elevation of the self above all others. Capitalism tells us to seek economic self-interest; American interest-group theory tells groups to pursue their political self-interest; dozens of pop psychological movements and magazines with titles like *Self* encourage us to turn inward rather than solve the problems of the world. A few years ago, President Jimmy Carter lamented that "in a nation that was proud of hard work, strong families, close-knit communities, and our faith in God, too many of us now tend to worship self-indulgence and consumption."[7] But Carter mistakenly assumed that this phenomenon was something new. It is a long-standing problem in American society.

The corollary of egoism in liberal capitalism is the competitive ethic. Competition rather than cooperation pervades American life, whether it be students competing for grades (instead of helping each other learn), athletes striving for prizes (rather than structuring games around joint efforts in which everyone is on the same team, lawyers vying for courtroom victory (rather than jointly pursuing a just outcome), or artists contesting prizes (rather than realizing that artistic achievement is unique and non-hierarchical). Even conservative Chief Justice Warren Burger has criticized the American legal system, arguing that "The entire legal profession—lawyers, judges, law teachers—has become so mesmerized with the stimulation of the courtroom contest that we tend to forget that we ought to be healers of conflicts."[8]

The opposite of egoism is a sense of community, and that is the area in which traditional conservatives have been most critical of capitalism. Capitalism is a dynamic system, in which the lives of individuals undergo profound changes as they seek economic advancement. Corporations uproot families, communities rise and fall with economic trends, advertising creates new wants and therefore new financial pressures on families. Technological innovations overturn social relationships, the automobile destroying the cohesive nuclear family and television obliterating joint family activities. Those who lament the destruction of the traditional family and social patterns should look to the dynamic of modern capitalism for a major culprit.

Inequality, materialism and egoism are surely not confined to the United States, or even to the narrowly defined capitalist world. However, I am contending that these vices are inevitable in any system predicated upon capitalist values. Whether they are inevitably part of human society is a difficult question, but it stands to reason that a system based upon other principles would have a greater chance of avoiding these ills.

CORPORATE CAPITALISM

While "liberal capitalism" is a good term for the theory that describes the way the United States considers itself, for more than a century the American socioeconomic system has been better described by the term "corporate capitalism." Defenders of the status quo would have us believe that the American economy is dominated by mom-and-pop grocery stores and the like. Instead, for many decades economic power has been concentrated in a relatively small number of huge enterprises; hence it is *corporate* capitalism.

Not only is the American economy dominated by large corporations, but the evidence is clear that this domination is growing. Even casual readers of the newspaper business pages in recent years know that mergers between corporate giants have become the order of the day, so that economic power is concentrated in fewer and fewer hands. These are only impressions, however, and in order to get a better picture it is necessary to look at some hard data. In 1950, the two hundred largest manufacturing corporations controlled 48 percent of the total manufacturing assets; by 1982, that figure was up to 61 percent. The top one hundred firms in 1982 held nearly half the total manufacturing assets.[9]

This increasing concentration of economic power clearly violates the traditional justification for the capitalist system. Classical capitalist theorists have long argued that the most efficient economic system is one in which power is decentralized, and thousands of producers and millions of consumers will share responsibility for economic decision making. However, if producer power is held by a relative few, then these advantages are lost. Defenders of the system often claim that corporate power is all right as long as there are at least a few corporations in each industry, preserving competition. However, this argument ignores the enormous difference between competition among many small firms and competition among a few giants, with all the potential for price-fixing and other conspiracies that this makes possible. Indeed, even the patron saint of capitalist thought, the eighteenth century Scottish philosopher Adam Smith, recognized this when he wrote that "people of the same trade seldom meet together, even for merriment and diversion, but the conversation ends in a conspiracy against the publick, or in some contrivance to raise prices."[10] Beyond the economic consequences of economic concentration, however, are the political consequences, about which new criticisms have been raised. The old criticisms are still valid, but added to them are others, including the following:

Greater inequalities

If liberal capitalism allows for inequalities that violate the promise of democracy, then the increasing concentration of the economy makes the situation all the more serious. If the effective exercise of legal and political rights is generally proportional to one's wealth, then corporations which have been amassing a greater and greater share of the nation's wealth have been acquiring the potential for more and more political power. Such power can take many forms, from sizable campaign contributions, to the financing of elaborate public relations efforts to influence public opinion (such as corporate expressions of political views on the guest editorial pages of newspapers) to the simple fact that any office-holder will be reluctant to adopt policies that might hurt the employer of so many of his or her constituents.[11]

Ignoring social goals

Every society makes numerous decisions that affect its members. Who shall live where? Who shall work, and at what jobs? Who shall get good medical care? Whose children shall be well educated? In a capitalist system, these decisions are largely made by the private sector, and under corporate capitalism they are made to a great extent by the managers of large corporations. Where people live depends on opportunities provided not only by the housing market, which is relatively decentralized, but also by banks; where people work depends on the job market, particularly on the hiring done by corporations; people's medical care depends on the health care industry and in particular on the health insurance subsidized by employers; their children's education, on how much revenue the government can raise from private sources. In most cases, the actions of corporate executives are very important, and in all cases, how much money people have is the crucial ingredient.

For society as a whole, basing such decisions on corporations' pursuit of profit and on people's wealth skews many public values. A community is devastated by the decision of a corporation to close a factory and seek higher profits elsewhere. The environment is despoiled because auto manufacturers produce vehicles that emit noxious chemicals and other firms release chemical wastes into soil and water. Inner cities become residues of poverty, unemployment and crime as suburbs attract the economic base of urban areas.

As the political economist Charles Lindblom has noted, in such cases business executives are in reality public officials, for the decisions they make are public in nature.[12] Yet they are not accountable to the people in the way that public officials are—they are not subject to elections, nor must they disclose their decision-making processes or the background of their decision-makers. And American politicians continue to lambaste public officials as though *they* were the most irresponsible power-wielders.

Many political scientists encourage such a view of power by discussing it only in government terms. Most introductory textbooks in American government discuss power as an attribute only of government. They contain many pages about such wielders of power as the president, members of Congress, bureaucrats and judges, but little or nothing about corporate executives, labor leaders, those who run the mass media, and other private power-wielders. By ignoring them, we insure their continuation in power.

Performance problems of capitalism

Another recent criticism of corporate capitalism is perhaps the most serious of all because it goes to the heart of capitalism's proudest claim, that it produces prosperity. Since the end of World War II, and especially since the late 1960s, the performance of American corporate capitalism has been declining in a number of respects. For example, over the long haul the unemployment rate has been going up. From World War II through 1974, only twice did the unemployment rate exceed 6 percent; from 1974 through 1984, it fell *below* 6 percent only once.

The same is true of inflation. After the post-World War II inflation died down in the late 1940s, inflation as measured by the Consumer Price Index only once exceeded 6 percent before 1973. From 1973 through 1983, it only fell *below* 6 percent twice. Likewise, the profitability of American business, as measured by the pre-tax profits as a percent of total capital, fell from the high teens in the early 1950s almost continually to around 10 percent by 1980.[13]

As intriguing as these and other data may be, this is not an economics text and I shall not explore them further in this chapter. My point is that the performance of corporate capitalism is slipping, and this will create enormous problems for both corporate elites and American government in the years ahead.

THE GOVERNMENT'S ROLE

As the social critic Thorstein Veblen once wrote, "the chief—virtually sole—concern of the constituted authorities in any democratic nation is a concern about the profitable business of the nation's substantial citizens."[14] In corporate capitalism, how does government serve corporate interests? There is a vast literature on this subject, and for the sake of brevity I shall simply touch on some of the main points.[15]

There is an important point that must be made here. When I argue that the political system caters to the corporate sector, I am not attributing this influence to bribery or to a grand conspiracy of the sort in a Jane Fonda movie, with sinister men in three-piece suits plotting in some skyscraper. Now will I emphasize, as some radicals do, the fact that so many people in government come from corporate or upper-class backgrounds.[16] If such factors were crucial in determining the scope of corporate influence, then the solutions would be easy: Catch the bribers, locate the conspirators and expose them, put people from working-class backgrounds into positions of power. Alas, it is not so simple a matter. As you read this book you will see the many ways in which people with decent intentions, *acting primarily out of a sincere concept of the public interest or, at worst, a desire to advance their careers,* do the bidding of corporate capitalism without having to be asked.

Let us begin with the proposition that capitalist states are not generally involved in the control of economic production. This would seem to follow from the definition of capitalism, although even in the super-capitalistic United States there are some government industries, from the Tennessee Valley Authority to the production of license plates in prisons. Nevertheless, the real task of government is to create and sustain the *conditions* under which the *private* sector can accumulate profits. How does the government do this?

One indispensable form of government aid to capitalism is what the American writer James O'Connor calls "social investment," or what the government spends to insure that profitable conditions prevail.[17] The West German scholar Claus Offe has itemized much of this social investment: "education, skills, technological change, control over raw materials, health, transport, housing, a structure of cities, physical environment, energy, and communication services."[18] Whenever the government builds an industrial park, improves a highway, or starts a new vocational program in the public schools or colleges, it is investing in capitalist growth—and therefore saving the private sector that much money. While it is argued that such spending benefits all of society, it clearly benefits corporations the most. Who gets more advantage from a well-built highway, the individual commuter or the company that has a faster way to get its product to market?[19]

While this book will be primarily concerned with domestic policy, no accounting of social investment would be complete without mentioning such investment in the foreign policy of the United States, and how often this nation's power is used to protect American and multinational corporate interests in other nations. While no single motive can "explain"

American foreign policy, surely a crucial part of that policy is the desire to protect private investments abroad, even to the point of overthrowing governments that seek to nationalize American businesses. American policy in Latin America and the Middle East cannot be understood without considering this "service" provided for the private sector.

O'Connor discusses another form of public investment that he calls "social consumption," which maintains the working class in conditions decent enough to insure its continuation as a work force.[20] This includes a variety of social services for the working class, above all Social Security, unemployment insurance, and workmen's compensation. While it took a great deal of working-class pressure to bring about such programs, these programs also serve the interests of the corporate world by keeping workers from falling to such a low economic level that they might turn to more radical alternatives. Moreover, a more satisfied work force is a more productive work force.

These forms of aid help capitalism in general, and so they are especially important in preserving it. However, when the subject of corporate influence in government comes up, Americans tend to think more of ways in which *individual* people and firms benefit—aid such as tax breaks and tariffs to specific industries, subsidies to particular firms such as the Chrysler bailout (remember *that* the next time you hear a corporation executive call for less government!), lobbying, and bribery. While all of these policies and activities do indeed go on, they are not nearly as significant in the broad picture as the ways in which the political system works to help all of capitalism across the board, *even over the opposition of many business people* (as with Social Security).

So far, I have been discussing rather straightforward ways in which government actively aids corporations, but there are also important ways in which government aids capitalism by fighting challenges to that system. Offe has shown that many political institutions screen out political demands that might undermine capitalism. Parties maintain a monopoly of political access, and often muddy the issues; interest groups, as I shall show in chapter 4, are geared only toward narrow, selfish concerns rather than broad social goals; and legislatures are increasingly ineffective.[21]

When dissident views arise, the government has far more direct means with which to suppress them. The Swedish sociologist Goran Therborn has listed four means of repression at the government's disposal, and despite the pride Americans take in the freedoms stated in the Bill of Rights, the United States has used each of Therborn's means of repression.[22] One is to outlaw dissident views, as when the Smith Act, passed in 1940, made it a crime "to teach and advocate the overthrow of the United States government by force and violence." This vaguely worded law—would someone be forbidden to say that in theory it would be a good thing if there were another American revolution, violent if necessary?—was used to destroy the Communist Party of the United States by jailing its entire leadership. Under the Smith Act, it was unnecessary to prove that people had actually engaged in revolutionary violence. The second of Therborn's means of repression is to restrict opposition within the system, including regulations limiting when, where, and how protest marches are conducted, and to set high hurdles for the establishment of third parties. This will be mentioned in the next chapter. The third means of repression is harassment and terror. The United States has employed this means in many instances, from the use of federal marshals to break up strikes in the late nineteenth century, to southern sheriffs' persecution of civil rights activists in the early 1960s, to the attempts by the FBI and other federal agencies to disrupt protest movements. Federal agency involvement had included anonymous letters from the FBI to Martin Luther King, Jr., suggesting that he kill himself and the use of gossip to break up radicals' marriages.[23] Finally, the government has resorted to surveillance of radicals, Therborn's fourth technique, for many years. The FBI underwent a massive effort to keep an eye on the Socialist Workers Party, a tiny, legal, and harmless group whose very existence seems to have offended people in high places.[24] In each of these cases, the groups and individuals being persecuted were guilty of no "crime" other than that of expressing their rights under the First Amendment.

Even the repressive functions of the government that are less overtly political than the measures just discussed tend to protect capitalism. The maintenance of "law and order" by the police, the courts, and the military is most beneficial to those who have the most at stake. "Law and order" most fundamentally means preserving the existing order, which is why conservative politicians have been much more enamored of the slogan than liberals and radicals have been.[25]

Offe points out, however, that the dependent relationship between corporations and the government is not one sided. In many respects, the government is dependent on the success of the private sector, if for no other reason than to be able to collect enough taxes to keep itself running. But the assiduous wooing of "business confidence" that we see occurring in Democratic as well as Republican administrations has other roots as well. Since capitalism is the basis of the economy, in the short run it is true that what is in the interest of General Motors is in the interest of the United States. What political leader wants to displease those who run the nation's economy and watch the stock market go down? Who would want to provoke an exodus of investment to other countries? Jimmy Carter was only the most recent Democrat to pride himself on how acceptable to business his economic policies were. In his memoirs, he proudly noted that in June 1980, "I had met with leaders of the key financial institutions on Wall Street and found them very supportive of our economic policies."[26]

All of these boons to corporate capitalism would not be enough to save the system if the mass of men and women in the United States were to decide that this inequalitarian, materialistic, and egoistic system should be replaced. Therefore one of the most important tasks of modern capitalism is to help reinforce people's belief in capitalist values. To preserve capitalism, it is necessary not only to aid in the process of accumulating profits, but also to promote the *legitimacy* of the system, the sense that the system is right. This is a function in which government plays a special role.

For all of the invasions of freedom of expression noted a few paragraphs above, the United States does have a wider range of such freedom than most nations. The strange thing is how little use is made of this liberty to dissent from liberal capitalist ideas.[27] According to many public opinion surveys, very few Americans believe in any other doctrine. Virtually no newspaper columnists, radio and television commentators, educational administrators, labor leaders, or public officials express views contrary to the public consensus. Even college professors, a radical group in many nations and sometimes accused of unorthodoxy here, overwhelmingly subscribe to liberal capitalist values.[28] The freedom to dissent beyond the mainstream is virtually never exercised, in the same way that a dog, let off its leash in a field, decides to run only in a small circle.

Defenders of the system argue that this near-unanimity of liberal capitalist values occurs because those values are, as the Declaration of Independence put it, "self-evident," and because capitalism has been so successful at providing prosperity.[29] But this does not explain why this level of consensus does not exist even in other relatively affluent capitalist nations with large socialist movements. Surely there have been powerful institutions promoting the consensus, so much so that the French philosopher Louis Althusser has written of the "ideological state apparatuses."[30] These are the institutions which promote capitalist values, and they include religion, the family, law, politics, labor unions, communications media, the culture, and, above all, the schools. While some of these institutions are not part of the state in a formal sense, Althusser included them because they all promote the values that reinforce the socio-political system of capitalism.

There are many obvious ways in which these institutions support the status quo. Schools teach the pledge of allegiance and the virtues of "free enterprise;" a high school textbook publisher warns authors to "avoid references that put the free enterprise system in a bad light;"[31] churches provide chaplains to the military and many members of the clergy preach conservative values; even public broadcasting carries subtle "commercials" identifying corporate sponsors; and so forth. Beyond these identifiable services, however, is a broader kind of propaganda. The capitalistic climate subtly defines who is respectable, and what ideas are acceptable. The business executive enjoys a higher status than the labor leader, whose demands are considered "greedy" by many people who do not examine the executive's degree of altruism. The successful capitalist is a community leader and even, like Lee Iacocca (whose "success" was largely due to a government bailout) talked about as presidential timber. Business leaders are appointed to the cabinet, and the nation admires their willingness to do without their seven-figure incomes for a few years while serving the government.

The ideas of these corporate executives, however stale and conventional, are taken as received wisdom by much of the press and population. Somehow the ability to turn a profit is translated into evidence of great moral and intellectual depth. On the other hand, the opinions of those who advocate social change are regarded as pie in the sky, the impractical musings of people who don't understand the "real world" and how it operates. Some reformers are even tolerated patronizingly, to show how "open" the system is. But as the American economist Robert Heilbroner once wrote, "the striking characteristic of our contemporary ideological climate is that the 'dissident' groups, labour, government, or academics, *all seek to accommodate their proposals for social change to the limits of adaptability of the prevailing business order.*"[32]

Among the most important ways in which the ideological apparatuses promote allegiance to capitalism is to reinforce individualism. The political system is vitally important in this regard; it encourages people to think of themselves as individuals, both as holders of rights and as voters. As one critic put it, the awareness of one's membership in a social class "can only be achieved and exercised *collectively,* whereas each worker is admitted to the ballot booth only as an isolated and atomized individual."[33] This may be one reason why voting is stressed so much; it fits right in with capitalist individualism.

Another capitalism-promoting function of the political process is to achieve in the minds of the citizens what another critic has called a "spurious equality,"[34] which is based on equal rights and the vote. The notion that you, the president, and the head of the Exxon Corporation each has one vote is important in fostering the legitimacy of the system and the myth of equal treatment. Here again, elections are vitally important to the maintenance of the system.

A third function of the political process that aids capitalism is to encourage the view that the ills of society can be "solved" by replacing the party in power with its opponent, rather than overturning the political and socioeconomic system entirely. The party out of power contributes to this function in its campaign rhetoric by attributing those societies' ills to the behavior of the incumbents.

Finally, through the political process the people are encouraged to express any dissent they may feel in socially acceptable ways, such as voting. Voting is like a safety valve; the voter expresses an opinion, confined to the narrow choice on the ballot, and does not resort to more potent means of challenging authority. Indeed, a report on local elections in China by an American journalist stressed that their purpose was to "restore confidence in the system," building "enthusiasm for the modernization drive," and "undercut[ting] the country's protest movement."[35] Perhaps those are the real functions of elections in the United States as well!

Legitimacy is built in other ways as well, notably through social welfare programs that give the poor just enough to live on and keep from the despair that can lead to radicalism.[36] This also helps capitalism in a more direct way by giving poor people spending money. It is no coincidence that conservative Republican Senator Robert Dole of Kansas has become one of the leading advocates of the food stamp program: food stamps are spent for food grown by Kansas farmers.

So the real function of elections, and of the whole political party system, begins to come into view. If the legitimacy of capitalism is to be sustained, then the party and electoral system will play a crucial role. It has become clear in recent years that the system of corporate capitalism faces the powerful dilemma of choosing between promoting the accumulation of profits and promoting the legitimacy of the system. The greater the emphasis given to promoting the fortunes of corporations, the more likely are the lower classes and their better-off allies to question the justice of the system. The more government provides to secure the allegiance of the worse off, the less will be available to insure that major corporations receive handsome profits.[37] This dilemma has great implications for the future of American politics, and it will be addressed again and again in this book.

AN ALTERNATIVE SYSTEM

As you have undoubtedly surmised, the conviction of this book is that the drawbacks of corporate capitalism considerably outweigh its virtues. There are many American reformers who seek to ameliorate these conditions while retaining the broad contours of capitalism. Some would add citizens to corporate boards of directors in order to represent the "public interest;" others would use government regulation as a means of reining in corporate irresponsibility; still others would try to use anti-trust policy to restore a pre-corporate, "mom-and-pop grocery store" form of capitalism. In the popular parlance, these people are known as liberals or progressives, believing that the ills of the system can be repaired within the capitalist framework.

Others see reform as futile. There is a profound logic within capitalism, a logic of inequality, private acquisitiveness and profit maximizing that will doom attempts to "erase poverty" or "end racism and sexism" or make the corporation a "good citizen." Poverty—economic inequality—is built into the very structure of capitalism. Racism and sexism are manifestations of capitalism's need to establish a source of inexpensive labor by defining some groups as underpaid and undertrained. As long as the purpose of the system is to acquire profits, piecemeal reforms will have only limited impact. That impact may make a significant difference to some people in some circumstances, but liberals are deceiving themselves if they think that such reforms will ever get to the root of the problem. Replacing Republicans with Democrats will not suffice. Indeed, even if Ralph Nader became head of General Motors, or Jesse Jackson became president of the United States, the constraints of his role and his institution would severely limit the amount of difference each would make.

There is an alternate vision, articulated for more than a century, that seeks an end to the dehumanizing qualities of capitalism and to replace them with a system sensitive to human needs. That system is democratic socialism, in which wealth is not concentrated in the hands of a few in a dog-eat-dog competitive system, but in which the means of production are shared by the people through collective enterprises such as worker control of the workplace, and government enterprises when appropriate. But the liberal capitalist consensus is so ingrained in Americans that the word "socialism" is a scare word, connoting Soviet gulags, harshly regimented lives, and oppressive government bureaucracy. In fact, socialism is nothing more than democracy carried out in the social and economic, as well as in the political, realm. If its name has been despoiled by tyrannical systems which claim it, such as the Soviet Union and North Korea, then so has the name of capitalism been despoiled in nations like South Korea, Chile, and South Africa.

But the purpose of this book is not to argue the cause of socialism. It will look instead, at the political party system of the world's foremost capitalist state, show how it operates, how it serves to buttress corporate capitalism, and what the potential is for change.

Further Reading

There are a number of American government textbooks written from a radical perspective. Among the better ones are Kenneth M. Dolbeare and Murray J. Edelman, *American Politics,* 4th ed. (Lexington, Mass.: D. C. Heath, 1981); Edward S. Greenberg, *The American Political System,* 3rd ed. (Boston: Little, Brown, 1983); and Michael Parenti, *Democracy for the Few,* 4th ed. (New York: St. Martin's Press, 1983).

The broader literature on the government under corporate capitalism is vast, and much of it is hard going for the student. Among the works that should not be too difficult are Ralph Miliband, *The State in Capitalist Society* (New York: Basic Books, 1969); James O'Connor, *The Fiscal Crisis of the State* (New York: St. Martin's Press, 1973); Claus Offe, "The Theory of the Capitalist State and the Problem of Policy Formation," in Leon N. Lindberg *et al.,* eds., *Stress and Contradiction in Modern Capitalism* (Lexington, Mass.: Lexington Books, 1975), 125–144; Claus Offe, "Structural Problems of the Capitalist State," in Klaus von Beyme, ed., *German Political Studies I* (Beverly Hills: Sage Publications, 1974), 31–57; Goran Therborn, *What Does the Ruling Class Do When it Rules?* (London: Verso Editions, 1980); and Alan Wolfe, *The Limits of Legitimacy* (New York: The Free Press, 1977). A brief and readable account of the development of liberal thought is found in C. B. Macpherson, *The Life and Times of Liberal Democracy* (New York: Oxford Univ. Press, 1977).

Notes

1. This emphasis on inter-system compatibility is a doctrine not only adhered to by radicals. See Harry Eckstein, "A Theory of Stable Democracy," reprinted in his *Division and Cohesion in Democracy* (Princeton: Princeton Univ. Press, 1966) 225–288.

2. For the classic observation, see Alexis de Tocqueville's *Democracy in America*, which is available in many editions. If you know any foreign students, ask them if they find Americans unusually individualistic.

3. According to one study, family background accounted for about half the variation in men's occupational status; see Christopher Jencks *et al., Who Gets Ahead?* (New York: Basic Books, 1979), 213–214.

4. For an extended discussion of the contradiction between liberal capitalism and democracy, see Alan Wolfe, *The Limits of Legitimacy* (New York: The Free Press, 1977), Part II.

5. Anatole France, *The Red Lily,* trans. Winifred Stephens (New York: Dodd, Mead, 1925), 91.

6. Quoted in Raymond Sokolov, *Wayward Reporter* (New York: Harper & Row, 1980) 3. Sokolov provides no source for the quotation.

7. Televised address of July 15, 1979, reprinted in the *Congressional Quarterly Weekly Report* (July 21, 1979) 1470.

8. Chief Justice Warren E. Burger, quoted in the *New York Times,* 19 February 1984, section 4, p. 20.

9. *Statistical Abstract of the United States 1982 83* (Washington: Government Printing Office, 1982) 535; and *Statistical Abstract of the United States 1984* (Washington: Government Printing Office, 1983) 538.

10. Adam Smith, *An Inquiry Into the Nature and Causes of the Wealth of Nations* (London: Strahan and Cadell, 1776), 1: 160.

11. See Charles E. Lindblom. *Politics and Markets* (New York: Basic Books, 1977), especially chapter 13.

12. Lindblom, *Politics and Markets,* 171–172.

13. Federal Reserve Bank of Kansas City data reported in the *New York Times,* 28 March 1983, p. D1.

14. Quoted in Ralph Miliband, *The State in Capitalist Society* (New York: Basic Books, 1969) 76.

15. This section of the chapter parallels the argument in Claus Offe, "The Theory of the Capitalist State and the Problem of Policy Formation," in Leon N. Lindberg *et al.,* eds. *Stress and Contradiction in Modern Capitalism* (Lexington, Mass.: Lexington Books, 1975), 125–127.

16. The classic such study was C. Wright Mills, *The Power Elite* (New York: Oxford Univ. Press, 1956).

17. James O'Connor, *The Fiscal Crisis of the State* (New York: St. Martin's Press, 1973), chapter 4.

18. Offe, "Theory of the Capitalist State," 134.

19. See Miliband, *The State in Capitalist Society,* 79.

20. O'Connor, *Fiscal Crisis,* chapter 5.

21. Claus Offe, "Political Authority and Class Structures," trans. Michel Vale, *International Journal of Sociology* II (Spring 1972), 83–93.

22. Goran Therborn, *What Does the Ruling Class Do When it Rules?* (London: Verso Editions, 1980), 222.

23. See David Wise, *The American Police State* (New York: Random House, 1976), and David J. Garrow, *The FBI and Martin Luther King, Jr.* (New York: W. W. Norton, 1981).

24. See Wise, *American Police State.*

25. See Ralph Miliband, *Marxism and Politics* (New York: Oxford Univ. Press, 1977), 90–92.

26. Jimmy Carter, *Keeping Faith* (New York: Bantam Books, 1982), 539; see also pp. 78, 528, and 568, and Miliband, *The State in Capitalist Society,* 147–155.

27. On the liberal capitalist consensus, see Louis Hartz, *The Liberal Tradition in America* (New York: Harcourt, Brace & World, 1955).

28. In 1969, only 5 percent of college faculty described their political views as leftist. See Everett Carll Ladd, Jr., and Seymour Martin Lipset, *The Divided Academy* (New York: McGraw-Hill, 1975), 158.

29. We might wonder how much of American prosperity is due to capitalism, and how much to abundant natural resources, and we might also wonder about the human costs of unbridled economic growth.

30 Louis Althusser, "Ideology and Ideological State Apparatuses (Notes toward an Investigation," in his *Lenin and Philosophy and Other Essays,* trans. Ben Brewster (London: New Left Books, 1971) 121–173.

31. "Self-Censorship," the *New York Times,* 6 June 1984, p. A26.

32. Quoted in Miliband, *The State in Capitalist Society,* 214; emphasis in the original.

33. Ernest Mandel, *Late Capitalism,* trans. Joris DeBres (London: Verso Editions, 1978), 496; emphasis in the original.

34. Bertell Ollman, *Alienation,* 2nd ed. (Cambridge, England: Cambridge Univ. Press, 1976), 213.

35. Linda Matthews, "Secret Ballot Returns in China Voting," *Los Angeles Times,* 26 December 1979, Section VI, pp. 1–3.

36. See Claus Offe, "Advanced Capitalism and the Welfare State." *Politics and Society* II (Summer 1972), 479–488; and O'Connor, *Fiscal Crisis,* chapter 6.

37. See Miliband, *Marxism and Politics,* 97; O'Connor, *Fiscal Crisis;* and Offe, "Advanced Capitalism."

3

America's Political Parties

Now that you have had a general overview of the role of political parties in the capitalist system, it is time to look at American parties. Right away there are a number of problems. One is to choose which features of the party system to describe; another is to decide how to assess those characteristics. Even when we observe a phenomenon, it is often difficult to evaluate its importance—as in the old example, Is the glass half full or half empty? For instance, one of the most important questions about a system of political parties is how far apart the major parties are on important issues of public policy. There are quite a few ways of measuring their distances—you will read about some of them in chapter 12. But even after we measure differences between the parties, by what standard can we conclude that those differences are great or small? If our parties are far apart on seven issues and close together on eight, what are we to infer about the distance between our parties? And how can we define "far apart" and "close together"?

One of the most useful ways that political scientists have to deal with such problems is the comparative approach, in which the question about inter-party differences changes from How far apart are our parties? to Are our parties farther apart or closer together than parties in comparable nations? Those "comparable nations" provide us with a standard by which our party system can be measured. Of course we must find comparable nations. It would not be very fruitful to compare our parties with those of nations that are radically different from our own in economic, social or political terms. If we find that our parties are quite different from those of one-party systems, or of third-world nations that are far less industrialized than we are, we would not know where to begin in finding the source of the differences, since those nations differ from ours in so many ways. Why does the Soviet Union have one party while the United States has two? Can this be attributed to their different histories, different cultures, different ideologies, different economic systems, different constitutions, different societies, or what? The differences are endless.

Like most political scientists faced with this problem about the United States, I shall use as comparable nations those that are highly industrialized and have competitive party systems with regular elections open to most adult citizens; all of them also have essentially capitalist economies. This chapter will implicitly compare the political parties of the United States with those of the nations of Western Europe, Canada, Israel, Japan, Australia, and New Zealand.

In choosing which features to examine, it will be helpful to think of a party as an organization; like any organization, it has a structure and goals. Therefore our first questions about American political parties are, How tightly structured are they? and What are their goals? We also need to know how many parties there are in a political system, and whether they have become stronger or weaker over time. (I will tentatively define a strong party as one that is tightly structured with a relatively high degree of internal cohesion, and plays a relatively significant role in politics as seen by both the masses and by political elites.)

In discussing these questions it is also necessary to use the concept of a "party system." This concept considers all the parties in a political system, how they interact with each other, and how they are related to the rest of the political system. Obviously we cannot determine how far apart parties are without considering more than one; but the concept of party system also implies that in the same political system there are often similarities between parties that overshadow their differences. Examples of both usages of the concept of party system will soon be apparent.

PARTY ORGANIZATION

Sometimes the diagrams we use to explain political parties in this country are highly misleading. We use a pyramid, at the top of which is the national committee of the Democratic or Republican party, with its members representing every state. Underneath the national committee are the fifty state committees, and under them are thousands of county and other local organizations. This illustration is misleading because it implies a military organization, with those on top giving orders to those beneath them, all down the chain of command. About our parties, nothing could be further from the truth.

Indeed, when we compare American parties with those of the comparable nations mentioned earlier, ours are much more decentralized, with little control exercised by those at higher levels of government over those at lower levels. The classic "bosses" of political lore, like William Tweed of New York City, Marc Hanna of Ohio, and Richard Daley of Chicago, were usually local or state party leaders. But power of the sort that they wielded has rarely, if ever, been exercised from the top of the national party pyramid. In 1980, when the leader of the Republican party in the United States Senate called a meeting of eight Republican county chairmen in New York to urge them to support the incumbent Republican senator for reelection, only four of them even bothered to show up.[1] Indeed, one political scientist, trying to come up with a word for how power is organized in our party system, settled on "stratarchy"—the autonomy of each level.[2] Even that does not capture the fact that for the most part, the strongest unit of party organization in this country has ordinarily been at the county level or lower.

A second fact about power in American parties can be illustrated by performing the following exercise. Before reading another sentence, jot down the names of the five or ten most important people in both the Democratic and Republican parties in the United States today. Now look over your lists. Chances are that your lists contain not the names of the national chairpersons, but of elected officials such as the president and the Speaker of the House, public officials appointed by them, such as leading cabinet officials, and former elected officials. (Indeed, can you even name the national chairperson of either party?) This suggests that the most influential national party leaders are not organization leaders. In fact, most everything that our party organizations do is tied closely to winning elections. But organizationally it means that elected officials cannot be dictated to by organization leaders. Indeed, it is the president whose wishes are ordinarily carried out by the party chairperson, not the other way around. So party organization is relatively weak in this country, both in its decentralization and, often, in its being less powerful than others in the party outside of the formal organization.

A third weakness of our parties lies in Americans' low level of commitment to party politics, with a resulting lack of eager workers. Only a small number of Americans—not much more than a tenth—participate in political campaigns to any extent.[3] In presidential elections, barely half of the eligible voters perform the most minimal political act of voting, and in congressional elections during presidential off-years, little more than a third vote. Even for party activists, politics is a seasonal, leisure-time activity. Our parties do little when there is no election campaign going on, which means that they are truly active only for several weeks in the fall of election years. Nearly all people who participate in politics do so as a hobby, devoting most of their labors to careers and other private pursuits. One effect of the relatively low rate of political participation by Americans is that even the smallest party organizations extend over sizeable areas, such as counties, cities and towns, partly in order to have a big enough population base from which to draw a sufficient number of activists.

While exceptions to these generalizations about American political parties exist, these characterizations are valid when comparable nations are taken into consideration. The classic comparative study of political parties was by a French scholar, Maurice Duverger, who called the basic organizational unit of our parties "*caucuses* which are narrowly recruited, rather independent of one another and generally decentralized."[4] Some European parties studied by Duverger also had the caucus structure, but others he called "branches." These are more tightly organized, bureaucratic in structure, and easier to join than caucuses; Socialist, Catholic, and Fascist parties are especially likely to be organized by branch.[5] Finally, Duverger wrote of parties organized by "cells," or small, well-disciplined groups established at workplaces; communist parties typically take this form.[6]

According to Duverger, then, both of America's major parties are caucus types. Since comparable nations have parties that take all three of the forms mentioned above, and since the branch and cell types are more disciplined than the caucus model, we can infer that, in general, our parties' organizations are considerably weaker than those elsewhere. There is also plenty of evidence that Americans participate in politics less than others do; see Table 3.1 for the data on voting turnout in national elections. The conclusion is clear: Americans vote less than the people of comparable nations do. Some say that this is only because other nations have easier voter registration laws, or fine people for not voting.[7] If we did likewise, they say, our turnout would be as high as other nations'. This only raises the question, Why don't we have the registration or nonvoter-penalty laws that they do? Why do they value voting more than we do?

Duverger also points out that other kinds of parties involve their members more than ours do, and make politics more than a leisure activity. He uses the example of the French Communist whose labor union is Communist, who reads the party newspaper to get news, who joins Communist athletic, cultural, and social clubs, who vacations at Party-run resorts, and whose entire family is involved in men's, women's, and youth groups affiliated with the Party.[8] Other parties in these nations also have ancillary groups, publications, and activities. Many years ago, Gabriel Almond and Sidney Verba established that Americans were less emotionally involved with their parties than the British, West Germans, Italians,

Table 3.1. Mean turnout in national elections, 1960–1978.

Italy	94	Norway	82	Chile	71
Netherlands	90*	Israel	81	Japan	71
Austria	89	New Zealand	81	Uruguay	71
Belgium	88	Venezuela	80	France	70
Denmark	87	Philippines	77	Turkey	62
Australia	86	Ireland	75	Jamaica	61
Sweden	86	United Kingdom	74	India	60
Greece	85	Costa Rica	73	United States	59
Finland	84	Sri Lanka	72	Lebanon	56
West Germany	84	Canada	71	Switzerland	53

Note: Figures represent average turnout as percentage of eligible age groups.

   *Compulsory voting

Source: G. Bingham Powell, Jr., "Voting Turnout in Thirty Democracies," in Richard Rose, editor, *Electoral Participation: A Comparative Analysis* (Beverly Hills & London: Sage Publications, 1980), 6.

and Mexicans. For example, citizens of those countries were far more likely than Americans to say negative things about other parties and even to care whether their son or daughter married a member of another party.[9]

PARTY GOALS

What is a political party supposed to do? As we look across the broad range of parties in the United States and abroad we find a number of possible answers. One of the first that usually comes to mind derives from the British politician Edmund Burke's famous definition of party: "A body of men united, for promoting by their joint endeavors the national interest, upon some particular principle in which they are all agreed."[10] Indeed, there are parties whose primary goal is to promote a point of view. People who join such parties are usually preoccupied with making sure that the party remains faithful to its philosophy, and that its candidates do not "sell out," even if the party viewpoint is unpopular with the electorate. Occasionally it is said of an American politician that, like Henry Clay, "he would rather be right than president." Running for president in 1964, Republican Barry Goldwater was so eager to promote his far-right-wing philosophy that he advocated unpopular positions like making Social Security voluntary or selling the Tennessee Valley Authority. In 1972, followers of Democratic presidential nominee George McGovern were accused of favoring "amnesty, acid, and abortion," despite the supposed lack of support for those positions among the American people.

However, most American professional politicians are not so single-mindedly committed to issue positions that they will not change them when the tide of public opinion shifts. What are the other goals that political activists have? Sometimes party activists simply want to control the party organization, even at the cost of electoral victory. Many years ago, when the South was overwhelmingly Democratic, the Republican organization in the region was run by a small group of people called the "post office Republicans." This was because their main purpose was to be available to receive patronage appointments—Federal jobs—whenever a Republican won the presidency, and the post office was a prime source of such appointments. Without much competition for such jobs, this little band of loyalists was happy to keep the party small. In the 1950s, however, when the Republicans started to make substantial gains in the South, the post office Republicans tried to resist because party growth would mean competition for patronage. Eventually, however, the post office group was driven out by the new Republicans and by the national party, which wanted campaign workers, not dead wood, in the South.[11]

While the post office Republicans were an oddity in American politics, controlling the organization is not an unusual motive. Party leaders often prefer candidates who are friendly to the organization, rather than candidates who, though they have a better chance of winning, are less willing to cooperate with the leaders. This has been especially true in the Democratic party, whose leaders are sometimes anything but the pragmatic operatives that some conservative political scientists claim. In 1984, for example, Democratic leaders stuck with Walter Mondale despite the greater popularity (as demonstrated in the polls) of the maverick Gary Hart; in earlier years they preferred Adlai Stevenson and Hubert Humphrey to more popular candidates who had offended the leadership.

Minor parties in the United States and some of the ideological parties elsewhere are guided by other motives. For example, some parties are primarily interested in promoting a point of view, even outside the electoral process. In the United States we have had socialist, prohibitionist, and anti-abortion parties that have not expected to win elections, and a recent prominent example from abroad has been the anti-nuclear Greens of West Germany. Some parties, with revolution as their primary goal, have agitated for that purpose through means violent and otherwise. In Germany in the Weimar era (1918–1933), the Nazis and Communists spent a great deal of effort disrupting each other's rallies and creating chaos in order to polarize the German people.[12]

But we have still not dealt with the main purpose of American political parties, and that is simply stated—*to win elections*. When winning and issues come into conflict, the former motive usually wins out over the latter. A study of delegates to both major parties' national conventions in 1980 looked at those who felt closer to one presidential candidate on the issues but thought that another candidate was more likely to win. The vast majority of such delegates voted for the candidate deemed more electable, not the one whose views they preferred.[13] We have already seen features of party organization in accord with this goal. For example, our parties are decentralized and therefore have the flexibility to respond to different local electoral situations. This has the effect of making both major parties electorally competitive all over the country. Since the early 1960s, for example, every single state has elected at least one Democrat and one Republican to the United States Senate or the governorship. Another pertinent organizational feature is the importance of elected officials and the relative lack of importance of party officials. Moreover, the seasonal nature of party activity in the United States is well suited to a system that has virtually no other purpose than election, and the same is true of the caucus mode of organization.

Before proceeding, I should make my position clear. I am not suggesting that issue-motivated activists do not play a sometimes significant role in American party politics. Rather, they and their concerns are usually overshadowed by the electoral motive, and more important, our parties are *structured* toward achieving electoral victory. For example, there is no mechanism for enforcing American party platforms. If there were, our parties would be compelled to take issues more seriously.

In a system that values electoral victory over everything else, it is not surprising that ideological factors play a relatively small role in our parties. The best way to illustrate this is to show that in comparison with other liberal capitalist states, our parties are rather close together. In many European nations there is a wide spectrum of political parties, resulting in large part from the more rigid class structure left over from the feudal heritage as well as from religious, ethnic, and geographic cleavages.[14] On the far left, especially in the Latin countries of Portugal, Spain, France, and Italy, are major Communist parties. Next come the Socialists, who want nationalization of the economy without the rigidities associated with Communism, followed by the various Social Democratic or Labor parties (names vary across nations), which are content to leave all but a few industries in private hands but want a full-blown welfare state. The Liberal or Radical parties are parties of "pure" capitalism and liberal democracy, and they are relatively small in Europe. On the right in all these nations are large Conservative or Christian Democratic parties, which are aligned with major industries and with a more traditional European-style conservatism which has ties with the remnants of the old landed aristocracy and is close to the established church. On the far right are the generally negligible Fascist parties.

This inventory does not apply to all liberal capitalist nations equally well, and parties like the West German Greens and various agrarian and ethnic parties are not accounted for at all. But the range of choice in most nations is wider than in ours. In Great Britain, for example, there are two major parties, the Conservative party, which combines what I have called liberal and Christian democratic tendencies, and the Labour party, which unites socialists and many social democrats. The British also have two smaller but significant parties, the Liberals and the Social Democrats, whose names imply their general positions.

It might help to visualize this configuration as a spectrum, from the Communists on the far left to the Fascists on the far right. Such a spectrum is illustrated in Figure 3.1. The father left you go, the less capitalist and more egalitarian are the parties. Now try to place the Democrats and the Republicans on this spectrum. Neither party has ever called for the nationalization of major sectors of the economy, nor even the kind of thoroughgoing welfare state to be found in much of the rest of the capitalist world. Neither party is fascistic, nor does either party ally itself with an established church (despite the religiosity of much of the American far right) or a landed aristocracy. At their most liberal, some Democrats are on the fringes of what would be considered social democracy in other nations, and at their most conservative some Republicans might feel at home in Christian Democratic parties. But clearly most partisans, and indeed most Americans, would identify with liberal parties abroad. In a sense, then, we are a one-party nation with two factions that we call Democrats and Republicans.[15]

Figure 3.1. Spectrum of political parties in many liberal capitalist political systems.

| | | Labor/ | Liberal/ | Chris. Dem./ | |
| Communist | Socialist | Soc. Dem. | Radical | Conservative | Fascist |

------ I --------------- I -------------- I --------------- I ---------------- I --------------- I ---

＊＊＊＊＊＊＊＊＊＊＊＊＊＊＊＊

Note: Asterisks represent ideological range of American parties.

Another way to understand this concept is to compare the nature of political competition here and abroad. In an election in one of these other nations, the choice may be titanic—between capitalism and socialism, between starkly conflicting concepts of democracy. In the United States, even the most vivid choice—say, if Ronald Reagan had run against Ted Kennedy in 1984—is much more muted. Reagan and Kennedy both support the essence of corporate capitalism, and neither wants to replace it with a truly socialist system. (Some right-wing rhetoricians have called Kennedy and his kind socialists, but they are simply revealing their ignorance of the meaning of the term socialism.) Kennedy and Reagan both support the American political system as it is—a system of limited government, divided power, and federalism. Neither would overhaul the constitution, and the amendments for which each man has voiced support (equal rights for Kennedy, anti-abortion and balanced budget for Reagan) would only peripherally modify our institutions. On the other hand, the leader of the left wing of Britain's Labour Party, Tony Benn, said in 1981 that Labour was "still a party that rejects the structures and values of capitalism."[16] Catch an American politician saying that![17]

One result of this limited political division is that there is less social division in voting in the United States than in most comparable nations. In most liberal capitalist nations, upper-class voters are predominantly in rightist parties, lower-class voters in parties of the left; and in most nations with religious differences, the parties claim different proportions of different religions. We hear this about American parties, too, with the Republicans considered the party of the rich and the Democrats thought of as the party of the poor, and Protestants more likely to be Republicans and Roman Catholics more likely to be Democrats. While there is a correlation between class and party in the United States, it is far lower than in the other countries I have been discussing. Using data compiled by G. Bingham Powell, Jr., Ivor Crewe discovered that out of nineteen nations, the class-party correlation in the United States ranked fourteenth. Using the same data, Crewe ranked our religion-party correlation eleventh out of thirteen.[18] The reason that we rank so low is presumably that, because the parties are not very far apart, people in most social groups do not overwhelmingly see one party as representing their interests.

It should be clear by now that American political parties, in comparison with other nations', are relatively weak both organizationally and ideologically (ideologically in the sense that our parties do not vigorously promote ideology). This is no coincidence. Why have a strong organization if you are not primarily interested in promoting an elaborate program? Political parties have only been organizationally strong when candidates have seen partisan organization as the key to election. In recent years, as I shall demonstrate, they have not.

THE TWO-PARTY SYSTEM

But we have not yet confronted what is surely one of the most important features of our party system, the fact that there are only two parties which get any reasonable number of votes or offices. For example, we have had twenty-two presidential elections in the twentieth century, and only five candidates have received as much as 5 percent of the popular vote without running on a major-party ticket. Since the Republican party's first victory in 1860, no third-party or independent presidential candidate has come remotely close to winning an election; nor have minor party candidates ever won more than a handful of seats in Congress.

Except during times of exceptional partisan instability, which we have not undergone since the 1850s, we have always had an essentially two-party system in America. This has led to a mythology, indeed even a fetish, about the two-party system that is shared by most Americans. They point to the famous multi-party horror stories: Weimar Germany (1918–1933), whose numerous parties coincided with an era of great instability that ended with the Nazi tyranny, and Fourth Republic France (1944–1958) and post-1945 Italy, whose cabinet coalitions have come and gone with great frequency. If the United States had a multi-party system, they say, we would suffer the same political instability, the same governmental ineffectiveness, and possibly even the same horrible consequence that Germany suffered.

There are several answers to this familiar refrain. One is that the United States manages to suffer governmental ineffectiveness despite our two-party system. But two-party proponents can argue, of course, that matters would be even worse under a multi-party system. There are, however, many stable, effective political regimes that have numerous parties. They include, to name a few, Belgium, Denmark, Finland, Israel, the Netherlands, Norway, Sweden, and Switzerland. Apparently a multi-party system does not necessarily cause instability.

Also at issue here is whether stability is the most valuable feature of a political system. It may not be surprising that Americans crave stability, but stability can mean stagnation, and it usually means that whoever has the most power and resources will continue to keep them. But even if you value stability, the above counterexamples of stable multi-party systems show that the number of parties may not be an important causal factor. Other factors, such as the degree of consensus in a nation, its level of prosperity, how long its institutions have existed, and the presence or absence of crises, are probably much more important determinants of stability or instability than the number of parties.

Anthony Downs has suggested one advantage of the two-party system: It supposedly makes voting a lot simpler for the voter. This is not only for the obvious reason that there are fewer parties from which to choose, a drawback if you don't like either of the parties on the ballot, but for strategic reasons. A voter in a multi-party system in which two or more parties have to form a coalition in order to run the government often does not know on election day which parties will be in the governing coalition. If there are three parties, the Left, Center, and Right, and you sympathize with the Left, you will be out of luck if you vote for the Left, and the Center and Right form a coalition after the election. You should have voted for the Center candidate, because then you would have strengthened the left side of the governing coalition. A vote for the Left is a wasted vote if the Left is not part of the government. In a two-party system, such complicated calculations are not necessary.[19] The problem with this line of reasoning, as logical as it is, is that it assumes that one vote will make a difference, an argument that I hope I refuted in the first chapter. Perhaps it is a stronger argument when applied to interest groups, newspaper editorialists, and others whose impact on elections is greater than the individual voter's.

Whether or not you think that a two-party system is superior to a multi-party system, there is no question that the extreme weakness of third parties in American politics is very important, for it limits the range of political choice.

THE DECLINE OF AMERICAN PARTIES

I have been presenting a picture of American political parties as relatively weak. Equally striking is the fact that this weakness has been increasing over time. Indeed, a frequent refrain among experts in American political parties is the decline of party. This does not mean that decline of the Democrats or the Republicans when compared with each other, but the decline of both parties and the party system as a whole. What do we mean by this?

One meaning of the decline of party is that the American people have become less and less favorable to parties over the past couple of decades. For example, nationwide public opinion survey data show a dramatic decline in the American people's favorable attitudes toward parties. Two questions are replicated in Table 3.2, and they show that people are much

Table 3.2. Attitudes of the American people toward political parties, 1964–1980, in nationwide public opinion surveys.

A.   How much parties help government pay attention to what people think:

Year	Not much	Some	A good deal	Don't know	Total
1964	13 %	39 %	41 %	7 %	100 %
1968	16	41	37	6	100
1970	19	43	33	5	100
1972	18	52	26	4	100
1974	19	55	22	5	101
1976	26	53	17	4	100
1978	22	53	21	5	101
1980	29	51	18	3	101

B.   "Parties are only interested in people's votes but not in their opinions."

Year	Agree	Disagree	Don't know	Total
1968	46 %	51 %	3 %	100 %
1970	54	43	3	100
1972	58	40	3	101
1974	58	37	5	100
1976	60	34	6	100
1978	62	33	5	100
1980	59	35	6	100

Note: Totals do not always equal 100 due to rounding.
Source: Warren E. Miller, Arthur H. Miller, and Edward J. Schneider, *American National Election Studies Data Sourcebook, 1952–1978* (Cambridge: Harvard Univ. Press, 1980), 261, 262; and my calculations from the 1980 American national election study.

more likely than they once were to believe that parties are uninterested in people's opinions, and much *less* likely to say that parties make government pay a good deal more attention to what people think. These trends are in keeping with a general trend away from confidence in many American institutions.

These attitudes are reflected in what is perhaps the most essential indicator of partisanship, the percentage of Americans who consider themselves independents. This is shown in Table 3.3, which reveals a jump in independents from the 20–25 percent range in the 1950s to the 34–38 percent range in the 1970s and early 1980s, except for a dip to 30 percent in 1982. Notice that this increase in the percentage of voters who consider themselves independents has come at the expense of both major parties; both the Democratic and the Republican percentages have declined since the 1950s. (Whether the slight rise in the Republican party in 1984 means a long-term rise in Republican fortunes is a subject for a later chapter.) Notice also that we can date the beginning of the rise of the independent percentage as occurring in the late 1960s.

Table 3.3. Partisan self-identification of the American people 1952-1984.

Year	Independents	Democrats	Republicans
1952	23 %	47 %	28 %
1954	22	48	27
1956	23	44	29
1958	19	49	28
1960	23	45	30
1962	21	46	28
1964	23	52	25
1966	28	46	25
1968	30	45	25
1970	31	44	24
1972	35	41	23
1974	37	39	22
1976	37	40	23
1978	38	39	21
1980	36	41	22
1982	30	44	24
1984	34	37	27

Note: Percentages do not include people who did not identify with any of these three categories.

Source: Warren E. Miller, Arthur H. Miller, and Edward J. Schneider, *American National Election Studies Data Sourcebook, 1952–1978* (Cambridge: Harvard Univ. Press, 1980), 81; and my calculations from subsequent American national election studies.

If you are the skeptical sort, you may be thinking, All right, people *say* they are less tied to the parties than they used to be; but does this mean that they are *behaving* any differently? After all, there are people who claim to be independents but who somehow always end up voting for the same party. One way to look at this is to observe volatility over time. If most people always vote for the same party, then election results would look the same year after year. But they don't. From 1960 to 1984, the American people have dealt the Democratic party every conceivable presidential election outcome: a landslide victory (1964), two close victories (1960 and 1976), a narrow loss (1968), and three crushing losses (1972, 1980 and 1984). Perhaps a better way to assess the behavior of individual voters is to look at ticket-splitting. How many voters are so detached from partisan ties that they will cast their votes for Democrats for some offices and Republicans for others? As seen in Table 3.4, ticket-splitters are indeed more numerous than they once were. People are more willing than they used to be to vote for a president of one party and a member of Congress of the other. Again, this trend seems to have begun in the late 1960s.

Another indication of weakening voter ties to parties is the electorate's greater willingness to vote for minor-party and independent candidates. Two were elected to the U.S. Senate in 1970, one to the governor-

Table 3.4. Percentage of voters who split their tickets between presidential candidates of one party and congressional candidates of the other, 1952–1984.

Year	President/Senate	President/Representative
1952	12%	12%
1956	16	16
1960	11	14
1964	17	15
1968	19	18
1972	28	30
1976	23	25
1980	24	28
1984	23	25

Note: Those voting for minor-party or independent candidates excluded. Read this table as follows: In 1952, 12 percent of the voters voted for a Republican for president and a Democrat for the U. S. Senate, or a Democrat for president and a Republican for the Senate. In other words, the remaining 88 percent of the electorate voted for the same party for both offices.

Source: Warren E. Miller, Arthur H. Miller, and Edward J. Schneider, American National Election Studies Data Sourcebook, 1952–1978 (Cambridge: Harvard Univ. Press, 1980), 385, 387; and my calculations from subsequent American national election studies.

ship of Maine in 1974, and a couple have won seats in the U.S. House of Representatives. The numbers are smaller, but higher than in previous decades. Until 1974, for example, the most recent non-major-party governor was elected in 1936.

These indicators do not necessarily mean that people are turning *against* parties. One researcher, Martin Wattenberg, has concluded that people are simply becoming apathetic about parties, and are decreasingly likely to think about them when the subject of politics comes up. Whether people are becoming hostile to parties or apathetic about them may not make much difference to the parties; either way, they have lost much of their prior significance in politics.[20]

If partisanship among the voters has become weaker, have party organizations also declined? This is a hard question to answer as precisely as we could answer the questions about voters, because there are no clear-cut measures of the strength of party organization that correspond to questions that can be asked on a survey such as "Do you consider yourself an independent?" But there is plenty of circumstantial evidence that party organizations are indeed not as strong as they used to be. Ask anybody you know who is over the age of fifty and has been involved in politics for a long time whether political parties are stronger or weaker than they used to be. It is likely that they will tell you that in their youth, politicians obeyed their party leaders much more than they do now. There is also a wealth of evidence that various local party organizations have declined, particularly in terms of their ability to win primaries. If a challenger can overcome the organization's candidate, then how strong can the leadership be?

The best example of this is the political "machine" that was once regarded as the strongest local organization in America. For fifty years, Chicago was dominated by the Cook County Democratic organization, led by Mayor Richard J. Daley from the 1950s until his death in 1976. Daley's successor, Michael Bilandic, was defeated in the 1979 primary by Jane Byrne, a political veteran who dared to defy the organization and beat its candidate. Four years later, it was Byrne's turn to lose her office. In a three-way race for the Democratic nomination, Daley's son and namesake challenged Byrne with the support of part of the Democratic machine, but the nomination was won by a black anti-organization candidate, U.S. Representative Harold Washington. Much of the Democratic machine then went so far as to work for Washington's Republican opponent, to a large extent due to racism but partly because Washington had threatened to destroy the machine. When Washington won the mayoralty, he immediately faced a bitter power struggle with the organization-dominated city council.

The point of this story is that the once-ironclad Democratic machine has suffered two consecutive losses in its own mayoral primary, and unity is a distant memory. This saga can be multiplied by many others across the nation; the fact that it happened in Chicago shows that no machine is invulnerable to insurgents within its own party. Because of the Democratic loyalties of the voters of Chicago, Democratic nominees continue to win the mayoralty, but they are not the candidates preferred by the machine.

When party machinery is on the wane, candidates and elected officials respond accordingly. A gallant few even switch parties, showing that old loyalties are no longer compelling. They include such notables as South Carolina's Senator Strom Thurmond and Texas's Senator Phil Gramm, who changed from Democrat to Republican, and Michigan's Senator Donald Riegle and Nebraska's Senator Edward Zorinsky, who changed from Republican to Democrat. Party switches used to be even rarer. More common is the tendency of candidates to build their personal campaign organizations and funding sources by going to personal supporters and interest groups, and by hiring professional campaign consultants and using the mass media, rather than relying solely on party literature to publicize their campaigns. No longer is the party looked to as the best source of campaign help.

Public officials are much less likely than before to toe the party line, and nowhere is this more evident than in Congress. For example, one way in which we can measure how important parties are in Congress is to look at the votes in which a majority of Democrats vote on one side, and a majority of Republicans vote on the other side. Presumably this indicates a real partisan issue. When there is such a "party unity vote," as the authoritative publication *Congressional Quarterly* calls them, does the average

member of Congress vote with his or her party? Of course it would not be
a party unity vote unless a majority of each party did so, but the trend
over time is worth looking at. Here we must look at four groups: Senate
Democrats, Senate Republicans, House Democrats, and House Republicans. Table 3.5 contains the data. From 1954 through 1966, the average

Table 3.5. Percentage of party-unity votes on which the average member of Congress voted with his or her party, 1954-1985.

Year	Senate Dems.	Senate Reps.	House Dems.	House Reps.
1954	77 %	89 %	80 %	84 %
1955	82	82	84	78
1956	80	80	80	78
1957	79	81	79	75
1958	82	74	77	73
1959	76	80	85	85
1960	73	74	75	77
1961	—	—	—	—
1962	80	81	81	80
1963	79	79	85	84
1964	73	75	82	81
1965	75	78	80	81
1966	73	78	78	82
1967	75	73	77	82
1968	71	74	73	76
1969	74	72	71	71
1970	71	71	71	72
1971	74	75	72	76
1972	72	73	70	76
1973	79	74	75	74
1974	72	68	72	71
1975	76	71	75	78
1976	74	72	75	75
1977	72	75	74	77
1978	75	66	71	77
1979	76	73	75	79
1980	64	65	69	71
1981	71	81	69	74
1982	72	76	72	69
1983	71	74	76	74
1984	68	78	74	71
1985	75	76	80	75

Note: Based on those in which a majority of Democrats vote one way and a majority of
    Republicans vote the other way.
Source: Congressional Quarterly data reported in John F. Bibby, Thomas E. Mann, and
    Norman J. Ornstein, Vital Statistics on Congress, 1980 (Washington: American En-
    terprise Institute, 1980), 104; and subsequent editions of the Congressional Quarterly
    Almanac.

party unity vote elicited from 77 to 81 percent support from the members of all four groups. From 1967 through 1985, however, the range was from 73 to 75 percent. The trend toward weaker partisanship is not a huge change, but considering that these loyalty scores must always be greater than 50 percent to be a party unity vote, any change is more significant than it appears.

This is just a sample of the many trends in American politics over the past couple of decades that point to a decline in the role of political parties in American politics. Most of them will be developed further in later chapters. For the moment, it is important to realize that not only are our parties less structured and less issue oriented than their foreign counterparts, but they are becoming even less effective as political instruments. The consequences of this for American politics are fundamental, and will be addressed in the next chapter.

SOME PROXIMATE CAUSES

Why do our parties exhibit these characteristics? One answer, central to this book, is that corporate capitalism requires that American parties take certain forms. But this is largely unconscious; our party leaders do not deliberately promote the social status quo. Short of this grand functional relationship between party politics and the socio-economic system, we can identify several factors that explain the direction our parties have taken. But bear in mind that all are in fact perfectly compatible with liberal capitalism.

Ideological underpinnings

To some extent, we have the kind of parties we have because of the content of the American ideological consensus. Americans define freedom as voluntary action; they treasure privacy and individualism; they have a preference for local initiatives rather than national-level efforts. These values are consistent with a caucus-based party system. Voluntarism is reflected in the fact that people must take the initiative to join a party; they are not automatically enrolled due to some other organizational membership such as a labor union. The American emphasis on privacy, broadly defined, keeps most people out of politics and busy with private pursuits. They prefer to segment their lives so that their other associations—jobs, families, communities—are not tied to party the way they are in some other nations. Individualism implies that only individuals can join parties, unlike, say, the British Labour party in which entire labor unions as well as individuals can join. Localism dictates a highly decentralized party structure in which county organizations are more important than state or national parties, and in such a system the appropriate type of party structure is the caucus. I could go on with other examples but broad ideological generalizations can take us only so far.

Social underpinnings

Who becomes active in politics? We can examine this question by looking at the people who participated in the 1984 presidential campaign either as campaign volunteers or as voters. Table 3.6 gives the results broken down by family income, and they confirm what scholars have long known about participation in American politics—it is a middle-class and upper-class activity. People in the top fourth of the nation in terms of family income were nearly twice as likely as those in the bottom fourth to belong to a political club or work for a political campaign. Moreover, upper-income people were considerably more likely than their lower-income counterparts to vote. In fact, we have reason to believe that the gap between rich and poor is even greater than this table indicates. After all, these data are based on what people *said* they did. Since only about 53 percent of the eligible citizens voted in November 1984, obviously some people were not being honest with the pollster; there is no income category here that reported less than a 60 percent turnout. In 1976, Michael Traugott and John Katosh went back and determined which survey respondents had actually voted, and they found that lower-income voters were roughly twice as likely as upper-income voters to report incorrectly that they had voted.[21] This means that the figures in Table 3.6 should be adjusted downward, especially for the poor. The result is that the gap between rich and poor is even greater than it appears in the table.

This correlation between class and political participation is one of the most important facts about American politics, for it reflects the locus of power in our society. Those Americans who genuinely believe that "all

Table 3.6. Participation in the 1984 presidential campaign, by family income quartile.

Family income (and percent of all families)	Percent who belonged to political club or were active in campaign	Percent who voted in November
$35,000 and over (24%)	19 %	87 %
$22,000-34,999 (26%)	15	79
$11,000-21,999 (25%)	14	71
$0-10,999 (26%)	11	60

Source: National survey, University of Michigan Center for Political Studies

men are created equal" and that the "American dream" means equal opportunity for everyone should confront this reality. Defenders of the system often dismiss the upper-class bias of American politics, saying that participation is open to everyone, and that if they wanted to, the poor could fully participate in the political system. This is a remarkably simplistic response to the situation, a variation on the theme of "blaming the victim." Something is discouraging lower-class people from getting involved in the political realm, and one of the purposes of this book is to find out what.

Two other facts about this upper-class bias should be stressed. One is that it is worse than in other comparable nations. One extensive study of political participation in seven nations, including the United States, found that the rich-poor gap in political participation was considerably higher in the United States than in Austria, Japan, the Netherlands, and even Nigeria; it was comparable to levels found in India and Yugoslavia, whose political traditions are far different than ours.[22] We regard most nations as more class-bound than ours, and yet even a society as traditional as Japan's has narrowed this gap far more than we have.

Why have comparable nations demonstrated far greater equality in political participation than we have, despite more traditional cultures? Why are the poor in the United States so reluctant to vote? There are a number of possible answers. Significant numbers of the poor are recent immigrants who may not have enough command of the English language to be able to participate in politics. Moreover, some blacks who grew up in the South at a time when they were forcibly kept from voting may never have developed the habit of voting. But these factors only explain the behavior of some segments of the poor; the widespread lack of participation of this group needs a more general explanation. Some have suggested that the answer lies in the fact that most of those comparable nations have political parties that are geared to working-class interests. Communist, Socialist, and Social Democratic parties are deliberately built on working-class bases, and they make a great effort to mobilize such people. In the United States, despite the Democratic party's rhetoric of being "the party of the working people," there is no counterpart. The implication of this assertion is that if we did have a mass party of the left, the participation gap between rich and poor would narrow.[23] Unfortunately, this cannot be proven or disproven. Ask most non-voting poor people, "Would you vote if there were a large Socialist party in this country?" and they are likely either to shrug because of their general lack of interest in politics, or to express the same aversion to such "un-American" ideas that most Americans share. We can only speculate about the consequences of a party catering to lower-class needs, but the example provided by foreign nations is suggestive.

It is also true that the upper-class bias of American politics is worsening. There has been a decline in the turnout of Americans in national elections since 1960, and the group that has been dropping out of the electorate the fastest is lower-income and poorly educated whites. Something has been convincing them that politics is becoming less and less relevant to their interests. Tragically, under the existing terms of American politics, they are probably right.

The fact that politics in America is a middle-to-upper-class activity helps explain some of the features of American political parties that I have been discussing. Since most activists are not economically needy, they regard politics as a pastime, and party politics is consequently a leisure activity. As noted above, in comparison with other nations our parties have similar social bases, with class and religious differences less pronounced here than elsewhere. This may explain why there are fewer differences between our parties than the differences found between parties in those countries. It may also provide a clue as to why we have only two parties: How many parties, after all, does the same social group need?

Origins

Duverger once hypothesized that parties can be divided into two types, those begun within government (especially the legislature) and those arising outside government. One is created by government officials, the other by people or organizations at the "grass roots." Duverger suggested that those begun inside government were more likely to be decentralized, to be dominated by elected officials, and to stress electoral aims over other (notably ideological) goals.[24]

As I shall discuss in chapter 5, American political parties were originally created by officials of the federal government—in the Cabinet and in Congress—in the 1790s. According to Duverger, then, it should not surprise us that our parties are relatively decentralized, dominated by elected officials, and devoted to electoral victory. While this may be true, it is probably a mistake to lay too much emphasis on developments of the 1790s to explain parties two centuries later.

Constitutional factors

Surely one of the most important influences on parties is the legal structure in which they must function. We can address those features contained in the Constitution as well as those included in statutes. In the American political system, the Constitution divides power among many institutions, with profound consequences for the parties. Federalism—the division of power among national, state and local levels of government—is probably the most important determinant of the decentralized structure of our political parties. It may help to explain the lack of differences between them as well, as state parties have enough autonomy to take a different tack from the national party in order to win their own areas. Since the 1930s, Democrats in the South have regularly departed from national Democratic party liberalism, and in recent years New England Republicans in Congress have been considerably less conservative than other Republicans. This is because the system of nominations and elections is decentralized, as our government is. There is precious little a president or national party chairperson can do to get rid of a member of Congress who deviates from the party line, just as there is little a president can do to a recalcitrant governor.

The other major way in which power is divided in the American political system is among the executive, legislative, and judicial branches of government. Because presidents and members of Congress can be nominated and elected without each other's approval, there is often a lot less party unity in Washington than there is in other national capitals. Political history is littered with the broken dreams of American politicians who naively assumed that power in one realm would lead to nomination in the other: Robert Taft, "Mr. Republican" of the 1940s and early 1950s, who despite his power in the Senate failed three times to win his party's presidential nomination; Lyndon Johnson, who as Senate majority leader was regarded as the second most powerful politician in America in the 1950s, but who ran a dismal second at the Democratic national convention in 1960; Henry Jackson, who failed miserably at two attempts to win the Democratic presidential nomination in the 1970s despite his tremendous power in the Senate; and Howard Baker, who as Republican leader of the Senate came nowhere near the 1980 Republican presidential nomination. The list could go on, and it can be matched by the presidents who erroneously thought that their prowess at winning the presidential nomination could be translated easily into control over Congress; Jimmy Carter was especially prone to that fallacy. This decentralization of the political process in Washington produces decentralization of our parties, with their multiple power bases.

Statutory factors

The Constitution was drafted before we had political parties, and consequently its provisions were not designed for any particular partisan advantage. The same cannot be said, however, for laws passed since parties arose. There are many laws which influence parties; two types of legislation in particular serve to maintain the two-party system by discriminating against minor parties.

Every time a legislature is to be elected the political unit (state, county, city, or whatever) can choose to elect the members in a variety of ways. Let us use the several representatives to Congress elected from the same state as an example. One way to elect them might be to have all the parties run statewide slates, and divide up the representatives according to the number of votes that each party gets. If a party gets 55 percent of the votes, for example, it then is entitled to 55 percent of the representatives. This is one form of "proportional representation." Another method, which is used in most elections in the United States, is the "single-member district" system, in which the state is carved up into several districts, with whoever receives the most votes in each district winning the seat in Congress.

It should become apparent that the single-member district system is usually far unkinder to minor parties than the system of proportional representation. In the single-member district system, a third party must concentrate its strength in a particular district in order to win. Any votes it gets in other districts are wasted; the voters might as well have stayed home. But in the kind of proportional representation system described above, every vote the party receives *anywhere* in the state counts toward its goal. And it need not win a plurality anywhere; as long as it gets a certain minimum share of the total statewide vote, it will be entitled to a representative. In the 1940s, the New York City Council was elected on a proportional basis; when Communists began winning seats, the single-member district system was reestablished.

If we had a proportional representation system, any vote cast for a minor candidate would not be wasted. But as long as the voter knows that a third-party candidate is unlikely to win, that voter will be likely to switch to another candidate. This is illustrated by the campaigns of three serious third-party or independent presidential candidates. In 1948, Progressive party candidate Henry Wallace received 7 percent in the March Gallup poll but only 2 percent of the votes in November. In 1968, George Wallace (no relation, political or otherwise) received 21 percent in a September poll, but only 14 percent in the November election. In 1980, independent John Anderson received 24 percent in a June poll, but only 7 percent in November.[25] Now, it is possible that each of these candidates lost votes because he ran a terrible campaign, but I think that a more important reason was that many of his supporters, knowing that he would lose, decided to switch to a candidate who had a chance of winning. If we elected presidents by a proportional system, in which, say, a candidate could win a seat in some sort of collective presidency by winning a certain proportion of the votes, then these candidates would probably have run better.

There is some indirect evidence for this proposition in some survey data from 1968 and 1980. The University of Michigan's national survey involved asking people to rate each presidential candidate on a scale from zero to one hundred—zero if you hated him, one hundred if you loved him, and any point in between. In 1968, those voters who rated Republican Richard Nixon above Democrat Hubert Humphrey and American Independent George Wallace gave Nixon 96 percent of their votes; those who rated Humphrey highest gave him 97 percent of theirs. But those who rated Wallace highest gave him only 81 percent. An even more extreme version of the same thing happened in 1980: 96 percent of the high Ronald Reagan scorers voted for him, 95 percent of the high Jimmy Carter scorers voted for him, but only 39 percent of the high John Anderson scorers voted for their candidate. In other words, even the people who rated Wallace and Anderson higher than their opponents were less likely—in Anderson's case, far less likely—to vote for them. And my hypothesis is that they voted against them because those candidates in a winner-take-all system were unlikely to win. The same calculation hurts alternative candidates in elections all over America.

Were this institutional feature not enough, legislatures dominated by the major parties have passed many laws intended to prevent alternative parties from overtaking them. The recent Federal Election Campaign Act provides tens of millions of dollars in public funds to major-party presidential nominees, but money only goes to minor-party candidates *after* the election, and only if they managed to win 5 percent of the popular vote. Of course, it would have been easier for the minor-party candidates to get 5 percent of the vote if they had had the money *before* the election. Limits on the size of campaign contributions also hurt new parties, because in the past they have relied on large contributors to get them off the ground; the Anderson campaign in 1980 had to spend an inordinate amount of time trying to raise funds. In 1979, Congress passed a law restricting low postal rates only to parties winning more than the magic 5 percent. Finally, many states have had laws making it very difficult for alternative candidates to get on the ballot. These include exorbitant numbers of necessary petition signatures, and requiring voters to abandon their existing party affiliation in order to help a new party get on the ballot.[26]

You have probably noticed that each characteristic of our parties can be explained by more than one of these causes. In other words, these traits are "over-determined." This suggests that our party system is all of a piece, which is in keeping with the argument of the previous chapter that the function of party system is to help to maintain the rest of the political, social, and economic systems. The rather neat dovetailing of the party system with ideological, sociological, historical, Constitutional, and legal factors is a fine illustration of the general theme of this book.

PHILOSOPHICAL UNDERPINNINGS

One final point remains to be made. There is a set of philosophical assumptions that underlies the kind of party system that exists in America, and not surprisingly it is compatible with the requirements of capitalism. We can best understand those assumptions by looking at some of the major arguments used by defenders of the American party system:[27]

Minimizing conflict

I suggested earlier that our parties are close together in part because they have similar social bases. Some have suggested that they can best be thought of as "umbrella parties," in which all social groups can be found under a broad umbrella-like tent. They argue that this is good, for it prevents the parties from being polarized around deep social divisions. If there are some rich people in both parties, some poor people, some Protestants, some Catholics, some Northerners, some Southerners, some liberals, some conservatives, some whites, some blacks, and so on, then no social group will despair when either party comes to power, and stability will be maintained.

There is even a terrible historical example that such theorists cite when making this argument—the Civil War. In 1860, a party that no white Southerner had voted for, the Republican Party, came to power. It won the presidency and the Congress, and was ready to replace the aging justices of the Supreme Court. The slaveholding South, despairing of its role in the national government, seceded from the union, and massive bloodshed ensued. Defenders of our party system argue that unless the parties can diffuse our social divisions by including a little something for everyone, and not standing far apart on issues, we can again be plunged into political violence.

Efficiency

With parties that are neither tightly disciplined nor ideologically far apart, compromise and flexibility are maintained in government, or so the system's defenders say. The parties can cooperate on major issues when necessary, especially when Congress is controlled by one party and the presidency by the other. Moreover, a change from presidency or Congress controlled by one party to a presidency or Congress controlled by the other party will not result in convulsive swings in policies. This makes for stability and order.

Imaginative leadership

If our parties were tightly disciplined and organized around their platforms, we are told, then political leaders would lack the ability to exercise bold, creative leadership. Every time a president or member of Congress wanted to depart from the party platform, he or she would have to contend with hordes of angry party members championing the platform of the past. If presidents had to be tied to their platforms, the defenders of the system ask, would Nixon have established relations with China? Would Franklin D. Roosevelt have unbalanced the budget in order to create needed social programs?

Each of these arguments can be refuted, notably by examining our comparable nations, most of which have more disciplined and ideological parties while maintaining social peace, governmental efficiency, and effective leadership. But rather than refuting these arguments, I want to show two ways in which they are consistent with a system of corporate capitalism. First of all, those who make such arguments seem to have a low regard for the mass of the American people. In brief, they assume that the people cannot be trusted to make electoral decisions based on serious policy considerations. If they are given half a chance, the argument goes, they will resort to political violence against each other; they need "umbrella parties" to keep them from one another's throats. If the people are able to choose between parties that stand behind their platforms, the result will be inefficiency in government and hamstrung leaders. Underlying these arguments is the belief that political elites know best: Let presidents and members of Congress deal with each other and decide their actions without the people looking closely over their shoulders.

Indeed, this is the corollary of the anti-populist philosophy behind the United States Constitution, as elaborated in several of the *Federalist Papers*.[28] It is also perfectly compatible with the spirit of capitalism, which in producing major inequalities in the social and economic realm, also creates a socioeconomic elite. The political result is a system that lacks the kind of popular control over that elite that a disciplined and ideological party system can provide.

The second way in which this party system is compatible with American capitalism is that it is profoundly oriented toward the status quo. Notice how often the concept of stability appears in the arguments presented above—social stability, and stability in government. Beyond this, there is an important truth about the role of government in a capitalist system. The only aggregation of power in the United States large enough to begin to change the economic and social order is the political order. Never in American history has the state come remotely close to an attempt to revise that socioeconomic order in a fundamental way. Yet the corporate establishment is quite nervous about its prerogatives, perhaps realizing the basic incompatibility between the norms of political equality and socioeconomic inequality. For whatever reason, corporate elites and their defenders are quick to cry socialism when even modest moves toward reform are made.

Despite such charges, government in America has grown, although usually in response to the demands of the private sector and far less than government elsewhere.[29] Nevertheless the corporate world realizes that government looms as its only serious potential challenger. If the American government ever wanted to mount such a challenge, it would have to overcome its own lack of coordination to do so. The American government is a perfect one for a nation which never wants to change things very much, for it is unwieldy and decentralized. Perhaps the only thing that could give government the will to try to force change on the rest of the system would be a disciplined and ideological party. Occasionally one of our parties gives a half-decent imitation of such a party, and changes which are *relatively* substantial for American politics occur. Consider, for example, the Democrats in the 1930s and the middle 1960s, and the Republicans in 1981; in each of those periods, the party in question voted as a bloc in Congress behind a bold presidential program, and significant changes in public policy ensued. But ordinarily our parties lack focus, and all who have an interest in keeping things pretty much as they are can breathe easily.

This is ultimately why our party system is so good for American capitalism, or any existing social order. Anyone who advocates major social change requiring political action should come to grips with the fact that a well-structured, well-coordinated political organization is probably the only means to achieve it. And it is difficult to think of such an organization without thinking of the political party.

Further Reading

This chapter was heavily influenced by Maurice Duverger's classics, *Political Parties,* trans. Barbara and Robert North (New York: John Wiley & Sons, 1963). A more recent work in the same vein is Giovanni Sartori's *Parties and Party Systems: Volume I* (New York; Cambridge Univ. Press, 1976). A major theme of any discussion of American parties must surely be their decline, and a breezy overview is William J. Crotty's *American Parties in Decline,* 2nd edition (Boston: Little, Brown, 1984).

Some scholars and activists have argued that parties have not declined, but are as strong as ever. Among them are Xandra Kayden and Eddie Mahe, Jr., in their book *The Party Goes On* (New York: Basic Books, 1985). Their argument is contradicted by much of the evidence of this and later chapters.

Notes

1. "Baker Fails to Induce G.O.P. Leaders to Back Javits," the *New York Times,* 17 May 1980, p. 25.
2. Samuel J. Eldersveld, *Political Parties: A Behavioral Analysis* (Chicago: Rand-McNally, 1964), 9. The term is from Harold Lasswell and Abraham Kaplan, *Power and Society* (New Haven: Yale Univ. Press, 1950).
3. In the national surveys conducted by the Center for Political Studies of the University of Michigan, the percentage of respondents who belonged to a political club, went to political meetings, or engaged in any other form of campaign work in presidential campaigns ranged from 9 percent to 16 percent from 1952 through 1984.
4. Maurice Duverger, *Political Parties,* trans. Barbara and Robert North (New York: John Wiley & Sons, 1963), 1; emphasis added.

5. Duverger, *Political Parties*, 1–2.

6. Duverger, *Political Parties*, 2–3.

7. For evidence of this, see Ivor Crewe, "Electoral Participation," in David Butler, Howard R. Penniman, and Austin Ranney, eds., *Democracy at the Polls* (Washington and London: American Enterprise Institute, 1981), 216–263, especially Table 10.4, 242–247.

8. Crewe, "Electoral Participation," 117–118.

9. Gabriel A. Almond and Sidney Verba, *The Civic Culture* (Princeton: Princeton Univ. Press, 1963), 131, 135–138.

10. Edmund Burke, "Thoughts on the Cause of Present Discontents," in *Works* (Boston: Little, Brown, 1971), I: 151.

11. On the post-office Republicans, see V. O. Key, Jr., *Southern Politics* (New York: Alfred A. Knopf, 1949), 292–297. Their fate in the 1950s is touched upon in Samuel Lubell, *The Revolt of the Moderates* (New York: Harper & Bros., 1956), 30–32.

12. For a fascinating account of how this worked in one German community, see William Sheridan Allen, *The Nazi Seizure of Power* (Chicago: Quadrangle Books, 1965).

13. Walter J. Stone and Alan I. Abramowitz, "Winning May Not Be Everything, But It's More Than We Thought," *American Political Science Review* LXXVII (December 1983), 945–956.

14. See Seymour Martin Lipset and Stein Rokkan, "Cleavage Structures, Party Systems, and Voter Alignments," in their edited volume, *Party Systems and Voter Alignments* (New York: Free Press, 1967), 1–64.

15. This comparison among nations is made in Giacomo Sani and Giovanni Sartori, "Frammentazione, Polarizzazione e Cleavages: Democrazie Facili e Dificili," *Rivista Italiana di Scienza Politica* VIII (Dicembre 1978), 339–362. Robert Harmel and Kenneth Janda, in their *Parties and Their Environments* (New York & London: Longman, 1982), chapter 3, come to a different conclusion based on data from 1957–1962, but in my opinion they are insufficiently sensitive to the differences between the Democrats in the United States and socialist and social democratic parties abroad.

16. "Laborites, Torn by Party Election, Press Ahead With Leftist Program," the *New York Times*, 29 September 1981, p. A10.

17. For example, in 1982 Walter Mondale said, "I'm a free competitive enterprise person. You don't hear any socialism out of me, or anything about a controlled economy." "Mondale on the Road for Distant Goal," the *New York Times*, 2 November 1982, p. D23.

18. Crewe, "Electoral Participation," Table 10.5, p.255. See also Robert R. Alford, *Party and Society* (Chicago: Rand-McNally, 1965).

19. Anthony Downs, *An Economic Theory of Democracy* (New York: Harper & Row, 1957), chapter 9.

20. Martin P. Wattenberg, *The Decline of American Political Parties 1952–1980* (Cambridge: Harvard Univ. Press, 1984).

21. Michael W. Traugott and John P. Katosh, "Response Validity in Surveys of Voting Behavior," *Public Opinion Quarterly* XLIII (Fall 1979), 359–377.

22. Sidney Verba, Norman H. Nie, and Jae-on Kim, *Participation and Political Equality* (New York: Cambridge Univ. Press, 1978).

23. See Walter Dean Burnham, "Party Systems and the Political Process," in William Nisbet Chambers and Walter Dean Burnham, eds. *The American Party Systems* (New York: Oxford Univ. Press, 1967), 301; Sidney Verba and Norman H. Nie, *Participation in America* (New York: Harper & Row, 1972), 208–210: and Howard L. Reiter, "Why Is Turnout Down?" *Public Opinion Quarterly* XLIII (Fall 1979), 297–311.

24. Duverger, *Political Parties*, introduction, especially pp. xxxiv–xxxvii.

25. Gallup results are from *The Gallup Opinion Index*, Number 183, December 1980. Election returns are from the *Guide to U.S. Elections* (Washington: Congressional Quarterly, 1976).

26. See Susan Blank, "Is the Race Fixed Against John Anderson?" in the American Civil

Liberties Union's publication, *Civil Liberties,* June 1980, 5–6; and Peter G. Samuels, "The Deck Is Stacked Against a Third Party," the *New York Times,* 1 April 1980, p. A19.

27. Among the authors who make the kinds of arguments to be discussed are Joseph A. Schumpeter, *Capitalism, Socialism, and Democracy,* 2nd ed. (New York & London: Harper & Bros., 1947), chapters 22–23; Herbert Agar, *The Price of Union* (Boston: Houghton Mifflin, 1950); Clinton Rossiter, *Parties and Politics in America* (Ithaca: Cornell Univ. Press, 1960); and Edward C. Banfield, "In Defense of the American Party System," in Robert A. Goldwin, ed., *Political Parties, U.S.A.* (Chicago: Rand McNally, 1961), 21–39.

28. See especially Numbers 6 and 10.

29. On the first point, see, for example, James O'Connor, *The Fiscal Crisis of the State* (New York: St. Martin's Press, 1973), and Alan Wolfe, *The Limits of Legitimacy* (New York: The Free Press, 1977). On the second point, see the data in Richard Rose and Guy Peters, *Can Government Go Bankrupt?* (New York: Basic Books, 1978), 253, 258; Robert W. Hartman, "The Budget Outlook," in Joseph A. Pechman, ed., *Setting National Priorities: The 1982 Budget* (Washington: The Brookings Institution, 1981), 193; and Arnold J. Heidenheimer, Hugh Heclo, and Carolyn Teich Adams, *Comparative Public Policy,* 2nd ed. (New York: St. Martin's Press, 1983), 173.

4

What Do Parties Do?

Political parties are an almost universal feature of political systems around the world today, and have been part of American politics almost uninterruptedly since the 1790s. Political observers, therefore, tend to take them for granted, and seldom wonder what functions parties perform that would not be carried out were parties not established. This chapter will examine party functions, for two reasons. First, because probably the most important question one can ask about any institution is: what exactly does it do and how would it be missed if it did not exist? This leads us to consider the decline of American parties described previously, a major theme of this book. If parties are weaker than they have been in many decades, what will be the impact on American society and politics? Only by thinking about what parties do can we begin to imagine those consequences.

One function of American political parties, already discussed in chapter 2, is in helping perpetuate the system of corporate capitalism by legitimizing the system in the eyes of the people. By legitimation, I mean giving the impression that the political system is open to all points of view, and that everyone has an equal role in choosing the leaders and policies of the nation. As parties and voting behavior have declined over time, we are led to wonder, first, if the American people are less enthusiastic than they used to be about how their political system works, and second, if parties are less able than before to help guide corporate capitalism through increasingly difficult times.

There are two considerations that impel us to explore the subject further. One is that parties may not be necessary for the perpetuation of corporate capitalism. Competitive elections, which existed in the United States before parties arose and which do not need parties, also serve the legitimizing function, as do the ideological apparatuses that teach people the values of liberal capitalism, while social welfare programs take the edge off the discontentment of the poor.[1] Parties are not the only agencies of legitimation, so it is entirely possible that corporate capitalism would survive in roughly its present shape even if parties did not exist. The second consideration is that parties perform other functions that make them important to the working of the political and social systems. By their very existence, they help to preserve corporate capitalism, but in other respects they affect how that system works. Exploring this is the task to which I now turn.

THE FUNCTIONS OF PARTIES

"Among political scientists," writes one of them, Leon Epstein, "virtually no anti-party, or nonparty, school has arisen to correspond to the anti-party sentiment of a substantial portion of the larger community."[2] Given a certain degree of ideological diversity among these scholars, this is indeed surprising. When academicians of left, right, and center all agree that parties are valuable institutions, we must ask if they are all describing the same thing when they discuss parties.

Conservative scholars have tended to agree with the premise of this book that parties promote the maintenance of the system, a function they heartily applaud. As Clinton Rossiter once wrote, "The American two-party system appears as one of the truly conservative arrangments in the world of politics."[3] Edward Banfield elaborated that the party system "has tended to check violence, moderate conflict, and narrow the cleavages within society; it has never produced, or very seriously threatened to produce, either mob rule or tyranny, and it has shown a marvelous ability to adapt to changing circumstances."[4] Conservatives are especially gratified that the vaguely defined Democratic and Republican parties have tended, in Banfield's words, to "narrow the cleavages." In other words, parties have reduced class divisions by failing to speak explicitly for class interests or to encourage the working class to use the political system to advance its interests.[5]

To many liberals, political parties are, in V. O. Key's words, "basic instruments for the translation of mass preferences into public policy."[6] The Italian scholar Giovanni Sartori points out that other institutions, such as public opinion surveys, can transmit mass preferences, but only parties "transmit demands *backed by pressure*."[7] This is of course the promise of liberal capitalism, and I argue that, in practice, this process is seriously limited.[8] It must be said, however, that the existence of parties may have some marginal effect on the tendency of people to think of serious issues of public policy rather than of the personalities of the candidates. After all, the party label induces people to think, in at least limited fashion, about what in the abstract unites the candidates who run on it, and that is likely to lead to considerations of policy. In 1978 a nationwide survey asked voters what they liked and disliked about the parties and the congressional candidates; 47 percent cited issues when discussing parties, while only 14 percent mentioned issues when reacting to candidates.[9] On the other hand, during campaigns, parties and candidates often seek to obscure issues in order not to antagonize voters.[10]

Scholars on the left include Walter Dean Burnham, who has called parties "the only devices thus far invented by the wit of western man that can, with some effectiveness, generate countervailing collective power on behalf of the many individually powerless against the relatively few who are individually or organizationally powerful."[11] This argument suggests that the lower classes benefit most from the existence of parties. The upper classes have a variety of available political resources, including control of the economic and social structure, knowledge of how the political system operates, leisure time in which to participate in politics, and campaign contributions. But those in the lower reaches of the socioeconomic structure have only one major political resource, their numbers. But numbers are a particularly dormant resource when concentrated among people with little knowledge of politics and scant leisure time. The only way to mobilize these numbers effectively is through organization, a cadre of people who concentrate on politics and how the masses can be educated politically and induced to participate in elections and lobbying. To the upper classes, a party provides only a marginal benefit when compared with all their other advantages; to the lower classes, a party organization stalwart's prompting may make all the differernce between political activism and apathy.

European political scholars and activists, being more used to thinking in class terms, have long argued this. Lenin wrote in 1902,

> I assert (1) that no revolutionary movement can endure without a stable organization of leaders maintaining continuity; (2) that the broader the popular mass drawn spontaneously into the struggle, which forms the basis of the movement and participates in it, the more urgent the need for such an organization, and the more solid this organization must be.[12]

During the same era, the non-revolutionary Swiss socialist Robert Michels argued that "the principle of organization is an absolutely essential condition for the political struggle of the masses," and, in the 1950s, the French scholar Maurice Duverger concluded from similar observations that parties "are always more necessary on the Left than on the Right" and that "a regime without parties is of necessity a conservative regime."[13] In other words, a regime without parties will not represent the interests of the lower classes, and will therefore be controlled completely by elites.

We seem to have come full circle, from Clinton Rossiter's calling the American party system conservative to Maurice Duverger's use of the same word to characterize non-party regimes. This raises again the question I asked earlier: Can these authors be writing about the same institution? I think they can, and this paradox can be explained in two ways. First, while American parties have always had the *potential* to represent lower-class interests, ever since the 1890s there have been powerful structural constraints that have kept them from doing so in the way that many European parties have.[14] To this extent, American parties are somewhat unusual. Second, and perhaps more to the point, there is no inherent contradiction between the Rossiter and the Duverger positions. Parties can both maintain the system *and* favor certain groups within that system, even if the favored groups are not the ones that benefit most from the system. Indeed, if the parties' primary function is legitimation, they *should* favor the lower classes; otherwise parties would be seen as just another bulwark of class privilege.

All in all, there is a common thread that unites these positive functions of parties. Whether parties are seen as defusing social conflict (the reason that conservatives love them), transmitting popular attitudes (the reason that liberals favor them), or mobilizing the lower classes (the reason that radicals are partial to them), they provide organization for social ends. Whether those ends involve the masses—pacifying them or mobilizing them—or the state—uniting a majority of legislators, providing common ground between executives and legislators—parties are an effective way of providing an ongoing basis for achieving their goals. As Sartori has put it, "No parties at all leaves a society out of reach, out of control."[15] For this reason, reforms that weaken party organization may make it difficult for anybody, left or right, to accomplish collective purposes.[16]

POLITICS WITHOUT PARTIES

Fortunately, the question of what politics would look like without parties need not be answered only by speculation. There have been two major studies of American politics in non-partisan situations, and they can help us envision a possible future for the United States should the decline of parties continue.

In the late 1940s, the political scientist V. O. Key traveled all over the American South and produced his classic monumental study of each state's politics.[17] At that time, the Republican party was a negligible force in most parts of the South, which was widely regarded as having a one-party system. Key, however, concluded that with no significant Republican threat, most southern Democrats felt no need for a cohesive organization; in effect there was no party organization of any kind. The result was a no-party system in which the Democratic party was merely a label for which candidates vied in the primary. In eight of the eleven states that Key examined, there were more votes cast in the Democratic gubernatorial primary than in the general election.[18] Therefore, among the Democrats, the South in the 1940s provides a test case of a political system with no real parties. For all the changes in the South since then, Key's analysis gives us a picture of such a system, perhaps with analogies to the entire nation in our own day. To what extent did that system lack the benefits that parties are supposed to provide?

A candidate running in such a primary, without the benefit of the backing of a party organization, often had to compete against a large number of other candidates, and making himself or herself known was a major hurdle. There was no organization to promote his or her name or to screen out fanatics, and many candidates therefore resorted to demagoguery to become known; in the old South racism was often the form of demagoguery used. "Perhaps a clue to the picturesque quality of many southern political leaders," suggested Key, a Southerner himself, "lies in the fact that attention-attracting antics function as a substitute for party machinery in the organization of support."[19] Support for Key's hypothesis lies in the example of California, a state with weak party organization which seems to produce candidates of unusual personal flamboyance (former governor Jerry Brown), nasty campaign tactics (Richard Nixon), or strong ideological appeals (Ronald Reagan).[20]

In this system, primary campaigns were frequently "the emptiest sorts of debates over personalities,"[21] and it was hard for the voters to tell the difference between candidates who supported the incumbents' policies and those who disagreed with them. In a partisan system party labels indicate that, generally speaking, candidates who share the party label of the incumbent are more likely to continue existing policies than those who belong to other parties. Without party labels, how could a voter endorse or reject existing policies? How could one know where each of many candidates stood? Even when a voter found a candidate to support, as soon as that candidate was no longer running it became difficult to see who else would carry out the same policies. Key demonstrated that often confused voters simply voted for the local or regional favorite, which he noted "may be an indicator of the absence of class politics or at least the disfranchisement of one class."[22] Finally, he noted that in the absence of a party organization that could provide a candidate with a ready-made team of campaign workers, many candidates secured adherents by promising all sorts of personal favors, thereby lowering the quality and ethics of state government.

Once in office, candidates had to provide those favors in order to maintain their coalitions. A system of personal factions also made government unstable, as policies could change rapidly when one candidate succeeded another, unbound by a common party tie. Moreover, noted Key, "A party system provides at least a semblance of joint responsibility between governor and legislature."[23] Without it, squabbles between the governor and legislature are more the norm than in systems where the party creates a bond between them.

Key's analysis concluded with the question, "Who benefits from political disorganization?[24] His answer was straightforward: the "haves rather than the have nots." Noting that "sustained programs of action . . . almost always are thought by the better element to be contrary to its immediate interests,"[25] Key concluded that only an organization—a political party—can carry through such programs.

It follows, if these propositions are correct, that over the long run the have-nots lose in a disorganized politics. They have no mechanism through which to act and their wishes find expression in fitful rebellions led by transient demagogues who gain their confidence but often have neither the technical competence nor the necessary stable base of political power to effectuate a program.[26]

When a governor speaking for the poor did emerge, there was no guarantee that his policies would survive his term. Alabama's Jim Folsom succumbed to alcoholism, and there was no sustained organization to carry on in his tradition. In Louisiana, the machine did survive Huey Long, but its adherents (including Long's son, former Senator Russell Long), were often anything but populists. In contrast, the New Deal survived Franklin Roosevelt in the form of the national Democratic party.

Another scholar who has studied the consequences of nonpartisanship is Willis Hawley, who examined a group of cities in California that elect their municipal officials in a nonpartisan fashion.[27] Examining data from those cities in the 1950s and 1960s, Hawley found indirect evidence for the proposition that parties tend to mobilize the lower classes. Hewley found that cities without parties were especially likely to elect Republicans to office (although of course their party identification did not appear on the ballot), to have low turnout (non-voting being, of course, usually highest among the poor), and to adopt public policies that were least favorable to lower-class interests. Hawley inferred from this that upper-class people do not need parties to educate them about politics, and unlike lower-class people they can look out for their own interests even in the absence of parties.

Between them, Key and Hawley seem to endorse most of the propositions about the functions of parties cited earlier in this chapter. In the old South, parties were not available to structure and confine social conflict, make it easier for the electorate to express its wishes, or help the lower classes to mobilize. In California's nonpartisan cities, this last function was missing as well. On the other hand, it is important to note that Key was not arguing that parties in northern states necessarily performed those functions either; nor was Hawley arguing that partisan cities necessarily represented the interests of the poor effectively.[28] As I shall stress again and again, the American party system has not been very effective in translating public opinion into public policy or representing the interests of the poor, most of whom do not even vote. The most appropriate conclusion to draw from Key and Hawley's studies is that without parties it is even less likely that such functions will be performed.

THE PARTY-INTEREST GROUP SEESAW

There is one more major consequence of the decline of parties to be discussed. It has long been argued that parties and interest groups are competitors in the political process, and that as one declines the other grows stronger. We might picture them as on a seesaw, one going down as the other rises. Numerous scholars have made this point:

- Key noted that in the old South, "individual corporations, individual industries, and particular groups, if they are skillful manipulators, can gain great immediate advantage in the chaos of a loose one-party factionalism," although he added that the unpredictability of such a politics could turn the tables on any particular interest.[29]
- Many observers have argued that where parties are weak, legislators are especially prone to the influence of pressure groups. Strong legislative party leadership enables a member to say to a lobbyist, "Sorry, my leader won't let me vote for your bill." Strong parties also provide campaign funds for candidates and make them less reliant on the support of interest groups, and provide guidance on voting for particular bills.[30]
- In an extensive analysis of state politics, Sarah McCally Morehouse found that states with strong parties had weak pressure groups, and vice versa. Nine of the fifteen strong-party states had weak pressure groups, and all fourteen of the weak-party states, for example, had strong groups.[31]
- Martin Wattenberg discovered that interest-group spending on campaigns for the U.S. House of Representatives in 1978 was highest where the party organization was considered weakest, and vice versa.[32]
- M. Margaret Conway has shown that throughout the 1970s, the proportion of congressional campaign funds that came from interest groups rose substantially, while the proportion coming from parties dropped.[33]

If there is an inverse relationship between parties and interest groups, then the decline of parties should provide new opportunities for the influence of private groups in politics. Indeed, some have linked the atrophy of parties to such a rise in interest-group power.[34] While it would be impossible to demonstrate conclusively that the decline of parties *caused* the proliferation of interest groups, there is much evidence that the latter phenomenon has occurred during the recent weakening of parties. Take, for example, political action committees (PACs), which are established by interest groups and others to raise and spend campaign contributions. In 1974 there were 608 PACs registered with the federal government; by 1984 there were 4,009. In 1972 PACs spent $19 million; twelve years later they spent $265 million. After accounting for inflation, that was a more than five-fold increase. From 1972 to 1982 PAC contributions jumped from 14 percent of donations to contests for the U.S. House of Representatives to 31 percent, and in Senate races the increase was from 12 to 19 percent. Those elected to the House in 1980 got 33 percent of their funds from PACs, and four years later the proportion was 44 percent. While federal law limits the amount that party committees can donate to candidates, in 1985 the Supreme Court ruled that Congress could not limit independent PAC spending on behalf of presidential candidates.[35]

One study found that in 1980 the number of people who gave contributions to PACs equalled the number who donated to candidates and was twice as great as the number who contributed to parties. In 1982 PACs raised almost as much as the parties did, $190 million compared with $218 million, respectively. Many observers have concluded that the PACs have weakened the parties.[36] There are also indications that another form of interest-group political action, lobbying, is on the increase. In 1977 there were about four thousand lobbyists in Washington, compared with ten to twenty thousand five years later. A study of a sample of Washington lobbyists published in 1983 found that at least half reported having increased such activities as forming coalitions with other groups, mounting grass-roots lobbying efforts, and donating to campaigns. A survey of major corporations discovered that while only 17 percent had a Washington office in 1968, 43 percent had established one ten years later.[37]

If it is true that the decline of parties is accompanied by a rise in the activity of interest groups, what impact is this likely to have on the American political system? Are interest groups to be welcomed or feared as an alternative to parties? We will now consider the debate over "pluralism," or the theory that politics is best understood as the interplay of various private interests.

PLURALISM—PRO AND CON

Capitalism, like any system based on the private concentration of economic power, is likely to encourage the activity of numerous privately based pressure groups in the political process. Americans have always been ambivalent about pluralism, happy to join and contribute to groups but concerned about their role in government. This had led to much controversy among scholars of American politics about whether pluralism serves the interests of the American people as a whole. This debate is the American equivalent of the far more profound conflict in most of the rest of the capitalist world between capitalists and socialists. In some respects, the American argument between advocates of pluralism and its critics is a watered-down version of the capitalist-socialist controversy.

Arguments for pluralism

The father of American pluralist thought was James Madison, and his best-known writings on the subject are contained in the tenth of the *Federalist Papers*. Madison was genuinely troubled about the effects of interest groups, which he called factions, because he was torn between the faith that society has a general good that overrides individual differences and the liberal capitalist emphasis on conflict among self-interested individuals.[38] However, he came down on the side of encouraging interest groups, first because he saw them as part of human nature ("The latent causes of faction are . . . sown in the nature of man"), and second because he believed that through conflict the many factions would balance each other out, making it impossible for a coalition of several of them to secure the permanent control of the government.[39] Madison's desire for a proliferation of interest groups is reflected in the First Amendment to the Constitution, which asserts "the right of the people peaceably to assemble, and to petition the government for a redress of grievances."

If Madison saw factions as necessary evils, it was left to others to describe the positive virtues of private groups. In the 1830s, the French observer Alexis de Tocqueville argued that such associations would be a "guarantee against the tyranny of the majority" by giving people in the minority on any issue a group of allies; they would enable great deeds to be accomplished in the absence of big government; they would help develop human sociability by encouraging people to interact with one another; they would provide a civic education to members (think of *Robert's Rules of Order*); and they would help prevent revolutions by giving people a stake in the existing order.[40] More than a century later, the American political scientist David Truman argued forcefully that groups provide access to government for everyone.[41] Note the conservative flavor of some of these arguments, with Madison and Tocqueville fearing majorities and de Tocqueville arguing that associations would help to prevent revolution.

Arguments against pluralism

The proposition that a political system based primarily on interest groups poorly serves the American public has been made on a variety of fronts. One of the most important of these arguments is that, as one member of Congress has put it, "the sum of all the PAC interests is not equal to the whole public interest."[42] A political scientist describes the PAC scene:

> The Peanut Butter and Nut Processors Association has its NUTPAC. The beer distributors have their SixPAC. Whataburger, Inc., operates Whata-PAC. There is a Bread-PAC (American Bakers Association), an EggPAC (United Egg Producers), a FishPAC (National Fisheries Institute), a Food PAC (Food Marketing Institute), and—to wash it all down—a Dr. Pepper PAC.[43]

With thousands of such organizations representing thousands of specialized interests, it is difficult to imagine optimal public policies resulting, in some mystical fashion, from the aggregation of all their demands, as the advocates of pluralism often claim. In contrast, argue champions of political parties, parties "are instrumental to collective benefits, to an end that is not merely the private benefit of the contestants." "A party is a part of a whole attempting to serve the purposes of the whole, whereas a faction is only a part for itself."[44] Particularly forceful on this point was the American political scientist E. E. Schattschneider, who wrote that "the parties are superior [to the special interests] because they must consider the problems of government broadly, they submit their fate to an election, and are responsible to the public."[45]

Nobody would deny that parties have often strong ties to interest groups, but advocates of strong parties argue that parties must necessarily address the broad public interest because it would be suicidal for a party to *claim* to be the "party of business" or the "party of labor" or whatever. In order to draw votes from outside those constituencies, parties must *claim* to be speaking for the public interest; at the very least, this means addressing a broad swath of issues that do not necessarily concern the narrow-based interest groups with which they are allied. Therefore, only parties, and not interest groups, can ever approximate the genuine public interest.

This raises one of the thorniest questions of political theory, whether there is such a thing as a "public interest" that broadly encompasses everyone in a society. Some extreme advocates of pluralism argue that there is no public interest, there are only group interests; the nation is too diverse to have its own interests.[46] Critics of pluralism counter that some groups are very diverse, too; if they have common interests, despite their heterogeneity, then why not the nation?[47] Radicals argue that in any society dominated by class interests, like the United States, there can be no general interest that unites all classes, and the concept of a "public interest" is a sham intended to fool the lower classes into supporting the interests of the upper classes.[48] The only political outcome that would truly be in everyone's interest would be a transformation to socialism.

I am inclined toward this radical viewpoint, but it is often overstated. Political institutions that use the rhetoric of the public interest in a capitalist system can play a small role in overcoming the egoistical orientation that is essential to liberal capitalism. Telling the public that there are broad interests shared by everyone suggests that narrow self-interest is not the only consideration in politics. Still, this is not an argument for the existence of a public interest. A more fruitful way to look at the matter, it seems to me, is to contrast narrow interests with broad interests. There are broad interests shared by large classes of people, such as tough consumer laws, clean air and water, and adequate public education. These may not be in everyone's perceived short-term interest—to a manufacturer, environmental and consumer regulations are sometimes seen as a burden, and a person without children in the public schools might oppose raising school taxes—but they are surely broader interests than, say, a tax benefit for a particular industry.[49]

In the contrast between broad and narrow interests, parties potentially have an advantage over interest groups. It has been pointed out by
many that narrow interests are more easily mobilized than broad interests;
for example, a very high proportion of oil producers are members of
various lobby or PAC groups, while only a small fraction of the nation's
consumers (who of course comprise the entire population) are members of
consumer groups.[50] "In the last decade," writes one analyst, "the PACs
with narrowly defined issues and very specific missions have made the
great leaps forward."[51] As argued earlier, parties must necessarily use the
rhetoric of broad interests and are more likely to address them than interest groups. However, party advocates exaggerate the extent to which
American parties truly represent such broad interests, for the bias in the
capitalist system is toward the interests of a few.

There are other arguments against a system based on interest groups.
One is that the leaders of such groups do not represent their members
adequately. Those who make this argument cite Robert Michels' "iron law
of oligarchy," which holds that all organizations sooner or later become
dominated by an unrepresentative leadership.[52] The classic illustration in
the literature of pluralism is labor unions, and a recent example is the
Mondale campaign of 1984. The labor federation AFL-CIO endorsed
Mondale in 1983 after polling fewer than a quarter of its members; only a
minority of AFL-CIO members in a *New York Times*/CBS News survey
sample reported that they favored the Minnesotan.[53] Despite the backing
of Mondale by an overwhelming majority of union leaders in the fall of
1984, roughly 43 percent of union members stayed home, and 23 percent
voted for other candidates. This means that only 34 percent of union
members voted for the man on whose behalf enormous resources of the
labor movement were committed.[54] Therefore the pluralist process did a
poor job of representing the views of most union members during the
1984 presidential campaign. On the other hand, "many corporate PACs
can hardly be considered showcases of democracy either."[55]

There are other problems with interest groups, too. One is that they
have carved out turf in many areas of public policy. Instead of bargaining
and compromising, as so many advocates of pluralism claim, many groups
concentrate on an executive agency and a congressional subcommittee and
dominate policy in that area virtually unchallenged. Among the serious
consequences of this, according to liberal critics, are a blurring of the
distinction between public and private power; a loss of accountability,
with the president and congressional leaders enjoying little sway over policy in these areas and the public being powerless to change policy through
the electoral process; and the fragmentation of public policy.[56]

These criticisms are generally valid, although it must be pointed out
that the capture of public policy by private forces is a natural consequence
of any capitalist system; even if this process were eliminated, elections
would still have little to do with changing policy. Surely the fragmentation

of policy has always been an integral part of the American political system, and it becomes particularly significant at a time when corporate capitalism needs all the coherent state backup it can get. But I have saved for last the most important problem with pluralism, and it is the focus of the next section.

PLURALISM'S UPPER-CLASS ACCENT

E. E. Schattschneider's best-known comment about pluralism was, "The flaw in the pluralist heaven is that the heavenly chorus sings with a strong upper-class accent."[57] In other words, the people whose interests are represented by interest groups tend to be those of the upper classes— business over labor, rich over poor.[58] This is the most profoundly undemocratic aspect of pluralism, and it requires some substantiation.

We start with a look at which Americans join politically relevant organizations. In Table 4.1 we can see, from a national survey taken in 1972, how many Americans of various social standings were members of groups of the sort that often become involved in politics. We can see that people of higher social standing are consistently more likely to join such groups, which suggests that the interest-group process is more likely to represent their interests than those of the non-joiners, who are of lower social status. It is important to recall the related fact that voting and other forms of political participation are also highly class-related.[59]

Table 4.1. Percentage of various social groups who were members of particular organizations in 1972.

Education	
0-8 years	17 %
9-12 years	30
At least some college	52
Family income	
Less than $10,000	24
$10,000 or more	48
Class self-description	
Working-class	28
Middle-class	41

Note: Read this table as follows: Of those people with 8 years of education or less, 17 percent belonged to at least one of the following types of organizations: business groups, professional groups, farm organizations, political clubs or organizations, civic groups, special-interest groups or lobbies, or labor unions.
Source: 1972 national survey, University of Michigan Center for Political Studies

An examination of PACs makes the point more directly. As the conservative Republican senator from Kansas, Robert Dole, has stated, "There aren't any Poor PACs or Food Stamp PACs or Nutrition PACs or Medicare PACs."[60] In the words of one scholar who generally downplays the fears that others have of PACs, "PACs on the conservative side of the spectrum, broadly defined, are giving more [to candidates] than their ideological rivals."[61]

Because the essential business of PACs is to raise and spend money, business PACs have an enormous advantage over labor and other liberal PACs. In one day alone in 1983, Amoco PAC collected $2,788 from company employees. Analysis of a sample of PACs in the early 1980s found that the average donation to a business PAC was $160 and to a labor PAC it was $14. When asked what kind of candidates they like to support, "if all else were the same between two candidates," nearly twice as many PAC managers said conservatives as said liberals, and they favored Republicans over Democrats by a margin of 27 to 21 percent. Business PACs have developed effective networks through such organizations as the Business and Industry PAC (BIPAC), the Chamber of Commerce, and the Public Affairs Council. A majority of PAC managers in the sample just cited reported receiving information from BIPAC, while fewer than a fourth used data from the AFL-CIO's Committee on Political Education. An overwhelming majority of the PAC money received by congressional leaders comes from corporate PACs.[62]

The net effect is that large majorities of the members of Congress get more money from business PACs than from labor PACs. About two-thirds of the people elected to the House of Representatives in 1984 were backed more by business than by labor, and the same was true of three out of four senators elected from 1980 through 1984. Small wonder that an official of BIPAC said of the Democratic senators up for reelection in 1984, "At least half of them have good records."[63]

There is every indication that the business advantage has been increasing. As one study put it, "the growth of PAC funding has generally favored incumbents and Republicans."[64] In Table 4.2 we can see that corporation and trade association PACs have been proliferating both in numbers and in wealth at a far greater rate than have labor union PACs. For example, labor PACs spent slightly more than corporate and trade association PACs did in 1972, but were outspent by the two business categories by a ratio of nearly two-and-a-half to one in 1984.[65]

Within the plush world of corporate PACs, their unrepresentativeness is compounded by the fact that large corporations dominate the scene. In 1978, for example, 70 percent of the 100 largest manufacturing firms had PACs, compared with only 33 percent of the next 400 firms, and 8 percent of the next 500 firms. Moreover, the larger the corporation, the wealthier the PAC. Michael Useem found that people who served on the boards of several large corporations were far more likely than directors of only one

Table 4.2. Growth of different kinds of political action committees (PACs), 1972–1984.

A) Number of PACs

	1974	1976	1978	1980	1982	1984
Labor	201	224	217	297	380	394
Corporate	89	433	784	1204	1467	1682
Trade assoc.	*	*	451	574	628	698
Other	318	489	201	476	896	1235
Total	608	1146	1653	2551	3371	4009

B) Spending by PACs, in millions of dollars

	1972	1974	1976	1978	1980	1982	1984
Labor	8.5	11.0	17.5	18.6	25.1	34.8	47.4
Corporate	8.0**	8.1**	5.8	15.2	31.4	43.3	59.0
Trade assoc.			**	23.8	32.0	41.9	53.9
Other	2.6	0.8	29.6	19.8	42.5	70.2	104.7
Total	19.1	19.9	52.9	77.4	131.1	190.2	265.0

*Trade association PACs were not counted as a separate category until 1977.
**Trade association PACs were combined with corporate PACs in 1972 and 1974, and were included in "other" PACs in 1976.
Sources: Larry J. Sabato, PAC Power (New York: W. W. Norton, 1984), pp. 12–14; "The PACs Are Proliferating," National Journal, February 9, 1985, p. 350; and press release issued by the Federal Election Commission dated May 19, 1985.

or two such firms to contribute to candidates (usually Republicans) and to make large donations in 1972. Corporations of the multi-board directors were more likely to have PACs, and to have lavishly funded PACs, than the others.[66]

Not only do business PACs far outspend labor PACs, and not only are business PACs likely to represent the interests of large corporations, but business derives many other benefits from the PAC process. First is the role of ideological PACs, which are heavily weighted to the right and support business interests. In 1984, for example, by far the biggest-spending such PAC was the National Conservative PAC (NCPAC), which spent well over $19 million; its closet competitor spent "only" $5 million. Next in order of spending in 1984 were the Fund for a Conservative Majority, [Jesse Helms'] National Congressional Club, the Republican Majority Fund, and the Ruff-PAC, established by a prominent financial consultant. All supported conservative candidates and policies.[67]

Business has other advantages, too. "Among the PACs of the right," notes the political scientist Frank Sorauf, "there is sharing of information, joint interviewing of candidates, overlapping leadership, and some cooperation in strategy and tactics."[68] This kind of network can, in effect, overcome the $5,000 limit on how much a PAC can give a candidate; PACs can far exceed that amount with coordinated contributions. The effectiveness of the networks is facilitated by the cooperation of Republican campaign committees that conduct surveys of congressional races and provide such data to PACs in order to help them decide whom to support. This was a factor in the Republicans' capture of the U.S. Senate in 1980.[69]

This imbalance has had some clear legislative effects, including a number of major conservative victories on congressional votes since the late 1970s on matters of consumer protection, labor law, regulation of used-car dealers, and taxes. On a key labor issue in 1977, eleven Democratic representatives switched to the pro-business position, and their votes were crucial to the defeat of the measure. Labor PACs retaliated by giving these representatives $69,000 less in 1978 than they had in 1976, but business and trade association PACs more than made up for the loss by increasing their donations by $169,000. In the tax battles of 1981, conservative groups had twenty-two times the lobbying budget of labor and other liberal groups.[70]

If interest groups are slanted to the right and parties are more likely to represent the interests of a broad cross section of the people, we should expect to find liberals more enthusiastic about parties and less happy about PACs, and conservatives just the opposite. While a clear test of the proposition may be unavailable, there are intriguing examples. In the 1790s, it was the more "liberal" politicians like Thomas Jefferson and James Madison who first organized parties, while "conservatives" like Alexander Hamilton did so only reluctantly.[71] Hamilton helped write George Washington's Farewell Address, with its famous attack on partisanship. A survey of House candidates in 1978 found conservatives far more supportive than liberals of PACs.[72]

PARTIES AND THE POLITICAL COMMUNITY

In this chapter, I have argued that the interest-group system has given many Americans a false impression that political equality is a meaningful reality in the United States. The theme of this book is that the American party system makes a similar claim, and that it too is deceptive. Does this mean that it makes no difference whether the United States bases its politics on parties or on pluralism?

Perhaps the best answer is that parties *can* perform some of the functions claimed by the scholars cited earlier in the chapter, but not the parties that Americans have become used to. Parties that are oriented primarily toward winning elections instead of representing classes or promulgating policies will never come close to fulfilling their potential. Because of that potential, having parties in the United States is preferable to not having them, but only marginally so. For example, consider this grim prophecy of a partyless United States by the liberal historian, Arthur Schlesinger, Jr.:

Political adventurers will roam the countryside like Chinese warlords or Iranian ayatollahs, recruiting personal armies, conducting hostilities against some rival warlords and forming alliances with others, and, as they win elections, striving to govern through ad hoc coalitions in legislatures. The prospect is not inviting. The crumbling away of the historic parties would leave political power in America concentrated in the adventurers, in the interest groups that finance them and in the executive bureaucracy.[73]

In the following chapters I shall demonstrate that this is a reasonably accurate picture of American politics today.

Understand that the de-emphasis upon parties is only symptomatic of a broader problem with the American view of politics. Christian Bay has written that politics and politicians are "the only agencies and agents that might potentially come to contribute a menace to the interests of the overprivileged; the only potentially rational, disinterested agencies and agents of justice and the common good."[74] A genuine politics is one in which the people decide their common fate in the resolution of public policies through public institutions. American capitalism has instilled in the people a great fear of public power, a distrust of popular institutions such as parties and legislatures, and a great trust in the great institutions of private power. Ever since the rise of the giant corporations in the late nineteenth century, there has been a tendency to remove politics from popular agencies, sometimes in the name of reform,[75] sometimes in the name of "scientific" public administration and expertise, sometimes in the name of bipartisanship in foreign policy. All of these trends, and others, were intended to insulate elites from popular power, whether those elites be public administrators, experts, or the foreign policy establishment.

In a political system that provides the public with an inadequate comprehension of major issues, keeping policy in the hands of elites seems sensible to many people. The price, however, is heavy. If the public does not decide policy, the private sector will, and it will decide it in the interest of a well-heeled few. Such a system also produces an apathetic citizenry prey to the most simplistic kinds of political appeals and a democracy in name only. True democracy involves mobilizing the public for public purposes, and political parties that organize classes and promote policies are the best vehicle for this. Instead, as Walter Dean Burnham has put it, we have "antiparties."[76] In the absence of true parties, the political system becomes an empty shell in which the privileged can compete for advantage.

Further Reading

A lively account of an American political system without effectively functioning parties is V. O. Key, Jr.'s classic *Southern Politics* (New York: Alfred A. Knopf, 1949); see the chapters on the various states, and especially chapter 14. Walter

Dean Burnham provides an incisive portrait of party decline and its significance in "The End of American Party Politics," *Trans-Action* (December 1969), 12–22. There is a vast literature on pluralism, pro and con. Classic statements are David B. Truman's *The Governmental Process* (New York: Alfred A. Knopf, 1951), which defends pluralism, and Grant McConnell's *Private Power and American Democracy* (New York: Alfred A. Knopf, 1966), which criticizes it. Research on political action committees is growing, and perhaps the most comprehensive account, which does not share this book's perspective, is Larry J. Sabato's *PAC Power* (New York: W. W. Norton, 1984).

Notes

1. See chapter 2 for a fuller discussion of these phenomena.
2. Leon D. Epstein, "The Scholarly Commitment to Parties," in Ada W. Finifter, ed., *Political Science* (Washington: American Political Science Association, 1983), 127–153.
3. Clinton Rossiter, *Parties and Politics in America* (Ithaca, N.Y.: Cornell Univ. Press, 1960), 64.
4. Edward C. Banfield, "In Defense of the American Party System," in Robert A. Goldwin, ed., *Political Parties, U.S.A.* (Chicago: Rand McNally, 1961), 22–23.
5. See Rossiter, *Parties and Politics,* 57–58; Banfield, "In Defense," 30–31; and Herbert Agar, *The Price of Union* (Boston: Houghton Mifflin, 1966), 689–690.
6. V.O. Key, Jr., *Public Opinion and American Democracy* (New York: Alfred A. Knopf, 1961), 433. See also Gerald M. Pomper, *Voters' Choice* (New York: Dodd, Mead, 1975), 164, 166, 183–184.
7. Giovanni Sartori, *Parties and Party Systems: Volume I* (Cambridge, England: Cambridge Univ. Press, 1976), 28; emphasis his.
8. See chapters 1, 7, and 8.
9. Martin P. Wattenberg, *The Decline of American Political Parties 1952–1980* (Cambridge: Harvard Univ. Press, 1984), 111.
10. See chapter 8, below.
11. Walter Dean Burnham, "The End of American Party Politics," *Trans-Action* (December 1969), 20.
12. V. I. Lenin, *What Is To Be Done?* (New York: International Publishers, 1969), 121.
13. Robert Michels, *Political Parties,* trans. Eden and Cedar Paul (New York: Collier Books, 1962), 62; and Maurice Duverger, *Political Parties,* trans. Barbara and Robert North (New York: John Wiley & Sons, 1954), 426.
14. See chapter 5.
15. Sartori, *Parties and Party Systems,* 42.
16. See chapter 6.
17. V. O. Key, Jr., *Southern Politics* (New York: Alfred A. Knopf, 1949).
18. Key, *Southern Politics,* 409.
19. Key, *Southern Politics,* 46.
20. See for example Garry Wills, *Nixon Agonistes* (Boston: Houghton Mifflin, 1970), 75–79. It is important to note, however, that party organizations that screen out bizarre or flamboyant candidates are also likely to eliminate those with views outside the mainstream, another way that parties protect the political system from dissident views.
21. Key, *Southern Politics,* 304.
22. Key, *Sothern Politics,* 302.
23. Key, *Southern Politics,* 308.

24. Key, *Southern Politics*, 307.

25. Key, *Southern Politics*, 308.

26. Key, *Southern Politics*, 307.

27. Willis D. Hawley, *Nonpartisan Elections and the Case for Party Politics* (New York: John Wiley & Sons, 1973).

28. This point, which has been missed by many scholars who have cited Key's work, has been argued by Hugh Douglas Price in "Rise and Decline of One-Party Systems in Anglo-American Experience," in Samuel P. Huntington and Clement H. Moore, eds., *Authoritarian Politics in Modern Society* (New York: Basic Books, 1970), 92–96; and Eric M. Uslaner, "Comparative State Policy Formation, Interparty Competition, and Malapportionment," *Journal of Politics* XL (May 1978), 409–432.

29. Key, *Southern Politics*, 309.

30. See, for example, Thomas Byrne Edsall, *The New Politics of Inequality* (New York: W. W. Norton, 1984), 108–109; and Frank J. Sorauf, "Political Action Committees in American Politics," in *What Price PACs?* (New York: Twentieth Century Fund, 1984), 79–80.

31. Sarah McCally Morehouse, *State Politics, Parties and Policy* (New York: Holt, Rinehart & Winston, 1981), 177.

32. Wattenberg, *Decline of American Political Parties*, 109–110.

33. M. Margaret Conway, "PACs, the New Politics, and Congressional Campaigns," in Allan J. Cigler and Burdett A. Loomis, eds., *Interest Group Politics* (Washington: Congressional Quarterly Press, 1983), 131, 133. Conway notes that some interest-group campaign committees are aligned with parties.

34. See Sorauf, "Political Action Committees," 84; Nicos Poulantzas, *Political Power and Social Classes*, trans. Timothy O'Hagan (London: Verso Editions, 1978), 315; and Claus Offe, "The Attribution of Public Status to Interest Groups," in Suzanne Berger, ed., *Organizing Interests in Western Europe* (Cambridge, England: Cambridge Univ. Press, 1981), 143.

35. "The PACs Are Proliferating," *National Journal* (February 9, 1985), 350; Larry J. Sabato, *PAC Power* (New York: W. W. Norton, 1984), 14; Sorauf, "Political Action Committees," 39, 91; "Political Action Funds Put at Record in House," the *New York Times*, 12 April 1985, p. B7; press release issued by the Federal Election Commission dated May 19, 1985; and "Court Strikes Down Limits on Independent PAC Outlays," *Congressional Quarterly Weekly Report*, 23 March 1985, 532–534. The judicial decision was Federal Election Commission v. National Conservative Political Action Committee. For more on the federal campaign finance law, see chapter 8.

36. One exception is the political scientist Larry Sabato, who has argued that the competition from PACs has inspired the parties to centralize and professionalize their operations, with the result that they are stronger in some ways than they used to be. This, however, is not a widely shared view. See Sabato, *PAC Power*, 152, 158–159, 163.

37. *Congressional Quarterly's Guide to Congress*, 3rd ed. (Washington: Congressional Quarterly, 1982), 792; Kay Lehman Schlozman and John T. Tierney, "More of the Same: Pressure Group Activity in a Decade of Change," *Journal of Politics* XLV (May 1983), 361; and David G. Moore, *Politics and the Corporate Chief Executive* (New York: The Conference Board, 1980), 3.

38. See chapter 5, below, for how this ambivalence affected Madison's view of parties.

39. In Clinton Rossiter's edition (New York: New American Library, 1961), see pp. 79 and 83.

40. Alexis de Tocqueville, *Democracy in America*, trans. Henry Reeve, Francis Bowen and Phillips Bradley (New York: Vintage Books, 1945), I: 201–202; II: 115–117, 124–125, and 127.

41. David B. Truman, *The Governmental Process* (New York: Alfred A. Knopf, 1951).

42. Representative Dan Glickman, Kansas Democrat, quoted in Sabato, *PAC Power*, 170. While not all interest groups have established PACs, and not all PACs are allied with interest groups, the arguments apply to both forms of organization.

43. Sabato, *PAC Power*, 25.

44. Both quotations are from Sartori, *Parties and Party Systems*, 25.

45. E. E. Schattschneider, *Party Government* (New York: Rinehart, 1942), 193.

46. See, for example, Truman, *The Governmental Process*, 50–51.

47. Grant McConnell, *Private Power and American Democracy* (New York: Alfred A. Knopf, 1966), 159–160, 364–365.

48. See Ralph Miliband, *The State in Capitalist Society* (New York: Basic Books, 1969), 207; and Murray Edelman, *Political Language* (New York: Academic Press, 1977), 153–154.

49. Even conservatives have their own perceived broad interests, such as keeping non-military government spending down and military spending up; I shall argue soon that pluralism serves conservative interests very well without requiring conservatives to resort to the rhetoric of the general interest.

50. Among those who have made this point are Schattschneider, *Party Government*, 31; McConnell, *Private Power*, 109–110, 365–366; Mancur Olson, *The Logic of Collective Action* (Cambridge, Mass.: Harvard Univ. Press, 1965); and Claus Offe, "Political Authority and Class Structures," trans. Michel Vale, *International Journal of Sociology* II (Spring 1972), 85–89.

51. Sorauf, "Political Action Committees," 80.

52. Michels, *Political Parties*, especially 342–356. See also Henry S. Kariel, *The Decline of American Pluralism* (Stanford, Calif.: Stanford Univ. Press, 1961), and McConnell, *Private Power*, 119–154, 355.

53. Sabato, *PAC Power*, 168–169.

54. These figures are from the survey of the Center for Political Studies of the University of Michigan.

55. Sabato, *PAC Power*, 169.

56. McConnell, *Private Power*, 7–8, 111–112, 164, 339; Kariel, *Decline of American Pluralism*, 213–251; and Theodore J. Lowi, *The End of Liberalism* (New York: W. W. Norton, 1969). See also Chapter 9, below, for further discussion of this phenomenon.

57. E. E. Schattschneider, *The Semisovereiqn People* (New York: Holt, Rinehart & Winston, 1960), 35.

58. Besides Schattschneider, see, for example, McConnell, *Private Power*, 342, 349; and Offe, "Attribution of Public Status," 151–155.

59. See chapters 3 and 7 in this book.

60. Quoted in Elizabeth Drew, *Politics and Money* (New York: Macmillan, 1983), 96.

61. Michael J. Malbin, "Campaign Financing and the 'Special Interests'," *The Public Interest* 56 (Summer 1979), 32.

62. Edsall, *New Politics of Inequality*, 130; Sabato, *PAC Power*, 46–48, 59, 74; and Michael Useem, *The Inner Circle* (New York: Oxford Univ. Press, 1984), 135.

63. Quoted in Sabato, *PAC Power*, 142. Data are from Michael Barone and Grant Ujifusa, *The Almanac of American Politics 1984* (Washington: National Journal, 1983), and Barone and Ujifusa, *The Almanac of American Politics 1986* (Washington: National Journal, 1985). One member of the House and one Senator reported receiving no PAC donations from business or labor, and data were missing for one other member of the House.

64. Study by the John F. Kennedy Institute of Politics at Harvard University, quoted in Edwin M. Epstein, "Business and Labor under the Federal Election Campaign Act of 1971," in Michael J. Malbin, ed., *Parties, Interest Groups, and Campaign Finance Laws* (Washington: American Enterprise Institute, 1980), 142.

65. I am grouping trade association PACs with corporate PACs because most trade association PACs are allied with corporate PACs, supporting the same kinds of candidates and policies. For example, in "Political Action Committees," 46, Sorauf reports that in 1982, trade association PACs gave 57 percent of their congressional contributions to Republicans; corporate PACs gave 66 percent to Republicans.

66. Epstein, "Business and Labor," 128–131; and Useem, *The Inner Circle,* 86–87, 137–138.

67. Press release issued by the Federal Election Commission dated May 19, 1985.

68. Sorauf, "Political Action Committees," 57. See also Sabato, *PAC Power,* 46–48.

69. Edsall, *New Politics of Inequality,* 132, 136–138.

70. Edsall, *New Politics of Inequality,* 108–109, 134–140; Malbin, "Campaign Financing," 38–39; Drew, *Politics and Money,* 38–52; and Benjamin I. Page, *Who Gets What from Government* (Berkeley, Calif.: Univ. of California Press, 1983), 47.

71. See chapter 5.

72. Cited in Sorauf, "Political Action Committees," 102.

73. Arthur Schlesinger, Jr., "Crisis of the Party System: II," *Wall Street Journal,* 14 May 1979, p. 20.

74. Christian Bay, "Thoughts on the Purposes of Political Science Education," in George J. Graham, Jr., and George W. Carey, eds., *The Post-Behavioral Era* (New York: David McKay, 1972), 97–98.

75. See chapter 6, for a discussion of progressive reformism.

76. Burnham, "End of American Party Politics," 22.

5

Party Development

How have American political parties developed over time? As with the study of the history of any institution, by knowing the past, we can understand how we arrived at the present. But this book is not primarily concerned with history. My major motive in discussing party development is to delineate the changes in our parties in the context of broader social, economic, and political change. In particular, which of these other changes led to changes in the party system, and how have changes in the party system affected society at large? In other words, my real concern is social change and how it occurs. If we understand that process correctly, we will not only understand how the past became the present, but we might also get an idea of how the present will become the future.

Think of the enormous changes that American society has undergone in two hundred years. From a rural nation of four million people clustered along the Atlantic coast, through the rise of capitalism, industrialism, and corporations, to a highly urban and suburban nation of a quarter billion people spread across the North American continent; from a population of whom most were Protestants from the British Isles, with most of the rest black slaves, through the emancipation of blacks, large-scale massacres of native Americans ("Indians"), and the immigration of millions of people from Ireland, the European mainland, and all parts of Asia, Africa, and Latin America—the amount of social and economic change has been mind boggling.

Despite all of these and many other social and economic changes, and despite a wide variety of political developments, it is remarkable how little fundamental change has occurred in the political system over the past two centuries. Louis Hartz once demonstrated how pervasive the doctrine of liberal capitalism has been in governing American political thought since the late eighteenth century, and Samuel Huntington once gave the institutional equivalent of Hartz's argument by stating that the United States has always had a "Tudor polity"—a set of political institutions that reflect sixteenth century English politics better than they address modern needs.[1]

If Hartz and Huntington are right, then our focus should be on the persistence of early American politics rather than the changes which are often emphasized. We sometimes marvel at the ideological and governmental changes in the United States in the past half century, when the New Deal changed Americans' expectations of the role of government. On the other hand, we should realize that the New Deal destroyed not capitalism but an outmoded variation of it; to use Franklin D. Roosevelt's own analogy, he saved the drowning capitalist but could not rescue the man's high silk hat. We should also understand that for all the growth of government since the 1930s, the fundamental institutional framework of the original Constitution, including federalism, separation of powers, and the like, survive. That politics should have remained so constant in the face of deep social change may be the most remarkable thing about the development of American public life.

In this context, we should expect political parties, as part of the political system, to have done relatively little "developing." This is the view of the political scientist Theodore Lowi, who has written that our parties "did not develop after a certain point in time, if development requires the functions of an institution to alter appreciably."[2] Moreover, the historian Paul Kleppner has written that "at least since the mid-1850s, party battles have been waged between the same major combatants, neither of which has effectively challenged, or even attempted to challenge, the dominant ideological and cultural hegemony of corporate capitalism."[3] Such a statement becomes meaningful when we again consider other advanced industrial nations, where constitutions and regimes have been overturned, political philosophies have been revised, and new kinds of parties have emerged to express the changing demands on the political system. There is nothing in our history since 1789 to compare with the rise of the British Labour Party, the advent of the Fifth Republic in France, or even Canada's emergence into nationhood.

It would indeed be misleading to leave you with the impression that nothing has changed; changes in our party system, while not so great as to turn our parties into tightly structured, ideological institutions, have been related to changes in the broader social and economic realm. I am not arguing any simpleminded economic determinism here; parties do not merely reflect economic influences, nor are they incapable of affecting the broader world. However, it would be inaccurate not to recognize that the same forces at work in the economy and the society affect the party system too. Most of this chapter will be a brief overview of American party developments in the light of those broader forces, which can perhaps best be summarized as the growth of the corporate capitalist state.

THE CONCEPT OF PARTY

At the close of the Middle Ages came a number of revolutions in religion, science, politics, and economics. The early stages of the economic changes that led to capitalism in Western Europe coincided with the beginnings of liberal political thought, for both were the vehicles of a newly emerging class of merchants and artisans who wanted to share power with the older feudal elites. The emerging commercial economy brought them wealth, and liberal political institutions like parliaments gave them a role in government and broke up the political monopoly of the aristocracy and the clergy. However, contrary to the arguments of radicals such as Karl Marx and conservatives like Milton Friedman, there is no necessary historical connection between capitalism and liberal political institutions such as limited government and the separation of powers; the world is full of oppressive capitalist regimes, notably in South Africa, Latin America and some other parts of the developing world.

While there may not be a necessary connection between rudimentary capitalism and liberalism, the trends were certainly linked in early American experience. Theorists influential in revolutionary America, notably John Locke, combined an emphasis on private property with a theory of government based on popular consent.[4] The Constitution was one that, if not part of a full-fledged capitalist system, paved the way for capitalist development by protecting private property and encouraging the state to foster economic expansion.[5] All of the essential features that we associate with American politics, including limited government, divided government, federalism, popular elections, and so forth, are in the Constitution, and were seen as compatible with, if not indispensable to, the commercial empire that was the aspiration of the founders.

However, there is one feature of American politics that was not envisioned in the founders' original theory, and that was the political party. Indeed, the very idea of party was anathema to them. Thomas Jefferson wrote in 1789 that "if I could not go to heaven but with a party, I would not go there at all."[6] In the very first of the *Federalist Papers*, Alexander Hamilton decried "party opposition," and in the most eminent of the papers, James Madison noted the common complaint that "the public good is disregarded in the conflicts of rival parties."[7] This was a frequent theme among political theorists of the eighteenth century, for they still held onto the ancient Greek notion that there is a general good that benefits all members of a society, while political subgroups, in contrast, are merely trying to achieve selfish goals. Other objections to parties stemmed from concern about their secrecy, and the charge that they got in the way of the voters' free exercise of the franchise.[8]

However, there was a profound inconsistency in the eighteenth century liberal faith that a general good overrides individual differences, because liberal capitalism elevates individual self-interest above anything resembling a general good. In economics, philosophers like Adam Smith told buyers and sellers to seek self-interest, rather than consciously try to achieve some ideal of the public interest; according to Smith, the public welfare would be taken care of automatically, by the famous "hidden hand." Similarly in politics, in the same essay in which he lambasted partisanship, Madison wrote:

> The latent causes of faction are. . . . sown in the nature of man. . . . [Such factions have] divided mankind into parties, inflamed them with mutual animosity, and rendered them much more disposed to vex and oppress each other than to co-operate for their common good.[9]

Madison assails partisanship at the beginning of his essay, and calls it an inevitable part of human nature a few paragraphs later. The sincere liberal capitalist, who emphasizes individualism and naked self-interest, is left with a tough choice: either try in vain to encourage in people a notion of public-spiritedness which is supposed to be contrary to human nature, or swallow your reservations and accept parties as a necessary part of the liberal-capitalist worldview. We know which path American politics took. Indeed, to have denied the validity of parties would have been to deny the very concepts of individualism and the pursuit of self-interest that underlie the capitalist mentality.

It was Madison himself who rose to the task of accepting parties as compatible with liberal thought. In his column in the *National Gazette* of January 23, 1792, Madison began by repeating the inevitability argument that he had made in the tenth *Federalist:* "In every political society, parties are unavoidable. A difference of interests, real or supposed is the most natural and fruitful source of them."[10] He proceeded to propose five ways to "combat the evil" that can arise from partisanship. The first required by establishing political equality among all. The next three means of insuring moderation in partisanship all involved insuring that economic equalities did not become too extreme; these suggestions were fundamentally incompatible with freewheeling capitalism, and they are the parts of Madison's formula that have been generally ignored by the American system. Finally, Madison proposed "making one party a check on the other."[11] Here we see the real role of parties in the liberal-capitalist order: just as producers and consumers are to limit each other's power in the marketplace, just as (according to Madison in the tenth *Federalist*) interest groups would check each other in the political realm, just as (according to Madison in the fifty-first *Federalist*) the institutions of the federal government would counteract each others' ambitions, so parties would keep an eye on each other. Once again, the energetic pursuit of naked self-interest—here by party politicians—would somehow lead to the achievement of the public good.

Other politicians of his day came to accept parties as well, Jefferson agreeing that partisanship is inevitable and that it induces each party "to watch and relate to the people the proceedings of the other."[12] Less sanguine was Hamilton, who lamented in 1802 that "we must renounce our principles and our objects, and unite in corrupting public opinion . . . employing the weapons which have been employed against us. . . ."[13]

Hamilton's frank cynicism alerts us to the fact that these were practical politicians, whose elaborate theoretical arguments were fostered by the fact that they themselves were the builders of the nation's first crude parties. These factional alliances began to develop over the policies of George Washington's administration. First came the disputes over the economic policies of Secretary of the Treasury Alexander Hamilton, designed to promote industry and worrisome to defenders of agrarian interests. Soon the focus shifted to foreign policy, notably whether the new nation's ties should be stronger with revolutionary France or with conservative Britain. This controversy reached its climax over the Jay Treaty with Britain in 1796, which was seen by its critics as conceding too much to that nation. By the end of the 1790s, two parties had taken their place at the center of American politics: the Federalists, led by the more conservative types like Hamilton and John Adams, and the Democrat-Republicans (the name varied from place to place), whose heroes were the more liberal Jefferson and Madison.

What were these early parties like? At the national level, there were loose alliances among compatible members of Congress in support of or in opposition to the president. Especially important to the Democrat-Republicans in Congress was their appointee as clerk of the House of Representatives, John Beckley, who not only served as a broker in congressional negotiations but also traveled all over the country building a network of party activists. Every four years, each party's "caucus" in Congress would meet to nominate a presidential candidate. Both parties also subsidized newspapers for purposes of propaganda, and when in power gave friendly editors (notably the Federalist John Fenno or the Democrat-Republican Philip Freneau) much government printing business. At the grass roots level, local "machines" tried to mobilize sympathetic voters, and the quadrennial presidential elections encouraged them to think in national terms. In New York City, for example, was Aaron Burr's Tammany Society, the forerunner of Tammany Hall. At the national level, presidents began to pay attention to people's partisanship when making governmental appointments. In 1801, Jefferson defended his patronage policy by arguing that "the will of the nation, manifested by their various elections, calls for an administration of government according with the opinions of those elected."[14]

By 1800, parties were so integral a part of presidential elections that a deadlock occurred in the electoral college. The original Constitution gave each presidential elector two votes, and there was no way for an elector to designate one of his votes as going for president and the other for vice president. Whoever received the most votes would be president, and the runner-up would be vice president. Among other considerations, this was supposed to insure that the vice president would be of presidential caliber. By 1796, with two parties developing, the election produced an odd combination: a Federalist president (Adams) and a Democratic-Republican vice president (Jefferson). Since the vice presidency has never been a powerful office, this was not a serious problem. In 1800, however, all of the Democratic-Republican electors voted for their presidential nominee, Jefferson, and their vice-presidential nominee, Aaron Burr. This resulted in a tie between Jefferson and Burr, and the election had to be decided in the House of Representatives. After thirty-six ballots, Jefferson finally won. By the next presidential election, the Constitution was amended to require electors to distinguish between their presidential vote and their vice-presidential vote, in order to prevent any future such deadlocks. This was a tacit recognition of the development of parties and of the discipline that parties were able to exert over their electors.

It is important to understand that these early parties were far from the institutions we think of today. In brief, there was little structure beyond the local machines. There were no national committees, no formal party leaders or organizations in Congress, and no presidential nominating system other than the congressional caucus, which was simply the gathering of all members of a party in Congress; only this small elite group participated in the choice. Party institutions were so weak that Jefferson called his congressional party "our rope of sand."[15] Moreover, the local machines were often alliances among local elites who did not necessarily have any overriding issue concerns, and voters often cast their ballots according to local considerations. After examining voting patterns in 1800, the historian David Hackett Fischer concluded:

> There was surely no simple symmetry of political conviction and economic interest, no clean-cut cleavage between wealth and poverty, between agriculture and commerce, between realty and personalty holdings, between city-dwellers and countryfolk, between northern merchants and southern planters, between subsistence and commercial farmers, between hardy frontiersmen and effete easterners, between orthodox Calvinists and other religious groups.[16]

Since the ballot was not secret, a voter was likely to be influenced by his local creditors.

These considerations have led one perceptive historian to argue that "scholars have overestimated the extent to which *institutionalized* parties structured politics before the 1830s."[17] If we bear this in mind, we can conclude that as far as parties were concerned, what the early decades of the federal system accomplished was the establishment of a rationale for accepting the existence of parties, and the rudiments of party organization.

PARTIES IN THE AGE OF CAPITALIST GROWTH

Now that the groundwork was laid for the rise of institutionalized parties, they could develop according to the needs of the socioeconomic system. In the nineteenth century, the economy developed into the most vigorous capitalist system in the world. It is difficult for us in the bureau-cratized and corporate late twentieth century to recapture the frontier spirit of early capitalism in all its vigor, so a couple of contemporary accounts will be useful. The French observer Alexis de Tocqueville wrote in the 1830s:

> In the United States a man builds a house in which to spend his old age, and he sells it before the roof is on; he plants a garden and lets it just as the trees are coming into bearing; he brings a field into tillage and leaves other men to gather the crops; he embraces a profession and gives it up; he settles in a place, which he soon afterwards leaves to carry his changeable longings elsewhere.[18]

More generally, and more poetically, Karl Marx and Friedrich Engels wrote of the rise of capitalism:

> All fixed, fast-frozen relations, with their train of ancient and venerable prejudices and opinions, are swept away, all new-formed ones become anti-quated before they can ossify. All that is solid melts into air, all that is holy is profaned, and man is at last compelled to face with sober senses, his real conditions of life, and his relations with his kind.[19]

A few statistics round out the picture. In the year 1790, only about 5 percent of the American people lived in places with populations over 2500; by 1860, 20 percent did. In 1810, only 3 percent of employed Americans were employed in manufacturing concerns; in 1860, 14 percent were.[20] Despite our image of expansion to the western frontier, urbanization and industrial-ization were powerful forces in early nineteenth-century America.

It sounds like an exciting time, with hordes of Americans buying, selling, and moving west, involved in all kinds of get-rich-quick schemes as the nation was in its "takeoff" stage of economic development. But unbri-dled growth had its costs, too. One was the "boom-and-bust" cycles of 1818–1823 and 1839–1843, in which periods of prosperity alternated with severe depressions; occasional briefer or more regional crises oc-curred in other years. Another was the increasing concentration of indus-try in the hands of a few, as large-scale manufacturing grew.[21] Along with this came accelerating inequality of wealth and income. Two economic historians have calculated that in 1774, the top one percent of free prop-ertied Americans held 13 percent of total assets, while in 1860, the top one percent held 29 percent of those assets.[22] About income disparities from 1816 to 1856, they concluded:

> In four short decades, the American Northeast was transformed from the "Jeffersonian ideal" to a society more typical of developing economies with very wide pay differentials and, presumably, marked inequality in the distri-bution of wage income.[23]

But occasional depressions and growing inequality were not the worst of it. As large-scale capitalism developed, so did the exploitation of the workers; with meager pay and oppressive working conditions, the fruits of workers' efforts went to the owners. Lewis Masquerier was one American who articulated this quite well when he wrote in 1844 that American laborers "have been reduced to the lowest state of degradation and misery by the almost universal usurpation of all property and power by a non-producing, tyrannical, and aristocratic class. . . ."[24] The condition of industrial labor was such that one prominent Southerner attempted to justify slavery by comparing it favorably with northern capitalism, telling the capitalist that "you retain your capital, and never labor, and yet live in luxury on the labor of others. Capital commands labor, as the master does the slave. Neither pays for labor. . . ."[25]

The costs of capitalist growth might have led to growing disillusionment with the political and socioeconomic systems, as neither the Jeffersonian ideal of small farms and businesses nor the "get-rich-quick" promise of capitalist ideology was fulfilled. But there was no widespread disillusionment, and this may have been due in great part to the rise of institutionalized political parties. Simply stated, my premise is that by appearing to give the mass of people real political power, parties gave them a sense of control over their fate and therefore prevented their economic disappointments from growing into full-fledged radicalism. How did this happen?

Until around 1830, political parties were still crudely formed, and mass participation in politics was still in the future. The Federalist party was so weak that by 1820 it did not even mount a presidential campaign. Both parties continued to choose their presidential nominees by congressional caucus; in many states presidential electors were chosen by the legislature. The early presidents all came from the Virginia or Massachusetts gentry, and property restrictions on voting were still in effect in many areas. The Madisonian model of party as a means by which one elite group of politicians kept an eye on another elite group of politicians still seemed valid.

By the 1830s all this had changed. Two vigorous new parties, the Democrats and the Whigs, had totally replaced their crude predecessors. In the 1832 campaign both parties adopted a new institution, the national nominating convention, which gave local and state party elites from all over the country the opportunity to participate in choosing a presidential candidate. By 1824, every state but South Carolina had given the electorate the power to vote for presidential electors. After 1824, presidential elections began to reflect the westward expansion of the nation as the voters began to choose presidents from states west of the original thirteen—Tennessee, Indiana, and Louisiana. Moreover, the size of the electorate expanded until 1840, when 80 percent of adult white males voted in the Harrison-Van Buren presidential contest, a turnout rate that has only twice been exceeded since.[26] In the 1840s, rudimentary national party committees were established. According to the historian Richard P. McCormick, "Voice voting and hand-written ballots gave way increasingly to printed ballots, polling units were reduced in area, and suffrage restrictions on white males, except in three states, were all but eliminated."[27]

The result of all these institutional changes was that partisanship took hold among the American people in a way never before seen anywhere in the world. With the advent of mass suffrage, party leaders sought to mobilize as many voters as possible, and politics became a form of mass entertainment—speeches, rallies, parades, signs, songs, buttons, and all of the paraphernalia to which Americans have since become so accustomed. A few disgruntled conservatives disapproved, like John Quincy Adams, who grumbled in his *Memoirs*:

> One of the most remarkable peculiarities of the present time is that the principal leaders of the political parties are travelling about the country from State to State, and holding forth, like Methodist preachers, hour after hour, to assembled multitudes, under the broad canopy of heaven.[28]

Opinion leaders began to express strong partisanship. Newspaper editors continued in the Fenno-Freneau tradition, and by 1850, 95 percent of American newspapers adhered to one party or the other. These editors became so influential that the parties eventually began considering them for the presidency: Horace Greeley was nominated by the Democrats in 1872, and William Randolph Hearst came in second at that party's national convention in 1904. Literary figures like Walt Whitman, John Greenleaf Whittier, William Cullen Bryant, and Nathaniel Hawthorne contributed their talents to campaigns, and college presidents were outspoken in their partisanship: One, Nicholas Murray Butler of Columbia University, was nominated for the vice presidency by the Republicans after the incumbent died at the height of the 1912 campaign, which was won by Woodrow Wilson, former president of Princeton. The historian Richard Jensen has called the usual campaign style of the nineteenth century "militaristic"—competing partisan armies mobilizing the troops.[29] These armies needed generals, and so a new career was established: the professional politician, exemplified by Martin Van Buren of New York. He was known as the "Little Magician" who was instrumental in building the Democratic party; he won a term in the White House in the process.[30]

Much is made of the notion of "Jacksonian democracy," and a myth that these changes really democratized American society has developed. It is important to bear in mind several points. First, the Jacksonians were not alone in fostering these changes. National conventions were started not by the Democrats but by the minor Anti-Mason party, and no mass mobilization tactic was more effective than the "log cabin and hard cider" campaign of the Whigs in 1840, which rallied support behind "Tippecanoe and Tyler too." Second, the available data suggest that the voters were not voting along class lines and expressing their economic interests; if anything, religious, ethnic and cultural divisions as well as local factors seem to have motivated the voters.[31] Therefore, the addition of large numbers of relatively poor voters to the political process was not enough to change the terms of the political debate.

The third point may be the most important of all. These institutional changes, as successful as they were in vastly expanding the political universe, did not really increaese the power of the mass of ordinary citizens. The most conspicuous new development, the convention, is a good example. The people who attend conventions, while more numerous than participants in congressional caucuses, have hardly been a cross-section of the American people. Especially in their early years, conventions were notorious for being controlled by a small coterie of party leaders, and their large size has always made serious deliberation by delegates impossible. In the word of one author, the chief impact of conventions in the Jacksonian era was "cosmetic."[32] Moreover, Jackson's election did not result in appointments to federal office of people whose social backgrounds were any less elitist than those of the previous era.[33] In sum, according to the historian William Shade, "Parties were 'invented' by politicians seeking power for their own diverse reasons by providing new means of interest aggregation, of political recruitment, and of rationalizing government at both levels of the federal system."[34] Articulating the interests of the mass of citizens is a goal missing from Shade's inventory.

The fourth and final reason that the politics of this period cannot be thought to have articulated the interests of people of limited means is in the ideology of the party elites. Sometimes the Whigs, with their advocacy of high protective tariffs, a national bank and federal aid for the building of roads and canals, are seen as the champions of capitalism, and the Democrats, who generally opposed these policies, are thought to represent other class interests. This is nonsense. The Democrats were equally capitalistic, but either wanted other levels of government to aid the growth of industry (*state* banks and road building) or wanted to protect the interests of planters (a low tariff to protect their export rights). According to the historian Richard Hofstadter, Jackson's main thrust was to open capitalism to newly rising elites, rather than dismantle the system—he sought to provide equal opportunity for entrepreneurs.[35] The lack of fundamental ideological differentiation between the parties is suggested by the fact that each one was strong in all areas of the nation.

All in all, then, what the first half of the nineteenth century saw was the growth of strong parties, the political mobilization of the mass of Americans, but at the same time a total lack of articulation of interests other than those of manufacturing, commercial, and agrarian elites. The mass of voters who might have been subject to radicalization were given the illusion of popular choice, which entailed the ability to vote out one set of liberal capitalists in exchange for another. In other parts of the world, elites encouraged the leftward drift of the masses by stubbornly holding out against universal male suffrage. In the United States, the "opening" of the political process saved the economic system in the long run.[36]

THE CRISIS OF THE SYSTEM SURMOUNTED

American parties had come to stay for the long haul, and this was demonstrated in the sectional crisis of the 1850s, which tore both parties apart. Hopelessly divided between their northern and southern wings, the Whigs gradually died out. A new party, the Republicans, strongly opposed to allowing slavery in the new Western territories acquired in the 1840s arose in the North. Most Whigs, and some antislavery Democrats, joined the new party, but in the South virtually all whites eventually became Democrats. That party was shattered at its 1860 national convention, and its northern and southern wings reconvened to nominate their own candidates. When later that year the Republicans gained control of both the presidency and Congress, and were poised to change the aging Supreme Court as well, the South seceded and civil war erupted.

When the war was over and the South, minus its "peculiar institution" of slavery, was compelled to rejoin the Union, the nation again settled into two-party competition. For all the change in American politics in this era, the fact of partisanship with all its trappings remained. The Republicans used their control of the national government in the 1860s to foster the growth of capitalism: high tariffs, a national banking system, land-grant colleges to train people in the new technologies, and aid to railroads. Across the North, they played on memories of the Civil War to win the presidency in all but two elections from 1860 until the end of the century. All of their nominees in this period were war heroes, and the "bloody shirt" campaigns featured the songs and slogans fondly remembered from the great war.

This period was the high water mark of American partisanship. The historian Richard Jensen has found that in the Midwest in this period, at least ninety-five percent of the voters identified with a party.[37] Indeed, partisanship became an offshoot of one's racial, ethnic, and regional identity: if you were a northern Episcopalian, you were a Republican *by virtue of* being a Northern Episcopalian. If you were a southern white, you were a Democrat *by virtue of* being a southern white. If you were black, you were a Republican *by virtue of* being black. If you were a Roman Catholic, you were a Democrat *by virtue of* being Catholic. And so forth. One did not have to agonize when deciding how to vote. As one United States senator put it in 1890 (allowing for partisan hyperbole and the prejudices of his class):

> The men who do the work of piety and charity in our churches, the men who administer our school system, the men who own and till their own farms, the men who perform skilled labor in the shops, the soldiers, the men who went to war and stayed all through, the men who paid the debt and kept the currency and saved the nation's honor, the men who saved the country in war and have made it worth living in peace, commonly and as a rule, *by the natural law of their being* find their places in the Republican party. While the

old slave-owner and slave-driver, the saloon keeper, the ballot box stuffer, the Ku Klux Klan, the criminal class of the great cities, the men who cannot read or write, commonly and as a rule, *by the natural law of their being,* find their congenial place in the Democratic party.[38]

But in other areas of American life, there were powerful changes occurring with the rise of the corporate state. From 1849 to 1899, the number of factories and other industries in the country quadrupled; from 1857 to 1900 the number of business concerns quintupled; from 1860 to 1900, manufacturing production increased sixfold; from 1865 to 1900, the total capital in manufacturing industries rose twenty-three times in constant dollars; from 1870 to 1900 the non-agricultural sector of the workforce rose from 48 percent to 60 percent; from 1850 to 1900 the percentage of the workforce in manufacturing increased from 15 percent to 20 percent; and in the same period the urban population rose from 15 percent to 40 percent.[39]

At the same time, the human costs of unbridled corporate capitalist expansion increased. The inequality of wealth and income seems to have remained high throughout the period from the Civil War to the Great Depression of the 1930s.[40] The business cycle continued to pull the population along an economic roller coaster, culminating in a devastating depression in the 1890s which put 18 percent of the labor force out of work.[41] Exploitation continued to be an issue with three large groups of the population: factory workers, western farmers, and southern blacks. As huge factories became the norm in the industrial Northeast and Great Lakes regions, working men and women turned to labor unions to protect themselves. This was the era of such federations as the Knights of Labor, the American Federation of Labor, and the Industrial Workers of the World. Attempts at non-confrontational settlement often turned into strikes, and strikes often became bloody battles when police and military forces were brought in by employers. One historian has called the period "the era of dynamite in American labor relations."[42]

Farmers were equally oppressed by industrial capitalism. The fluctuations of the marketplace drove many farmers into bankruptcy, and their troubles were augmented by high loan rates from bankers and high shipping rates from railroads. It has often been argued that the relationship between the rural South and West and the industrial Northeast was like the relationship between a colony and an imperial nation, with the former sending raw goods for the manufacturing process to the latter, at exploitative rates. As late as 1948, Harry Truman campaigned in North Carolina telling the people that "the greedy Wall Street interests that want cheap labor and the cheap farm products" treat "the South and the West as colonies to be exploited commercially and held down politically."[43]

Like their urban counterparts, the farmers sought relief by organizing. This gave rise to such groups as the Granger movement and the Farmers'

Alliance; in the famous words of one organizer, farmers were told to "raise less corn and more hell." Like the laborers, farmers were sometimes met with official violence when they pressed their cause.[44] In the South, black farmers had fewer means of exerting pressure on the political system, due to the white monopoly on the use of force.

It was not long before these claimants turned to a device that had been around for decades as a symbol of popular participation in politics, the party. If parties could be organized for the rivalries of elite groups in society, and to organize masses of people to play a subsidiary role in those rivalries, then why not use parties to mobilize masses of people to challenge the rule of the elites? *This* was a role for parties which James Madison never advocated.

For the greater part of this era, the major parties were wedded to corporate capitalism. The Republicans stood behind the high tariff in order to prevent foreign competitors from challenging the emerging industrial giants, and the gold standard in order to keep inflation down so that the banks could count on getting their loans repaid in dollars just as valuable as those loaned out. As for the Democrats, while their preference for low tariffs tended to help farmers (especially large farmers with much produce to export), in most other ways they backed the interests of various commercial sectors. Indeed, any business firm which relied on exports wanted low tariffs, lest other nations retaliate by raising their own. On other issues, there was little or no difference between the major parties. The only Democrat elected president from 1860 until 1912, Grover Cleveland, was a firm supporter of the gold standard.

And so the late nineteenth century witnessed a succession of parties organized to press the claims of protesters, with increasing electoral success. Farmers first formed the Greenback party, which sought to inflate the currency and enable farmer-debtors to pay back their loans in cheaper currency. The party amassed about 75,000 votes in the 1876 presidential election, and more than 300,000 and 175,000 in the 1880 and 1884 campaigns respectively. The Union Labor party gained 146,000 in 1888, but the breakthrough came with the People's party in 1892, whose million popular votes constituted 8.5 percent of the national total. That party, commonly called the Populists, carried four states, and throughout the 1890s won the governorships of eight midwestern and western states. It managed to coalesce urban workers, farmers, and Southerners of both races.[45]

These parties stood for increasingly radical policies, as their platforms illustrated. The 1880 Greenback platform decried "the barbarism which imposes upon the wealth-producers a state of perpetual drudgery" and denounced the major parties for encouraging the rise of large corporations.[46] Continuing this theme, the party's 1884 platform called for "such governmental action as may be necessary to take from such monopolies the powers they have so corruptly and unjustly usurped, and restore them to the people, to whom they belong." Vague on this point, the Greenbackers were more specific about more moderate reforms like a graduated income tax, safe working conditions, and women's suffrage.

The Union Labor platform of 1888 adopted most of the Greenbackers' recommendations, and called for public ownership of the means of transportation and communication and arbitration of labor disputes. Finally, in 1892 the Populists declared that "wealth belongs to him who creates it," a position shared by socialists, and echoed the call for public ownership of railroads, telegraphs, and telephones. To the defenders of corporate capitalism, these were ominous words indeed. The crisis of the 1860s had been minor compared to the potential explosion of the 1890s; it was less repugnant to divide one capitalist nation into two, as the Civil War threatened, than to lay the seeds for the destruction of capitalism altogether. Capitalists must have looked with apprehension at the rise of mass socialist parties in Europe, and when a severe depression began in 1893, it must have sounded like a death knell to many businessmen.

To make matters worse for the adherents of corporate capitalism, the Populists in 1896 forged an alliance with the Democrats, whose more populistic wing took over the convention and nominated a 36-year-old Nebraskan, William Jennings Bryan, for president. This "Fusion" or, as its detractors called it, "Popocrat," coalition threatened to put Populists in the national government. While Bryan himself was hardly radical, he was seen as the dupe of more extreme elements. Conservative Democrats deserted the ticket, and the Republicans began a campaign of vilifying Bryan and predicting further economic collapse if the Nebraskan won.[47]

If political parties could be used as the vehicle of mass discontentment, then the task for the defenders of the system went beyond sending Bryan back to Nebraska. Parties had become a two-edged sword, and the task now was to blunt the sword. By 1896, corporations were already a dominant force in American politics, and business alliances for the purpose of lobbying grew rapidly in this era: the National Association of Manufacturers was born in 1895, and the Chamber of Commerce of the United States seventeen years later. With the support of the political establishment (even Bryan was not anti-capitalist), and with its new organizational vehicles, the business community could get along quite well without strong party mechanisms. The only people who really needed parties to promote their views were those without establishment support or well-heeled lobbying groups, and these were the masses of the sort who supported Populism. If the strong ties that Americans felt toward parties could be loosened, then parties might never again constitute a potential threat to the socioeconomic system.

Fortunately for those with an interest in destroying strong parties, this process was already underway. In the 1880s and 1890s, political corruption had led to a number of changes designed to reduce the power of party leaders. Since these leaders relied on patronage—government jobs—as incentives for people to work in their organizations, one of the first reforms was to take patronage out of the hands of politicians and distribute jobs on the basis of civil service examinations. On the national level, the first civil service law was passed in 1883, two years after President Garfield was assassinated by a disappointed job seeker; patronage was literally becoming a life-and-death issue. Soon election laws were changed to prevent party leaders from exercising ballot fraud. These changes included stricter registration laws and the secret or "Australian" ballot. The Australian ballot also involved the government in printing ballots that listed all parties' candidates. No longer would voters get their ballots from their favorite party; by being shown all the candidates' names, they would be encouraged to split their tickets. In such ways were the psychological bonds between voters and parties weakened.[48]

But the task of weakening the parties could not be accomplished by legal changes alone. The national elites of the Republican party began to see that victory rested on getting away from the ethnic and cultural cleavages of their era. In state elections in 1890, the party had been badly defeated by too close an association with fundamentalist Protestant groups which advocated prohibition, the closing of shops on Sunday, the use of the Protestant Bible in schools, and other issues that frightened many non-fundamentalists. One of the Republicans who lost that year was William McKinley, who failed to win the Ohio governorship. From that time on, McKinley and his chief adviser, the industrialist Marc Hanna, knew that the political agenda had to be changed. The Republican party's relationship with the corporate elite had to be solidified, and the masses had to be induced to get beyond cultural issues.

The first task was accomplished easily enough, as Hanna created a massive fund for the party based on corporate contributions. McKinley himself was present at the formation of the National Association of Manufacturers in 1895. Big business was only too eager to help its friend reach the White House, especially when it became clear that the alternative was the Popocrat Bryan. The McKinley war chest amounted to $3,350,000, by far the largest to that date in history.[49]

When it came to persuading voters to forget their old partisan ties, McKinley and Hanna enjoyed remarkable luck. First, the economic depression that occurred under Democratic rule made prohibition and Sunday closings seem like rather unimportant issues. Second, the old relationship between the Republicans and the fundamentalists was turned on its head by the nomination of Bryan, who was the 1890s equivalent of a "Moral Majority" politician. Almost incapable of making a speech without biblical allusions, as his famous "Cross of Gold" speech illustrates, Bryan supported most of the fundamentalist issues. As Woodrow Wilson's secretary of state years later, he would forbid the serving of alcoholic beverages at diplomatic receptions, and he ended his life attacking the teaching of evolution in the public schools.

Bryan's nomination in 1896 sent fear through the various religious and ethnic communities that saw fundamentalism in government as a threat to their traditions. Seeking to avoid being implicated in what was generally regarded as a Catholic-Protestant dispute, the Republicans had a rabbi give the invocation at their national convention. Knowing that they no longer had to be on the defensive about such issues, McKinley and Hanna concentrated on elevating economic prosperity to the top of the agenda, and promised a "full dinner pail" to every worker, the 1896 equivalent of two cars in every garage or a color television in every living room. For once, the American voter was asked not to vote on the basis of who won the Civil War or whose religious and ethnic values were more attractive, but on who could promise more. This had profound implications for parties, for it meant that voters would no longer be bound to one party or the other, but would rather be available to the highest bidder. While such a party system was in a sense economic, it reduced economics to individual benefits rather than the interests of broad social classes, and therefore, lowered the level of working class consciousness.[50]

In the immediate task of defeating Bryan, the McKinley-Hanna strategy was a blazing success. All over the industrial parts of the nation, workers fearful of losing their jobs and immigrants worried about Bryan's social values cast their votes for McKinley. The Republican percentage of the presidential vote shot up from what it had been in the previous election: 12 percent higher in New York, 18 percent in Massachusetts and Rhode Island, 16 percent in Connecticut, 10 percent in Pennsylvania and Illinois. (The Republican vote percentage dropped during the same period in nine states in the South and West.) McKinley became the first Presidential candidate in twenty years to win an absolute majority of the popular vote, and his party was to control the White House for 28 of the next 36 years and Congress for 26 of the next 34.

Perhaps more importantly, the 1896 election seems to have occasioned a profound weakening of the ties between voters and parties. Partly as the result of the election law changes described above, but partly as a result of the changes I just discussed, voters began to behave less partisanly. They appear to have split their tickets more, they cast fewer votes for offices lower down on the ballot, they turned out less in non-presidential election years, and in general their turnout dropped precipitously. In 1896, the turnout was 79 percent of the eligible (adult male) electorate; by 1912, it had dropped to 59 percent. Eight years later, with the arrival of women's suffrage, it would decline still further. All over the country, voters were losing their attachment to the parties and to the electoral process, a trend which continues to the present day.[51]

This process was encouraged by a variety of legal changes that followed on the heels of civil service, registration laws, and the Australian ballot. In the early years of the twentieth century came the direct primary, intended to take control of nominations away from party leaders. The initiative, referendum, and recall also aimed to reduce the discretion of party elites. Two constitutional amendments played a role here. The direct election of United States Senators deprived party leaders in state legislatures of control over that office, and women's suffrage was advocated by many as a way to "clean up" politics.

Political candidates began to respond to these deep changes in the political order. As Woodrow Wilson told a partisan audience in 1915,

> My friends, what I particularly want you to observe is this, that politics in this country does not depend any longer upon the regular members of either party. There are not enough regular Republicans in this country to take and hold national power; and I must immediately add there are not enough regular Democrats in this country to do it, either. This country is guided and its policy is determined by the independent voter. . . . I say to the independent voter, you have got us in the palm of your hand.[52]

No longer could politicians hope to win merely by mobilizing the faithful. Instead, persuading the uncommitted became the task of every national campaign. Theodore Roosevelt had complained in 1896 that Hanna "advertised McKinley as if he were a patent medicine," but advertising would now become a crucial part of the political process. Newspapers, too, were affected. Partisan organs throughout the nineteenth century, they came to rely more and more on commercial advertisers and less and less on circulation for their profits. Circulation wars ensued, and papers became less and less blatantly partisan on their news pages in order both to attract advertisers and to woo readers.[53]

The decline of parties was reflected in high executive appointments to the national government. Traditionally, a president has the greatest degree of flexibility in appointing a cabinet when he has succeeded a president of the other party; when he succeeds a president of his own party, there may be pressure to keep certain people on, and when he makes changes in his own cabinet, lower-ranking officials are often promoted to the cabinet. If we look at the initial cabinets of those presidents who succeeded presidents of the other party, going back to the Jacksonian era, we find that all such presidents from 1829 to 1849 composed their cabinets entirely of people who had served in elective office or the United States Senate, and all such presidents from 1853 through 1889 appointed a majority of their cabinets from such sources. In 1893, Grover Cleveland became the first president whose cabinet was only half composed of such officials, and the trend has been downward ever since. The lows have been Eisenhower in 1953 (20 percent), Carter in 1977 (27 percent), and Reagan in 1981 (31 percent). Moreover, in the nineteenth century cabinets, those who had not held elective office were always party activists, but all of the twentieth century cabinets have had a sizeable number—usually more than a third—who had no partisan experience at all.[54] At the turn of the century, presidents began to look away from their parties as sources of high appointments.

The net result of all these changes, many of which came about because of the sincere activities of well-meaning "reformers," was to save the capitalist system from the kind of challenge it was undergoing in many European nations. Those who stopped voting came disproportionately from the lower classes. This was especially so in the South, when blacks (who had been part of the Populist movement in many areas) were forcibly deprived of the vote and many poor whites could not meet new suffrage requirements such as literacy tests and poll taxes. But the national twenty-percent drop in turnout was not merely a southern phenomenon. All over the North, corporate-tied Republicans held a hammerlock on public office. From 1900 to 1930, states as sizeable as California, Iowa, Pennsylvania and Wisconsin never had a Democratic governor, and Connecticut, Illinois and Michigan only elected Democratic governors when the Republicans were split from 1910 to 1914.

In state after state in the North, the Republicans were in firm control, and the same was true for Democratic elites in the South. Large numbers of voters saw that they had little or no chance of affecting the outcome, especially when their own interests went unrepresented. On the national scene, large interest groups speaking for business and other conservative interests—the Chamber of Commerce, the American Farm Bureau Federation, the American Medical Association—continued to be formed. The beginnings of the bureaucratic state also emerged during this period, relatively unhampered by the party machines that were so powerful in the previous era. America's new foreign policy of interventionism abroad—in Cuba, the Philippines, China, and increasingly all over Central America and the Caribbean—sought to make foreign markets safe for American investment. Bryan tried to make imperialism an issue when he ran against McKinley for the second time in 1900, but he lost again. The gold standard and high tariffs were the most obvious domestic policies serving the interests of entrenched big capital.[55]

We also remember the early twentieth century as a time of positive reform, including regulatory commissions, state laws improving working conditions, and some "trust-busting." It is important to note how limited many of these programs were, how easily they were circumvented by major corporations, and how in many instances business elites *wanted* the new programs in order to exercise control over them. One chairman of the Federal Trade Commission in the supposedly reformist Wilson Administration told a group of businessmen:

> In my position on the Federal Trade Commission I am there as a business man. I do not mind telling you that when I was offered the place I told the President that all I knew was business, that I knew nothing about the new laws nor the old ones, and that I would apply the force that I might have in the interest of business.[56]

There were, it is true, far-sighted corporate leaders who saw that a degree of social reform might be necessary to pacify the masses, and they supported some of the changes on the state level: safer working conditions, restrictions on child labor, inexpensive life insurance through savings banks, and so on. Despite these improvements, the new Socialist party made inroads into the electorate, winning six percent of the presidential vote in 1912—the fifth-highest showing for a non-major-party effort in the twentieth century. But in 1917, the First World War and the Bolshevik revolution in Russia gave the authorities the excuse to repress domestic radicals, and that, in combination with factors to be discussed in the next chapter, stopped the growth of a mass socialist movement in the United States.

All in all, though, the changes that came to a head in the 1890s were the best insurance that corporate capitalism had against mass political mobilization. The twentieth century has witnessed a continuation of the trends of that era, with the weakened parties and the depoliticized, demobilized mass population that I have discussed in earlier chapters.

NEW CRISIS, NEW SOLUTION

While new policies and institutions, American imperial expansion, and the assault on partisanship in the 1890s may have gotten corporate capitalism through its worst crisis up to that time, the old problems remained. The business cycle continued to take the nation through booms and busts, severe inequalities remained, and the old discontentments over exploitation still festered. In the 1930s, the system again underwent a crisis that was both economic and political, but the corporate elites were unable to surmount it with a political coalition and a national administration of their own making as they were in the 1890s.

In a number of key respects, the buildup to the crisis of the 1930s looked as though the history of the 1890s was repeating itself. First, there were longstanding agrarian and industrial grievances that at their peak took the form of a strong third-party movement. Throughout the 1920s farmers suffered economic hardships, and conservative Republican presidents Harding, Coolidge, and Hoover vetoed legislation designed to ease their plight. In 1924, rural and urban dissidents backed the presidential candidacy of Senator Robert LaFollette, a Wisconsin Republican who ran on the Progressive party ticket with the endorsement of the Socialist party. With a platform that called for redistributive taxes and public ownership of water power and railroads, the senator carried one-sixth of the total popular vote, the second-highest third-party showing from the Civil War to our own day. LaFollette died the following year, and unlike the Populists, the Progressives were unable to sustain their showing beyond one election.

The second parallel with the 1890s was the resurgence of ethnic conflict. The Democratic party became the battleground between rural fundamentalist Protestants and urban cosmopolitans, many of whom were

Roman Catholics. Bitter convention battles in the 1920s over Irish independence, prohibition, and whether to condemn the Ku Klux Klan split the
party. In 1928, when the Republicans were expected to win the presidency,
the urban wing was allowed to nominate one of its own without serious
opposition. He was Governor Alfred E. Smith of New York, the first Roman Catholic major-party presidential nominee. His nomination created the
same wave of fear and revulsion among rural fundamentalists that Bryan's
nomination had set off among urban voters, and a tidal wave of vicious
anti-Catholic hate literature flowed all over the nation's "Bible Belt." As a
result, Republican Herbert Hoover carried the normally Democratic states
of Florida, Kentucky, North Carolina, Oklahoma, Tennessee, Texas, and
Virginia. At the same time, Smith carried the normally Republican (but
heavily Catholic) states of Massachusetts and Rhode Island, and nearly
carried New York. While his nomination may have temporarily driven from
his party many fundamentalists, he seems to have drawn back many ethnic
and urban voters who had been attracted to McKinley and some other
Republicans. Moreover, Smith's candidacy appears to have increased the
turnout in many urban precincts."[57]

The third and most obvious parallel between the 1890s and the 1930s
was economic depression. The one that began with the stock market crash
in 1929 made the 1890s look like prosperity: by the end of 1932, one-
fourth of the work force was unemployed. This time the Republicans were
in power, and the Democrats were able to make political hay out of hard
times. And just as McKinley and Marc Hanna devised an ingenious new
strategy to make the Republicans the majority party, so did Governor
Franklin D. Roosevelt of New York and his chief strategist, James Farley,
for the Democrats, as they produced a new formula for electoral victory. It
did not emerge in the 1932 campaign; all Roosevelt had to do that year
was to be an alternative to President Hoover, and make as few promises as
possible.

Indeed, the early New Deal—Roosevelt's appropriately vague name
for his program—was no great departure from the policies of the Progressive era. There were measures to help the farmers, like the Agricultural
Adjustment Act, the Tennessee Valley Administration, and various commodity control acts; programs to provide short-term jobs for the unemployed, such as the Civilian Conservation Corps, the Civil Works Administration, and the Works Progress Administration; and policies to restore
public confidence in capitalism, like the Home Owners' Loan Act (to help
bankers), the Securities and Exchange Commission (to keep the stock market dependable), and above all the National Recovery Administration,
which enabled corporations to regulate their share of the economy with
government sanction. These measures were passed to a great extent in
order to forestall mass protest and as alternatives to more radical
proposals.[58]

As Roosevelt's first term wore on and the Depression continued, those more radical alternatives loomed larger. Minnesota's Governor Floyd Olson said that if capitalism could not cure the Depression, "I hope the present system of government goes right down to hell."[59] More potent critics included Louisiana Senator Huey Long, who, until his assassination in 1935, was considered a possible candidate against Roosevelt; Francis Townsend, who had a scheme to end poverty in California; and the demagogic priest Father Charles Coughlin, who lambasted the New Deal in his radio program. In order to undercut these challengers, Roosevelt in 1935 began to endorse more radical-sounding legislation—Social Security, which laid the groundwork for America's watered-down version of the welfare state; the National Labor Relations (Wagner) Act, which protected unions' right to organize; a so-called "soak-the-rich" tax; and some regulatory measures. The tax and regulatory bills were watered down by Congress without serious opposition from Roosevelt; Social Security relied on a regressive[60] tax on current workers and excluded the neediest people from coverage; and the Wagner Act was hardly a challenge to capitalism.

The real purpose of the New Deal was expressed by Roosevelt himself. Those who chose to see him as a radical could point to his sometimes bitter attacks on the greedy capitalists who, the president charged, had brought on the Depression. When Roosevelt accepted his party's second-term nomination in 1936, for example, he said, "I should like to have it said of my first Administration that in it the forces of selfishness and of lust for power met their match. I should like to have it said of my second Administration that in it these forces met their master."[61] This kind of rhetoric was important in building Roosevelt's coalition. But at the same time, Roosevelt himself never departed from his insistence that the *system* of capitalism was worth saving, even if the old elite had to be displaced. In one speech in 1936, he told the following parable:

> In the summer of 1933, a nice old gentleman wearing a silk hat fell off the end of a pier. He was unable to swim. A friend ran down the pier, dived overboard and pulled him out; but the silk hat floated off with the tide. . . . Today, three years later, the old gentleman is berating his friend because the silk hat was lost.[62]

In another speech that year, Roosevelt affirmed his support for "private enterprise as the backbone of economic well-being in the United States," and declared that it was his administration that had "saved the system of private profit and free enterprise after it had been dragged to the brink of ruin." About the businessmen he had saved, Roosevelt added, "some of them are even well enough to throw their crutches at the doctor."[63] Two years earlier, he had written that "one of my principal tasks is to prevent bankers and businessmen from committing suicide."[64]

How did Roosevelt save capitalism? One way was to involve the government in stabilizing the economy and preventing the extremes of the business cycle that had plagued American capitalism. This involved bringing all major interests in society into the political process. Roosevelt expressed his theory of government in 1936 as follows:

> It is the problem of Government to harmonize the interests of these groups which are often divergent and opposing, to harmonize them in order to guarantee security and good for as many of their individual members as may be possible. The science of politics, indeed, may properly be said to be in large part the science of the adjustment of conflicting group interests.[65]

This is the real significance of the Wagner Act. Given the pro-capitalist attitudes of most labor leaders, insuring unions the right to organize simply added another constituency to the political scene, and guaranteed that the labor movement would not turn socialist as it had throughout Europe. Indeed, no less stalwart a defender of the existing order than Marc Hanna had written in 1920:

> To have success in conciliation, or arbitration, there must be thorough and effective organization on both sides. I believe in organized labor, and I have for thirty years. I believe in it because it is a demonstrated fact that where the concerns and interests of labor are entrusted to able and honest leadership, it is much easier for those who represent the employers to come into close contact with the laborer, and, by dealing with fewer persons, to accomplish results quicker and better.[66]

The other way in which capitalism was saved during the Great Depression was by giving the masses of poor and unemployed the sense that government was being responsive to their needs. Roosevelt's personal magnetism and the modest programs to alleviate the pain contributed to this feeling. While economic historians are quick to point out that the New Deal did not end the Depression, which was only terminated when the Second World War led to an economic boom, a different perception was created. Roosevelt was reelected in 1936, carrying every state but Maine and Vermont, and he won two more terms in 1940 and 1944. Unlike the 1932 election, when all sectors of a desperate nation turned to him as the only alternative to Hoover, the 1936 election divided the nation socioeconomically. Roughly speaking, the rich went Republican and the poor and middle-class voted Democratic. The class gap, though still muted compared with voting in comparable nations, was unprecedented for an American election.

This was Roosevelt and Farley's contribution to American party politics—to introduce a muted class dimension, and give the economically oppressed the sense that there was a party that represented their interests. Modern American liberalism, a doctrine of mildly redistributive programs administered by the national government, was thus born in the 1930s and gave rise to a political coalition of the following groups, that still survives in Roosevelt's Democratic party.[67]

Southern whites

Many southern whites found their attachment to the Democratic party strengthened by the New Deal's agricultural policies, especially regional programs such as the Tennessee Valley Authority. For southern conservatives, decades of tradition and the political stake they had in the Democratic party postponed massive defections to a later period when race became a more overt issue in national politics.[68] Their political stake included congressional committee chairmanships that would have to be sacrificed if the South went Republican, and "bonus votes" for heavily Democratic states at Democratic national conventions. The bonus votes were a sop to the South after the party in 1936 abolished its requirement that presidential nominees win two-thirds of the convention votes. That two-thirds rule was seen by southerners as an effective veto over hostile nominees, and when it was repealed the bonus votes gave the South some compensation.

White ethnics

Al Smith's legacy was to keep ethnic voters firmly in his party, and Roosevelt capitalized upon this. Many of his high appointees were Roman Catholics and Jews, and perhaps his most dramatic appeal to ethnics came at the height of the 1944 campaign, in a speech in ethnic Boston:

> Today, in this war, our fine boys are fighting magnificently all over the world and among those boys are the Murphys and the Kellys, the Smiths and the Joneses, the Cohens, the Carusos, the Kowalskis, the Schultzes, the Olsens, the Swobodas, and—right in with all the rest of them—the Cabots and the Lowells. . . . It is our duty to them to make sure that, big as this country is, there is no room in it for racial or religious intolerance—and that there is no room for snobbery.[69]

The major change here was the movement of American Jews into the Democratic party. Attracted by Roosevelt's liberalism and then by his leadership against Nazi Germany during the Second World War, Jews have remained a predominantly Democratic group to the present day.

The labor movement

The Wagner Act and other laws favorable to labor, such as the minimum wage, gave the Democratic party overwhelming support from labor unions. United Mine Workers president John L. Lewis said of Roosevelt in 1936 that "labor owes him a debt of gratitude that can be liquidated only by casting its solid vote for him at the coming election."[70] Said one worker, "Mr. Roosevelt is the only man we ever had in the White House who would understand that my boss is a sonofabitch."[71] Thus began a decades-long alliance between most of the labor movement and the national Democratic party.

Farmers

The New Deal's agrarian policies solidified for the time being the alliance with agriculture that began in the days of William Jennings Bryan. However, of all the elements of the coalition, farmers were the first to defect, and since then they have been considered a "swing" group of American politics, as well as a continually diminishing proportion of the American population.

Liberal reformers

During the Progressive era, reformers who sought to increase the role of government as a regulator of the public health and safety were divided between the followers of Woodrow Wilson (Roosevelt's mentor) in the Democratic party and those of Theodore Roosevelt (Franklin's distant cousin) in the Republican party. The New Deal appointed so many of these reformers to high office and adopted so many of their policies that the Democratic party became the primary home for liberals. Much was made of Roosevelt's "brains trust," the professors and professionals who came to Washington to implement the agenda of early twentieth century progressivism.

Blacks

Perhaps the most extreme shift came among black Americans, who heeded the words of one prominent black editor when he wrote, "My friends, go turn Lincoln's picture to the wall. That debt has been paid in full."[72] To a great extent, blacks were responding to the New Deal in the same way that lower-income whites were, but with an added dimension. While Roosevelt was uninterested in legislation to help blacks as a group, including federal measures to prevent lynchings of blacks by white mobs, others in his administration were willing to engage in symbolic gestures of great appeal to blacks. Most notably, Roosevelt's wife Eleanor and Secretary of the Interior Harold Ickes publicized their professional contacts with blacks, and made sure that the singer Marian Anderson gave a concert on government property after the Daughters of the American Revolution refused to let her use their hall. Such acts helped cement the wholesale movement of blacks away from the Republican and toward the Democratic party. Later generations of black activists might have regarded blacks in the 1930s as too willing to respond to mere symbolism, but blacks were no more easily seduced than the working-class whites who found the modest programs of the New Deal so enticing.[73]

These were the major components of the Neal Deal coalition, whose stability was tested after Roosevelt died and the far less magnetic Harry Truman had to lead the party in 1948. Despite a left-wing threat from former vice president Henry Wallace, whose Progressive ticket challenged the cold war assumptions of the Truman administration, and the right-wing opposition of Strom Thurmond, whose States' Rights ticket ran against Truman's civil rights policies, and despite his low standing in the polls, Truman won the election by reviving the New Deal coalition and showing that it did not depend solely on Roosevelt's personal skills.[74]

The significance of the New Deal for party politics was twofold. First, it created a new majority coalition that has retained the allegiance of a plurality of American voters ever since. Despite the many changes in American politics since that time, documented throughout this book, any understanding of current American politics must begin with the party that Roosevelt and Farley forged during the Great Depression. In a broader sense, that coalition saved American capitalism by altering it, through regulatory and mildly welfarist policies. McKinley-style capitalism in the United States was dead.

The second long-term effect of the New Deal on party politics was to erode further the ties between the masses and political parties. While Roosevelt inspired strong allegiance to his party in the short run, the increased dependence on government services loosened the bonds between the needy and the party machines that had provided the equivalent of such services. As one scholar has put it, "A governmental order in which party destroyed bureaucracy gave way to a governmental order in which bureaucracy destroyed the integrity of party."[75]

THE REALIGNMENT CYCLE AND PARTY DEVELOPMENT

This chapter began with the assertion that American parties have undergone precious little developing in the past two centuries, and has continued with a description of how, at key moments in the American past, parties served to maintain the socioeconomic order. Now it is time to integrate these two themes by developing an overview of the process of partisan change.

Many historians and political scientists have concluded that the development of American parties has involved neither random fluctuations nor complete stability. Instead, they have discerned long periods of relative stability alternating with briefer periods of instability that mark the beginnings of new partisan eras. There are terms for these time blocs. The stable periods are called *party systems,* which can be thought of as periods when the parties in contention, the coalitions comprising them, their institutional composition, and the issues on the public agenda remain rather stable.[76]

The eras of instability are called periods of *realignment*, when parties and voters literally realign themselves around new issues, new partisan allegiances, and new political institutions.[77] Some have argued that realignments reach their peak in a single *critical election*, but it is difficult to imagine a single election having the lasting impact that so-called critical elections are supposed to.[78]

American history, then, displays party systems lasting about three decades, which are interrupted by realigning eras of several years' duration, which in turn lead to new three-decade party systems. According to this scheme, the periods discussed in this chapter look like this:

1. The first party system, which witnessed the gradual triumph of the Democrat-Republicans over the Federalists from the 1790s to the 1820s;
2. The first realignment, in which factions of the old parties created the Democratic and Whig parties;
3. The second party system, which saw the Democrats and the Whigs compete from the late 1820s until the 1850s;
4. The second realignment, in which the Whigs died out, the Republicans rose to power, and members of the old parties joined the Republicans or the newly constituted Democrats;
5. The third party system, which saw relatively evenly matched Democrats and Republicans vying for power from the 1850s until the 1890s;
6. The third realignment, described above, which reached its peak in the 1890s;
7. The fourth party system, in which the Republicans dominated American politics from the mid-1890s until the early 1930s;
8. The fourth realignment, occasioned by the Great Depression and the New Deal;
9. The fifth party system, in which the Democrats outnumbered the Republicans.

Whether the fifth party system, which arose in the 1930s, has lasted until the present day or broke up in the turmoil of the 1960s is a question that has preoccupied political scientists, journalists and politicians for years. A major question is whether the decline of partisanship means that realigning cycles are no longer possible.[79]

The question for the moment is, Why have there been these thirty-year cycles? One author has suggested that thirty years or so is approximately the length of a generation, and realignments occur when one generation displaces another. With newer interests and concerns, the younger generation finds the established parties irrelevant to its needs, and the parties must adapt to those needs.[80] The problem with this argument is that generations are always dying out and being replaced; it is an ongoing process. Why should the breaks in party politics have occurred when they did, instead of at other times?

A more fruitful explanation is offered by Walter Dean Burnham, who identifies realignments with more general crises in the political system. They are marked, he points out, by an unusually high intensity of feeling about politics and an exceptional degree of ideological polarization among the American people.[81] Elections in realigning eras have also been marked by more divisive national conventions, and by the use of the Supreme Court as a campaign issue.[82] It is as though the entire legitimacy of the political system is called into question.

Burnham's view is consistent with the theory that realignment coincides with major watersheds in American history—the onset of the Jacksonian era, the sectional crisis that led to the Civil War, the agrarian and urban violence of the end of the nineteenth century, the schisms of the Great Depression. Realignments have marked major changes not only in party politics, but also great changes in American history. Old orders change, and new coalitions take power. The ascendancy of the West in the 1820s, of industrialism in the 1860s, of large corporations in the 1890s, and of organized labor in the 1930s were all facilitated by realignments. Some would argue that a similar change occurred in the 1960s, when first blacks and then southern and western white conservatives began to play an unprecedented role in American national politics. This suggests that the question of whether we have been undergoing a realignment in recent years is more significant than whether the Republicans will get more votes than the Democrats; realignments have coincided with major upheavals in American history, altering all of politics.

How can we reconcile the argument that American parties have not developed with the changes from party system to party system? One important point is that for all these changes, American parties have continued to represent liberal capitalist values, and have been more concerned with winning elections than with raising issues. In that sense, there has been profound stability despite the rise and fall of various party coalitions, institutions, and issues. But Walter Dean Burnham suggests a deeper significance of the realignment cycle. Pointing out that the nation has undergone profound social and economic changes, Burnham argues that the political system has never been geared primarily toward fostering social change. Indeed, how could it have, when issues have been of secondary importance at best in American party politics? However, at several times in American history, the popular demand for change has become so great that the political system has been unable to respond in an orderly fashion. Lacking the capacity either to guide the change or to respond to it comprehensively, the party system responds only when there is a political crisis. The response, realignment, is not nearly proportional to the social need, but it is enough to take the pressure off for the time being. This is what a realignment does—it accommodates the political system to the social and economic system just enough to forestall more radical changes. In a phrase, realignment is "America's surrogate for revolution."[83]

There is an irony and a threat in this process. The irony is that a political system that prides itself on its propensity for compromise and its flexibility is actually quite rigid. Not only is it bound tightly within a liberal capitalist framework, but it permits limited accommodation within that framework only after disruption and violence erupt. The threat is that should the realignment process ever end, the system would need another surrogate for revolution. It is Burnham's belief that no such surrogate exists, and liberal capitalism would have a difficult time surviving.

We are left with a picture of a party system that has developed squarely within the bounds of liberal capitalism, changing over time in a limited fashion. It has responded both to perceived and potential challenges to the capitalist order, as in the 1830s, 1890s and the 1930s, and to the desire of new social groups to claim a role in national politics. There has been change, but circumscribed within the assumptions of the system. This is a problem if those assumptions are inadequate to meet the needs of the nation's social and economic development. Can the nation meet the needs of the twenty-first century with an eighteenth century constitution and a declining nineteenth century party system?

Further Reading

The best single volume to introduce the student to American party development is Everett Carll Ladd, Jr., *American Political Parties* (New York: W. W. Norton, 1970). Like this chapter, but from a different perspective, it ties party development to broader social changes. The more advanced student will benefit from the excellent essays in William Nisbet Chambers and Walter Dean Burnham, eds., *The American Party Systems* (New York: Oxford Univ. Press, 1967). Perhaps no one has contributed more to our understanding of the subject than Burnham, both in his *Critical Elections and the Mainsprings of American Politics* (New York: W. W. Norton, 1970) and in his shorter pieces collected in *The Current Crisis in American Politics* (New York: Oxford Univ. Press, 1982). A different perspective, far more sanguine about American political development, is found in James L. Sundquist, *Dynamics of the Party System*, revised ed. (Washington: The Brookings Institution, 1983). Other good collections are Joel H. Silbey, Allan G. Bogue, and William H. Flanigan, eds., *The History of American Electoral Behavior* (Princeton: Princeton Univ. Press, 1978), and Paul Kleppner *et al.*, *The Evolution of American Electoral Systems* (Westport, Conn.: Greenwood Press, 1981).

For readings on particular historical periods, see the notes in this chapter.

Notes

1. Louis Hartz, *The Liberal Tradition in America* (New York: Harcourt, Brace & World, 1955); and Samuel P. Huntington, "Political Modernization: America vs. Europe," in his *Political Order in Changing Societies* (New Haven: Yale Univ. Press, 1968), 93–139. A

precursor of Huntington's argument can be found in Talcott Parsons, "The Distribution of Power in American Society," *World Politics* X (October 1957), 133–134.

2. Theodore J. Lowi, "Party, Policy, and Constitution in America," in William Nisbet Chambers and Walter Dean Burnham, eds., *The American Party Systems* (New York: Oxford Univ. Press, 1967), 274.

3. Paul Kleppner, "Critical Realignments and Electoral Systems," in Kleppner *et al.*, *The Evolution of American Electoral Systems* (Westport, Conn.: Greenwood Press, 1981), 3.

4. See Locke's *Second Treatise of Government*, which is available in many editions. The most incisive interpretation of that school of thought remains C. B. Macpherson's *The Political Theory of Possessive Individualism* (New York: Oxford Univ. Press, 1962).

5. A useful collection of essays about the linkages between capitalism and the Constitution is Robert A. Goldwin and William A. Schambra, eds., *How Capitalistic Is the Constitution?* (Washington: American Enterprise Institute, 1982). Most of the contributors, regardless of their ideology, answer the question with "very." One exception is Forrest McDonald, whose essay, "The Constitution and Hamiltonian Capitalism," argues that "The Constitution was not originally designed to establish capitalism in America, but constitutional government and capitalism became inextricably intertwined at the outset." (p. 74)

6. Quoted in Richard Hofstadter, *The Idea of a Party System* (Berkeley and Los Angeles: Univ. of California Press, 1969), 123.

7. In Clinton Rossiter's edition (New York: New American Library, 1961), these quotations are on pp. 34 and 77 respectively.

8. Austin Ranney, *Curing the Mischiefs of Faction* (Berkeley and Los Angeles: Univ. of California Press, 1975), 30–37.

9. In the Rossiter edition, this quotation from the tenth *Federalist* is on p. 79.

10. Gaillard Hunt, ed., *The Writings of James Madison,* (New York: G. P. Putnam's Sons, 1906), VI: 86.

11. Gaillard Hunt, ed., *The Writings of James Madison*, VI: 86.

12. Quoted in Hofstadter, *The Idea of a Party System*, 115.

13. In Noble E. Cunningham, ed., *The Making of the American Party System* (Englewood Cliffs, N.J.: Prentice-Hall, Inc., 1965), 81.

14. In Cunningham, editor, *The Making of the American Party System*, 171. On this period, see William Nisbet Chambers, *Political Parties in a New Nation* (New York: Oxford Univ. Press, 1963); Joseph Charles, *The Origins of the American Party System* (New York: Harper & Bros., 1961); and Hofstadter, *The Idea of a Party System*.

15. Quoted in James Sterling Young, *The Washington Community* (New York: Colum bia Univ. Press, 1966), 130.

16. David Hackett Fischer, *The Revolution of American Conservatism* (New York: Harper & Row, 1965), 201.

17. Ronald P. Formisano, "Deferential-Participant Politics: The Early Republic's Political Culture, 1789–1840," *American Political Science Review* LXVIII (June 1974), 474 (emphasis in the original).

18. Alexis de Tocqueville, *Democracy in America*, trans. Henry Reeve, (New York: Colonial Press, 1899), II: 144-145. The book was first published in 1835 and remains the best account of the social psychology of liberal capitalism.

19. Karl Marx and Friedrich Engels, *Manifesto of the Communist Party*, in *Selected Works in Three Volumes* (Moscow: Progress Publishers, 1969), I: 111. This most concise and readable summary of Marxist thought first appeared in 1848.

20. *Historical Statistics of the United States*, (Washington: Government Printing Office, 1975), Part 1: 12–13, 139.

21. See Douglass C. North, *The Economic Growth of the United States 1790–1860* (Englewood Cliffs, N.J.: Prentice-Hall, 1961), 163.

22. Jeffrey G. Williamson and Peter H. Lindert, *American Inequality* (New York: Academic Press, 1980), 36.

23. Williamson and Lindert, *American Inequality*, 68.

24. "Declaration of Independence of the Producing from the Non-Producing Class," in Philip S. Foner, ed., *We, the Other People* (Urbana: Univ. of Illinois Press, 1976), 66.

25. George Fitzhugh, *Cannibals All!* (Cambridge, Mass.: Harvard Univ. Press, 1960), 17. This remarkable work was first published in 1856.

26. Walter Dean Burnham's presidential election turnout estimates from 1824 to 1968 can be found in the *Congressional Record,* (December 11, 1970), 41223–41224.

27. Richard P. McCormick, *The Second American Party System* (Chapel Hill: Univ. of North Carolina Press, 1966), 343–344.

28. Quoted in Alexander Heard, *The Costs of Democracy*, abridged ed. (Garden City, N.Y.: Anchor Books, 1962), 352.

29. Richard Jensen, "American Election Campaigns: A Theoretical and Historical Typology," unpublished paper presented to the 1968 annual meeting of the Midwest Political Science Association. This paper is the source of my information about newspapers and literary figures.

30. See Robert V. Remini, *Martin Van Buren and the Making of the Democratic Party* (New York: Columbia Univ. Press, 1959), especially p. 193.

31. See Lee Benson, *The Concept of Jacksonian Democracy* (New York: Atheneum, 1964); and Ronald P. Formisano, *The Birth of Mass Political Parties* (Princeton: Princeton Univ. Press, 1971).

32. McCormick, *Second American Party System*, 349. See also James S. Chase, *Emergence of the Presidential Nominating Convention* (Urbana: Univ. of Illinois Press, 1973), 288–289.

33. See William G. Shade, "Political Pluralism and Party Development," in Kleppner *et al., The Evolution of American Electoral Systems*, 98.

34. Shade, "Political Pluralism and Party Development," 105.

35. Richard Hofstadter, *The American Political Tradition* (New York: Vintage Books, 1948), 56.

36. In *The Liberal Tradition in America,* Hartz called this process the "law of Whig compensation."

37. Richard J. Jensen, *The Winning of the Midwest* (Chicago: Univ. of Chicago Press, 1971), 6–7.

38. Quoted in Theodore H. White, *The Making of the President* 1960 (New York: Atheneum, 1961), 358 (emphasis added).

39. *Historical Statistics of the United States*, Part 2: 666, 912–913, 667, and 683; and Part 1: 127, 139, and 12–13.

40. Williamson and Lindert, *American Inequality*, 46–47, 75.

41. *Historical Statistics of the United States*, Part 2: 135.

42. Quoted in Richard Maxwell Brown, "Historical Patterns of Violence in America," in Hugh Davis Graham and Ted Robert Gurr, eds., *Violence in America: Historical and Comparative Perspectives, A Report to the National Commission on the Causes and Prevention of Violence,* (Washington: Government Printing Office, 1969), I: 54.

43. *Public Papers of the Presidents of the United States: Harry S. Truman 1948* (Washington: Government Printing Office, 1964), 824.

44. Brown, "Historical Patterns," pp. 52–54.

45. On the Populist alliance, see Norman Pollack, *The Populist Response to Industrial America* (Cambridge: Harvard Univ. Press, 1962), and Lawrence Goodwyn, *The Populist Moment* (New York: Oxford Univ. Press, 1978).

46. For this and all other party platforms, see Donald Bruce Johnson and Kirk H. Porter, *National Party Platforms 1840–1972* (Urbana: Univ. of Illinois Press, 1973).

47. A highly readable account of the campaign is Paul W. Glad, *McKinley, Bryan and the People* (Philadelphia and New York: J. B. Lippincott, 1964).

48. On the importance of institutional changes in this period, see Philip E. Converse,

"Change in the American Electorate," in Angus Campbell and Philip E. Converse, eds., *The Human Meaning of Social Change* (New York: Russell Sage Foundation, 1972), 263–301; and Jerrold G. Rusk, "The Effect of the Australian Ballot Reform on Split-Ticket Voting: 1876–1908," *American Political Science Review* LXIV (December 1970), 1220–1238. See also note 51 below.

49. Herbert E. Alexander, *Financing Politics* (Washington: Congressional Quarterly, 1980), 5. On the growing relationship between the Republicans and corporate elites, see Robert D. Marcus, *Grand Old Party* (New York: Oxford Univ. Press, 1971).

50. This general interpretation of the changes of the 1890s is based on Samuel P. Hays, "Political Parties and the Community-Society Continuum, " in Chambers and Burnham, *The American Party Systems, 152–181*. Hays' students have produced excellent regional accounts of this process. On the Midwest, see Paul Kleppner, *The Cross of Culture* (New York: The Free Press, 1970), and Jensen, *The Winning of the Midwest*. On the Northeast, see Samuel McSeveney, *The Politics of Depression* (New York: Oxford Univ. Press, 1972).

51. The classic account of these changes is Walter Dean Burnham, "The Changing Shape of the American Political Universe," *American Political Science Review* LIX (March 1965), 7–28. Burnham has engaged in a lively debate with the authors cited in note 48, above, disagreeing with their stress on the importance of institutional changes in explaining these changes in voting behavior. See the *American Political Science Review* LXV (December 1971), 1149–1157, and LXVIII (September 1974), 1002–1057. In my view, Burnham is correct to place the electoral reforms in the broader context of the manipulation of the masses by political and socioeconomic elites.

52. Woodrow Wilson, *The New Democracy,* ed. Ray Stannard Baker and William E. Dodd, (New York: Harper & Bros., 1926), I: 238, 247.

53. Jensen, "American Election Campaigns." The Roosevelt quotation is in note 20.

54. Data on the background of cabinet members can be found in Robert Sobel, ed., *Biographical Directory of the United States Executive Branch 1774–1977* (Westport, Conn.: Greenwood Press, 1977).

55. On turnout, see E. E. Schattschneider, *The Semisovereign People* (New York: Holt, Rinehart & Winston, 1960), chapter 5; J. Morgan Kousser, *The Shaping of Southern Politics* (New Haven: Yale Univ. Press, 1974); and Paul Kleppner, *Who Voted?* (New York: Praeger Publishers, 1982), chapter 4. On the rise of interest groups in this period, see David B. Truman, *The Governmental Process* (New York: Alfred A. Knopf, 1951); and Grant McConnell, *Private Power and American Democracy* (New York: Alfred A. Knopf, 1966). On the rise of the new bureaucratic state, see Stephen Skowronek, *Building a New American State* (New York: Cambridge Univ. Press, 1982).

56. Quoted in Gabriel Kolko, *The Triumph of Conservatism* (Chicago: Quadrangle Books, 1967), 274–275. This book makes a comprehensive argument about the effects of the Progressive movement. See also Samuel P. Hays, *The Response to Industrialism* (Chicago: Univ. of Chicago Press, 1957), and Robert H. Wiebe, *The Search for Order* (New York: Hill & Wang, 1967).

57. On the Democrats' ethnic conflicts in the 1920s, see David Burner, *The Politics of Provincialism* (New York: Alfred A. Knopf, 1968). On Smith's effect on turnout, see Kristi Andersen, *The Creation of a Democratic Majority 1928–1936* (Chicago: Univ. of Chicago Press, 1979).

58. See William E. Leuchtenberg, *Franklin D. Roosevelt and the New Deal* (New York: Harper & Row, 1963), on which much of this discussion is based.

59. Quoted in Leuchtenberg, *Franklin D. Roosevelt,* 96.

60. A "regressive" tax is one not based on the ability to pay, and therefore it hurts lower-income taxpayers more than higher-income payers.

61. *The Public Papers and Addresses of Franklin D. Roosevelt,* (New York: Random House, 1938), V: 568–569.

62. *Public Papers and Addresses,* 385.

63. *Public Papers and Addresses,* 487–488.

64. Quoted in Arthur M. Schlesinger, Jr., *The Coming of the New Deal* (Boston: Houghton Mifflin, 1958), 503.

65. *Public Papers and Addresses,* p. 148.

66. Quoted in Edward S. Greenberg, *Understanding Modern Government* (New York: John Wiley & Sons, 1979), 85. Much of my interpretation of the New Deal was inspired by this little book. See also Theda Skocpol, "Political Response to Capitalist Crisis," *Politics and Society* X (1980), 155–202.

67. The best review of the electoral trends of the New Deal and post-New Deal era is Everett Carll Ladd, Jr., with Charles D. Hadley, *Transformations of the American Party System* (New York: W. W. Norton, 1975), Part I.

68. For the sectional strains within the Democratic party in Congress in the late 1930s, see James T. Patterson, *Congressional Conservatism and the New Deal* (Lexington: Univ. of Kentucky Press, 1967).

69. *The Public Papers and Addresses of Franklin D. Roosevelt* (New York: Harper & Bros., 1950), XIII: 398.

70. Quoted in Arthur M. Schlesinger, Jr., *The Politics of Upheaval,* (Boston: Houghton Mifflin, 1960), 593.

71. Quoted in Eric F. Goldman, *Rendezvous with Destiny* (New York: Alfred A. Knopf, 1958), 345.

72. Quoted in Leuchtenberg, *Franklin D. Roosevelt,* 187.

73. On black politics in this period, see John B. Kirby, *Black Americans in the Roosevelt Era* (Knoxville: Univ. of Tennessee Press, 1980), and Nancy J. Weiss, *Farewell to the Party of Lincoln* (Princeton: Princeton Univ. Press, 1983).

74. There are many books on the 1948 campaign, two of the best being Irwin Ross, *The Loneliest Campaign* (New York: New American Library, 1968), and Allen Yarnell, *Democrats and Progressives* (Berkeley: Univ. of California Press, 1974).

75. Skowronek, *Building a New American State,* 290. See also Sidney M. Milkis, "Franklin D. Roosevelt and the Transcendence of Partisan Politics," *Political Science Quarterly* C (Fall 1985), 479–504.

76. I infer this definition from Chambers and Burnham, editors, *The American Party Systems.*

77. Major studies of the realignment process are Walter Dean Burnham, *Critical Elections and the Mainsprings of American Politics* (New York: W. W. Norton, 1970); Bruce Campbell and Richard J. Trilling, eds., *Realignment in American Politics* (Austin: Univ. of Texas Press, 1980); and Jerome M. Clubb, William H. Flanigan, and Nancy H. Zingale, *Partisan Realignment* (Beverly Hills: Sage Publications, 1980).

78. The "critical elections" concept first appeared in V. O. Key, Jr., "A Theory of Critical Elections," *Journal of Politics* XVII (February 1955), 3–18.

79. See Burnham, *Critical Elections,* 91–134.

80. Paul Allen Beck, "A Socialization Theory of Partisan Realignment," in Richard G. Niemi *et al., The Politics of Future Citizens* (San Francisco: Jossey-Bass, 1974), 199–219.

81. Burnham, *Critical Elections,* 6–7.

82. On conventions, see Burnham, *Critical Elections,* 6–7; the Democratic conventions of 1860 and 1896 come to mind. On the Supreme Court and realignments, a good starting point is David Adamany, "The Supreme Court's Role in Critical Elections," in Campbell and Trilling, editors, *Realignment in American Politics,* 229–259. The court was an issue in the campaigns of 1860 (the Dred Scott decision), 1896 (the anti-income tax decision of 1894), and 1936 (various anti-New Deal decisions), as well as 1968 when Richard Nixon accused the Court of being insufficiently attentive to "law and order."

83. Burnham, "Party Systems and the Political Process," in Chambers and Burnham, eds., *The American Party Systems,* 289. This discussion is based on Burnham, *Critical Elections,* 181–182.

6

Party Organization

A social and economic system that wanted to perpetuate itself could hardly do better than to have a party system like ours: issues are downplayed so that serious questions about the structure of society are never raised, and structure is kept weak so that, were such questions ever raised, it would be very difficult to mobilize resources to change the system. This chapter will look closely at party organization in two respects. First, the strongest party organizations in American history will be examined, with an eye to how they served to maintain the social and economic order. Second, the question of party reform will be considered, concentrating on recent changes in national parties and the implications for the possibilities of social change.

MACHINE RULE

One of the distinguishing features of the American party system is the lack of ideological distance between the major parties. Since virtually all of the nations with which I compared the United States have major socialist or social democratic parties, we can more specifically ask the question that was phrased by a German socialist in 1906: "Why is there no socialism in the United States?"[1]

Indeed, the more we think about the question, the more paradoxical it is that in the early twentieth century the United States did not develop a lasting mass socialist movement, as Britain, France, and even more repressive nations like Germany and Russia did. After all, like most of those other countries, the United States was transformed by the Industrial Revolution into an urban, industrial nation with a mass of working-class people who elsewhere formed the basis for socialist and social democratic parties. Although native-born American workers may have grown up with the liberal capitalist values that have long dominated this nation, the early twentieth century was a time when millions of immigrants, a good number of them radicals, entered the country. The Russian revolutionary Trotsky lived in New York before the Russian Revolution, and in Massachusetts,

two Italian anarchists, Sacco and Vanzetti, were executed for armed rob-
bery and murder after a trial in which their ethnicity and politics heavily
influenced their fate. Radical immigrants might well have provided the
inspiration for homegrown socialism.

As noted in the previous chapter, parties of the Left did run up some
impressive vote totals around the turn of the century. In presidential elections, the Populists received 8.5 percent of the popular vote in 1892, the
Socialists 6.0 percent in 1912, and the Progressives 16.6 percent in 1924.
Some leading American intellectuals were attracted to Marxism in the early
years of the century and during the Great Depression of the 1930s, and their
writings might have helped the leftist cause. If all of these factors were in
place, then why did no permanent mass socialist movement develop?

Answering such a complex question would involve discussing many
factors, including material aspects (such as a higher standard of living), a
general lack of class consciousness traceable to the lack of a feudal tradition, and governmental repression during and after the First World War,
but here I shall concentrate on the first answer that the German socialist
gave in 1906: no permanent socialist movement developed because of the
political machine. While party organization has declined substantially in
the past couple of decades, in most major cities in the late nineteenth and
early twentieth centuries politics was dominated by powerful party "machines" (the term you used if you didn't like them) or "organizations"
(what their members preferred to call them). These machines (I shall use
"machine" and "organization" interchangeably, intending neither praise
nor condemnation) were led by the "boss" or "leader" (again, depending
on what you thought of him; again, I shall use both terms). The classic
urban machine was usually Democratic and its base was in the working
and lower classes and in the immigrants who flooded into the cities. Yet I
shall argue that it was anything but a vehicle for the true interests of such
people.

How did these machines function? What was the basis of their power?
I shall argue that they engaged in two kinds of relationships, those based
on personal relationships and favors, and those based on money.

Personalism

Moisei Ostrogorski, a Russian liberal who visited the United States in
the 1880s and 1890s to study American politics, produced one of the
classic descriptions of the boss:

> The boss owes help and protection to his henchmen, he must defend
> them with his person, must forward their political ambitions, if they have any,
> ensure them a livelihood if they are not well off, as is the case with most of his
> lieutenants, procure them places in the public service, keep them there, how-
> ever great their incompetence or their neglect of their duties. He will move
> heaven and earth to place his men, he will risk his influence to achieve it. This

is the first reward which he claims, regardless of himself, from the boss above him, or from the head of the executive power who makes appointments. He must have a place for his henchmen.[2]

Ostrogorski compares his boss to a mafia chieftain, and we might generalize this to any feudal relationship, the knight swearing personal fealty to the king, and in turn being responsible for the vassals who pledge their fealty to him. These are relationships based on *personal* obligations, and in order to understand the functioning of the machine we must consider this kind of human relationship. The sociologist Herbert Gans once distinguished between people who are "object-oriented" and those who are "people-oriented." The former aspire to abstract "objects," such as moral, ideological, material, cultural, or social goals. The latter want to be part of a group of people, and take their goals from the group.[3] While Gans denies that any broad class of people is object-oriented, he does describe the professional upper-middle class as "particularly object-oriented."[4]

Does a person aspire to goals which are abstractions, or to those which involve particular human relationships? The scheme that Gans develops has great implications for politics. Daniel Elazar has divided American regions into three political cultures, one of which, the "traditionalistic," is confined largely to the South and will not be considered here. Another is what Elazar calls "moralistic," and loosely corresponds to Gans's object-orientation. "Politics," says Elazar in describing this culture, "is considered one of the great activities of man in his search for the good society—a struggle for power, it is true, but also an effort to exercise power for the betterment of the commonweath."[5] Such concepts as "the good society," "power," and "the betterment of the commonwealth" fit Gans's object-orientation quite neatly, as do issues, with which Elazar says those members of the moralistic culture are preoccupied.

In Elazar's scheme, the counterpart to Gans's person-orientation is the "individualistic culture:"

> In its view, government is instituted for strictly utilitarian reasons, to handle those functions demanded by the people it is created to serve. . . . The individualistic political culture holds politics to be just another means by which individuals may improve themselves socially and economically. . . . Political life within an individualistic political culture is based on a system of mutual obligations rooted in personal relationships.[6]

With these comparisons, we can begin to understand how the party organizations of the turn of the twentieth century appealed to their members and the voters. The immigrants who filled American cities during this period came largely from the European peasant class that was not far from the Middle Ages in its culture. In Europe, government had meant oppression: in Ireland it was the English, in Poland the Russians, in Italy a host of foreign invaders, and to Jews government meant pogroms. In many cultures, the social structure of the peasantry revolved around the extended family, and formal education was meager. Consequently, the idea of government as an instrument of abstractions such as class interest or patriotism or a particular issue of public policy was not within the experience of the immigrant masses of the great cities, and would have to be developed over time. In the contemptuous formulation of the British liberal, H. G. Wells, the American immigrants "have no ideas and they have votes."[7]

To those who worked for the machine, the incentive was straightforward—government jobs, or patronage. This was the ideal motivation for an American party organization, for it was simple and material. It required no battles over issues, and no controversial considerations of the general good. It could be parcelled out to individuals one by one. The only goal was victory, for in victory the jobs would flow. It was also a good way to keep people working for the party, for if their jobs were at stake, their allegiance and hard work could be counted on.

If patronage was the way to motivate the organization's workers, other personal favors could capture the allegiance of the voters. For the poor, a bucket of coal in the winter and a Christmas turkey were examples of the machine's largesse. More broadly, the local politician was the voter's liaison with city government. In the 1930s, one such worker in a lower-class area of Chicago described his work:

> When anyone gets into trouble with the law—petty thieving, trouble with a relief investigator—or when he loses his job or is about to be evicted, or when a kid gets in with a bad gang and starts staying out all night, in cases like this it is not the relief agency or social welfare agency that the harassed voter first goes to, but rather to the precinct captain who stands in with the law, who will not talk down to him but will treat him as a friend in need, and who is waiting for him in the local tavern or in the ward headquarters, where there is a full-time secretary who knows just who can handle the situation.[8]

Said a New York politician at the turn of the century:

> If there's a fire in Ninth, Tenth, or Eleventh Avenue, for example, any hour of the day or night, I'm usually there with some of my election district captains as soon as the fire engines. If a family is burned out I don't ask whether they are Republicans or Democrats, and I don't refer them to the Charity Organization Society, which would investigate their case in a month or two and decide they were worthy of help about the time they are dead from starvation. I just get quarters for them, buy clothes for them if their clothes were burned up, and fix them up till they get things runnin' again. It's philanthropy, but it's politics, too—mighty good politics. Who can tell how many votes one of these fires brings me?[9]

Notice that all of these favors were individualized, personal favors. The machine was not primarily in the business of seeking legislation to prevent unjust evictions or improve the building codes in order to prevent fires. While such laws would have helped large numbers of people, the organization wanted mainly to create gratitude among specific individuals. If one were to help large masses of people, they might not know who had helped them and therefore whom to support at the polls. Individualized gratitude, not class action, was the aim of the machine.

This was no secret to the machine politicians, who saw issues as an irrelevancy. Here is one New York politician on William Jennings Bryan's favorite issue in 1896:

> In two Presidential campaigns, the leaders talked themselves red in the face about silver bein' the best money and gold bein' no good, and they tried to prove it out of books. Do you think the people cared for all that guff? No. They heartily endorsed what Richard Croker said at the Hoffman House one day in 1900. "What's the use of discussin' what's the best kind of money?" said Croker. "I'm in favor of all kinds of money—the more the better." See how a real Tammany statesman can settle in twenty-five words a problem that monopolized two campaigns![10]

On inter-party differences, his policy was:

> When Tammany's on top I do good turns for the Republicans. When they're on top they don't forget me. Me and the Republicans are enemies just one day in the year—election day. Then we fight tooth and nail. The rest of the time it's live and let live with us.... You see, we differ on tariffs and currencies and all them things, but we agree on the main proposition that when a man works in politics, he should get something out of it.[11]

In short, issues—the concern of Gans's object-oriented or Elazar's moralistic person—had no place in politics. Politics was about jobs for organization workers and favors for the voters, and issues would only confuse matters and lose support for the machine.

A politics that revolves around personal relationships and kinship ties is one in which ethnic identity becomes very important. As soon as an ethnic group became sizeable enough to claim a significant share of the electorate, it joined the arena in which nominations had to be traded off. In New York City by the 1930s, the three-person citywide ticket had to represent the "three I's," Ireland, Italy, and Israel; a few years later in Connecticut, the U.S. Representative at Large had to be Polish; and so on. Voters were expected to vote their loyalties to their own ethnic group, again putting personal considerations above issues. Moreover, to the ambitious young immigrant, politics was one of the few avenues of upward mobility.

In this personalized politics, corruption played a special role. To the object-oriented person, corruption would be a violation of the abstract quality of honesty in government. To the person-oriented adherent of the machine, it meant doing favors for your friends, just as nepotism meant doing favors for your family. What kind of upstanding person would put an abstraction like integrity or meritocracy above one's relationships with one's peers? Every so often in a number of cities, enough voters would be appalled by one scandal or other to elect a reformist administration, and usually it would be voted out again as soon as the wave of outrage died down.[12]

How did such a style of politics serve to maintain the social and economic order? First, merely by downplaying issues it reduced the likelihood that people would start to analyze the social system. Major political transformation requires that people understand the need for change, how the current system stands in the way of such change, and how change can be accomplished. All of these steps require analysis, and, therefore, a style of politics that involves thinking about substantive issues, and not merely about who is giving what to whom.

The second way in which this style of politics perpetuates the status quo is that by promoting the persistence of ethnic identity, it divides the lower class against itself. Lower-income Irish-Americans can choose to think in class terms or in ethnic terms. If they think in class terms, they will ally themselves with lower-class Italian-Americans, Jews, blacks, and so forth, and oppose upper-class Irish-Americans as well as the elite of other groups. In this way, a cross-ethnic alliance of the lower class will form, and may pose a threat to the established order. On the other hand, if lower-class Irish-Americans think in ethnic terms, they will refuse to join in a coalition with other lower-class ethnic groups, at least around class interests. The established order will not be threatened. Therefore a party system that stresses ethnicity, like the machines of old, prevents a class coalition from forming and creating the possibility of major social change.

Finally, by the system of individualized favors, the machines bought off the lower classes and reduced the discontentments that might have led to more radical action. The bucket of coal, the prevention of an eviction, the emergency assistance, the city job, may have provided just enough relief to give the recipient some measure of hope. It is like the realignment process discussed in the previous chapter: just enough minor change to forestall a major upheaval. The machine politicians prided themselves on their patriotism. The aforementioned Croker, leader of the infamous Tammany machine in New York, boasted:

> Think what New York is and what the people of New York are. One half, more than one half, are of foreign birth. . . . They do not speak our language, they do not know our laws, they are the raw material with thich we have to build up the state. . . . There is no denying the service which Tammany has rendered to the Republic. There is no such organization for taking hold of the untrained, friendless man and converting him into a citizen. Who else would do it if we did not?[13]

Croker's henchman, George Washington Plunkitt, claimed half in jest that patronage kept young men from becoming radicals. When civil service laws jolted the machine by requiring that one pass an examination in order to get a municipal job, Plunkitt related:

There was once a bright young man in my district who tackled one of these examinations. The next I heard of him he had settled down in Herr Most's saloon smokin' and drinkin' and talkin' socialism all day.... That young man is today one of the wildest Anarchists in town. And just to think! He might be a patriot but for that cussed civil service.[14]

One response to all this is to regard the machine nostalgically as a service agency for the poor and an educator of the immigrant. No doubt the machine alleviated some human suffering in individual cases, but if it destroyed the potential for a classwide movement that could have brought more fundamental relief for wide strata of society, then history's verdict may be a more profound indictment than condemnation of its corruption alone.

Cash

Where did the organization get the funds for all of the services it provided to constituents? In 1918, the German sociologist Max Weber described the American party boss as a "political capitalist entrepreneur who on his own account and at his own risk provides votes." According to Weber, while the party raises funds from members' contributions, assessments on the salaries of officeholders, bribes, and tips, these sources are insufficient:

> The boss is indispensable as the direct recipient of the money of great financial magnates, who would not entrust their money for election purposes to a paid party official, or to anyone else giving public account of his affairs. The boss, with his judicious discretion in financial matters, is the natural man for those capitalist circles who finance the election.[15]

The notion of the leader as a calculating businessman is in stark contrast to Ostrogorski's portrait of the feudal chieftain building a network of personal favors. Weber did not overlook that aspect of machine rule, but his portrait is more complete. Just as the machine held on to its workers by the use of patronage, and to its voters by the distribution of individualized favors, it raised large contributions from those businesses that needed the cooperation of the municipal government for licenses, contracts, and other benefits. The heyday of these organizations was the period of vast municipal building projects, such as ports, aqueducts, subways, schools and other public buildings, parks, highways, and so forth. Fortunate was the construction company that received the contract for such projects, and shrewd was the businessman who made the appropriate donation to the party that controlled the city government that decided who would get that contract.

In his cheerfully cynical fashion, Plunkitt defended the process:

> The civil service gang is always howlin' about candidates and office-holders puttin' up money for campaigns and about corporations chippin' in.

They might as well howl about givin' contributions to churches. A political organization has to have money for its business as well as a church, and who has more right to put up than the men who get the good things that are goin'? . . . If a corporation sends in a check to help the good work of the Tammany Society, why shouldn't we take it like other missionary societies? Of course, the day may come when we'll reject the money of the rich as tainted, but it hadn't come when I left Tammany Hall at 11:25 A.M. today.[16]

Weber described the boss as 'absolutely sober,"[17] and this portrait of the boss as organization man fits a number of self-descriptions that party officials have produced. Ed Flynn, the Democratic leader of the Bronx and a close confidante of Franklin Roosevelt, wrote in his memoirs that the "personal element" had played too great a role in his organization. He set out to change that, in terms that would do a business school graduate proud:

> There was too much talk, too much waste of time, with too little accomplished. I wanted to streamline the organization. I intended to keep my personal life entirely separate from my political life. . . . Personal relationships in any business (and a political machine is my business) are apt to cause jealousy and dissatisfaction. No one in the Bronx can say that he was ever "closer to the Boss" than anyone else.[18]

Even the colorful Plunkitt maintained sobriety in his personal life. Here is his description of a victory celebration on election night in 1897:

> A lot of small politicians followed us, expectin' to see magnums of champagne opened. The waiters in the restaurant expected it, too, and you never saw a more disgusted lot of waiters when they got our orders. Here's the orders: Croker, vichy and bicarbonate of soda; Carroll, seltzer lemonade; Sullivan, appolinaris; Murphy, vichy; Plunkitt, ditto. Before midnight we were all in bed, and next mornin' we were up bright and early attendin' to business, while other men were nursin' swelled heads. Is there anything the matter with temperance as a pure business proposition?[19]

In its relations with the business world, the machine helped to perpetuate capitalism in a variety of ways. The most direct way, as noted, was to provide individual firms with licenses, contracts, and other benefits. These aids have not gone unappreciated by the corporate class. Indeed, when Chicago's mayor Richard Daley was elected to a sixth term in 1975, this pillar of the Democratic party was praised by none other than the arch-Republican editorialists of the *Wall Street Journal,* who wrote, "We don't suggest that a patronage machine is the essence of civic enlightenment, but no one seems to have come up with a better way to get schools built, streets maintained, trash and garbage collected." Daley's machine was described as "wasteful but reasonably effective."[20] It is important to pay close attention to the kinds of services the *Journal* was praising: building schools (without attention to the quality of education within), maintaining streets (without attention to the quality of housing on those streets), collecting garbage (without attention to broader environmental issues). All are services that can easily be contracted out to private businesses, and therefore serve the interests of both the machine and the corporate sector. Any concern with the quality of human services was largely irrelevant to both the Daley organization and the corporate world.

In a broader sense, however, the machine helped the corporate sector by placating the masses with its services. This kept down the level of discontentment and made the cities safer for investment. Just as multinational corporations are intensely concerned with the political stability of third world nations, lest unrest result in a loss of investments, domestic corporations want to invest in places where unrest is low and the government is not levying high corporate taxes in order to fund major social services. In these regards the old party organizations were happy to cooperate.

The machines that I have been describing are nearly all extinct. The causes of their demise can to a great extent be inferred from the foregoing discussion. First, patronage was dealt a series of severe blows by civil service reforms, in which people wanting government jobs no longer had to woo party leaders, but could secure employment by passing the kinds of examinations that Plunkitt believed created radicals. In recent years this kind of legislation has been augmented by a series of judicial decisions: in Elrod v. Burns (1976), the Supreme Court held that "nonpolicymaking, nonconfidential" city employees could not be fired merely for belonging to the wrong party, and in Branti v. Finkel (1980), it ruled that in order to dismiss a public employee for partisan reasons, the government had to show that partisanship is "appropriate" to the job.[21]

Other weapons of the machine were blunted over time. With the establishment of a number of social welfare programs in the 1930s, poor people came to rely less and less on the party for subsistence favors. Sometimes this process is overstated, exaggerating both the largesse of public welfare programs and the speed with which the New Deal destroyed the old parties. During the New Deal period, in fact, local party organizations administered many of these welfare programs and were able to channel aid to favored individuals.[22] But surely over time this control was eroded and professional administrators eventually took over.

This last point brings up another factor that eroded the machines, population mobility. This took several forms, one of which was the movement of whites to suburbs after the Second World War. Combined with the migration of blacks and Puerto Ricans to many northern cities in this period, the emigration of whites changed the racial composition of major cities. In most areas, the white machines simply were not open to nonwhites on an equal basis, and by the 1960s growing nonwhite militancy created enormous pressures on city politics. Gradually more and more cities elected black mayors, until by the middle 1980s Los Angeles, Chicago, Detroit, Philadelphia, Cleveland, Gary, and Newark had done so. These elections usually involved the defection of large numbers of white

Democratic voters who supported the white Republican candidate rather than a black candidate of their own party, and in Gary and Chicago prominent white Democratic politicians backed the Republican.[23] At the same time, the diminishing economic base of the cities created more severe fiscal problems, with bankers coming more and more to control urban pursestrings, as in the "bailout" of New York City in the 1970s.

In the 1950s, major cities became the scene of increased political activism by young white professionals who were attracted to the cultural and social opportunities found there. Not only were such people in no need of the Christmas turkeys, patronage jobs, and other benefits of the machines, but they were Gans's object-oriented and Elazar's moralistic prototypes. Viewing politics as an arena for deciding issues of public policy, they had little patience for the personalistic style of the old organizations, and in many areas they fought to replace machine politics with a type more suited to their culture.[24] The "reforms" for which they fought will be the focus of the rest of this chapter.

THE POLITICS OF "REFORM"

Comparing machine and reform politicians, one historian has suggested that they merely provide "competing modes of protecting the economic and social privileges of local elites," and that both balanced "the frequently conflicting claims of community and accumulation"[25]—the major task of the American political system in general. This description is useful, for it keeps us from seeing reformers and machine politicians as "good guys" and "bad guys" and guides us to an understanding that each type, in its way, serves the interests of capitalist elites.

In the early twentieth century, the Progressive movement was the prototype of anti-machine reformism. Here I am not referring primarily to the Progressive party that ran Theodore Roosevelt for president in 1912 (or to a later Progressive party that ran Robert LaFollette for President in 1924), but rather to a widespread political movement that had adherents in that party as well as within both major parties. It has often been argued that the differences between the Progressives and the party organizations involved social and ethnic antagonisms. Progressives were, it is said, middle-class Protestants who wanted to cripple the only political base that the poor and the immigrants had.[26] All of the Progressive reforms that ostensibly "cleaned up" politics, such as the direct primary, civil service, registration laws, and the direct election of United States senators, were designed to undercut those who spoke for the urban masses. Even women's suffrage, so uncontroversial today, was seen as a way to "purify" politics by adding to the electorate the supposedly more moral sex. In fact, when women's suffrage took hold everywhere in 1920, women who were middle and upper-middle class or native-born were considerably more likely than their lower-class and immigrant counterparts to turn up at the polls. This was due to the higher education levels of middle-class and native women, as well as to the fact that the more traditional immigrant culture placed women in a socially more subservient role, consequently discouraging them from taking part in public life. Therefore, those who wanted to undercut the machines derived a great short-term advantage from the Nineteenth Amendment.[27]

There is no question that the Progressives adhered to a liberal version of capitalism and wanted to make the hurly-burly economic and political systems of the late nineteenth century more professionalized and efficient. In regulating the marketplace and in reforming politics, they believed that they were preparing American capitalism for the new century. In politics, this meant displacing the machines which had substituted personal favoritism for impersonal efficiency. On the other hand, there was no real class conflict between the Progressives and party organizations; each simply adhered to a different variant of capitalism, and each served business interests in a different way. As the twentieth century developed, the progressive vision gradually caught on.

In recent decades, there has been a revival of this progressive impulse to clean up party politics. For the most part, it has been localized in the Democratic party, among some of the adherents of presidential candidates Adlai Stevenson in the 1950s, Eugene McCarthy in the 1960s, and George McGovern in the 1970s. However, the admirers of Republican John Anderson in 1980 fit the progressive description as well. Like the Progressives of an earlier era, these reformers are primarily the more educated middle and upper-middle classes. Take Anderson, the most recent example. Because he ran for president as an independent, we know that the support he received from different kinds of voters was not too heavily influenced by their partisan background, unlike Stevenson, McCarthy and McGovern. The *New York Times*/CBS News survey of voters in the 1980 campaign revealed that while 3 percent of black voters, 6 percent of Hispanic voters, and 2 percent of those white voters who had not graduated from high school had voted for him, Anderson was backed by fully 12 percent of those white voters who had graduated from college.[28]

Since the mid-1960s, the new Progressives have played a major role in changing the rules of the national Democratic party. Like their predecessors, they have primarily been middle- and upper-middle-class whites, and their reforms in recent years have been aimed at increasing their leverage within the Democratic party. Some of the issues involved in these disputes are similar in nature to the machine-reform controversies of an earlier era; for example, the role of issues in politics and various electoral reforms such as direct primaries. But there are differences, too, due largely to the fact that the arena is national rather than local politics. While the opponents of the reformers have included leaders of local machines, the real focus of controversy has been the rules governing presidential nominations. Moreover, the national parties in the United States have never had the organizational coherence that strong local machines have had. So while there are similarities between local disputes and the battles over national rules, there are significant differences as well.

What issues have been at stake in the controversies over national party rules? One was where to locate power within the party. Should the party leaders have a dominant role, and therefore should their attendance at conventions be guaranteed? Those who advocate this position argue that the party can only be strong if it has powerful leadership looking out for its interests and coordinating its activities. A party without strong leadership is likely to be divided, ineffective, and unable to win elections. Whatever will lead to party unity is attractive to such people. On the other side are those neo-Progressives who want the party to be controlled by "the people." Democracy, they argue, means not only popular control in November, but popular control at every step of the electoral process as well. Party leaders should have no special role in the delegate selection process. While no reform commission has ever required that states adopt primaries, these reformers tend to applaud the trend toward more and more primaries since 1968.

Another controversy has been over how issue-oriented the party should be. Machine politicians want to downplay issues lest the voters be offended by an issue stance with which they disagree. Progressives usually argue that the main purpose of a party should be to advocate issues. Republicans are divided over this issue, too, and behind these proposals is the faith that if each party stresses issues, the voters will have a clear choice between the parties and one's own party will emerge victorious.

A third controversy has been over affirmative action. Should the party exert itself to represent groups that in the past had been excluded deliberately or due to oversight? Machine politicians, no strangers to the ethnically balanced ticket, have tended to draw the line at this issue. Some argue that affirmative action is divisive, and ask why other groups besides women, racial minorities and young people are not included. Advocates of affirmative action seek not only to redress past inequities but also to woo those groups to the party by increasing their representation at the national convention.

The first demand for party reform in the 1960s came from civil rights workers, who came to the Democratic national convention in 1964 to demand fair representation in the racist Democratic parties of the South. One of them, a black woman named Fannie Lou Hamer, told of losing her job and being arrested and beaten severely in jail, merely for trying to register to vote in Mississippi. In the true spirit of American politics, the convention "compromised" by giving only two seats on the delegation to Ms. Hamer's group, and letting the all-white party regulars keep the rest of the seats if they would merely sign a "loyalty oath" to the national ticket.[29]

For the 1968 Democratic convention, the national party adopted new rules that stipulated that delegations had to be "broadly representative" of their states, and the national convention forcibly integrated the Georgia and Mississippi delegations in more than token numbers. But the hotter issue within the party that year was the war in Vietnam. Two antiwar senators, Eugene McCarthy of Minnesota and Robert Kennedy of New York, won all of the contested primaries between them and in the polls ran ahead of Vice President Hubert Humphrey, a defender of the war policies of President Lyndon Johnson. In June, Kennedy was assassinated, and his delegates split among McCarthy, Humphrey, and Senator George McGovern of South Dakota, who entered the race to provide a rallying point for the Kennedy people.

In the course of the nominating battle, the McCarthy and Kennedy forces discovered that the party regulars who backed Humphrey enjoyed numerous benefits that went beyond the bounds of fairness. For example, many national convention delegates were appointed by the party organization; some states had "winner-take-all" procedures, in which the majority faction won all the delegates even if there was a sizeable minority faction; and many procedures were not well publicized and were therefore known only to the friends of the party organization. At the national convention itself in Chicago, the Johnson administration forces ran the proceedings with an iron hand, brutally ignoring the parliamentary rights of the antiwar faction. Outside the convention hall, the Chicago police engaged in what an official report later called a "police riot" in their zeal to repress antiwar demonstrators. Despite the fact that he had not won a single contested primary, Humphrey was easily nominated on the first ballot.[30]

The frustration and rage that the whole nominating process aroused among so many Democrats inspired the convention to authorize the appointment of two reform commissions to change the party rules in the direction of greater fairness. One, called the McGovern-Fraser Commission after its chairs, Senator McGovern and Representative Donald Fraser of Minnesota, was concerned with the delegate selection process. The second was the O'Hara Commission, named for Representative James O'Hara of Michigan, and it dealt with the national convention itself. The recommendations of these two commissions were adopted by the party and went into effect at the 1972 convention. Thus began years of drafting and re-drafting party rules. In the wake of the 1972 convention came two more commissions, one chaired by Baltimore City Councilwoman (and later Representative) Barbara Mikulski, which produced the delegate selection rules for the 1976 national convention. The other, chaired by former North Carolina governor Terry Sanford, drafted a "party charter," which produced the party's first national convention held in a non-presidential year (1974). To draft the rules for the 1980 convention, a commission was formed under Morley Winograd, former party chair in Michigan. Then Governor James Hunt of North Carolina chaired the commission that wrote the rules for the 1984 convention. Most recently, the Fairness Commission, headed by party chair Donald Fowler of South Carolina, prepared rules for the 1988 convention. There have been other, less important rules-changing commissions as well, and over the years the Republicans have made some minor modifications in their national party rules.

What have these commissions wrought? What principles guided them? It would be very time-consuming and beside the point to go through a detailed elaboration of all the changes that each commission made, so instead I shall list their major goals and give examples of how each commission tried to address them.[31] The commissions will be identified both by name and by the year of the convention whose rules it wrote (not by the year in which it met). Then I shall consider some of the difficult issues raised by these aims and the philosophy that guides them.

Fair play

Probably the least controversial accomplishment of the McGovern-Fraser Commission (1972) was to clean up some of the blatantly unfair practices of 1968 and earlier years. Among these changes were that no longer would there be:

- High fees levied on delegates in order to go to the convention;
- Unwritten rules and unpublicized meeting dates and times, known only to party leaders;
- Inaccessible times and places for meetings;
- Delegates selected before the election year.

While party leaders may have grimaced at being deprived of some of their favorite power devices, it would be difficult for anyone to defend any of these practices on principle.

Fair representation

Starting with McGovern-Fraser (1972), all delegate-selection commissions have wrestled with the question of how to insure that candidates with a certain degree of support within the party can have that support translated into convention delegates. In other words, a candidate who has the support of 40 percent of the party should not end up with only 15 percent of the delegates. To begin with, the McGovern-Fraser (1972) and Mikulski (1976) Commissions outlawed the "unit rule." This was a practice by which a majority of the people choosing delegates or voting at the national convention could compel the minority to vote unanimously with the majority. If Candidate A had 60 percent of a state's delegates and Candidate B had 40 percent, the unit rule would result in a vote of 100 percent for Candidate A.

The Mikulski (1976) Commission went further, by requiring that any candidate receiving at least 15 percent of the vote in a state primary, caucus or convention must receive that same percentage of the delegates to the national convention. Generally, then, Candidate *B* in the preceding example would end up with about 40 percent of the delegates. This rule abolished winner-take-all selection procedures, such as in the California primary, in which all the delegates went to whoever came in first, regardless of what the winning percentage was.

In an attempt to roll back some of the Mikulski reforms, in the belief that the earlier commissions had gone too far in the liberal direction, the Winograd (1980) Commission made two changes in this area. One was to get around the winner-take-all ban by allowing for districts (smaller than congressional districts) which would choose one delegate each. The other was to change the 15 percent rule whereby candidates had to get at least 15 percent of the vote in a state primary, caucus or convention in order to get their proportional share of national convention delegates. The Winograd Commission voted to allow the figure to exceed 15 percent (thereby depriving the less successful candidates of any share of delegates), especially as the delegate selection process wore on. The effect would be that later in the contest, it would be harder and harder for anyone except the couple of leading candidates to win any delegates. The Hunt (1984) Commission continued in this vein, opting for requiring candidates to get 20 or 25 percent in order to win delegates, allowing states to give the winning candidate "bonus votes" (extra delegates besides those won in the normal process), and accepting certain kinds of winner-take-all procedures. Jesse Jackson vehemently protested this rule in 1984, claiming that it deprived him of his fair share of delegates; he succeeded in obtaining only slight modifications by the Fairness Commission which wrote the rules for 1988.

Affirmative action

Surely the most controversial part of the McGovern-Fraser (1972) changes were those that increased the proportion of delegates who were women, blacks, or younger than thirty. This was a carryover from the 1964 and 1968 conventions which were forced to address the question of racism in some of the southern delegations. While the McGovern-Fraser report called only for a "reasonable relationship" between each group's percentage of a state's population and its percentage of the delegation from that state, critics charged that quotas were being established. Several delegations, including Mayor Daley's from Chicago, were excluded from the 1972 convention because of these rules. The effect was to increase the percentage of women delegates from 13 percent in 1968 to 40 percent in 1972, of blacks from 5 percent to 15 percent, and of young people from 3 to 22 percent.[32] Subsequent commissions have tended to relax the McGovern-Fraser guidelines, resulting in a drop-off for blacks and young people. The

Winograd (1980) and Hunt (1984) Commissions required, however, that half of each state's delegation be female.

Party-building

Several of the commissions considered ways in which the Democratic party could be strengthened as an institution. The concept of party strength is one that has had several meanings in the United States, some mutually exclusive. Five of these meanings can be identified in the work of the commissions.

1. *The party charter.* The Sanford Commission, which delivered its report in 1974, proposed the drafting of a kind of constitution called the party charter. This charter was adopted later that year, and called for a set of institutions that would give the party a permanent structure. These were to include a judicial council to settle disputes about party rules, a national finance council, and an annual financial report. In the following decade, these provisions had little effect on party affairs; there has been no getting around the organizational weakness of America's national parties.

2. *Nationalization of the parties.* One of the consequences of these rules changes and new institutions has been a concentration of party power at the national level. As the national party claimed the right to make the rules for state parties, a tension began to develop between them. The 1972 convention produced two Supreme Court decisions that gave the national Democratic party rules supremacy over state party rules, and a Supreme Court decision in 1981 enabled the national party to refuse to seat delegates from Wisconsin who had been chosen according to the state law that allowed Republicans to vote in Democratic primaries. In other words, national party rules were to take precedence over state law.[33]

3. *The off-year convention.* Attempting to deviate from the American tradition of parties doing little other than trying to win elections, the Sanford Commission also proposed that the party conduct national conventions in the middle of presidential terms. This would presumably get the party to think about other matters than nominations, such as its organization and issues, and thereby "build the party." From 1974 to 1982 the Democrats conducted three such conferences, and they have been the exception that proves the rule: no important policy or institutional innovations emerged from any of the off-year conventions, but they were used by prospective presidential candidates as opportunities to make contacts. In 1985 the party abolished them outright.[34]

4. *Platform accountability.* Platforms are generally regarded as meaningless expressions of pie in the sky, although careful exami-

nation suggests that they provide a reasonably good indication of a party's policy goals.[35] In any case, American political parties have never had any mechanism to insure that platforms would be carried out. One kind of proposal made by Democratic reformers has been to make the platform "meaningful." To such reformers, strong parties are those united behind coherent policy stands. At the 1980 Democratic national convention, a rule was adopted that required candidates to respond to the platform in writing, "including a pledge to carry out the recommendations . . . along with any reservations to specific provisions."[36] There was no way to enforce the pledge. The same convention established a Platform Accountability Commission, whose mandate was to determine ways to strengthen the platform and its role in party affairs. As one scholar has put it, "it is unlikely that the commission can move beyond nibbling at the edges of an area that speaks to the most fundamental of weaknesses ingrained within the current (American) party operations."[37]

5. *Representation of party leaders.* To some, party strength means vesting power in the leadership. By removing some of the unfair practices that the bosses had used before 1972, the McGovern-Fraser Commission made it harder for leaders to control their delegations (although their power was declining even before the new rules were adopted). It also ruled that nobody could be a delegate merely because he or she held some other party or public office. The Mikulski (1976) Commission also adopted this rule, but encouraged the Democratic National Committee to extend delegate privileges (but not votes) to high party and public officials.

As in so many other areas, the Winograd (1980) Commission reversed the trend set by its predecessors. It added to each delegation 10 percent more seats, to be reserved for party and public officials. The Hunt Commission upped this figure to approximately 25 percent for the 1984 convention.

Much ink and wind have been expended on all these issues, and to many middle-class activities the Progressives have had the rhetorical advantage of seeming to speak for democracy, fair play, political seriousness, and justice. It is my contention, however, that these matters are largely symbolic and rhetorical. The real issue is power, and who will exercise it within the Democratic party. In reality, the reformers are seeking personal and political advantage over the more traditional party elites, and these debates are window-dressing for a contest in which very little that is fundamental in politics is at stake. In short, whoever writes the rules for the Democratic future will not be changing the basic structure of American politics or its socioeconomic context, and therefore the battle is over less titanic matters than much of the rhetoric would suggest.

THE HIDDEN AGENDAS OF "REFORM"

Most of these reforms, then, are best understood as ways to increase the power within the party of upper-middle-class activists, rather than as a means to change the underlying basis of American politics. This can be shown in two ways.

Personal advantage

As the new reforms are adopted, which social groups gain representation at national conventions and in the rest of the nominating process? First, we should consider the question of "opening up" the party to broader participation. Reformers give the impression that through primaries and similar mechanisms, huge numbers of people who represent the American masses, take part in the process of delegate selection. This is totally misleading, first because only a small minority of eligible voters participate in primaries. In 1976, for example, only about 28 percent voted in the presidential primaries; and in 1980 and 1984, only about 21 and 15 percent respectively voted in the Democratic presidential primaries.[38] Second, voters in primaries are not at all a cross-section of the population. Study after study has shown that they overrepresent middle and upper-middle-class whites—*exactly the constituency of contemporary Progressivism*. For example, the national survey of the University of Michigan's Center for Political Studies found that in 1980, 59 percent of whites who had graduated from college had voted in presidential primaries, compared with 33 percent of all other voters. In 1984, the *New York Times* surveyors found that while those who had attended college comprised 27 percent of all Democrats, they made up 53 percent of the Democrats who had voted in primaries.[39] This suggests that one of the effects of increasing the number of primaries is to increase the leverage of that group. This is true even if their motivation is not overtly class related, and despite the rise in black voter participation due to Jesse Jackson's campaign.

Other reform positions are also geared to the interests of upper-middle-class whites. The increased emphasis on issues, taken within the present context of American politics, means that the better-educated and more articulate activists will have a greater impact on party affairs. They, and not working-class people, are likely to know fine points of parliamentary procedure, have the self-confidence that formal education confers on people to express themselves in public, and have the leisure time and desire to read about issues. It is easy for them to advocate turning parties away from patronage, since they do not rely on patronage jobs for their livelihood to the extent that the machine constituents did.[40]

Even affirmative action, seen as a way to help the disadvantaged, has interesting consequences when seen from this perspective. Who are the women who benefit from increased female representation at national conventions—cleaning women and working-class housewives, or the Gloria Steinems and Phyllis Schlaflys of the world? Which young people are likely to attend conventions, college students or their high school classmates who now work in gas stations and beauty parlors? Which blacks become delegates, professionals or those from the underclass? These questions answer themselves. Affirmative action may indeed have a number of genuine benefits for the groups affected—in the old days, even black professionals were excluded—but we should not delude ourselves that conventions genuinely represent the American people.

It is important to remember that with the exception of women, the most populous group of Americans who have suffered from discrimination is lower-class people. Why, then, has neither party made a concerted effort to represent *this* group at national conventions? In 1980, the average Democratic national convention delegate had an annual family income of $37,000, compared with $47,000 for the mean Republican delegate—both figures several times greater than the national average. In addition, only 2 percent of the Republicans and 4 percent of the Democrats had blue-collar jobs. In 1984, 57 percent of the Republican delegates and 42 percent of the Democratic delegates had family incomes that exceeded $50,000.[41] This underrepresentation of the lower classes is perfectly consistent with the self-proclaimed values of liberal capitalism, which stress equal opportunity for both sexes and all races, but countenance grossly unequal treatment for the classes. So embarrassing has this discrepancy been to the Democrats, who claim to be the "party of working people," that they have begun to engage in taking gingerly steps to broaden the class representation at the convention. A commission was established by the 1980 convention under the chair of Representative Mickey Leland of Texas to deal with the problem, and the Hunt Commission called for efforts to increase the representation of low-income people through affirmative outreach. But these efforts are likely to remain only lip service.

Political advantage

Not only have the reforms benefited upper-status activists, but when this group has supported certain liberal candidates, the reforms have served their political interests as well. Much of the impetus for reform has been a reaction to the relative conservatism of old-line party leaders, the sort who backed Humphrey and the Johnson war policies in 1968. Therefore, "opening up the party" has meant taking power from those who are currently on top.

The reforms helped liberal activists in less direct ways as well. Few people vote in primaries, and those who do are unusually likely to be concerned with issues and ideology. Within the Democratic party, such people tend to be liberals, and within the Republican party, they are likely to be conservatives. In recent years, liberal Democrats and conservative Republicans have indeed received a higher share of the vote in primaries than their share of the support of their fellow partisans, as measured by Gallup polls. In 1972, liberal Democrats George McGovern, Shirley Chisholm, John Lindsay and Eugene McCarthy had the support of about 27 percent of fellow Democrats in the polls, but liberal mobilization netted them 33 percent of the vote in primaries. In 1976, liberal Democrats Morris Udall, Jerry Brown and Frank Church had 15 percent in the polls but 20 percent in the primaries. In 1980, Edward Kennedy had 31 percent in the polls and 42 percent in the primaries. Similarly, on the Republican side, Ronald Reagan won 36 percent in the polls in 1976 but 47 percent in the primaries. It seems clear that ideologues are more likely than others to show up at the polls during primaries.[42] Therefore, increasing the number of Democratic primaries increases the opportunities for liberals to play a role in the nominating process.

Advocates of affirmative action also hoped that the new female, black, and young delegates would be liberals. In 1972, the first year that affirmative action took effect, that was indeed the case. According to a survey of Democratic delegates, two-thirds of the delegates who were younger than thirty backed liberal candidate McGovern, while fewer than half of those over thirty voted for him; and nearly two-thirds of women delegates supported McGovern, compared with fewer than half of the men.[43] Black delegates were not so enamored of McGovern, but certainly blacks in general have been one of the most liberal population groups in the United States. In 1976, on the other hand, women, black, and young delegates were slightly more likely than other delegates to favor Jimmy Carter, who was considered *less* liberal than most of his competitors. On the Republican side, in 1980 Ronald Reagan was no less likely than his opponents to secure women delegates, despite his difficulties in appealing to women voters in November.[44] While most affirmative action categories may have worked to the advantage of the reformers' hero in 1972, it is hard to demonstrate a similar edge since then.

In general, then, the reforms seem to have provided some short-term benefits to the reformers, both personally and politically. This argument is made not only by radicals, but by defenders of the older form of organizational politics as well.[45] While I share the conservatives' view that the reforms can best be understood as a way to increase the power of the reformers, my argument differs from theirs primarily in that I do not regard the organization stalwarts as generally preferable to the reformers. Organizational leaders today are not an especially underprivileged group, nor can it be said that they have represented the true interests of the lower classes any better than reformers have. The reformers and the party leaders simply stand for different segments of middle-class opinion. Let me repeat once again that organization politics and machine politics have each done their share to maintain corporate capitalism.

EVALUATING THE REFORMS

Regardless of who benefits from the reforms, do they make sense? Here a number of scholars have made some telling criticisms of the reforms, some of which are essentially unrelated to one's ideology.[46] In short, among the various reform goals there are massive contradictions that demonstrate the shallowness of progressive thought in the United States. These are contradictions in principle, not necessarily in reality, although I shall provide from experience some examples of each.

The first contradiction is between "opening up" the party to "the people" and pushing issues. These goals could become contradictory if "the people" do not want to raise issues. Indeed, there is empirical evidence that in the United States party elites are *more* issue-oriented than the masses. For example, in 1984 the University of Michigan's Center for Political Studies asked respondents to its national survey to identify themselves as one of seven ideological types, from extremely liberal to extremely conservative. Fully 84 percent of Democrats who belonged to a political club or had been active in the presidential campaign that year were able to identify themselves ideologically but only 66 percent of the non-activists did so. Among Republicans, 89 percent of the activists and 78 percent of the non-activists did so. This suggests that activists are more aware of, and interested in, some of the standard ideological categories of American politics. The consequence is that under current conditions, with conventional understandings of the meaning of issues, we are more likely to have issue-based parties by keeping them in the hands of leaders than by "opening them up" to the masses. Under a different socioeconomic system, the American people might be more oriented toward issues.[47]

Similarly, there may be a contradiction between "opening up the party" and promoting a particular ideology. There is a great deal of evidence from many sources that party elites are more ideological than the party masses. In particular, Democratic elites are more liberal than the Democratic masses, and Republican elites are more conservative than the Republican masses. One example is found in the University of Michigan survey cited in the preceding paragraph. Among Democrats who *did* identify themselves ideologically, 50 percent of the activists called themselves liberals, while only 36 percent of the non-activists did so. On the Republican side, 82 percent of the activists adopted the conservative label, compared with 62 percent of the non-activists. Similar results were found in a CBS News survey of national committee members and party masses in the spring of 1981. While 40 percent of the members of the Democratic National Committee who adopted a label deemed themselves liberals, only 25 percent of the rank and file did. Among Republicans, 66 percent of the National Committee members called themselves conservatives, compared with 54 percent of the masses.[48] Such survey results have consequences in the real world of politics, where primaries can be won by illiberal Democrats like George Wallace and Jimmy Carter over the opposition of more liberal candidates backed by party leaders. This is a qualification of the argument made above that Democratic primaries tend to favor liberal candidates. But if *everyone* in the party voted in primaries, liberal candidates might well be disadvantaged. Those who think that maximizing the participation of "the people" in politics is currently compatible with more ideological parties are likely to be disappointed more often than not.[49]

The preceding contradictions imply a third: "Opening up the parties" may well be incompatible with delineating clearcut differences between parties on the issues. A wealth of data over many years has shown that the Democratic and Republican elites are farther apart on the issues than the Democratic and Republican masses. This is true regardless of how we define the elites. A *New York Times*/CBS News survey of congressional candidates and party masses in 1978 found little or no difference between the average Democrat and the average Republican on a large federal tax cut, balancing the Federal budget, or abortion, while Democratic and Republican congressional candidates differed dramatically. On the issue of national health insurance, the opinions of rank-and-file Democrats diverged from those of grass-roots Republicans, but the candidates differed even more dramatically.[50] The CBS News survey of national committee members found similar results in 1981 on a wide variety of issues. For example, 48 percent of grass-roots Democrats and 60 percent of the Republican rank and file wanted more money spent on the military, compared with only 22 percent of the Democratic National Committee and a whopping 89 percent of the Republican National Committee.[51] Finally, numerous studies of national convention delegates since 1956 have shown again and again that Democratic and Republican delegates are farther apart on the issues than their grass-roots counterparts.[52]

Again, such findings have consequences in political campaigns. One of the most unusual was a bizarre practice in California politics called "cross-filing," in which a candidate could run in *both* parties' primaries for the same office. This certainly was the maximum in grass-roots democracy, for it allowed party members to vote for anyone, even a member of the other party. In 1948, for example, Representative Richard M. Nixon ran in both parties' primaries for reelection, and won both of them. In November, the voters had a choice between Richard Nixon, Republican, and Richard Nixon, Democrat! In this way, giving the mass of party identifiers total leeway in the choice of a nominee resulted in a total lack of difference between the candidates in November.

The last contradiction to be discussed is between affirmative action and proportional representation of each candidate's followers. While ordinarily it will not be difficult for a major candidate to secure an adequate number of women, blacks, youths, and other such people as delegates, there may be problems when the candidates's appeal effectively rules out a group. One such situation occurred in 1972, when Alabama governor

George Wallace, whose national reputation had been based on thinly veiled racism, had to come up with black delegates in order to meet the requirements of the McGovern-Fraser reforms. Wallace managed to do so, by finding the most atypical blacks who by definition were totally out of touch with the needs and desires of fellow blacks. One of them addressed the national convention, telling a series of jokes poking fun at the civil rights movement.

Notice that in these contradictions, the goal that most frequently appears is intra-party democracy, what is often called "opening up the party" to "the people." While the control of parties by machine rule has not usually produced a concern with issues, ideological appeals, or striking inter-party differences, it is important to realize that primaries and other forms of more widespread participation need not do so, either. If intra-party democracy is one's only goal—and for most people in politics, it is not—this is not a problem. But those who think that other goals will be achieved via more "open" parties might be disappointed.

In short, most of the contradictions among these reform proposals would be eliminated if the goal of broader participation were dropped.

ORGANIZING FOR SOCIAL CHANGE

If one were concerned with neither perpetuating machine rule nor with replacing it with misguided and shallow reformism, what kind of party would one prefer? Specifically, if we want parties to be vehicles for social change, willing to challenge and even overturn whatever should be altered or eliminated in the social, economic and political order, what kind of party is needed? It seems clear that one minimum requirement is a party that is concerned with issues, for without raising issues, how is a party to mobilize a constituency that is willing to address these matters? Presumably candidates' personalities, ethnicities, and similar matters of limited relevance to issues will always play at least a minor role in politics, but any party that is content to downplay issues will never be able to raise the consciousness of the voters to a high enough level to mount the kind of challenge to the established order that is required. Such a challenge would rule out the kinds of patronage parties that used to dominate American politics.

So far the neo-Progressives will agree with me. In the next requirement we part company. For a party to be organized effectively enough to carry out a radical agenda, it must have enough internal discipline to speak with a coherent voice in campaigns and to mobilize officeholders to carry out that agenda as public policy. While "internal discipline" does not require the monolithic, dictatorial practices of conspiratorial, revolutionary parties, it is a departure both from American practice and the reformers' goal of a wide-open party. A party that lacks discipline is unlikely to achieve any significant policy changes because the resources of the defenders of the status quo are so prodigious that it would take only the most disciplined opposition to prevail. Even within the limited confines of traditional American politics, the periods of greatest political change have occurred when the party in power was unified.

This in turn means that the leadership of the party must have the tools to run the party effectively and to enforce as much discipline as is compatible with the goals both of carrying out the agenda and maintaining the political rights of the members. These political rights include some orderly means of replacing an irresponsible leadership cadre, or, failing that, leaving the party. But short of that kind of revolt, the leadership must be given a special role. Among its tasks would be to speak for the party, draft its issue agenda, play an important role in selecting candidates for elective and appointive office, and enforce discipline among officeholders. A party which does not give such a role to its leadership is forsaking any role in promoting social change, whether liberal or radical.

Consequently, any party worthy of its name should avoid a number of the "reforms" which have burdened the American parties in recent years. Freezing the leadership out of the nominating process and vastly increasing the number of primaries are changes that sound democratic, but, by hampering leadership, have the effect of preventing parties from becoming vehicles for change. Primaries not only make discipline impossible but also turn the nominating process into orgies of public-relations campaigns and interest-group penetration. Moreover, primaries make parties hostage to whoever feels like participating, regardless of their commitment to the party and its agenda. As argued earlier, this is likely to result in an influx of issue-oriented activists, but there is no guarantee that those activists will be in sympathy with the party's overall orientation. Some states allow non-members to vote in a party's primary, while most have very lenient requirements as to how far ahead of a primary voters can declare their party membership. Parties thus become reduced to empty vessels, waiting to be filled by whatever slick candidate with whatever well-heeled support can attract whatever manner of voter. At a bare minimum, a party should restrict its affairs to those people who have demonstrated a genuine commitment to it.[53]

Michael Walzer, a democratic socialist theorist, has addressed these matters. He has concluded that caucuses, which are meetings that are open to those party members who have the energy and will to attend, are preferable to primaries, but that conventions are even better. Conventions can be comprised of delegates who are chosen through other means, such as primaries and caucuses open only to party members, and party leaders can be guaranteed a major role there. The business of the party—rule-making, agenda-setting, and nominations to elective office—can be conducted face to face and with an arena for whatever bargaining and accommodation may be necessary.[54]

The horrified Progressive will cry, Where is popular rule? What choice is there for the people? The limited answer is that the people have input on election day. Once each party has set forth its agenda and chosen its candidates, it is up to the electorate to choose from among them. This choice *between* the parties is the ultimate electoral accountability, and it is more important than any democratic-looking process *within* a party. Of course, the first chapter of this book argued that the electoral process is in general a very limited way to influence politics. It is typical of American political thought that Progressives seek to legitimize parties by incorporating the electoral process within them. In other words, they see the solution for the problems of power within parties in simple terms: let people conduct elections (called primaries) within parties, and everything will be fine. The problem is that parties often become ideologically incoherent, as different (usually middle-class) groups take them over during different primaries. If, instead, one sees the political process as most effectively influenced by concerted, organized action, then an issue-oriented, *disciplined* institution is the best way to achieve it. Neither patronage machines nor "reformed" parties will do the trick—and that is why they have survived for so long.

Further Reading

Our modern understanding of machines begins with Robert K. Merton, *Social Theory and Social Structure* (Glencoe, Ill.: Free Press of Glencoe, 1949), 71–81. The notes in this chapter cite numerous studies of particular machines, and a good feel for traditional machine politics can be derived from the often funny ruminations of a Tammany Hall stalwart, recorded in William L. Riordon, *Plunkitt of Tammany Hall* (New York: E. P. Dutton, 1963). The best study of the contrast between machine politics and reform politics, which glorifies the former at the expense of the latter, is James Q. Wilson, *The Amateur Democrat* (Chicago: Univ. of Chicago Press, 1962).

Much has been written about the reforms of the national Democratic party since 1968. A good overview which is sympathetic to those reforms is William Crotty, *Party Reform* (New York: Longman, 1983). Hostile accounts abound, among them Jeane Kirkpatrick, *The New Presidential Elite* (New York: Russell Sage Foundation and the Twentieth Century Fund, 1976); Nelson W. Polsby, *Consequences of Party Reform* (New York: Oxford Univ. Press, 1983); and Byron E. Shafer, *Quiet Revolution* (New York: Russell Sage Foundation, 1983). These accounts all tend to attribute more consequences to the reforms than are plausible; after all, parties began to decline long before the McGovern-Fraser Commission first met.

Notes

1. This is the title of a short book by Werner Sombart. See the reprint edited by C. T. Husbands (White Plains, N.Y.: M. E. Sharpe, 1976).

2. M. Ostrogorski, *Democracy and the Organization of Political Parties, Volume II.: The United States,* Seymour Martin Lipset, ed. (Garden City, N.Y.: Anchor Books, 1964), 184–185.

3. Herbert J. Gans, *The Urban Villagers* (New York: The Free Press, 1962), 89–90.

4. Gans, *The Urban Villagers,* 260. See all of chapter 11.

5. Daniel J. Elazar, *American Federalism,* 2nd ed. (New York: Thomas Y. Crowell, 1972), 96.

6. Elazar, *American Federalism,* 94–95.

7. Quoted in C. T. Husbands' introduction to Sombart, *Why Is There No Socialism in the United States?* xxix. Joel Arthur Tarr, in *A Study in Boss Politics* (Urbana: Univ. of Illinois Press, 1971), argues that religious groups differed in their propensity to be issue-oriented or susceptible to machine appeals.

8. Quoted in Harold F. Gosnell, *Machine Politics* (Chicago: Univ. of Chicago Press, 1937), 70. See also Robert K. Merton, *Social Theory and Social Structure* (Glencoe, Ill.: Free Press of Glencoe, 1949), 73–74.

9. William L. Riordon, *Plunkitt of Tammany Hall* (New York: E. P. Dutton, 1963), 27–28. This fascinating work was first published in 1905.

10. Riordon, *Plunkitt of Tammany Hall,* 88.

11. Riordon, *Plunkitt of Tammany Hall,* 38.

12. Merton notes that such reform administrations failed because they could not fulfill the functions that machines did. See his *Social Theory and Social Structure,* 79–80. It has also been argued that reform administrations suffered from their inability to deliver on their pledge of greater efficiency. See Melvin G. Holli, "Urban Reform in the Progressive Era," in Lewis L. Gould, ed., *The Progressive Era* (Syracuse: Syracuse Univ. Press, 1974), 147–151.

13. Quoted in Arthur Mann's introduction to *Plunkitt of Tammany Hall,* xix.

14. Riordon, *Plunkitt of Tammany Hall,* 12.

15. Max Weber, "Politics as a Vocation," reprinted in H. H. Gerth and C. Wright Mills, eds., *From Max Weber* (New York: Oxford Univ. Press, 1946), 109. See also Merton, *Social Theory and Social Structure,* 74–79.

16. Riordon, *Plunkitt of Tammany Hall,* 73.

17. Weber, "Politics as a Vocation," 109.

18. Edward J. Flynn, *You're the Boss* (New York: Viking Press, 1947), 60–61.

19. Riordon, *Plunkitt of Tammany Hall,* 79–80.

20. "Postponing the Last Hurrah," *The Wall Street Journal,* 4 March 1975, p. 22.

21. Elrod v. Burns, 427 U.S. 347 (1976); Branti v. Finkel, 445 U.S. 507 (1980).

22. In the South, this gave local elites the opportunity to administer these programs on a racist basis. See Gunnar Myrdal, *An American Dilemma* (New York: Harper & Bros., 1944), I: 258–259, 348–357, 360–362. Local control of New Deal programs in Pittsburgh is described in Bruce M. Stave, *The New Deal and the Last Hurrah* (Pittsburgh: Univ. of Pittsburgh Press, 1970). In general, see Lyle W. Dorsett, *Franklin D. Roosevelt and the City Bosses* (Port Washington, N.Y.: Kennikat Press, 1977).

23. On Gary, see the news stories in the *New York Times* dated 30 September, 27 October, and 3 and 7 November 1967; and on Chicago, see in the same paper the news stories dated 17 and 26 March and 3 and 10 April 1983.

24. The classic study of these urban professionals is James Q. Wilson, *The Amateur Democrat* (Chicago: Univ. of Chicago Press, 1962). For a different view of the relationship between constituent desires and political incentives, see Martin Shefter, "Party and Patronage," *Politics and Society* VII (1977), 403–451.

25. Terrence J. McDonald, "Comment," *Journal of Urban History* VIII (August 1982), 460. "Community and accumulation" is a formulation devised by John H. Mollenkopf.

26. A number of scholars have shown that Progressive candidates often derived the bulk of their support from lower-class and immigrant voters. See Michael Paul Rogin and John L. Shover, *Political Change in California* (Westport, Conn.: Greenwood, 1970), 35–89; and Roger E. Wyman, "Middle-Class Voters and Progressive Reform," *American Political Science*

Review LXVIII (June 1974), 488–504. Such voters may have indeed been wise to have supported Progressives when the alternative was conservatism, a cruder form of liberal capitalism with fewer concessions for the have-nots.

27. Aileen S. Kraditor discovered that some of the leaders of the women's suffrage movement were motivated by social and ethnic considerations; see her *The Ideas of the Woman Suffrage Movement* (New York: Columbia Univ. Press, 1965). According to Alan P. Grimes, these factors motivated many of the male politicians who voted for women's suffrage; see his *The Puritan Ethic and Woman Suffrage* (New York: Oxford Univ. Press, 1967). Stuart A. Rice found that in Illinois in 1920, women were more likely than men to vote Republican; see his *Quantitative Methods in Politics* (New York: Alfred A. Knopf, 1928), 178–179. Walter Dean Burnham later discovered that women in the suburbs of Cook County had a higher turnout than women in Chicago, when compared with male turnout. See his "Theory and Voting Research," *American Political Science Review* LXVIII (September 1974), 1013. The complexities of mass support for women's suffrage are revealed in Eileen L. McDonagh and H. Douglas Price, "Woman Suffrage in the Progressive Era," *American Political Science Review* LXXIX (June 1985), 415–435. On Progressivism as capitalist reformism, see works as diverse as Richard Hofstadter, *The Age of Reform* (New York: Alfred A. Knopf, 1963), and Gabriel Kolko, *The Triumph of Conservatism* (Chicago: Quadrangle Books, 1967).

28. In this connection it is worth pointing out that Anderson's voting record in Congress had revealed general support for business and opposition to labor, as ratings that he received from business and labor groups over the years confirmed. According to ratings published over the years, in *The Almanac of American Politics,* Anderson's mean score from the AFL-CIO's Committee on Public Education from 1968 through 1978 was 34, while the National Association of Businessmen gave him a mean rating of 79. If he was the candidate of the "liberals," his record and his constituency showed how meaningless such a label can be even within the context of the narrow American ideological range, and how compatible with upper-class interests Progressive heroes can be.

29. On this incident, see Stokely Carmichael and Charles V. Hamilton, *Black Power* (New York: Vintage Books, 1967), 86–97. Fannie Lou Hamer's chilling testimony is quoted in Judith H. Parris, *The Convention Problem* (Washington: The Brookings Institution, 1972), 66.

30. The best of the many accounts of the tumultuous presidential campaign of 1968 is Lewis Chester, Godfrey Hodgson, and Bruce Page, *An American Melodrama* (New York: Viking Press, 1969).

31. For a comprehensive summary of the work of these commissions, on which this discussion relies heavily, see William Crotty, *Party Reform* (New York: Longman, 1983).

32. These data are from Warren J. Mitofsky and Martin Plissner, "The Making of the Delegates, 1968–1980," *Public Opinion* (October/November 1980), 43; reprinted in Crotty, *Party Reform,* 136.

33. The decisions referred to are O'Brien v. Brown, 409 U.S. 1 (1972); Cousins v. Wigoda, 419 U.S. 477 (1975); and National Democratic Party v. LaFollette, 450 U.S. 107 (1981).

34. For an account of the first midterm conference, see Denis G. Sullivan, Jeffrey L. Pressman, and F. Christopher Arterton, *Explorations in Convention Decision Making* (San Francisco: W. H. Freeman, 1976). On their abolition, see "DNC Approves Kirk's Plans to Alter Democrats' Image," *Congressional Quarterly Weekly Report,* 29 June 1985, p. 1287.

35. Gerald M. Pomper with Susan S. Lederman, *Elections in America,* 2nd ed. (New York: Longman, 1980), 128–178. See also chapter 12, below.

36. *Official Report of the Proceedings of the Democratic National Convention* (Washington: Democratic National Committee, undated), p. 171.

37. Crotty, *Party Reform,* 109.

38. The figure for 1976 is from Austin Ranney, *Participation in American Presidential Nominations, 1976* (Washington: American Enterprise Institute, 1977), 20. The 1980 estimate is from Elaine Kamarck, "Openness, Participation and Party Building," a paper pre-

pared for the Hunt Commission in 1981, 2–4; cited in Stephen J. Wayne, *The Road to the White House*, 2nd ed. (New York: St. Martin's Press, 1984), 91. The 1984 data can be found in the *Congressional Quarterly Weekly Report*, 7 July 1984, p. 1619.

39. The 1984 data can be found in Adam Clymer, "Turnout Cheers Democrats," the *New York Times*, 17 June 1984, section 4, p. 4. On the demographic unrepresentativeness of primary voters in general, see Austin Ranney and Leon D. Epstein, "The Two Electorates," *Journal of Politics* XXVIII (August 1966), 609–612; Austin Ranney, "The Representativeness of Primary Electorates," *Midwest Journal of Political Science* XII (May 1968), 228–231; Austin Ranney, "Turnout and Representation in Presidential Primary Elections," *American Political Science Review* LXVI (March 1972), 26–27; and James I. Lengle, *Representation and Presidential Primaries* (Westport, Conn.: Greenwood Press, 1981), 15–28.

40. Wilson, *The Amateur Democrat*, 353–355.

41 Mitofsky and Plissner, "The Making of the Delegates," 41; and the *New York Times*, 24 August 1984, p. A10. These sources reveal that labor union members have been well represented at recent Democratic conventions, but almost not at all at Republican conventions. Even at Democratic conventions, large numbers of labor delegates—perhaps a majority—are white-collar professionals such as teachers.

42. For more evidence, see Ranney and Epstein, "The Two Electorates," 613–615; Ranney, "The Representativeness of Primary Electorates," 231–235; and Lengle, *Representation and Presidential Primaries*, 52–63. Ranney found contrary evidence in 1968; see his "Turnout and Representation in Presidential Primary Elections," 29–34.

43. Figures calculated from Jeane Kirkpatrick, *The New Presidential Elite* (New York: Russell Sage Foundation and the Twentieth Century Fund, 1976), 86, 430.

44. Unpublished analyses of 1976 Democratic and 1980 Republican delegates by CBS News.

45. For example, see Penn Kemble and Josh Muravchik, "The New Politics and the Democrats," *Commentary*, December 1972, 78–84; Kirkpatrick, *The New Presidential Elite;* Everett Carll Ladd, Jr., *Where Have All The Voters Gone?* (New York: W. W. Norton, 1978), 59–63; and Byron E. Shafer, *Quiet Revolution* (New York: Russell Sage Foundation, 1983).

46. The classic statement of the kind of criticism I shall be making is E. E. Schattschneider, *Party Government* (New York: Rinehart, 1942), especially chapter 3.

47. As discussed below in chapter 7, there is evidence that the American people have become more issue oriented in recent years. Nevertheless my contention is that this would be even more the case were there a different socioeconomic system.

48. "CBS News Democratic National Committee Survey" and "CBS News Republican National Committee Survey," press releases dated 5 June and 12 June 1981, respectively. See also the data on national convention delegates shown in the table in the *New York Times*, 13 August, 1980, p. B2.

49. A similar point is made in Claus Offe, "Political Authority and Class Structures," trans. Michel Vale, *International Journal of Sociology* II (Spring 1972), 85.

50. "Poll Indicates Congress Candidates Were More Extreme Than Voters," the *New York Times*, 9 November 1978, p. A21.

51. See note 48, above.

52. The groundbreaking study was Herbert McClosky, Paul J. Hoffman, and Rosemary O'Hara, "Issue Conflict and Consensus Among Party Leaders and Followers," *American Political Science Review* LIV (June 1960), 406–427. See also Kirkpatrick, *The New Presidential Elite*, chapter 10; John S. Jackson III, Barbara Leavitt Brown, and David Bositis, "Herbert McClosky and Friends Revisited," *American Politics Quarterly* X (April 1982), 158–180; and the *New York Times*, 24 August 1984, p. A10.

53. The Democrats adopted such a rule for their 1984 delegate selection process, but dropped it for 1988.

54. Michael Walzer, "Democracy vs. Elections," *The New Republic*, 3 and 10 January 1981, p. 19.

7

Nonvoters and voters

One of the most influential, if least remembered, of the founders of the American republic was James Wilson of Pennsylvania. A signer of the Declaration of Independence and framer of the Constitution, he served as an associate justice of the first U.S. Supreme Court. In a speech delivered on the last day of 1789, Wilson enumerated the many advantages of the right to vote. He spoke of its "powerful tendency to open, to enlighten, to enlarge, and to exalt the mind." The person who can vote "will naturally turn his attention to the contemplation of publick men and publick measures." Not only would the right to vote benefit the individual, according to Wilson, but society would gain as well. Patriotism would grow, as the voter would feel a "bond of union" with elected officials.[1]

In maintaining that allowing people to vote would increase their allegiance to the political system, Wilson was confirming my argument in chapter 2 that the real purpose of parties and elections is to sustain that system. But surely voting can also promote a person's awareness of "publick men and publick measures," as Wilson said, and is therefore part of any decent and free system. In addition, the nineteenth century English liberal philosopher John Stuart Mill argued, each person "is the only safe guardian of his own rights and interests."[2] This notion that political life is the interplay of self-oriented interests fits neatly into liberal capitalist thought, and provides yet another rationale for the right of suffrage.

Whatever the purpose of electoral rights, the striking fact about recent American political development is that the effective exercise of those rights is declining. A smaller and smaller percentage of Americans is choosing to exercise the alleged benefits of voting, and it is said of many who do that they are preoccupied with anything but "publick men and publick measures."

NONVOTERS

One of the most widely discussed trends in recent years is the tendency of Americans not to show up at the polls.[3] For example, about 63 percent of those eligible voted for president in 1960, but during the twenty years after that election turnout declined, until in 1980 it was only 53 percent. The 1984 election saw a very slight rise in turnout over the level in 1980, interrupting the longest continuous decline in American history. Similarly, the turnout in congressional off-years dropped from 46 percent in 1962 to a low of 35 percent in 1978, rising a bit to 38 percent in 1982.[4]

In chapter 3, the unusually low turnout in the United States was compared with that of other advanced capitalist nations. At that time I responded to the argument that our low turnout is due merely to the fact that American registration laws are more restrictive than those of other nations; if that were so, I asked, why are our laws more restrictive? In particular, I noted (and displayed in Table 3.6) that the turnout of low-income Americans is particularly low. It is, in other words, an electoral system tilted toward the well-to-do.

The phenomenon of low turnout, and in particular the low turnout of the disadvantaged, is one that American political scientists often ignore or dismiss. Very few pages of textbooks about American voting patterns are devoted to the nearly 50 percent of the adult population who do not vote, and when confronted with the evidence, some suggest that nonvoters are so satisfied with present conditions that they contentedly stay at home on Election Day.[5] The fact that so many Americans choose not to exercise the minimal form of political participation deserves more attention than it has received, and it is hard to imagine that this largely low-income group refrains from voting because they are satisfied with the system. Indeed, the nationwide survey conducted by the Center for Political Studies of the University of Michigan in 1984 found that nonvoters were far more likely than voters to agree with the statements "People like me don't have any say about what the government does," "I don't think public officials care much what people like me think," and "Somehow politics and government seem so complicated that a person like me can't really understand what's going on."

Some of the common explanations of why turnout has dropped seem unpersuasive. Some blame dissatisfaction over the Vietnam War or Watergate, but there was no widespread discontentment with the war until after 1964, and with Watergate until after 1972. Moreover, by 1976 both had ceased to be American preoccupations. Yet turnout dropped during *all* years from 1960 to 1980. Some have blamed the 26th Amendment to the Constitution, which gave eighteen to twenty-year-olds the vote in 1971. It is true that young people have very low levels of voting, and adding them to the electorate had the effect of lowering the overall turnout. But turnout of voters of *all* ages has been declining.[6]

One important social group that cannot be blamed for the decline in turnout is blacks. With the support of the civil rights movement and new federal laws in the 1960s, southern blacks overcame the unfair administration of the laws and the government-backed terrorism that had kept them from voting. While the rest of the nation was experiencing a decline in turnout, that of southern blacks rose dramatically from perhaps the lowest in the nation to rates comparable to others'. In the North, black turnout has fluctuated but has not declined consistently as whites' has.[7]

Indeed, in certain respects the decline in turnout has been truly paradoxical, for there have been trends that suggest that it should *rise,* not fall. First, many registration requirements have been dropped or loosened. The poll tax, a tax on voting, was outlawed by the 24th Amendment to the Constitution in 1964; most literacy tests have been outlawed; and length-of-residence requirements have been drastically shortened in many areas. Second, as Americans are becoming more educated and have held more white-collar jobs, they have entered groups whose turnout is relatively high. This should have augmented voting levels. Finally, Americans are living longer, and despite some popular misconceptions, the voting level of the elderly is high.[8] Having more older Americans in the population should drive up turnout.

After an extensive examination of whose turnout has been declining most among white voters, I found that the answer is that *low-income whites have been dropping out of the electorate the most.* (See Table 7.1) As noted above in chapter 3, these surveys tend to exaggerate the turnout, and one study found that low-voting groups tend to exaggerate the most. This means that the gap between rich and poor is even wider than the data suggest.[9] Nevertheless, there is no reason to believe that the trends over time are not as the table indicates. The turnout of low-income whites has dropped almost five times as much as the turnout of upper-income whites, and the gap between the two groups has nearly doubled.

We can picture what has been happening if we imagine the electorate as a strip of elastic tacked to a wall at one end, and dangling vertically. The top of the strip represents high-income, high-turnout white voters, and the bottom represents low-income, low-turnout white voters. Someone pulls the free end of the elastic strip downward, to represent the lowering

Table 7.1. Turnout of whites in presidential elections by income, 1960–1984.

	1960	1964	1968	1972	1976	1980	1984	Change, 1960–1984
Above median income	86.2	84.3	86.0	83.7	80.6	80.8	84.0	− 2.2
Below median income	76.7	74.6	69.7	65.1	65.0	64.9	66.2	− 10.5
Difference	9.5	9.7	16.3	18.6	15.6	15.9	17.8	

Note: Read this table as follows: In 1960, 86.2 percent of whites with family incomes above the national median for whites voted in that year's presidential election.

Source: National surveys, University of Michigan Center for Political Studies

of turnout. Those at the bottom are pulled down the farthest, while those at the top are pulled down very little. The distance between the very top and the very bottom increases.

That lower turnout can be attributed to the dropping out of the lower-income population seems to be substantiated by the rise in turnout in 1982 over 1978, the previous congressional off-year. According to a massive survey by the Census Bureau, the sharpest rise in turnout from 1978 to 1982—nearly 7 percent—occurred among the unemployed.[10] Similarly, rising turnout in some of the 1984 Democratic presidential primaries can be attributed to Jesse Jackson's appeal among low-voting blacks. The four places in which turnout in the 1984 Democratic primary was at least 50 percent higher than in 1980 were Alabama, the District of Columbia, Georgia, and Vermont.[11] All but Vermont have large concentrations of black voters. Apparently the only way to reverse a trend that is spearheaded by low-income people is to find a way to interest such people in the political process. Possible ways to lure their interest include severe recessions, as in 1982, or charismatic candidates who speak for the dispossessed, as in the spring of 1984.

Indeed, in 1984 a number of liberal and social service organizations tried to get the poor registered, with only mixed success. The numbers of newly registered poor voters were disappointing, and matched by those of more conservative voters registered by Republicans and religious fundamentalists.[12]

What is the significance of this remarkable trend toward lower-class nonvoting? First, it demonstrates that a political system geared to the "haves" is showing diminishing appeal to the "have-nots." With both major parties appealing to "business confidence" and adopting policies geared to the maintenance of the corporate capitalist order, low-income whites see less and less reason to vote. Indeed, instead of deploring their lack of civic responsibility, we might applaud them for their sophistication. They may understand better than voters do how small the difference is between America's major parties.

As I noted in chapter 3, political systems which offer a broader choice, including social democratic, socialist, and communist parties that aspire to represent the interests of the working class and the poor, are characterized by a far higher turnout among those groups than in the United States. While this would seem to imply that a broad-based American socialist party would draw most nonvoters to the polls, it is impossible to prove this because low-income Americans have not shown much more affinity for the label "socialist" than their wealthier counterparts have.

The reader may well wonder why black Americans, no less underprivileged than low-income whites, have not shown the same decline in turnout. (It is important to remember in this connection that while black turnout has not declined, blacks still tend to vote less than whites.) Perhaps the reason is that since 1960 there have been some government policies directed mainly at blacks, from enforcement (or lack of enforcement) of the Civil Rights and Voting Rights Acts, to affirmative action programs, to desegregation. Moreover, on racial issues, more than on most others, there are differences between the parties, and most blacks perceive the Democrats as more favorable to their interests. So they have more incentive to maintain voting levels than poor whites do. (The fact that white turnout declined throughout both liberal and conservative administrations makes implausible the theory that the decline was due primarily to resentment at black gains in the 1960s.)

The other implication of low-income whites' dropping out of the electorate is that, in Mill's words, they will be less able to defend their "rights and interests." Political strategists have taken note of this trend and have adjusted their advice accordingly. The last time a Democrat was elected president, in 1976, his pollster drafted a post-election memorandum which included the following:

> *The labor vote.* Carter received almost two-thirds of the labor vote, which was an important ingredient of his success. . . . On the negative side, like many of the components of traditional [sic] Democratic coalition, the "labor vote" has been shrinking.
>
> *The poor.* Carter did exceptionally well with poor voters, whether white or black. Again, the number of these voters in the electorate is declining.
>
> *White-collar and professional, the college-educated.* This is the largest rising group in the population. It must be attracted in significant numbers if Democrats are to be successful in the future. These are voters who are often, however, cautious on the questions of increased taxes, spending, and particularly inflation, an issue which mobilizes this group in a conservative fashion.[13]

Such comments provided political justification for the conservative economic policies of the Carter administration, and help to explain why the turnout of low-income whites continued to decline four years later. Only when such people perceive the political system as pertinent to their interests will we see an increase in turnout. But it seems unlikely that, under corporate capitalism, American parties will ever provide the lower classes with enough incentive to participate minimally in public life.

ONE VERSION OF HOW AMERICANS VOTE

How do those people who do show up at the polls decide how to vote? For most of American history, scholars took it for granted that elections were concerned with "publick men and publick measures." Historians and political scientists would read party platforms, campaign speeches, and newspaper editorials, and conclude that Lincoln was elected because of the slavery issue, McKinley because of free silver, and Harding because of the League of Nations. In the 1930's, however, the technique of sample surveying was developed enough so that researchers could get a good idea of how a population, such as the entire American electorate, would answer a series of questions merely by asking a carefully chosen group of no more than about 1,500 of them. For more than fifty years, pollsters and scholars have been trying to deduce how people vote by using such surveys.

What have they concluded? The simple answer is that there is no clear-cut and generally agreed-upon theory of American voting behavior. Almost any reasonable guess as to what people use to make up their minds has been demonstrated in one study or another. We can review a number of such studies before attempting to integrate their findings.

Group identity

The first major scholarly studies of American voting behavior were conducted during the 1940 and 1948 presidential campaigns by a team of researchers from Columbia University. They concluded that people vote according to the cues provided by the social groups to which they belong.[14] Such groups can include face-to-face groups such as family, friends, and co-workers, as well as broader collectivities with which one identifies, such as one's religion, race, class, or geographic section. This is perfectly in keeping with one way in which Americans have always discussed politics, with the Democrats winning the votes of white southerners, blacks, blue-collar workers, Roman Catholics, and Jews, while Republicans have done better with upper-income voters and Protestants outside the South.

Indeed, in 1984 we can find evidence of different social groups voting far differently from each other. According to the *New York Times*/CBS News survey, blacks gave 90 percent of their votes to Mondale; white Protestants gave Reagan 73 percent of theirs; Reagan won 55 percent of the Catholic vote, and Mondale received 66 percent of the Jewish vote. Those with family incomes under $12,500 backed Mondale by 53 percent, while those earning over $50,000 gave Reagan 68 percent. And so on.[15]

Why do people "vote their group"? The Columbia team concluded that people like to behave in accordance with others with whom they identify, and that this is reinforced by the fact that people tend to associate with others like themselves.[16] In a particularly telling example, they pointed out that not only did most Catholics vote Democratic in 1948, despite the fact that religious issues were not part of that campaign, but moreover, "Catholics closely identified with their religion vote Democratic more than Catholics not so identified."[17] This seemed to confirm the Columbia team's view that voting is an act that involves almost mindless conformity to group norms, regardless of the circumstances of a campaign. Blacks voting for Jesse Jackson, "yuppies" voting for Gary Hart, labor union members voting for Walter Mondale, or Westerners voting for Ronald Reagan might be good examples from our own time.

It is important to add that to Americans, more than to voters abroad, "group" is less likely to mean socioeconomic class than race, religion, or geographic section.[18] Despite James Madison's assertion that "the most common and durable source of faction has been the various and unequal distribution of property," American parties, and hence voting behavior, have relatively little to do with the great economic issues that form, in Madison's words, "the principal task of modern legislation."[19] This alone is a telling comment on the vacuousness of American electoral politics.

Party identification

In the 1950s researchers from the University of Michigan produced a series of studies concluding that one of the most important factors in the mind of the voter was what they called "party identification."[20] What party does the voter identify with, and how closely? Most voters, they argued, use such an identification as a filter through which they view the political world. When someone who has no experience in electoral politics becomes established in a party, like General Dwight Eisenhower with the Republicans at the time the Michigan group was conducting its study in 1952, voters will respond accordingly. Strong Democrats began to notice hitherto unnoticed flaws in Eisenhower's character, while strong Republicans started seeing the general as even more heroic than before.[21]

A wealth of studies has demonstrated that partisanship is usually the strongest correlate of a voter's choice. In the 1984 *New York Times*/CBS News poll, for example, Mondale won the votes of 73 percent of the Democratic identifiers, while Reagan was garnering 92 percent of the Republican vote. Independents backed Reagan by 63 percent.[22] Although Mondale's showing among Democrats looks low, it has generally been true that Republican voters are more loyal than Democratic voters to their respective presidential nominees, and that independents tend to go for the Republican candidate. These are two reasons why Republicans won six out of nine presidential elections from 1952 to 1984, despite the fact that Democratic identifiers far outnumbered Republican identifiers in that period.[23]

Why is partisanship so important? The Michigan researchers concluded that most people form their partisan allegiance early in life, influenced by their families, and then use it as a screening mechanism for interpreting the political world, as described above. It becomes a kind of crutch for an electorate that is not very interested in politics, a handy guide to politics that does not require a lot of cogitation when it comes to voting.[24]

Candidate image

If partisanship was so important, then why did the Republicans win the presidential elections of the 1950s? For the answer, the Michigan researchers turned to the second major factor in their explanation of voting, which is commonly referred to as "candidate image." Because the word "image" has so many connotations of salesmanship and media manipulation, it is important to stress that the Michigan scholars were interested simply in those factors associated with the candidate himself, rather than with his party. Reagan's personality, his association with the wealthy, his views on the Equal Rights Amendment, and his being from California are all part of what we might call his "candidate image." In the 1950s, Eisenhower's image was so positive that for many voters it overcame the negative associations they had with his party.

In 1984, too, there was evidence of the role of the image of the candidates. The University of Michigan survey asked respondents if Reagan was a "moral" person. Those who said yes gave Reagan 68 percent of their votes, while those who said no backed Mondale with 86 percent. Bear in mind, however, that some Reagan voters might have perceived Reagan as moral because they had already decided to vote for him on other grounds, rather than deciding to vote for him because they thought he was moral.

It should not be surprising that Americans are particularly influenced by the images of the individual candidates. If, relatively speaking, parties are hard to distinguish and offer little choice on broad policy questions, why not look at the personal characteristics of the candidates? While those personal characteristics can include legitimate factors, such as how honest a candidate is or how inspiring a leader, any observer of American elections knows how much of it is trivial. Billy Carter's peccadilloes, Nancy Reagan's expensive tastes, Gary Hart's name change, countless campaign ads with the candidate's smiling family and dog, all constitute what Sidney Lens considers "politics by psychoanalysis" and Walter Dean Burnham has called "American politics as understood and reported by *People* magazine"[25]— colorful people, charming anecdotes, and everything you've ever wanted to know about them except the public policies they would implement. How many times do Americans react to a candidate by complaining that he or she is boring, as though they were choosing a date for Saturday night, or as though the point of politics was to put on a good show! As I shall argue in the following chapter, the mass media play a great role in fostering such an approach, and it fits a relatively issue-less politics perfectly.

There is another reason that Americans are especially obsessed with candidates' personal characteristics. The organizational weakness of American political parties means that elected officials have more independence from party than do their counterparts in other countries. Therefore the individual qualifications of a candidate assume greater significance here.

The role of issues

These classic studies of American voting patterns emphasized groups, parties, and candidates, everything except what earlier scholars had stressed—issues. The voters did not know much about what the researchers knew were the great issues of the day, they did not know where the candidates stood on those issues, and when asked what they liked and disliked about the parties and candidates, they did not use standard ideological terms such as liberal and conservative. Voters tended to assume that candidates they liked shared their opinions, even when the candidates did not.[26]

This sorry picture of the voters' inability to deal with issues seems to be confirmed by the many indications that the voters are woefully ignorant of essential political facts. In the nationwide survey conducted by the University of Michigan's Center for Political Studies in 1972, nearly three-fourths of the respondents did not know how long a United States senator's term and barely more than half knew that the election that year kept the Democrats in control of the House of Representatives. Many surveys have shown that about half the respondents could name their representative in Congress off the top of their heads.[27]

What can be concluded from such findings? The Columbia University researchers wrote in 1954:

> For political democracy to survive, other features are required: the intensity of conflict must be limited, the rate of change must be restrained, stability in the social and economic structure must be maintained, a pluralistic social organization must exist, and a basic consensus must bind together the contending parties. . . . How could a mass democracy work if all the people were deeply involved in politics?[28]

For the authors of those sentences, such conservative conclusions logically followed from the portrait they painted of the American voter, portraying a person rather incapable of intelligently dealing with issues and easily swayed by his or her peers. These authors' recommendation, therefore, was to muddy the differences between the parties, and keep the masses from deciding public policy disputes, lest they contaminate the process with their ignorant views. The scholars concluded with a call for a "division of labor" in politics between the few who knew about issues and the many who did not.[29]

The Michigan scholars drew two conclusions from their similar findings about voters and issues. First, "the electoral decision typically will be ambiguous as to the specific acts government should take."[30] If voters cannot deal intelligently with issues, they asked, how can we conclude that an election provides a "mandate" for the winner to take specific actions? If Ronald Reagan won because people voted for him due to peer pressure, or because of his cowboy image, then how can anyone conclude that voters were endorsing his policies?

Consequently, the second conclusion of the Michigan team was that "the electoral decision gives great freedom to those who must frame the policies of government."[31] If Reagan and other incumbents are not getting policy cues from the electorate, then they can pretty much do what they please about public policy. The thrust of the early Michigan studies, as well as that of the Columbia research, is elitist.

Finally, the conclusions of both groups of scholars imply that if voters respond to group cues, partisanship, and candidate image, the wise candidate will be the one who plays up those factors in campaign ads. Lots of smiling family pictures and patriotic symbols are in order, rather than thoughtful issue-oriented appeals which the public will misperceive and forget. As one scholar wrote about campaigners, "If they see voters as most certainly responsive to nonsense, they will give them nonsense."[32] This is a subject for the next chapter, but suffice it to note that mindless campaign appeals surely follow from a portrait of the electorate in which issues are downplayed.

Such a portrait of "democracy" comports well with the maintenance of corporate capitalism. Reread the quotation from the Columbia study, with its references to limited conflict, restrained change, stability, consensus, and the noninvolvement of the people in politics, and this should become apparent. Indeed, if keeping the mass of people out of politics removes one potential threat from the system, then it should be no wonder that there have not been greater efforts to increase turnout in the United States.

Other conclusions just cited also fit the goal of the maintenance of the system. Providing a division of labor between the politically knowledgeable and the politically ignorant, and leaving elites free from any policy directives that might come out of elections, are ways to insure that the status quo will be maintained. Running shallow, issueless campaigns will insure that the public will not obtain the information necessary to formulate an independent and perhaps critical judgment about the system.

A SECOND OPINION

But what if the theory of voting behavior just outlined is wrong? What if there are ways of interpreting the data that are more charitable to the electorate than the previous inferences?

To begin with, bloc voting by social groups might signify something other than mindless conformity. After all, members of the same group have similar educations and similar life experiences. Why should it surprise us when most Catholics vote for the same candidate, even when religion is not an overt campaign issue, if Catholics share a religious tradition that has implications for many public issues? What is irrational about blacks forming a voting bloc, if all have suffered the effects of racism and most of them perceive one party as preferable on that issue?[33]

Similarly, party identification and candidate image may be more rational motivations than popular lore grants. In the words of one author, party identification is "a *standing decision,* a decision that motivates political behavior in the *absence* of intervening, politically relevant events and issues."[34] In other words, many voters identify a party as a reasonably good approximation of their political views, and until and unless they perceive a particular candidate or issue that shakes up that assumption, they will stick with that party. Given the lack of ideological distance between American parties, and given the few incentives that most people have to pay a lot of attention to politics, who can say that this is not reasonable behavior?[35] As for candidate image, I have already noted that much of what people evaluate in a candidate is perfectly appropriate.[36]

Finally, we must confront the question of the voters' failure to deal intelligently with issues. A number of critics have pointed out that this allegation is based on unfair tests of voters' knowledge and intelligence. For example, when a pollster asks a respondent about an issue that the pollster decides is important, and the respondent does not know much about it, is this proof of the respondent's stupidity? Or does this simply mean that the issue was not one in which the respondent was interested? Social scientists use the concept of "salience," or how important a subject is to a person. If the pollster decides to ask about something that is not salient to the respondent, we should not be surprised if that respondent does not deal very effectively with that issue. If I were to ask you about, say, American foreign policy toward Tanzania, and you demonstrated little knowledge of that policy and no well-formed opinion about it, you would justifiably be resentful if I then concluded that you don't know very much about public policy. You might well respond, "Why don't you ask me about something I'm interested in!" Indeed, the best studies of the issue orientation of the voter begin by making sure that the issues involved are salient to the respondent.[37]

Another problem involves those studies that conclude that voters lack sophistication about issues because they do not use concepts like liberal and conservative when discussing parties and candidates. There are three responses to this conclusion. The first is the rather obvious point that if the parties and candidates are not far apart ideologically, why should we expect voters to use ideological concepts when discussing them?[38] Expecting people to discuss ideology when talking about parties and candidates presupposes that the parties and candidates are so ideologically distinct that it is impossible for an intelligent person to converse about them without mentioning ideology. A major theme of this book is that parties and ideology need never be mentioned in the same conversation, so little do they have to do with one another.

The second point is that it may be unfair to expect the average person to be as articulate about politics as the social scientist, the journalist, or the politician. As one researcher has put it, "people who feel uneasy in 'talking politics', out of their element, slightly threatened and not very self-confident should tend to become flustered, to begin to trip over their own words, to hash syntax, lose trains of thought, and go blank on many important points of fact."[39] Surely many students have experienced this kind of problem on examinations! Voters who are capable of thinking in a sophisticated fashion may not be very articulate about their views. The surveys may be tapping verbal expression more than mental ability.

Finally, there may be many kinds of political sophistication that may go beyond the standard liberal–conservative spectrum. A voter may, for example, be a libertarian, against "big government" in all areas (but not, in typically American fashion, against concentrations of power in the private sector). Such a person will be against spending a lot on social programs *as well as* on the military. Some observers would call this inconsistent, since those we call liberals usually want more spent on social programs than on the military, while conservatives usually want the priorities reversed. But who is to say that libertarianism is any less intelligent a way to view politics? There may be many other political doctrines that contradict orthodox patterns but do not signify lack of intelligence on the part of the electorate.[40]

The voter has taken a lot of abuse, too, on the subject of ignorance. It is difficult to explain their lack of knowledge about numerous issues, the facts of American government, and even the name of their representative in Congress. But the matter of salience is again pertinent. If a foreign policy issue does not affect a person's daily life, we should not be surprised if that person does not walk around with much knowledge of it in his or her head. A similar point can be made about the facts of American government. Just because someone thinks that a United States senator's term is, say, four years long, does not mean that the person cannot make an intelligent choice between the candidates contending for that term. Just how much detailed information should we expect a voter to have at the tip of one's tongue?[41]

Voters do have more necessary information on tap than we think. Recall that only about half could give the name of their representative off the top of their heads. However, when shown a list of several names, more than 90 percent could correctly pick out their representative,[42] demonstrating that while they were unable to spout the information upon request, it was stored in their minds, accessible when necessary. Consequently, whenever these voters were confronted with news about their representative in the mass media or in conversations they would be able to identify the representative as their own. How much more should we expect of citizens in a regime that does not encourage a high level of political participation?

But to establish that voters can intelligently deal with issues, it is necessary not only to criticize the earlier studies, but also to present some positive contradictory evidence. There have been many studies that have done so, and here I shall briefly review only a few of the most influential:

- In 1966, ground was broken by V. O. Key's posthumously published book, *The Responsible Electorate*. As the title implies, Key's point was that "voters are not fools."[43] He attempted to demonstrate this with data from most of the elections from 1936 through 1960, comparing voters who shifted from one party's presidential nominee in one election to the other's in the next with those who did not shift. The shifters were more likely to agree with the policy positions of the candidate to whom they defected than were those who stood pat. Key also argued that voters vote "retrospectively," emphasizing the hard evidence provided by the record of the incumbent party rather than either party's promises for the future.

· In 1971, David RePass showed that in 1964, voters were especially likely to vote for the party that they thought would do a better job on the issues that they found most salient.[44]

· In 1972, Richard Boyd demonstrated that in 1968, people with particular positions on issues were willing to defect from their party's presidential nominee in predictable ways. For example, voters who took a liberal stand on an issue were more likely to vote for the Democrat than other voters with a similar partisanship.[45]

· In 1975, John Jackson concluded from examining data from the 1964 election that people identify with parties to a great extent as a result of their beliefs about issues, rather than letting their party affiliation determine their opinions. Moreover, this implies that people will change their partisanship "if their positions on various issues change, if the parties modify their positions, or if new issues arise which divide the existing party coalitions."[46]

· In 1978, Edward Tufte provided evidence that since World War II, when the economy (measured by the population's after-tax income and accounting for inflation) is doing well, the incumbent party has done well in the elections. This suggests that the voters are capable of intelligently evaluating their short-term economic self-interest.[47]

· In 1981, Morris Fiorina elaborated upon Key's notion of the "retrospective vote" by arguing that voters use the incumbent's performance to try to project what his party will do in the future. To demonstrate this, Fiorina used data from the late 1950s and middle 1970s; he also maintained that using the past record as a voting guide is an intelligent use of the "hardest data" one has in an election.[48]

This inventory only begins to scratch the surface of the many studies that have taken seriously the voters' ability to deal intelligently with significant political concerns, such as the public policies advocated by the candidates and the record of the incumbent. Like group identity, party identification and candidate image, concern with issues played a part in the 1984 presidential campaign. The University of Michigan's survey that year revealed that people who wanted to increase spending for the military voted for Reagan by 72 percent, while those who wanted to reduce such spending backed Mondale by 68 percent. Advocates of more spending for food stamps, on the other hand, supported Mondale by 76 percent, while opponents of this policy backed Reagan by 77 percent. In their books about the 1980 campaign, the journalists Jack Germond, Jules Witcover, and Jeff Greenfield argued that Reagan's victory was due to serious policy concerns on the minds of the electorate.[49]

What are the implications of such a portrait of the voter? We can look at the conclusions drawn from the less attractive picture given in the previous section. First, if voters are dealing intelligently with campaign issues, then do elections "say something" beyond that fact that Candidate A defeated Candidate B? In the first chapter, I tried to show that elections are a poor way for the public to express its views in politics; nothing in this chapter contradicts that contention. However, I must distinguish between two questions: Can *elections* express the "public will," and do *individual voters* behave intelligently? The scholars discussed in the previous section argue that the answer to both questions is "no." Some other scholars, noted in chapter 4, argue on the basis of studies like the ones just cited that the answer to both questions is "yes." I am suggesting, before presenting my own view, that there is nothing inconsistent about saying "no" and "yes": elections cannot express the public will nearly as well as other modes of political participation, but voters *are* able to decide how to vote on the basis of issues. In fact, the hypothetical voters I discussed at the beginning of the first chapter were all motivated by serious electoral concerns.

The second implication of the earlier studies of voters is that elections give public officials no guidance, leaving them to do pretty much as they please, immune from being fairly accused of letting down the voters who elected them. This follows from the meaninglessness of elections. If, on the other hand, voters do vote on the basis of issues, does this mean that officials have a "mandate" from the voters that they ignore at their peril? Some say so. Again, I would maintain that only rarely, if ever, does a single issue so dominate a campaign and produce so clear a contrast between candidates that the result produces a mandate. However, there is a big difference between saying that Reagan won because people liked his personality or were responding to peer pressure, and saying that he won because of many different issue concerns of many voters, no single one of which dominated the campaign or the electorate. The latter interpretation at least puts the officeholder on notice that a thinking electorate will be watching his or her performance.

Finally, there is a clear implication for the kind of campaign a candidate should run. If the voters are capable of considering issues, then an issue-oriented campaign can work. I say "can work," because any kind of advertisement can backfire if it is incompetently produced or if its message is offensive to most voters. But a candidate need not confine his or her campaign advertising to smiling family portraits and similar drivel.

I argued earlier that issueless campaigns help to preserve the social and economic system by diverting the attention of the electorate from the kinds of issues that might cause it to call that system into question. We might therefore conclude that a campaign based on issues can threaten the corporate capitalist order. Certainly the potential exists. However, it is only a potential, and not a likely one. First, most issues that are raised in American campaigns fall well within the confines of capitalism, and pose no threat to the system. Indeed, much of the Reagan campaign in 1980 was based on issues, but his proposals hardly threatened corporate capitalism. Second, even if campaigns took a more radical approach, Americans are socialized and conditioned against appeals that violate liberal capitalist norms; the socialist label has been enough to condemn even the mildest reform proposals.

SYNTHESIS: THE CONDITIONALITY HYPOTHESIS

By now, you are probably very confused about how Americans vote. Many eminent scholars have argued and shown that voters vote on the basis of trivial concerns, while others of equal distinction have argued and shown that voters are no fools. Sometimes students conclude that since the latter research was conducted more recently, it is superior to the former, proving the earlier scholars wrong. Do not fall into this kind of simple-mindedness. Americans often assume that newer is better. I tried to demonstrate the error of this kind of reasoning by showing that *all* of these theories can be substantiated by surveys from the most recent presidential campaign.

How can we integrate these theories? A fruitful place to begin is in the first major study of issue voting, V. O. Key's *The Responsible Electorate*:

> The voice of the people is but an echo. The output of an echo chamber bears an inevitable and invariable relation to the input. As candidates and parties clamor for attention and vie for popular support, the people's verdict can be no more than a selective reflection from among the alternatives and outlooks presented to them. Even the most discriminating popular judgment can reflect only ambiguity, uncertainty, or even foolishness if those are the qualities of the input into the echo chamber.... If the people can choose only from among rascals, they are certain to choose a rascal.[50]

In effect, Key was arguing that it is pointless to discuss what the voter is "really" like, because it is impossible to imagine a voter outside the context of a campaign and an election. A voter's behavior is dependent on the nature of the choices that he or she is given.

A little exercise will make his point clear. Imagine that your political science professor brings two people into the classroom and asks you to vote for one of them for Congress. Each of them smiles and says something vague about how much he or she wants to do for the country if elected—but says nothing about specific issues. How will you vote?

Chances are, you will base your choice on what you saw—their looks, their speaking ability or their race, ethnic group, sex or age. If your professor then told you that you were an irresponsible voter for basing your decision on such trivial criteria, you might justifiably answer, "How do you expect me to vote? That's all the information I had."

If, on the other hand, each "candidate" spoke out on a variety of issues that are important to you and presented contrasting views, chances are you would vote on the basis of those issues, even if it meant voting for the ugly one or the one of the "wrong" sex. This is what Key was getting at: voting behavior depends on the nature of the choice presented to the voter. Or, as computer jocks put it, "Garbage in, garbage out." If candidates give the voters garbage in their campaigns, the voters will vote on the basis of that political garbage. Political scientists have made this argument more and more frequently over the years.[51] It might be called the "conditionality hypothesis": the criteria that people use in deciding how to vote depend on the *conditions* of the election, notably the kind of choice that the candidates present. But more important than making this argument is proving it; indeed the conditionality of voting behavior has been demonstrated empirically by researchers.

In 1972, Gerald Pomper showed that from 1956 to 1968, there was an increase in (1) the voters' ability to distinguish between the parties' stands on issues, (2) their tendency to identify the Democrats as the more liberal party, and (3) the tendency of liberals to identify as Democrats, and conservatives to identify as Republicans. While not strictly a study of voting behavior, Pomper's findings have obvious implications for the voters' ability to vote issues. For our purposes, the most important point is that Pomper saw these increases begin in 1964, and he attributed this to the presidential campaign that year in which the Republicans nominated Senator Barry Goldwater of Arizona, their most conservative standard-bearer in a generation. Pomper concluded, "When there *are* party positions and differences, the voters can perceive them."[52] Pomper later updated his findings with data from the 1972 election.[53]

In 1975, Pomper looked directly at voting behavior, adopting the conditionality hypothesis. In 1956, a year when both presidential candidates, Republican Dwight Eisenhower and Democrat Adlai Stevenson, were widely perceived as "moderates," Pomper found that issues played a negligible role in how people voted. In 1964, however, when the ultraconservative Goldwater ran on the Republican ticket, and in 1972, when the very liberal George McGovern was nominated by the Democrats, issues played a far greater role (and party identification a smaller role) than in 1956.[54] Apparently the nomination of a more ideological candidate will lead the voters to vote more ideologically.

Norman Nie and Kristi Andersen showed in 1974 that the public was far more likely in the 1960s and 1970s than in the 1950s to have ideologically "consistent" views on the issues. They suggested that this was because the electorate became more interested in politics over time, which is one condition that might be incorporated in the "conditionality hypothesis." But they also noted in passing that in order for this greater ideological consistency to be translated into issue voting, parties and candidates must offer the voters real choices.[55]

In 1976, Nie, Sidney Verba, and John Petrocik discovered a sharp growth in the issue orientation of the American populace from the 1950s to the 1960s. People discussed parties and candidates more in ideological terms, showed more ideological consistency in their own views, and voted more on the basis of issues than they had before.[56] Perhaps the most striking and original of their proofs of the conditionality hypothesis was a series of survey questions in 1973 in which people were asked to "vote" in hypothetical match-ups between well-known politicians. When the choice was between Democrat Hubert Humphrey and Republican Charles Percy, widely perceived as "moderates," three out of four voters stuck with their own party's standard-bearer. However, when asked to choose between Goldwater and McGovern, nearly half voted for the other party's candidate. The defectors tended to be the people we would expect: conservative Democrats attracted to Goldwater, and liberal Republicans drawn to McGovern.[57]

While most of the research on voting has focused on Presidential elections, the conditionality hypothesis has been demonstrated on other levels as well. For example, Alan Abramowitz has shown that in races for the United States Senate in 1978 in which the two major party candidates were ideologically far apart, voters were especially likely to (1) perceive differences between them, (2) regard the Democrat as (correctly) more liberal, and (3) vote for the candidate closer to themselves ideologically.[58] Similarly, Gerald Wright discovered that in contests for the U.S. House of Representatives in 1966, the farther apart the candidates were, the more likely people were to vote on the basis of issues.[59]

One way to see how conditionality works is to look at how various groups voted in the past several presidential elections. Using the University of Michigan surveys, I have divided the voters into partisan and ideological groups, depending on how they identified themselves. This may be an erroneous way to assign people to ideological categories, since a person might call himself or herself a liberal, for instance, while holding what you or I would consider conservative beliefs on most issues. However, for the sake of simplicity, people will be grouped according to the way they identify themselves.

In Table 7.2 are the various groups and how they voted. Notice that in 1972, Democrats were intensely divided over whether to vote for their standard-bearer George McGovern. Eight-three percent of liberal Democrats voted for him while only 31 percent of conservative Democrats did, a fifty-two percent difference, as the fourth line of the table shows. A similar difference occurred among Independents. As for Republicans, party members of all stripes heavily backed Richard Nixon.

Table 7.2. How self-identified partisans and ideologues voted for president, 1972 to 1984.

	McGovern, 1972	Carter, 1976	Carter, 1980	Reagan, 1980	Mondale, 1984
Democrats:					
Liberals	83	88	78	10	90
Moderates	53	77	58	37	72
Conservatives	31	59	70	22	65
Liberal minus Conservative	52	29	8	−12	25
Independents:					
Liberals	66	63	40	23	68
Moderates	25	48	21	60	37
Conservatives	13	22	17	75	13
Liberal minus Conservative	53	41	23	−52	55
Republicans:					
Liberals	13	42	6	81	5
Moderates	2	19	12	76	8
Conservatives	2	6	2	92	3
Liberal minus Conservative	11	36	4	−11	2

Note: Read this table as follows: In 1972, Democratic liberals cast 83 percent of their votes for McGovern, as did 53 percent of Democratic moderates and 31 percent of Democratic conservatives. The difference between liberal and conservative Democrats was 83 minus 31, or 52 percent.

Source: National surveys, University of Michigan Center for Political Studies

In 1976, the picture was far different. In that year, a majority of Democrats of all persuasions voted for Jimmy Carter, and the difference between liberal and conservative Democrats dropped dramatically from the 1972 figure of 52 percent to 29 percent in 1976. Among independents, the difference dropped less precipitously from 53 to 41 percent. Republicans were again the exception, with the difference rising substantially to 36 percent.

What happened in 1980? The 1972 and 1976 races are relatively simple to analyze, because they were essentially two-candidate races. However, because of the relatively strong showing of John Anderson's Independent ticket in 1980, it is necessary to show how the partisan and ideological groups voted for both Carter and Ronald Reagan that year, as the results differ. In most cases, ideology had *less* of an impact in 1980 than it had had in the two previous elections. Similarly in 1984, Democrats and Republicans heavily supported their parties' nominees regardless of their own ideological learnings. Only among independents were there marked differences between liberals and conservatives in terms of how they voted.

Why were the Democrats more influenced by ideology in 1972 than in any of the three later elections? The conditionality hypothesis suggests that the conditions were different in 1972, especially regarding the choice offered by the candidates. And indeed, surveys from those years reveal that voters saw more differences on the issues between McGovern and Nixon in 1972 than between Carter and Gerald Ford in 1976.[60] The voters were responding to broader differences between the candidates in 1972, and were more likely to vote their ideology.

Moreover, voters in 1980 did not perceive a great gulf between Carter and Reagan, nor did the voters in 1984 see vast differences between Reagan and Mondale. The University of Michigan's national survey asked respondents in each presidential election since 1972 to place the major-party nominees in one of various ideological categories, and the results appear in Figure 7.1. This figure is slightly misleading, because I have averaged the respondents' scores for each candidate as though they saw each pair of adjacent ideological categories to be the same distance from each other as all the other pairs; this is not necessarily the case, but in the absence of better data I shall use these. Figure 7.1 shows that the respondents saw about the same distance between Ford and Carter in 1976 as between Carter and Reagan in 1980 and between Reagan and Mondale in 1984. On the other hand, McGovern was seen as much farther to the left than the other Democratic nominees in Figure 7.1, and this resulted in the widest perceived choice between a pair of candidates in any of the years. That is why 1972 stands out in Table 7.2.

The fact that Reagan was perceived to be not much different from Nixon or Ford in Figure 7.1 may be the most surprising of all. After all, Ronald Reagan was widely viewed by political analysts as the most conservative nominee the Republican party had had in fifty years. Apparently the voters in 1980 agreed that he was farther to the right than Nixon or Ford, but with Carter's growing conservatism they did not see the choice as very wide. As a consequence, ideology played only a limited role in their voting patterns in 1980. In 1984 the Democrats nominated a slightly more liberal candidate than Carter had been, but Reagan was considered to have moved slightly to the left of where he had previously been as well. Therefore, the distance between the candidates was seen to be rather constant over the years from 1976 to 1984.

THE MALIGNED VOTER

Does the voter focus upon "publick men and publick measures"? In many ways, he or she does not. Huge numbers of people do not vote at all, and many who do vote judge candidates by trivial criteria. However, I

Figure 7.1 Mean placement of Democratic and Republican presidential nominees on ideological scale, 1972 through 1984.

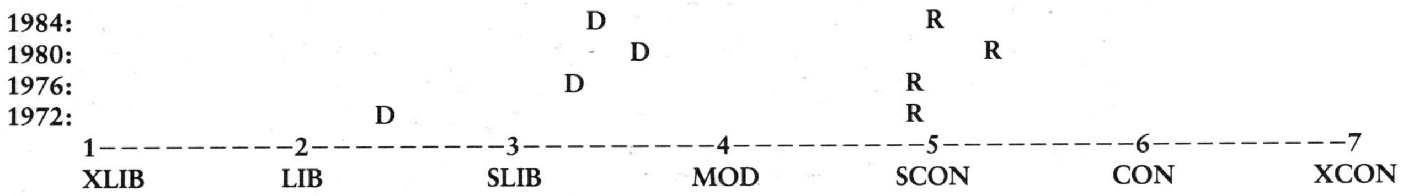

```
1984:                        D                R
1980:                    D                 R
1976:               D                      R
1972:         D                            R

      1------2------3------4------5------6------7
      XLIB   LIB    SLIB   MOD    SCON   CON    XCON
```

XLIB = Extremely Liberal
LIB   = Liberal
SLIB = Slightly Liberal
MOD   = Moderate
SCON = Slightly Conservative
CON   = Conservative
XCON = Extremely Conservative

Note: Read this diagram as follows: In 1972, the average respondent placed the Democratic nominee at point 2.4 on the scale, and the Republican nominee at point 4.9 on the scale.

Source: National surveys, University of Michigan Center for Political Studies

have tried to show that voting behavior depends on what kind of choice the parties and candidates give the voter. Therefore, the smug put-downs of the voter by those who accuse the electorate of being incapable of behaving intelligently are a case of blaming the victim. The voters are victimized by *campaigns* that underplay "publick measures." Exactly how such campaigns do so is the focus of the next chapter.

Further Reading

My comments on the decline of turnout are based on my article, "Why Is Turnout Down?," in *Public Opinion Quarterly* XLIII (Fall 1979), 297–311. For an exhaustive study of the phenomenon confined to a finite period, see Raymond E. Wolfinger and Steven J. Rosenstone, *Who Votes?* (New Haven: Yale Univ. Press, 1980).

The voting behavior literature is truly massive, with many of the most important works cited above. Much of the literature can only be understood by readers with some understanding of quantitative methods. A good beginning and overview is William H. Flanigan and Nancy H. Zingale, *Political Behavior of the American Electorate,* 5th ed. (Boston: Allyn & Bacon, 1983). The best of the classics are Bernard R. Berelson, Paul F. Lazarsfeld, and William N. McPhee, *Voting* (Chicago: Univ. of Chicago Press, 1954); Angus Campbell, Philip E. Converse, Warren E. Miller, and Donald E. Stokes, *The American Voter* (New York: John Wiley & Sons, 1960); and V. O. Key, Jr., *The Responsible Electorate* (Cambridge: Harvard Univ. Press, 1966). These books are not only rich in theory, but also reasonably clear to the novice.

For a penetrating radical view of recent electoral trends, see Alan Wolfe, *The Limits of Legitimacy* (New York: The Free Press, 1977), Part II.

Notes

1. Robert Green McCloskey, ed., *The Works of James Wilson,* (Cambridge: Harvard Univ. Press, 1967), II: 787–789. The argument that political participation promotes patriotism is an old one; see *The Politics of Aristotle,* ed. and trans. Ernest Barker (New York: Oxford Univ. Press, 1962), 124–125.

2. John Stuart Mill, "Representative Government," in his *Utilitarianism, Liberty, and Representative Government* (London: J. M. Dent & Sons, 1926), 208.

3. This section of this chapter is a revised version of my article, "Why Is Turnout Down?," in *Public Opinion Quarterly* XLIII (Fall 1979), 297–311. Similar findings are published in Thomas E. Cavanagh, "Changes in American Voter Turnout, 1964–1976," *Public Opinion Quarterly* XCVI (Spring 1981), 53–65.

4. Data through 1980 are from the *Statistical Abstract of the United States 1984* (Washington: Government Printing Office, 1983), 262. The 1984 estimate is based on the total presidential vote in the *Congressional Quarterly Weekly Report,* 13 April 1985, 687, and the estimate of the population over age eighteen in "Voting and Registration in the Election of November 1984," Series P–20, Number 397 (Washington: Bureau of the Census, January 1985), 5. For historical trends, see Walter Dean Burnham's estimates in the *Congressional Record,* 11 December 1970, 41223–41224.

5. See, for example, the remarks of Everett Carll Ladd in *Public Opinion*, August/September 1982, 6–7.

6. See my "Why Is Turnout Down?", 300–301.

7. These and later generalizations are based on the national surveys of the University of Michigan's Center for Political Studies.

8. Raymond E. Wolfinger and Steven J. Rosenstone, *Who Votes?* (New Haven: Yale Univ. Press, 1980), chapter 3.

9. See Michael W. Traugott and John P. Katosh, "Response Validity in Surveys of Voting Behavior," *Public Opinion Quarterly* XLIII (Fall 1979), 359–377.

10. "Jobless Were More Likely to Vote in '82 Than in Previous Off Years," the *New York Times*, 18 April 1983, pp. A1, A12.

11. *Congressional Quarterly Weekly Report*, 7 July 1984, 1619.

12. See, for example, Frances Fox Piven and Richard A. Cloward, "Prospects for Voter Registration Reform," *P.S.* (Summer 1985), 582–593; and Cloward and Piven, "Trying to Break Down the Barriers," *The Nation*, 2 November 1985, 433–437, and "How to Get Out The Vote in 1988," *The Nation*, 23 November 1985, 547–549.

13. Patrick H. Caddell, "Initial Working Paper on Political Strategy" (10 December 1976), 11, 21. I am indebted to my colleague, Everett Ladd, for making it available to me.

14. See Paul F. Lazarsfeld, Bernard R. Berelson, and Hazel Gaudet, *The People's Choice* (New York: Duell, Sloan, & Pierce, 1944), and Berelson, Lazarsfeld, and William N. McPhee, *Voting* (Chicago: Univ. of Chicago Press, 1954).

15. Data can be found in Gerald M. Pomper *et. al.*, *The Election of 1984* (Chatham, N.J.: Chatham House Publishers, 1985), 67–68.

16. Berelson *et. al.*, *Voting* 81, 83.

17. Berelson *et al.*, *Voting*, 79.

18. See Robert R. Alford, *Party and Society* (Chicago: Rand McNally, 1963), and Ivor Crewe, "Electoral Participation," in David Butler, Howard R. Penniman, and Austin Ranney, eds. *Democracy at the Polls* (Washington and London: American Enterprise Institute, 1981), Table 10.5, 255.

19. These famous statements, from the tenth *Federalist*, can be found on p. 79 of the Clinton Rossiter edition (New York: New American Library, 1961).

20. Angus Campbell, Gerald Gurin, and Warren E. Miller, *The Voter Decides* (Evanston, Ill.: Row, Peterson, 1954), and Campbell, Philip E. Converse, Miller, and Donald E. Stokes, *The American Voter* (New York: John Wiley & Sons, 1960).

21. See Campbell *et. al.*, *The American Voter*, 30–31.

22. Data in Pomper *et al.*, *The Election of 1984*, 67.

23. See Table 3.3 in chapter 3 for the percentage of self-identifiers since 1952.

24. See Campbell *et al.*, *The American Voter*, 120–167.

25. Sidney Lens, "What Socialists Can Do in 1984," *The Nation*, 21–28 July 1984, 41–42; and Walter Dean Burnham, "Foreword" to Martin P. Wattenberg, *The Decline of American Political Parties 1952-1980* (Cambridge: Harvard Univ. Press, 1984) xii.

26. Berelson *et al.*, *Voting*, 215–233; Campbell *et al.*, *The American Voter*, 168–265; and Philip E. Converse, "The Nature of Belief Systems in Mass Publics," in David E. Apter, *Ideology and Discontent* (New York: The Free Press, 1964), 206–261.

27. See Thomas E. Mann, *Unsafe at Any Margin* (Washington: American Enterprise Institute, 1978), 26–30.

28. Berelson *et al.*, *Voting*, 313, 314.

29. Berelson *et.al.*, *Voting*, 321.

30. Campbell *et al.*, *The American Voter*, 544.

31. Campbell *et al.*, *The American Voter*, 544.

32. V. O. Key, Jr., *The Responsible Electorate* (Cambridge: Harvard Univ. Press, 1966), 6.

33. See Key, *The Responsible Electorate*, 3–4; Walter Berns, "Voting Studies," in Her-

bert J. Storing, ed, *Essays on the Scientific Study of Politics* (New York: Holt, Rinehart & Winston, 1962), 1–62; and Arthur S. Goldberg, "Social Determinism and Rationality as Bases of Party Identification," *American Political Science Review* LXIII (March 1969), 5–25.

34. Peter B. Natchez, "Images of Voting," *Public Policy* XVIII (Summer 1970), 582; emphasis in the original. The notion of a "standing decision" first appears in V. O. Key, Jr., and Frank Munger, "Social Determinism and Electoral Decision," in Eugene Burdick and Arthur J. Brodbeck, eds., *American Voting Behavior* (Glencoe, Ill.: The Free Press, 1959), 286.

35. See also Benjamin I. Page, *Choices and Echoes in Presidential Elections* (Chicago: Univ. of Chicago Press, 1978), 104.

36. See Arthur H. Miller and Warren E. Miller, "Ideology in the 1972 Election," *American Political Science Review* LXX (September 1976), 833–834.

37. See David E. RePass, "Issue Salience and Party Choice," *American Political Science Review* LXV (June 1971), 391.

38. See RePass, "Issue Salience and Party Choice," 398–399, and John H. Kessel, "Comment: The Issues in Issue Voting," *American Political Science Review* LXVI (June 1972), 461.

39. Karl Boughan, "The Forgetful Voter," unpublished paper presented to the 1974 annual meeting of the American Political Science Association, 11. See also John Plamenatz, "Electoral Studies and Democratic Theory: A British View," *Political Studies* VI (1958), 8–9.

40. See Boughan, "The Forgetful Voter," 14–17.

41. See E. E. Schattschneider, *The Semisovereign People* (New York: Holt, Rinehart & Winston, 1960), 135.

42. Mann, *Unsafe at Any Margin*, 30–34.

43. Key, *The Responsible Electorate*, 7.

44. RePass, "Issue Salience and Party Choice."

45. Richard W. Boyd, "Popular Control of Public Policy," *American Political Science Review* LXVI (June 1972), 429–449.

46. John E. Jackson, "Issues, Party Choices, and Presidential Votes," *American Journal of Political Science* XIX (May 1975), 181.

47. Edward R. Tufte, *Political Control of the Economy* (Princeton: Princeton Univ. Press, 1978), chapter 5.

48. Morris P. Fiorina, *Retrospective Voting in American National Elections* (New Haven: Yale Univ. Press, 1981). Besides Key's work, Fiorina relied heavily on Anthony Downs, *An Economic Theory of Democracy* (New York: Harper & Row, 1957). Unlike the authors being reviewed here, Downs did not use empirical data to prove his theory. See also Arthur H. Miller and Martin P. Wattenberg, "Throwing the Rascals Out," *American Political Science Review* LXXIX (June 1985), 359–372.

49. Jack W. Germond and Jules Witcover, *Blue Smoke and Mirrors* (New York: Viking Press, 1981); and Jeff Greenfield, *The Real Campaign* (New York: Summit Books, 1982).

50. Key, *The Responsible Electorate*, 2–3. He anticipated this passage in his review essay, "The Politically Relevant in Surveys," *Public Opinion Quarterly* XXIV (Spring 1960), 56.

51. See Berns, "Voting Studies," 7–8; Kenneth Prewitt and Norman Nie, "Election Studies of the Survey Research Center," *British Journal of Political Science* I (October 1971), 491–492; and Page, *Choices and Echoes*, 281.

52. Gerald M. Pomper, "From Confusion to Clarity," *American Political Science Review* LXVI (June 1972), 427 (emphasis in the original).

53. Gerald Pomper, *Voters' Choice* (New York: Dodd, Mead, 1975), chapter 8.

54. Pomper, *Voters' Choice*, chapter 9.

55. Norman H. Nie with Kristi Andersen, "Mass Belief Systems Revisited," *Journal of Poltiics* XXXVI (August 1974), 540–591.

56. Norman H. Nie, Sidney Verba, and John R. Petrocik, *The Changing American Voter* (Cambridge: Harvard Univ. Press, 1976), chapters 7–10.

57. Nie, Verba, and Petrocik, *The Changing American Voter*, chapters 17–18.

58. Alan I. Abramowitz, "Choices and Echoes in the 1978 U.S. Senate Elections," *American Journal of Political Science* XXV (February 1981), 112–118.

59. Gerald C. Wright, Jr., "Candidates' Policy Positions and Voting in U.S. Congressional Elections," *Legislative Studies Quarterly* III (August 1978), 445–464.

60. See, for example, the second edition of Nie, Verba, and Petrocik, *The Changing American Voter* (Cambridge: Harvard Univ. Press, 1979), chapter 20; and Page, *Choices and Echoes,* 94–97.

8

Campaigning for Office

At the beginning of the preceding chapter, I quoted some comments on voting by James Wilson, one of the early leaders of the American republic. Wilson included in his remarks the responsibilities of the voter during a political campaign: "He should be employed, on every convenient occasion, in making researches after proper persons for filling the different departments of power; in discussing, with his neighbours and fellow citizens, the qualities that should be possessed by those who fill the several offices; and in acquiring information, with the spirit of manly candour, concerning the manners, and history, and characters of those, who are likely to be candidates for the publick choice."[1] In this fashion, political campaigns would educate the electorate on the candidates and the issues.

This is an attractice picture of political campaigns, but most Americans know that it is inaccurate. Too often are campaigns an education for the masses in nothing but trivia. Frequently, this is because there seems to be little difference between the candidates, but even when the contrast between them is stark, campaigns seem to fall short of the liberal capitalist ideal. In 1964, for example, the Republicans gave the American people what they called "a choice, not an echo," by nominating an ultraconservative senator, Barry Goldwater, for President against a liberal Democratic incumbent, Lyndon Johnson. Yet even this campaign was unsatisfactory to many voters. As one news magazine put it:

> The 1964 Presidential campaign has been one of the most disappointing ever. It was going to be a confrontation between opposing philosophies; it turned out to be a wrestling match between volatile personalities. It was going to prove the vital difference between two strong political parties; it has merely shown that one, the G.O.P., is in need of great repair. . . . It was not going to be a "me too" campaign; it has turned out to be one in which the principals largely shout "You're another."[2]

The task of this chapter is to delineate exactly how and why campaigns diverge from the ideal. First, however, we should consider the dilemma that liberal capitalism would face if campaigns accomplished what they ideally are supposed to. If campaigns were truly educational, then the public would learn about issues in sufficient depth to be able to question the fundamentals of corporate capitalism. They would not necessarily call those elements into question, but the possibility would exist. Such information could be empowering; that is, it could put enough data into the minds of the masses for a serious examination of the American social and economic system, and it could be followed by political action. Such an examination is to be feared by corporate elites.

PROFESSIONAL CAMPAIGN CONSULTANTS

In the past several decades, the process of campaigning for high office has been transformed by the rise of a new kind of political operative, the professional campaign consultant. This is a person who hires out his or her services to any candidate able to pay the price and whose race the consultant is willing to handle. Especially grateful to the consultant is the inexperienced winning candidate. After his first election as governor of California in 1966, Ronald Reagan said of the consulting firm of Spencer-Roberts, "I'd never run for office again without the help of professional managers like Spencer and Roberts."[3] And he never did.

What do these consultants do? Different consultants provide different services, but almost any modern major-party campaign for president, U.S. senator, or governor, and increasingly for U.S. representative or big-city mayor, will use the following:

Polling

Ever since the young George Gallup ran a poll for his mother-in-law's race for secretary of state of Iowa in 1932, politicians have increasingly relied on sample surveying to read the minds of the voters. We often think of surveys in the way that the mass media do, as ways to tell who is ahead or behind in a contest. But this is really not very useful to the candidates. How can the person who is ahead stay ahead? How can the person who is behind catch up?

Louis Harris, who was President Kennedy's chief pollster, once wrote that candidates rely on three uses of polling.[4] As we proceed through them, we can illustrate each of Harris' uses of polling with memoranda written by a key Reagan adviser, Stuart Spencer, at the height of the 1984 campaign.

· First, with a survey, a candidate can learn what various social groups are thinking about the race, so that his or her coalition-building strategy can be planned. Wrote Spencer:

> Our base of support from 1980 is still available to us. We can expect to improve our support from two groups, younger voters between the ages of 18 and 24 and suburban ticket-splitters. Our key constituency, how-

ever, remains middle-income working people. Farmers, middle-income people, and small business owners should be the focus of our efforts throughout the campaign.[5]

· Second, polls show what the voters think of the candidate's personal qualities (and, although Harris did not say so, his or her opponent's qualities as well). Spencer studied the surveys to learn how Reagan was coming across to the public:

> He is perceived as decisive, a strong leader, a good man in a crisis and a President who can get things done. The campaign must reflect the same kinds of attributes and characteristics.[6]

· Finally, surveys can ascertain what issues are important to the voters, and what they think about those issues. Spencer concluded:

> Our President's outstanding vulnerabilities are issue-oriented: foreign affairs (the need for a safer more peaceful world), the economy (residual fear over unemployment and fair treatment for all Americans), the role of government (education and medicare).[7]

Because surveying is a highly technical craft that requires skill in choosing a representative sample of people to interview, designing questions that will solicit the information one wants in an unbiased manner, summarizing the results by computer, and interpreting the findings, candidates need specialists to poll for them. Therefore pollsters are a fundamental element of the modern campaign consulting operation.

Advertising

Perhaps the most controversial of all the modern campaign advisers is the media consultant. Using survey findings to determine what "image" a candidate should "project," and to which voters, the media consultant will produce ads and place them on television and radio, in newspapers and magazines, and on signs and billboards. For television ads, which consumer the largest part of the media budget, the options include whether to push the candidate's personality or issue positions; whether to present the candidate or attack his or her opponent; whether to have the candidate talk directly to the audience, use "candid" shots, or keep the candidate out of the picture entirely; and which audience to select. A commercial shown with an afternoon soap opera will have a different audience than one run with "Saturday Night Live." One shown in Fargo, North Dakota may need a different emphasis than one aired in San Francisco.

Here are a couple of examples of television advertising. Both are taken from the ads of Malcolm Wallop, a right-wing Republican elected to the U.S. Senate in 1976. The first was a positive ad about Wallop, but with no issue content. It showed him riding a horse at the head of a band of cowboys, like someone out of a cigarette ad, while the announcer said:

Go forth for Wyoming, Malcolm Wallop. Tell them in the United States Senate that the people of Wyoming are proud of their land and life, and a Wyoming senator will fight every intrusion upon it. That you, Malcolm Wallop, will serve the nation best by serving Wyoming first—the very special needs of this great state. And in doing so share its blessing with America. Malcolm Wallop for U.S. Senate. Ride with us, Wyoming!

The second Wallop ad was aimed at his opponent, and raised an issue while showing a letter addressed to Mrs. John Smith:

We paid exactly four cents to mail a first-class letter in 1959. That's about the time Senator Gale McGee came to the United States Senate. Since then a lot has happened. [Stamps begin to pile up on the letter.] Oh, yes, McGee is chairman of the Senate Post Office Committee. And, oh, yes, Mrs. Smith is still waiting for the letter. Join the Wallop Senate Drive.

That November, McGee was "walloped" and lost his seat in the Senate.[8]

Research

Major campaigns also have a need for useful information, and hire research staffs to get it. Of course, polling is a kind of research on the voters. In addition, any candidate who hopes to be taken seriously has people studying the issues and developing positions on them. In his campaign for governor of California in 1966, for example, the political novice Ronald Reagan went around carrying a chunk of four-by-eight-inch "fact cards" with information about his state.[9]

Research on a candidate's opponent is important as well, and recent campaigns have been marked by unethical and sometimes illegal examples of it: the 1972 Nixon campaign's break-in at Democratic national headquarters at the Watergate, and the 1980 Reagan campaign's receipt of debate briefing papers from the Carter campaign. In a more savory category was Gerald Ford's campaign consultant's unearthing of a 1975 proposal by Reagan to cut $90 billion in federal expenditures. This was used to devastating effect against Reagan in the following year's New Hampshire primary, since the enactment of Reagan's proposal would have forced that state to raise taxes drastically to make up for the loss in federal aid.[10]

Even research on the candidate can be useful. When Richard Nixon ran for president in 1968, after more than twenty years in national politics, his staff compiled sixty-seven issue positions of his and put them into a computer that could be used to mail letters to voters with particular issue concerns.[11]

Direct mail

In recent years, some consultants have organized mass mail campaigns to raise funds for candidates and political groups. These specialists compile lists of thousands of names of potential contributors from such sources as subscribers to sympathetic magazines (such as *National Review* for conservatives or *The Progressive* for liberals), past donors to similar candidates or causes, members of compatible organizations, and so on. Then they draft a letter designed to tickle money out of the wallets of those people, and send the mailing out in droves. While the percentage of return may be small, the volume of mail is so great that enormous sums can be raised. In 1975, the National Republican Congressional Committee spent less than $60,000 to send a mailing to 210,000 past contributors, and raised $635,000—with only about one out of nine recipients of the letter responding.[12]

There is no question that the foremost direct mail consultant in American politics has been the right winger Richard Viguerie. Operating out of his Virginia headquarters, Viguerie claims to have amassed a list of millions of names of past and potential conservative contributors.[13] Like most other direct mail consultants, Viguerie tries to make his appeals as emotional as possible. He told an interviewer, "A lot of my clients don't like the copy because they say it sounds too cornball, too conversational, it's not dignified. But people respond to emotionalism."[14]

CAUSES AND EFFECTS OF THE CONSULTANTS

What gave rise to these campaign specialists? We can identify four causes of particular importance, and the first is central to the theme of this book. Campaign consultants fill the vacuum left by weak parties. It is no accident that California was the home of the first campaign consultant firm, Whitaker and Baxter, in the 1930s.[15] California has long been known for the absence of strong party organization, and with an electorate that lacked the cues that party organization provided in many other states, candidates wanted someone to organize their campaigns and give them an "image" that would enable voters to remember them. The state became the home of several early campaign consultant firms, as well as a style of campaigning in which the manipulation of images was the key to success. Three of its sons became presidential candidates: Richard Nixon, who rode the "Red scare" to the Senate in 1950 in a campaign that vilified his opponent as the "pink lady"; Jerry Brown, whose notion of leadership was wrapped up in trendy symbolism; and Ronald Reagan, who combined nostalgic ideology with the best gestures Hollywood could teach him. All were typical products of a media-based political system.

Why did the system spread from California eastward? In a sense, the whole nation has become California, as party organization and party voting have declined everywhere. In chapter 5, I noted that the trend toward independence from parties began to be discerned very early in the twentieth century, and candidates had to figure out ways to appeal to uncommitted voters. Campaign consultants, therefore, arose to fill a need. Some consultants are proud to be part of the decline-of-party syndrome. Joseph Napolitan, a longtime Democratic media consultant, once wrote that before television, a candidate had to work through the party to communicate with the voter, but no longer; "I for one think this is good, not bad."[16]

Another causal factor, suggested by Napolitan, was the rise of new techniques and technologies. Public relations as a specialty began in the early twentieth century, and its methods were soon applied to political persuasion. By the 1920s, radio had begun to be used to broadcast political speeches, and Franklin D. Roosevelt, with his rich voice and his eloquence, was the first national politician to master the new medium. In the 1930s, as noted above, sample surveying was developed and was soon used to study the electorate. The 1952 presidential campaign was the first to make widespread use of television, including the broadcasting of conventions and campaign speeches, advertising, and Richard Nixon's direct appeal to the voters to extricate him from a fund-raising scandal. Finally, computers have been used extensively, from analyzing surveys to sending out mailings to potential donors. In all these cases, candidates had to turn to people trained in the new methods rather than rely on machine politicians who were technologically in the Stone Age.

Declining parties and developing technologies are two widely cited reasons for the rise of campaign consultants,[17] and the political scientist Larry Sabato suggests a third: "rising campaign costs (and expenditure and contribution limitations) have placed a premium on the wise use of every campaign dollar."[18] This raises a point to be developed below, that money can be spent wisely or foolishly, and as long as the consultants convince the candidates that they know what they are doing, candidates will be willing to lavish money upon them. Perhaps equally important is Sabato's last point, that "everyone now needs [consultants] if only because everyone else has them."[19] Many candidates hire consultants partly in order to convince people that they are serious about running.

This raises a fundamental question: how effective *are* the consultants? This is difficult to determine for two reasons. The first is that there is a lot of nonsense being written about the subject. Much of it is hype written by consultants to blow their own horn, complete with "hard-nosed" attitudes toward politics and life, as well as bloated statistics on their ratio of wins to losses.[20] Much of the rest is the gee-whiz treatment by journalists who are only too willing to accept every wild claim by the consultant being interviewed.[21]

The other, more serious problem with trying to figure out how good the consultants really are is that scientific tests of their accomplishments are virtually impossible. If Consultant Jones works for Candidate Smith in a campaign, and Smith wins, how can we tell what Jones' contribution was? Maybe Smith would have won without Jones' help, perhaps by an even larger margin. The scientific way to test Jones' effectiveness would be to run the campaign all over again, this time without Jones. But obviously this is impossible.

A related difficulty is the *"post hoc, ergo propter hoc* fallacy," which simply means that just because one event follows another does not mean that the first event *caused* the second. If Candidate Smith accepts Consultant Jones' advice and puts a new commercial on television, and then goes up in the polls, how can we know for sure that the commercial was responsible? Ronald Reagan's consultant in his 1966 gubernatorial campaign, Stuart Spencer, was candid enough to say of it, "I never saw an easier campaign in my life: Everything fell into place. We got a great reputation out of it but it wasn't that hard."[22]

The best-known example of the overstated puffery about campaign consultants came to light in 1969, when a reporter named Joe McGinniss published a book entitled *The Selling of the President.*[23] McGinniss had sat in on the media strategy sessions for Richard Nixon's 1968 presidential campaign, and his book was an insider's account of how carefully Nixon's public image was stage-managed. Besides the television commercials, the centerpiece of the campaign was a series of programs in which Nixon would sit around a table with an unrehearsed group of people, answering their questions. The carefully selected questioners were mostly friendly, with an occasional hostile person thrown in to make the show look less packaged than it was. However, the audience was full of Nixon partisans who were guaranteed to applaud any strong response Nixon might give.

The media razzle-dazzle, combined with the book's title and the fact that its cover had a picture of Nixon's face on a pack of cigarettes, led many to conclude that Nixon has been sold to the American people like a commercial product. But the real message of the book is that his carefully designed media campaign did not prevent Nixon from falling from a huge lead in the polls around Labor Day to an extremely close victory two months later. His opponent, Hubert Humphrey, had a notoriously underfinanced campaign with little opportunity for the kind of lavish media spending that Nixon had; and yet he went from a landslide loser to a near-winner. The American people might well have been voting in 1968 on grounds other than showmanship.

Perhaps the best attempt to test the effects of media campaigns scientifically was that of the political scientists Thomas Patterson and Robert McClure, who interviewed a sample of citizens before and after being shown television ads from the 1972 presidential campaign between Nixon and Democrat George McGovern. They found that the ads had relatively little effect on people's feelings about the candidates, that "people see in candidates' commercials pretty much what they want to see."[24] For example, after seeing a series of McGovern ads, one viewer predisposed toward the Democrat said, "It was honest, down-to-earth," while a Nixon fan responded, "Those commercials are so phoney."[25] However, the real effect of the commercials was to inform the electorate about where the candidates stood and about some of the factual information conveyed in their ads.[26] This suggests that the voters may react more intelligently to advertising than media consultants would have candidates believe.

Whatever their effect in particular campaigns, what is the more general impact that consultants have on the political process? One consequence is that they contribute to the decline of parties. This is a vicious cycle: the decline of parties, as noted above, made consultants more appealing to candidates, and, as time goes on, these candidates have become more and more dependent on consultants and less and less so on parties. To whom does a victorious candidate owe gratitude, his or her party or his or her consultant? If the latter, then why should the elected official work with his or her fellow partisans?[27] One study of the 1978 congressional campaign found that the campaigns that spent the most on advertising were the ones in which the voters were most likely to think in terms of candidate images and the least prone to think in terms of party.[28]

On the other hand, a determined and well-heeled party organization could use these campaign techniques to exert discipline over candidates. For many years, the Republican national party has offered coordinated services to congressional candidates.[29] In recent years, with its growing financial advantage over the Democrats, the party has accelerated these efforts, and coordinated fund-raising and allocation, polling, advertising, and recruiting candidates.[30] During a congressional battle over the budget in August 1982, the deputy chairman of the Republican National Committee won over two wavering Republican representatives to the Reagan position by promising to "max out" or raise the legally permitted maximum in campaign funds for them, and went on: "We'll help you do a quick-and-dirty newsletter, make a commercial, organize a town meeting. Boom. Boom. Boom."[31] If a party united itself in this way, then the new campaign methods could reverse the decline of party organization, but it is difficult to imagine such a development withstanding not only all the trends in the other direction, but also the fundamentally decentralized nature of American politics.

Another widely noted consequence of the new use of consultants is that it has driven up the cost of campaigns. A few years ago, a typical consultant charged in the tens of thousands of dollars for a major campaign, or even a hundred thousand;[32] surely the figures have risen since then. Later in this chapter I will address the question of burgeoning campaign costs more generally, but consultants' fees are certainly a major share of a modern campaign's expenses. If consultants are effective at what they do, then their high charges make the notion of equal access to high office for all Americans a bitter joke. Most candidates need either a lot of personal wealth or access to well-heeled contributors.[33]

A third set of consequences involves ways in which consultants shape candidates' appeals. One effect is the homogenization of personal styles. It sometimes seems as though every young man running for high office today uses a blow-dryer, and every young woman wears a "dress-for-success" suit, presumably because, like young anchorpersons, they were told by their media consultants that it makes them look better on television. Along with this is a nationwide tendency for politicians to use their nicknames in order to appear folksy. While many presidents have had nicknames, not until 1976 did the American people elect a man who used his officially. The directory of the 99th Congress listed twelve Bills (and one Billy), seven Bobs (and one Bobbi), six Dans (and one Danny), six Toms (and one Tommy), six Dons—nearly a fourth of the members listing nicknames as their official names. And in terms of personal style, regional differences among candidates seem to have declined, with no recently elected southern senators wearing white linen suits and string ties.[34]

More serious is the fact that so many consultants stress personalities rather than issues. The previous chapter cited several of the many studies that show that voters can respond intelligently to issues, and the Patterson-McClure study cited earlier confirmed this. And as further evidence, Ronald Reagan was elected president using ads that presented issue positions, such as one in which he said:

> I didn't always agree with President Kennedy. But when his 30 percent federal tax cut became law, the economy did so well that every group in the country came out ahead. Even the government gained $54 billion in unexpected revenues. If I become President, we're going to try that again.[35]

Even those who differ profoundly with Reagan on the issues can recognize that such commercials did address policy questions, and did not rely primarily on Reagan's fabled personality. Moreover, there is evidence that voters are more prone to favor candidates who use issue commercials than those who stress image.[36] But despite such evidence, many consultants downplay the significance of issues. Here is a sample of their wisdom:

> Our studies show that there is no correlation between how the voter feels about an issue and the candidate of his choice.
> —John Deardourff, 1976 Ford consultant[37]

> I agree with what John says, and that is probably the last thing we will agree on for the rest of this campaign.
> —Gerald Rafshoon, 1976 Carter consultant[38]

> People don't vote on issues, they vote on trust.
> —Douglas Bailey, 1980 Baker consultant[39]

> Voters are really looking for character more than positions.
> —Peter Hart, Democratic pollster[40]

> In most elections, the issue isn't foreign policy or inflation. The issue is really the human being.
> —Robert Goodman, Republican consultant[41]

Too many good people have been defeated because they tried to substitute substance for style.

—Patrick Caddell, Democratic pollster[42]

Most issues today are so complicated, so difficult to understand, and to have opinions on that they either intimidate or, more often, bore the average voter.

—Harry Treleaven, Republican consultant[43]

I tell people I have no interest in goverment and don't know anything about it and they think I am joking, but I'm not.

—Joseph Napolitan, Democratic consultant[44]

Accompanying this lack of issue orientation sometimes is a pose of unsentimental toughness. Media consultant Gene Jones told Joe McGinniss, "For the money, I'd do it for almost anybody," and consultant Sanford Weiner acknowledged, "We have all, from time to time, represented clients whom we didn't particularly love, but who could help us pay the overhead."[45] As Professor Sabato put it, "They are businessmen, not ideologues."[46]

These last several quotations illuminate one of the most profound effects of the consultants, going far beyond the underplaying of campaign issues. In many ways, these consultants turn politics into a game without substance, and act as though there really were no difference between selling a candidate and selling soap. Napolitan is not the only consultant who expresses no interest in what politics is supposed to be about, that is, determining the policies of government,[47] and those who offer their services to almost anybody obviously see little advantage in one set of political principles over another.

Indeed, as perverse as it is, this is an appropriate way to run politics in a corporate capitalist system. Just like corporate leaders who are trained to look only at the "bottom line" and not at the social consequences of their actions, so do consultants become mesmerized with technique rather than with the real issues of politics. Although, as I stated above, most of them do set limits on the partisan or ideological characteristics of the candidates for whom they work, the fascination with technique is evident to anyone reading their books or interviews. Seldom does one of them say, "I'm really sorry that my candidate lost that election, because he/she had wonderful ideas about the issues." And in their war stories, there is remarkably little animosity toward the opposition. After all, how many soap companies get emotional about other soap companies?

In a variety of ways this elevation of technique over policy hurts the chances of the American political system's ever becoming anything but a prop for the corporate capitalist order. Just as specialization in the factory deprives the individual worker of any identification with the product on which one is working, specialization in campaigning alienates the consultant from the candidate, who is seen as just one product of many. Moreover, the candidate becomes alienated from oneself and comes to feel like a product. If you are Malcolm Wallop, you ride a horse because your consultant thought it would look good. What do you suppose Malcolm Wallop felt like as he made the other ad in which he had to ride a horse while carrying a portable toilet seat as a spoof on health and safety regulations?[48] Any candidate with a shred of self-respect is likely to react like John Anderson, who has called the process "dehumanizing."[49]

But besides the dehumanizing effects on consultants and candidates, perhaps the most serious consequences of all are for the people. As the political scientist David Lee Rosenbloom has argued, a system of campaigning based on professional consultants is one in which political power lies with a small group of expensive technicians, with the voter left to watch the ads passively.[50] Is it any wonder that turnout is declining, as politics is less and less oriented toward mass participation and more and more toward political consumerism? To the consultant, the best world is one in which the voter receives no information other than what the advertisements contain; to the corporate elites, this is ideal because the people will be increasingly conditioned to accept what is prepared for them. And if they become so cynical that they drop out of politics altogether, they will be even less of a threat to the status quo.

CAPITAL IN POLITICS

Media campaigns cost money, and no discussion of American political campaigns would be complete without considering the role of campaign contributions and spending. This is a lively and often controversial subject, and there are a few famous aphorisms about it. "The three most important things in politics," a prominent Republican senator once said, "are money, money, and money."[51] Said an equally prominent Democrat, "Money is the mother's milk of politics."[52] The problem with such glib remarks, however, is that they can obscure some of the important truths about money in American politics.

The role that money plays in campaigns is shaped by the capitalist context. This implies, first of all, that as with most other enterprises in American life, the role of government is minimal. Until a few years ago, the government did virtually no regulating of campaign spending, and its only important role was as regulator of the broadcasting industry and enforcer of such policies as the "equal time" doctrine that was supposed to protect all candidates' right to equal coverage. However, when it suited the interests of the major parties to exclude minor parties from participation in the 1960 presidential debates, that policy was suspended.[53]

In recent years, just as the capitalist state has bailed out weak corporations, it has also stepped in to give major parties and candidates much of their funding in presidential campaigns. Some states have followed suit in lower-level campaigns. The details and implications of the federal government's role in campaign financing will be explored below, but it is important to stress that just as the federal rescue of various corporations and banks leaves those firms essentially under private control, federal contributions are used by parties and candidates as they see fit. Most important of all, perhaps, is that these parties and candidates must purchase virtually all of their advertising. In Great Britain, by contrast, political advertising on television is forbidden, but each party is guaranteed free time on all stations.[54]

In the capitalist setting, where the government provides no aid for most offices and candidates need to buy all advertising, campaigns are expensive. The staggering cost of campaigning rises year after year. According to the nation's leading authority on the subject, Herbert Alexander, the cost of all American political campaigns at all levels in 1952 was $140 million; in 1980, it was $1.203 *billion*.[55] The skeptical reader will rightly observe that these figures overdramatize the increase, first, because the electorate has increased in size and therefore more money is needed to reach the voters, and second, because inflation has made the cost of *everything* rise. If we divide each year's total spending by the size of the electorate, and convert the result to constant 1967 dollars, we conclude that politicians in 1952 spent about 2.9 cents per voter, while in 1980 they spent 5.6 cents—nearly double the 1952 figure. And it should be noted that this rise *underdramatizes* the trend, because there were only thirteen gubernatorial elections in 1980, compared with the thirty in 1952.

To get a more focused look at this trend, we can observe the spending by major-party presidential campaigns after the conventions. We will not look at *all* presidential candidates, because if we did, the trend would be influenced by how many third-party and independent candidacies there were in a particular year; similarly, if we were to look at preconvention spending, the trend would be influenced by how many candidates were seeking their parties' nominations that year. With these stipulations, Table 8.1 shows the trend from 1948 to 1980, and it reveals that the major party candidates spent nearly seven times in 1972 what they had spent in 1948 on each voter. Since 1972, federal contributions to the parties have at least ostensibly kept spending down; but more on that later.

Notice from the table that there were three years in which spending per voter in 1967 dollars increased by at least a dime. The first year was 1952, when for the first time both parties invested substantially in television. The second was 1968, when the Republicans dramatically increased their television budget for the Nixon campaign, discussed earlier. The third was 1972, when spending on broadcasting actually declined while the use of other media, notably direct mail, rose sharply.[56] Clearly the rise in the cost of presidential campaigns can be attributed to the use of professional consultants and the techniques discussed earlier in this chapter.

Congressional campaigns have seen similar rises, presumably for similar reasons. In 1980, the total cost of Senate and House campaigns was

Table 8.1 Total cost of major-party presidential campaigns, general elections, 1948–1980.

Year	Total Cost, Current Dollars	Cost Per Voter	Cost Per Voter, 1967 Dollars
1948	$ 4,863,630	$ .10	$ .14
1952	$11,641,549	$ .19	$ .24
1956	$12,885,353	$ .21	$ .26
1960	$19,925,000	$ .29	$ .33
1964	$24,783,000	$ .35	$ .38
1968	$36,996,000	$ .51	$ .48
1972	$91,400,000	$1.18	$ .94
1976	$43,586,641	$ .53	$ .31
1980	$58,541,656	$ .68	$ .27

Source: Estimates of Herbert E. Alexander, compiled by Stephen J. Wayne, *The Road to the White House* (2nd edition: New York: St. Martin's Press, 1984), 29.

nearly a quarter of a billion dollars, which in 1967 dollars worked out to $1.12 per voter; the comparable figure for 1972 was only 68 cents. The average cost of a victorious Senate campaign in 1982 was more than $2 million; a successful House campaign cost about $250,000. In constant dollars, the cost of congressional campaigns in 1982 was more than double what it had been only eight years earlier.[57]

The implication of all this, of course, is that political candidates must either be wealthy themselves, or become dependent on well-heeled individuals or interest groups in order to raise enough capital to win high office. Seldom will lots of small contributions do it, and in order to reach the small contributors a candidate needs a sizable budget for media or direct mail. So much for the notion of equal access to such offices. There are always candidates who get there despite meager spending, but they are increasingly the exception.

The need for huge amounts of campaign capital implies in turn, that people will not reach positions of substantial political power unless they are minimally acceptable to groups and individuals with a big stake in the preservation of the system. Liberal candidates, often accused by their political foes of being farther to the left than they truly are, provide vivid examples. In recent years, liberal candidates including Eugene McCarthy in 1968, George McGovern in 1972, and John Anderson in 1980 relied upon wealthy individuals such as Stewart Mott, whose family controlled General Motors, Wall Street investment banker Donald Petrie, and California businessman Max Palevsky. In 1980, more than 40 percent of Edward Kennedy's presidential campaign contributions from individuals were in amounts of $500 and over.[58] Such contributions may well have reflected the fact that these candidates were not as threatening to the system as their critics suggested.

But it is not liberals who benefit most from a system based on the ability to pay to get one's message across. The party more closely tied to wealthy and corporate interests will be favored more in such a system, and in the United States that has been the Republican party. As campaign costs rise, the disparity between the parties' abilities to finance campaigns grows. Republican committees at all levels spent about twice as much as Democratic committees in 1976, three times as much in 1978, nearly five times as much in 1980, and well over five times as much in 1982: $214 million versus $40 million in 1982. The same kind of advantage accrues to nonparty groups. In the 1980 election, nonparty groups spent more than $13 million attacking Democrats or praising Republicans; nonparty groups taking the opposite view spent less than $200,000. Among ideological organizations, conservative groups spent more than $27 million in 1980, while liberal groups spent only $2 million. In 1984, more than 90 percent of the nonparty spending in the presidential race benefitted Reagan.[59] And so forth.

But these examples should serve a cautionary purpose, because despite the colorful comments about the role of money in politics, there are numerous examples of the fact that while it helps, it does not guarantee victory. After all, Republicans have traditionally raised more money than Democrats, but since 1930 the Democrats have won most elections. From the election of 1932 until presidential campaign spending was limited by legislation passed in 1974, there were eleven presidential campaigns; the candidate who spent more won only five of them.[60] At the beginning of the 1980 presidential campaign, John Connally raised more than any other Republican, and ended up winning exactly one delegate. The biggest congressional spenders in 1982, Minnesota Senate candidate Mark Dayton and New Jersey House candidate Adam Levin, both Democrats, lost their contests. At the beginning of the 1984 presidential campaign, the second most well-heeled Democrat was John Glenn, and fifth out of eight was Gary Hart; Glenn soon dropped out of sight, while Hart ran a strong race against Walter Mondale.[61]

Despite these examples, no campaigner would turn down an opportunity to raise more funds than his or her opponent. After all, the Democratic nominee in 1980, Jimmy Carter, was the biggest spender, as was Walter Mondale in 1984. Moreover, in 1982 the winner outspent the loser in nine out of the twelve closest U.S. Senate contests, and forty-six out of the seventy-six closest races for the U.S. House of Representatives.[62] Money may not guarantee victory, but everyone agrees that having it is preferable to the alternative.

"REFORMING" CAMPAIGN FINANCES

American political history has been filled with examples of the abuses of campaign funding. While candidates of both major parties have been guilty of those abuses, the all-time nadir was reached during the Nixon reelection campaign in 1972. That campaign was almost a textbook case study of how to expand the role of money in politics illegally, and space permits only a few illustrations.

When several Nixon campaign workers were arrested for breaking into Democratic national headquarters at the Watergate complex, they were carrying thousands of dollars from a bank account in Miami that was used to "launder" money, or serve as a repository of funds that had been passed through numerous other banks and individuals (some in Mexico).[63] The purpose of the "laundering" was to hide the identity of Nixon contributors, especially if the donation was intended to influence government policy (in other words, if it was a bribe), and conceal massive contributions to the Nixon campaign. Some Democratic contributors, moreover, would have been embarrassed if it were known that they were helping Nixon. One contributor, New York Yankees owner George Steinbrenner, was directed to give various amounts to committees with names like "Dedicated Americans for Government Reform" and "Loyal Americans for a Better America," which were fronts for the Nixon campaign. Moreover, Steinbrenner minimized his overt involvement by giving bonuses to business associates and having them donate an equal amount to Nixon. When all this was revealed, Steinbrenner was convicted of a felony and fined $15,000.[64]

Obscuring the sources of campaign money was nothing new in politics. Speaker Thomas "Tip" O'Neill once recalled a donors' breakfast for John Kennedy in Missouri during the 1960 presidential campaign. Kennedy and O'Neill collected $12,000 in cash and $17,000 in checks, and in the men's room Kennedy told O'Neill to give the checks to one of Kennedy's top aides and the cash to Kennedy himself. As Kennedy pocketed the money, O'Neill said, "Geez, this business is no different if you're running for ward leader or president of the United States."[65] There was a Kennedy family tradition of dealing with cash contributions casually; the president's father, Joseph, would collect anonymous donations for Franklin Roosevelt's 1932 presidential campaign and then write the campaign a check, implying that he had given all of the money.[66]

But the real concern about money in campaigns is that it is used to influence government policy. One of the contributors to the Miami bank account implicated in the Watergate affair received a bank charter from Nixon's Comptroller of the Currency; George Steinbrenner was trying to get a shipbuilding firm he owned out of an obligation to build a ship for the federal government, and also wanted Justice Department approval of a bid to purchase other businesses; International Telephone and Telegraph was accused of trying to influence antitrust policy when it offered to underwrite part of the cost of the 1972 Republican national convention; and ambassadorships have often gone to big party contributors including Ruth Farkas, who was appointed ambassador to Luxembourg by Nixon after giving his campaign $300,000 (most of it after the election was over).[67] One would-be donor to the 1972 presidential campaign of Democrat Edmund Muskie offered him $200,000 and said:

> You understand, there will be a quid pro quo. I want to be an American ambassador. Not a big country, you understand, not France or England. I couldn't afford those anyway. But can you give me a little one, Switzerland or Belgium?[68]

Muskie threw him out.

The revelation of such abuses led to a major overhaul of the government's role in presidential and congressional campaign finances, in the form of the 1974 amendments to the Federal Election Campaign Act of 1971. The law has since been amended further, and its contours were shaped significantly by a Supreme Court decision, Buckley v. Valeo.[69] The following is a brief summary of a complex set of laws and regulations:

Contribution limits

In order to prevent the recurrence of many of the above abuses, the law limits overt contributions that individuals and groups can give to candidates. Individuals may not donate more than $1,000 to any candidate for the presidency or Congress, or more than $25,000 to all candidates and committees in any year. As mentioned in chapter 4, the law authorizes businesses, labor unions, and other organizations to form "political action committees" (PACs) which solicit voluntary contributions for candidates from members of those groups. Individuals may donate up to $5,000 to a PAC, and PACs may give up to $5,000 per candidate, with no limit on total contributions by PACs. Individuals may also give up to $20,000 to a national party committee per year.

As the journalist Elizabeth Drew has pointed out, these limits can be easily and legally circumvented. Because they apply to the nominating process as well as to the election itself, an individual can give a candidate $1,000 for a primary, $1,000 for a primary runoff, $1,000 for a convention, and $1,000 for the fall campaign—up to $4,000 in all. The same kind of multiplier effect applies to PACs. Moreover, by donating to party committees and PACs that are known to favor a particular candidate, an individual may indirectly contribute up to $25,000 a year to that candidate. Candidates who want to get around these limits can set up their own personal PACs, which can be used to build their own careers by donating to other candidates. Among the politicians who have done so have been Ronald Reagan, Edward Kennedy, Walter Mondale, and Jack Kemp.[70]

But the most ingenious way around the law, Drew reports, is "soft money," money that the law allows state parties to spend on general campaign activities such as get-out-the-vote drives, ads directed toward state campaigns, and buttons and bumper stickers. Since state laws differ in their contribution limits, with some states not imposing any limits, a donor could give as much as he or she wants to a party by contributing to the party in a state without such limits. Indeed, some states even allow corporations and unions to spend money on parties and candidates directly out of corporate and union funds, which cannot be done legally on the federal level. The national parties, especially the Republicans, have coordinated these funds so that money raised in one state, legally under that state's laws, can be shipped to another state where that kind of fund-raising would have been illegal. As the deputy chairman of the Republican National Committee told Drew, "If Mobil Oil wanted to give you twenty million bucks, I think they could give you twenty million bucks, and you don't have to show it."[71] All these loopholes allowed brewer Joseph Coors and his family to donate almost $150,000 to the Republican cause in reported money alone, despite a federal law that suggests individual spending limits of $25,000 per year.[72]

Disclosure

In the belief that the exposure of corrupt influences is the best way to prevent such influences from arising, the law requires all contributions to candidates, parties and PACs over $200 to be reported and published. Perhaps the biggest loophole in this provision is "soft money" collected by state parties, which is not reported at the federal level even though its use will help federal campaigns. After all, when a state spends money in ads and souvenirs that tell voters to support that party, and engages in get-out-the-vote drives, it is helping presidential and congressional candidates of that party as well as state candidates.[73]

Matching funds, federal grants, and spending limits

Of all elections, the most substantially affected by the new system are presidential elections. Candidates who run for their party's presidential nomination are eligible for funds from the U.S. Treasury if they meet certain criteria designed to screen out fringe candidates. They must raise $250 in each of twenty states from small donors (those who have given $250 or less), for a total of $5,000, and then the government will match the first $250 of each contribution they receive from individuals. If they receive less than ten percent of the vote in two consecutive primaries, they receive no more matching funds until they start doing better. In 1984, Ronald Reagan and all eight Democratic candidates qualified for matching funds. Reagan received $10.1 million, Mondale $9.5 million, Hart $5.3 million, and Jackson $3.1 million.[74]

Those candidates who accept matching funds must also accept limits on how much they can spend in each state as they seek the nomination. In 1984, that limit was $20.2 million for the nation, plus another $4.04 million for fund-raising expenses, with state limits varying widely.[75] Candidates who do not accept the funds may spend as much as they can. In the past two elections, only Republican John Connally in 1980 refused the funds. Connally apparently believed that he could raise more than the federal limits, but this defiant gesture only confirmed his image as a well-heeled wheeler-dealer.

The law also provides money to the major parties to run their national conventions; in 1984 this amounted to $8.08 million per party. For the postconvention campaign, each major-party presidential candidate is given a huge federal grant, $40.4 million in 1984, and not allowed to accept contributions from individuals or PACs. This is intended to remove all private influences from the campaign; it also serves as a limitation on what candidates can spend. If a candidate other than the Democrat and Republican obtains more than 5 percent of the popular vote, he or she will receive some money—after the election. John Anderson did so in 1980, and received more than $4.2 million; Reagan and Carter had each been granted more than $29.4 upon receiving the nomination.[76]

The fund from which matching funds and convention and general election grants are derived comes from a check-off on federal income tax forms. Each taxpayer may check a box on Form 1040 to contribute one dollar to the fund. Checking it off does not increase an individual's taxes. In 1977, about 38 percent of the taxpayers checked the box, with wealthy people slightly more likely than others to do so.[77] Of course, anyone who contributes to the fund will see at least half of that dollar go to candidates whom he or she opposes. The tax code also encourages donations to political campaigns by allowing each taxpayer to deduct from his or her taxes half of all contributions up to $100. If in a presidential nominating campaign you give your favorite candidate $100, the candidate will get another $100 in matching funds and you will get half of your donation back when you file your income tax—thereby parlaying a net contribution of $50 into a $200 gift to your candidate.

Drew points out that many of the loopholes that make a mockery out of limits on contributions make presidential campaign spending limits equally misleading. Soft money, which is supposed to be spent only on state campaigns, has a spillover effect to the benefit of presidential campaigns as noted above. Some of the Republican television ads paid for in this way in 1982 even mentioned Ronald Reagan by name, and soft money paid for a new Republican national headquarters in 1980 and a new Democratic radio and television studio in 1982. According to Drew, the Republicans raised $9 million in reported soft money in 1980, compared with $1.6 million for the Democrats; and this does not include money unreported at the national level.[78]

Another loophole in the spending limits is the ability of "independent" committees to spend money in support of a candidate without affecting that candidate's spending totals. The Supreme Court allowed such committees on the theory that people should have the right to express their free speech by paying for ads backing the candidates they favor; in a capitalist society, freedom equals money. The stipulation is that such efforts must be truly independent of the candidate's campaign, lest these committees in reality be adjuncts to the campaign and a way around the spending limits. In 1980, as noted earlier, such committees spent $13 million in support of Republicans, and only $200 thousand backing Democrats. In 1982, these committees spent $5.2 million, mostly to elect Republicans. In 1984, they spent $23.4 million, and more than 90 percent of the presidential spending was pro-Reagan or anti-Mondale.[79]

Independent committees are a clever way around the law, because in most cases they are anything but separate from the official campaign. Two of the biggest such spenders in 1980 were headed by Republican senators, Jesse Helms of North Carolina and Harrison Schmitt of New Mexico; to assume that they had no contact with the Reagan campaign, whose head was Senator Paul Laxalt of Nevada, strains credulity. Organizers of "independent" committees freely acknowledged to Drew that much information passed between their organizations and the official campaign, either surreptitiously or through press accounts.[80]

These committees raise other problems as well. The chairman of the National Conservative PAC said in 1980, "A group like ours could lie through its teeth and the candidate it helps stays clean."[81] Indeed, in 1980 a group affiliated with that PAC ran an ad against Democratic Senator Frank Church of Idaho, alleging that he had weakened national defense by opposing the Titan missile; the truth was that Church had advocated a more effective replacement for the Titan.[82] Such tactics can prove embarrassing to the candidates the groups are trying to help. When Geraldine Ferraro's finances became an issue in 1984, that same group planned to film commercials of Anne Burford, former administrator of the Environmental Protection Agency, attacking Ferraro. This was contrary to the strategy of the Reagan campaign, which did not want to create a wave of sympathy for Ferraro or remind voters of the dismal environmental record of Burford, a former Reagan appointee.[83]

The Federal Election Commission

To administer this system, the law created an agency called the Federal Election Commission. Its six members, like most high federal officials, are appointed by the president and confirmed by the Senate.

EFFECTS OF THE SYSTEM

From the many loopholes in the law, including those mentioned above, we can begin to deduce the real effects of the legislation.

Symbolic victory

Many "reforms" in American politics have foundered to the extent that they ran into the assumptions of corporate capitalism. Since campaign financing is one important way in which businesses exert influence in politics, it should not be surprising that reform in this area has failed to rid the system of the corrupting influence of money. As the political scientist Larry Sabato put it, "Corporate money and all other special interest money has always found its way into the political system, and severe limitations on it will almost inevitably be frustrated."[84] Elizabeth Drew discusses how in 1981 both parties vied to use changes in the tax code to treat corporations better, partly in order to woo PAC contributions.[85] This influence is often insidious; instead of an outright bribe, the contribution is frequently used to give the lobbyist entry into the congressperson's office. One Democratic representative told Drew:

> The corruption and the evil is not only in people seeming to sell access or in some cases perhaps even their votes; it lies in the preoccupation of legislators, many of them very fine men and women, who have to spend a large part of their lives panhandling, going around to all these groups saying, "I would just love to have a check from you." That shouldn't be.[86]

Drew also points out how many of Ronald Reagan's appointees were fund-raisers in his 1980 campaign, including his Secretary of Labor, chairman of the Securities and Exchange Commission, and his ambassadors to Great Britain, Italy and Denmark.[87]

Some defenders of the system argue that these effects are exaggerated. Michael Malbin quotes one of the Democratic leaders in the house, Thomas Foley of Washington, as saying that "money follows votes and not the other way around.[88] In other words, a PAC gives money to a legislator only after the legislator has already decided to back that PAC's stands. But even if this is true, won't the *anticipation* of PAC money influence how that legislator votes? Malbin cites three academic studies that show that there was indeed a correlation between PAC contributions and how members of Congress had voted, and two other studies that found that PAC contributions influenced congressional votes, but were less influential than members' ideologies—which brings us back to the point that the anticipation of PAC money may influence members' ideologies as measured by their prior voting records.[89] Moreover, both Drew and Malbin provide quotations from members of Congress showing that they *perceive* that PACs are influential, and in politics the perception of power is itself a form of power.

This new system of regulating campaign finances may have been intended to limit or abolish the corrupting effects, and through matching funds and spending limits make it easier for poorly financed candidates to get started. Its most important effect, however, may have been to address the issue with symbolism while leaving its basic contours intact. This, too, is typical of American politics. As the political scientist Murray Edelman has written, we in the United States "routinely institutionalize our symbolic reassurances in the form of constitutional or statutory guarantees and in the creation of administrative organizations."[90] In other words, the Federal Election Commission as well as most other regulatory agencies have the primary aim of soothing the public's concern over corruption, and therefore legitimizing that continuing corruption.

The "incumbent protection act"

Some have argued that the new system also benefits incumbents. Indeed, PACs commonly support congressional incumbents more than challengers: in 1984, PACs gave nearly $75 million to incumbents, and only $17 million to their foes. It has been argued that being excluded from the fall presidential campaign has driven PACs into congressional campaigns: PAC donations to congressional campaigns increased from 1972 to 1980 more than two-and-a-half times in constant dollars. Moreover, argues the political scientist Gary Jacobson, any limitation on the availability of campaign funds works to the advantage of incumbents, since it is challengers who need to raise a lot of money in order to overcome the incumbents' visibility edge.[91] Given the loopholes itemized earlier, perhaps the law will never equalize campaign spending; but it is the incumbents who are especially likely to take advantage of those loopholes.

Guarding against third parties

Finally, the new system provides extra protections for the major parties. Non-major-party presidential candidates only receive federal money in the fall if they receive at least 5 percent of the popular vote; but how can they do so without enough money to get their message across? Anderson did get his money, but only after the election was over and it could not do him any good in the 1980 campaign. Ironically, the money could have been carried over into 1984 had Anderson chosen to run; but 1980 was the year in which he was eager to run and somewhat popular with the voters. The new system also hurts new parties by preventing their organizers from raising a lot of money from a few wealthy supporters.

In a variety of ways, the Federal Election Campaign Act as amended helps to perpetuate the current operations of the American political system. It makes a largely symbolic stab at reducing corruption, attempting to make people think that the problem has been dealt with while allowing it to flourish in new forms. It helps incumbent legislators win reelection and adds another nail to the coffin of would-be third parties. It is a fine example of how political "reform" ends up changing nothing essential to the functioning of the corporate capitalist order.

CAMPAIGN JOURNALISM

As important as a candidate's ads and the money behind them can be in influencing voters, most of the electorate's impressions of a campaign come from journalism. In recent years, there has been a fascination with the mass media, particularly television, and their impact on American politics. Scholars speak in hyperbolic terms: "Television is the new political god;" "Television is the most profound change that has occurred in all advanced industrial societies, including America, since the end of World War II;" "It is now the networks that act as the shadow cabinet."[92] It is claimed that Howard Baker was chosen minority leader of the Senate in 1977 because he is "photogenic," despite the fact that the majority leader chosen at the same time was the decidedly unphotogenic Robert Byrd.[93]

What has been the role of the news media in covering political campaigns in recent years? What impact have journalists had on the poltical process? How has the coverage affected the parties and the system as a whole?

The question of bias

For a number of years, conservatives have claimed to detect in television and much of the print media a clear bias toward liberals and Democrats. When the American people support liberal ideas and candidates, it is supposedly because they have been influenced by prejudicial reporting. Vice President Spiro Agnew voiced such suspicions in a couple of notorious speeches in 1969, and they have been picked up by many right-wing publicists.[94]

Is there any evidence of partisan bias in the news media? One attempt to answer this question involves taking surveys of journalists. One of the most extensive such studies, conducted in 1971, found that journalists are pretty reflective of the partisanship of other Americans, but those in the "elite press" were less likely to identify themselves as Republicans or conservatives. A study of newspaper reporters that was published in 1985 also found them to be less Republican and conservative than the population as a whole. Most studies of people working in the elite media, such as the three major broadcasting networks, *Time, Newsweek,* the *New York Times,* and the *Washington Post,* have likewise found them to be more likely than the average American to identify themselves as liberals and to vote Democratic.[95] However, the question remains as to what they mean by the term liberal. Walter Cronkite once defined himself as a liberal: "not bound by doctrines or committed to a point of view in advance."[96] Similarly, a *Newsweek* editor described his kind of liberal as "an open-minded, fair person, but also one who is bemused and ironic."[97] So "liberalism" may not mean ideology here, and the studies of journalists' views based on the closest observation conclude that they are rather middle-of-the-road.[98]

In the many attempts to test theories of liberal bias in the media, the strong conservative orientation of many of the most prominent journalists is often overlooked. Edwin Diamond observes:

> The most widely distributed syndicated columnists are conservatives James J. Kilpatrick (514 dailies) and George Will (375). . . . Elsewhere in print, the two biggest magazines are both conservative in their political outlook: *Readers' Digest* and *TV Guide*. So are the editorial pages of the two largest circulation papers in the country—the *Wall Street Journal* and the *New York Daily News*. Even in broadcasting, where liberal demons are said to infest the air, the conservative voice of Paul Harvey carries farther than any big-city, statist commentator.[99]

Moreover, the overwhelming majority of newspapers in the country endorse Republicans for the White House, with the only exception in history occurring in 1964. In 1984, for example, Reagan was endorsed by more than six times the number of papers that backed Mondale.[100] In 1981, Representative Jack Kemp, the Reagan loyalist, accurately observed of the publisher of the *New York Post*, "Rupert Murdoch used the editorial page, the front page and every other page necessary to elect Ronald Reagan President."[101]

Regardless of the personal views of reporters or publishers, is there much evidence of partisan bias in what is broadcast or published? The most exhaustive studies have been Richard Hofstetter's monitoring of the three major networks during the 1972 presidential campaign, and Michael Robinson and Margaret Sheehan's observation of CBS News and United Press International in 1980. Both measured how much coverage each candidate received, how many stories were favorable or unfavorable, and so forth. Such exercises can be deceptive, because events in the real world can be unfavorable to a candidate—questions of financial impropriety, a weak performance in a debate, a poor showing in the polls. If the coverage of such events therefore hurts that candidate, this might not reflect journalistic bias.[102] In any event, both campaign studies concluded that, in Hofstetter's words, "partisan bias was not a significant factor in news coverage."[103] In a follow-up study in 1984, Robinson concluded that "there is virtually no ideological bias on evening news. There is no partisan bias on evening news."[104] This should not be too surprising. After all, a reporter is trained to subdue his or her personal preferences when writing a story, and editorials can be confined to one page in a newspaper or one minute on the air. The public can rest assured; they are not being brainwashed by partisan bias in televised campaign coverage, or in the dispatches of UPI.

In recent years, in fact, there is some evidence that the public has perceived, if anything, a *Republican* bias in the news. Nineteen percent of the public in the mid-1980s saw their daily newspaper as too favorable toward Republicans, and only 12 percent saw a pro-Democratic slant. When asked if the media were making Reagan look better or worse than he really is, nearly twice as many said better as said worse, and for Jimmy Carter the ratio was three-to-one in the direction of making him look worse.[105]

Even when the news is slanted, its effects may not be as great as many fear. To begin with, there is the phenomenon of "selective perception," in which people tend to see only what confirms what they already believe. In a study of TV news in 1972, Thomas Patterson and Robert McClure found that, just as with the ads cited earlier in this chapter, people tended to see their favored candidate looking good and the opponent looking bad. In the 1976 presidential primaries, Patterson discovered that partisans were more likely to remember stories about their party's candidates than about the other party's and also that a candidate's supporters were more likely than his detractors to react favorably to stories about him. In studies of how newspaper endorsements affect voting, John Robinson found that in general, strong partisans and those who had made up their minds early were least affected by such cues.[106]

There is perhaps no better example of selective perception than how people respond to presidential debates. In 1984, for example, the CBS News/*New York Times* surveyers asked people which candidate had done the best job or won the first Reagan-Mondale debate. Respondents who were predisposed to support Reagan picked him as the winner of a 50-to-21 percent margin, while Mondale backers chose Mondale, 83 to 5 percent. The same kind of difference was seen in studies of the presidential debates in 1960, 1976, and 1980.[107]

Finally, it seems clear that for all the mystique of those who control the media, they have only a limited impact on the political process. No presidential candidate in recent years has enjoyed as favorable coverage as John Anderson did in the spring of 1980. According to Robinson and Sheehan, in March he received more time on CBS than any other candidate, despite the fact that he never won a primary. The massively favorable treatment even surprised the CBS reporter who was covering Anderson, and led to speculation that Walter Cronkite would be Anderson's running mate.[108] Despite this, Anderson continued to lose every primary in which he ran, and he finally dropped out of the Republican primaries in frustration—living proof of the limits of the power of the electronic media.

The structure of the media.

It would appear that television and other standard national news media play less of a role than is commonly supposed in persuading people to vote for one candidate or another. We would, however, be foolish were we to conclude from this that the media have no impact on American politics. The way to sketch this impact is to look not at overt signs of partisanship, but rather at the structure of the news media and what they are trying to accomplish.

Perhaps the most important fact to bear in mind about the mass media is that, like so much else in American life, they are big business. This means, first of all, that there is a high concentration of economic and social power in a small number of news institutions. More than nine out of ten viewers in the United States are covered by ABC, CBS, NBC and their affiliates. Ninety-nine out of hundred news outlets are fed by one or both of the major wire services, AP or UPI. Ninety-eight out of a hundred cities in the United States have only one daily newspaper, and nearly three-fourths of newspaper readers read papers that are part of large national chains. The number of daily papers has declined by 27 percent since 1920, and on a per-capita basis there are fewer dailies in the United States than in at least fourteen European (including some Communist) and five non-European comparable nations. All in all, twenty corporations now control most of the newspapers in America. The liberal capitalist vision of the nation's founders, in which many newspapers would carry many versions of the news and the enlightened citizenry would be able to construct a good picture of reality, has given way to the corporate capitalist reality of control of the media by a few. This trend has been increasing, and it is augmented by the fact that the boards of the major news outlets are often dominated by representatives of other large corporations.[109]

What does this imply about the gathering and dissemination of the news? Like any other large corporation, the typical news organization is run by the capitalist norms of competition and profit. Numerous students of the media have pointed out how pervasive is the spirit of competition, among the various media (newspaper reporters resenting "flashy" television journalists), among units within a medium (networks vying to be the first to "call" the election, reporters looking for a "scoop"), even among reporters within the same outfit.[110]

A personal experience is pertinent here. During the election of 1980, I was a survey consultant at CBS News. In the weekend before the election, CBS held a "rehearsal" to prepare for election night, and the climax of the occasion was a series of pep talks by network executives. The last to speak was Walter Cronkite, who was preparing for his last election as anchorman. The closing words of his pep talk were:

> On election night, whether the winner is the Gipper [Reagan], the Farmer [Carter], or the Spoiler [Anderson], the real winner will be the Eye.

The eye, of course, is the symbol of CBS, and in this way Cronkite was saying that the real contest of the evening was not who would be president, but which network would win.

Win what? As in any capitalist enterprise, the point is to win profits, and the primary way that a television network or newspaper obtains profits is to sell advertising time or space. In order to charge advertisers high rates, the media corporation must show them that their message will reach a lot of people, and on television this means high ratings. To view the news media as a public service is to miss what they themselves see as their main function—to advertise for profits.[111]

What impact do these facts of life have on the way in which news is presented? First, media corporations assume that most people have only a limited interest in hard news; this assumption fits the American political culture of low political involvement. Since hard news programs on TV are expected to draw small audiences, comparatively little time or money is put into them. The evening news, scheduled for only half an hour, shrinks to about twenty-two minutes after time for credits and ads are subtracted. This leaves a series of stories that average little more than a minute each, providing what Cronkite has referred to as a "headline service." As Walter Mondale put it during the 1984 campaign, "I get 45 seconds on the networks each night and Reagan gets 45 seconds."[112] Indeed, one network executive calculated that the text of one CBS broadcast would take up less than two columns of print in the *New York Times*. And a good deal of those twenty-two minutes is taken up with feature stories. This is the medium from which two-thirds of the American people get their news.[113]

There are other signs of the low priority put on the coverage of news on television. Low budgets mean that reporters are only stationed in a few metropolitan centers, which means that the news reported tends to come from only a few areas. Moreover, only a few predictable "newsmakers," notably government officials, are covered. Nor is there much money for documentaries to cover issues in depth, for research facilities, or for long stories about political campaigns. In 1985, the three major commercial networks produced among themselves only fourteen hours of documentaries. Most reporters are shunted about from beat to beat, with no time for specializing in a subject. And most of them do not see this as a serious problem. Nor are newspapers a vast improvement over the shallowness of television. When space devoted to ads, crossword puzzles, sports, comics, horoscopes and the like are factored out, the average newspaper has five pages of hard news out of sixty-six.[114]

When hard news is reported, the media tend to focus on what the corporation thinks will attract an audience, and that will be what is flashy: sensational crimes, natural disasters, celebrities. What can be shown with a vivid picture is valued over less animated stories, especially, of course, on television, but even in the print media. Edward Jay Epstein tells of a Republican governors' conference in which the newspaper coverage involved serious issues, but because there was no film of the issue discussions, NBC's story dealt only with the governors riding horses and wearing cowboy hats.[115]

Local television stations are often the worse offenders, peopled, as they are, by reporters with bland manners and an emphasis on "happy news." The *New York Times* summed it up with a headline about a local station in New York: "A New Approach At WCBS News: Emphasis On Reporting."[116]

What does all of this imply about the coverage of political campaigns? It means, first of all, that campaigns as "serious" news are likely to be underemphasized, and indeed there are few stories about campaigns compared with the remaining content of newspapers, magazines or television. For example, six urban California television stations devoted less than 2 percent of their time in the fall of 1974 to the state's gubernatorial campaign. A study of two major newspapers and the three major news magazines found that the number of stories about presidential campaigns declined from 1952 to 1980.[117] By 1984, the networks had reduced their coverage of the national party conventions to just a few hours, not wishing to sacrifice all of that big-audience prime time in which more popular shows could be broadcast. But the most widely commented upon effect of the search for audiences has to do with how campaigns are reported.

An illustration will be useful here. During the 1984 campaign, the *New York Times,* regarded as perhaps the most "serious" paper in the country, ran an article headlined "Ferraro Assails President's View of Nuclear War."[118] The first thirty-one lines of the story indeed dealt with that issue, but they were followed by sixty-eight lines about John Zaccaro's finances, and then by twenty-one lines about nonissue aspects of the campaign such as the size of the crowds Representative Ferraro was attracting. Roughly speaking, this is a good example of how American journalism covers campaigns:

1. *Downplay issues.* Jimmy Carter said in 1976 that "the traveling press have zero interest in any issue unless it's a matter of making a mistake."[119] A reporter who covered a congressional campaign in 1978 told researchers, "The straight issues are not good news because there's only one story in it, and it doesn't lead anywhere, or build any excitement"—in other words, readership.[120] Every study of the content of campaign coverage has found that only a small minority of stories or parts of stories deal with the issues; when issues are covered, they are generally dealt with only insofar as they involve the candidates directly, and only when there is a *new* issue position raised. And the situation is getting worse; Doris Graber found that the proportion of stories devoted to issues in presidential campaigns in the *New York Times* plummeted from 65 percent in 1968 to 35 percent in 1972 to 30 percent in 1976 to 18 percent in 1980.[121]

2. *Downplay parties.* In his study of journalists at CBS, NBC, *Newsweek* and *Time,* Herbert Gans concluded that their values were like those of the old Progressive movement discussed in chapter 6, and one of the central tenets of that movement was a revulsion toward parties. For whatever reason, parties are given short shrift by American journalism. In 1972, the networks dealt with parties in only a quarter of their stories, and the proportion of stories about

parties in major newspapers and new magazines has dropped sharply since 1952.[122]

3. *Stress personalities.* If issues and parties are downplayed, what is emphasized? As in all aspects of American journalism, there is a heavy stress on personalities, the more colorful the better. This was indeed the emphasis in the *Times* story about Ferraro, dominated despite its headline by news about her husband and their finances. Similarly, in the 1980 Robinson and Sheehan found 140 stories about Billy Carter, compared with nineteen on the Strategic Arms Limitation Treaty with the U.S.S.R. Nor do most Washington reporters see this as a serious problem. Again, the situation is getting worse, as the ratio of candidate-related stories to party-related stories has risen sharply since 1952.[123] The mad frenzy of American journalists to find colorful stories is captured in the commands of an NBC director to his camera crew during Jesse Jackson's speech at the 1984 Democratic national convention:

> Three, six, five! Hold it, nine! Go, baby go! O.K., get me a white face, get me a black face, good baby, good! O.K., hold it! Give me Julian Bond! . . . Oh yeah, yeah, yeah! Young people please, young people on everything but the far camera! This lady is good. Hold her.[124]

4. *Play up the horse race.* The subject that dominates campaign coverage is the race itself. As one media critic has put it, according to journalists "politics is essentially a game played by individual politicians for personal advancement, gain, or power."[125] Like most competitive games, the question is who wins and who loses, not what issues are at stake. The president of ABC News said in 1984, "I rarely root for teams; I root for close games."[126] The Washington journalist Charles Peters adds, "Above all else, I want the game to be interesting. And that is just what I think reporters want from a political campaign."[127] The majority of stories about campaigns are devoted to this aspect: who is ahead, who won the latest primary, and who is likely to win the race. It is as though the victory of a personality were all that is at stake—and often it is. Stories about the campaign itself, such as debates and the size of crowds, become the focus, and in 1980 CBS spent more time covering whether there would be any debates than covering the hostages in Tehran or the economy. Again, the trend is toward more and more emphasis on such topics.[128]

An ironic consequence of this is to distort the horse race itself by making too much of isolated events. There is a huge emphasis placed on early events such as the Iowa caucuses and the New Hampshire primary.[129] When George Bush beat Ronald Reagan in the 1980 Iowa caucuses by a couple of thousand votes, much of the press was set to award Bush the nomination. "Ronald Reagan is politically dead," said an NBC reporter; "Reagan does not look like he'll be on the Presidential stage much longer," agreed a *Boston Globe* colleague.[130] Four years later, when Gart Hart edged ahead of George McGovern by fewer than 1,500 votes in the same caucuses for a distant second-place finish to Walter Mondale, the press began to build up Hart and ignore McGovern. This coverage helped Hart win in New Hampshire and elsewhere in New England, when journalists began to sound a premature death knell for Mondale. *Newsweek* called him a "dethroned front runner," and the *New York Times* asked, "How could Mr. Mondale lose such a commanding lead so fast?"[131] In fact, at no time did Mondale ever lose his lead in delegates.

CONSEQUENCES OF CAMPAIGN JOURNALISM

What are the effects of this kind of campaign coverage on American politics? In a variety of ways, American journalism serves to perpetuate the corporate capitalist order. This is not because of any conspiracy to brainwash the public; it is a natural consequence of the patterns of behavior described above.

First, it is worth pointing out that for all the controversy over whether journalists are liberals or conservatives, the overriding fact is that they support the contours of the capitalist system. A survey of journalists at elite institutions found that large majorities agreed that "private enterprise is fair to workers" and that "less regulation of business is good for [the] USA," and equally large majorities disagreed that "big corporations should be publicly owned" or that "institutions need overhaul;" additionally, most cited a stable economy as the most important goal for the nation in the 1980s. In another study, Gans concluded that the values of journalists could be summed up as "ethnocentrism, altruistic democracy, responsible capitalism, small-town pastoralism, individualism, and moderatism," all supportive of the system.[132]

The "moderatism" that Gans cited is reflected in the journalistic belief that objectivity means a bland middle-of-the-road stance that is inherently biased against any political groups that want change. As the chairman of CBS once put it, "In this country play it down the middle."[133] Playing it down the middle means ignoring "inflammatory" speeches, as an NBC producer once directed his staff; it means not running stories hostile to business; it means relying on "official sources" and not dissidents; it means ignoring third-party candidates in campaign stories; and in the words of the Federal Communications Commission, which regulates broadcasters, it means that the "fairness doctrine" does not "make time available to Communists or to the Communist viewpoints."[134] This exclusion of ideas that are out of the mainstream reinforces the proclivity of Americans to shy away from noncapitalist ideas.

Some have accused the media of fostering disrespect for the system by focusing on scandals, from Chappaquiddick to Watergate to members of Congress accepting bribes from FBI informants. Journalists are notoriously cynical, and one scholar claims to have discovered that people who follow TV news are more cynical than those who do not.[135] However, such cynicism does not really threaten the political system. First, the message of scandals is that the system is fine, but not some of the people in it—if only they were apprehended, all would be fine. When Nixon resigned, Ford said, "Our long national nightmare is over;" but to critics of the system, replacing one president with another does nothing about the underlying problems of corporate capitalism. The second reason that media-fed cynicism does not threaten the system is that the normal response to cynicism is to drop out of politics altogether, which does not threaten anybody.

THE MISGUIDED ELECTORATE

This chapter began with a quotation from an eighteenth century politician who laid down some guidelines for voters in a liberal capitalist setting. Central to his theory was the ability of the voters to obtain information about the candidates and the issues. In recent years, we have seen how far the United States has moved from this idyllic picture of an informed citizenry.

We first observed the role of professional campaign consultants with their new campaign techniques. They have been responsible for much of the rising costs of campaigns, which has turned politics into big business affordable primarily by those with large budgets. Moreover, most of them have based their appeals on image gimmickry and the notion that the voter is a passive consumer. Then we studied the burgeoning costs of campaigns and recent legal changes which have had the effect of cementing the advantages of incumbents and major parties. Finally, we analyzed the role of the press, finding it highly centralized and doing a minimal job of bringing sophisticated analysis of campaign issues before the voters. All in all, we find candidates with great financial resources with an edge over those without, and voters without the means of, in Wilson's words, "making researches" into the electoral choice.

If this picture is ill suited to the liberal capitalist dream, it fits the corporate capitalist reality very well indeed. Were the media to present penetrating analyses of the political, social and economic system, and were the candidates to stress their stances on issues, and were dissident candidates to have access to the funds and the media exposure to compete on an equal footing, many voters might come to question the assumptions of the status quo. Better for the system that voters become passive and cynical.

It is important to emphasize that no claims of conspiracy are being advanced here. Campaign consultants and journalists are not plotting to preserve capitalism; consultants are trying to earn a living by winning elections, and journalists are trying to earn a living by giving the public what they think it wants, by adhering to such professional norms as "objectivity." In such indirect ways is the system reinforced, and if those professionals were ever to behave in ways that were threatening to the system, they would be stopped.

Finally, this discussion should round out our picture of both the American nonvoter and the American voter as presented in the previous chapter. We saw there an electorate in which half the people do not bother to vote, with the other half too often responding to less than serious considerations. We concluded that the people were merely responding to the nature of the political choices that candidates gave them. Now we can see how campaigns so often do little to encourage them to do otherwise. The mystery is that Americans so often continue to think of campaigns as opportunities for public education, rather than means to lull the populace into apathy.

Further Reading

The most recent comprehensive treatment of professional campaign consultants is Larry J. Sabato's *The Rise of Political Consultants* (New York: Basic Books, 1981). On campaign finance, the works of Herbert E. Alexander are regarded as definitive; see, for example, his *Financing the 1980 Election* (Lexington, Mass.: Lexington Books, 1983). Elizabeth Drew's *Politics and Money* (New York: Macmillan, 1983) is a fine piece of reporting that exposes the enormous loopholes in the Federal Election Campaign Act.

The best study of television journalism is Edward Jay Epstein's *News from Nowhere* (New York: Random House, 1973). Some media studies that more or less share the perspective of this book are Ben H. Bagdikian, *The Media Monopoly* (Boston: Beacon Press, 1983); Robert Cirino, *Don't Blame the People* (New York: Random House, 1971); Todd Gitlin, *The Whole World is Watching* (Berkeley and Los Angeles: Univ. of California Press, 1980); and David L. Paletz and Robert M. Entman, *Media Power Politics* (New York: The Free Press, 1981). For a delightful but ultimately disturbing account of what it is like to cover a presidential campaign, see Timothy Crouse, *The Boys on the Bus* (New York: Ballantine Books, 1974).

Notes

1. Robert Green McCloskey, ed., *The Works of James Wilson* (Cambridge: Harvard Univ. Press, 1967), II: 788.

2. *Time* Magazine, 30 October 1964, 27.

3. Quoted in James M. Perry, *The New Politics* (New York: Clarkson N. Potter, 1968), 16.

4. Louis Harris, "Polls and Politics in the United States," *Public Opinion Quarterly* XXVII (Spring 1963), 3–8.

5. The memorandum, dated August 1984, is reprinted in Peter Goldman and Tony Fuller, *The Quest for the Presidency 1984* (New York: Bantam Books, 1985), 417.

6. In Goldman and Fuller, *Quest for the Presidency,* 415.

7. In Goldman and Fuller, *Quest for the Presidency,* 415.

8. The text of the advertisements can be found in Larry J. Sabato, *The Rise of Political Consultants* (New York: Basic Books, 1981), 149.

9. Dan Nimmo, *The Political Persuaders* (Englewood Cliffs, N.J.: Prentice-Hall, 1970), 71.

10. Sidney Blumenthal, *The Permanent Campaign,* rev. ed. (New York: Simon & Schuster, 1982), 175–176.

11. Lewis Chester, Godfrey Hodgson, and Bruce Page, *An American Melodrama* (New York: Viking Press, 1969), 612–613.

12. Sabato, *Rise of Political Consultants,* 230.

13. In 1977, Viguerie claimed to have 30 million names, of whom 4.5 million had donated money; see Sabato, *Rise of Political Consultants,* 222. In 1980, he used the figure of 11 million; see Blumenthal, *Permanent Campaign,* 236. It is difficult to know how much exaggeration is involved here.

14. Quoted in Blumenthal, *Permanent Campaign,* 246.

15. On Whitaker and Baxter, see Stanley Kelley, Jr., *Professional Public Relations and Political Power* (Baltimore: The Johns Hopkins Press, 1956), and Nimmo, *Political Persuaders.*

16. Joseph Napolitan, *The Election Game* (Garden City, N.Y.: Doubleday, 1972), 112.

17. See, for example, Robert Agranoff's introduction to his edited volume, *The New Style in Election Campaigns* (Boston: Holbrook Press, 1972), 8–17.

18. Sabato, *Rise of Political Consultants,* 11.

19. Sabato, *Rise of Political Consultants,* 11.

20. See for example Napolitan, *Election Game.*

21. See, for example, Perry, *The New Politics,* and Blumenthal, *Permanent Campaign.*

22. Quoted in Sabato, *Rise of Political Consultants,* 21. See also Sabato, 13–23, and Agranoff, *New Style,* 21–22.

23. Joe McGinniss, *The Selling of the President* (New York: Trident Press, 1969).

24. Thomas E. Patterson and Robert D. McClure, *The Unseeing Eye* (New York: G. P. Putnam's Sons, 1976), 113.

25. Patterson and McClure, *The Unseeing Eye,* 114.

26. Patterson and McClure, *The Unseeing Eye,* 166.

27. See Nimmo, *Political Persuaders,* 197; Agranoff, *New Style,* 43–44; and Sabato, *Rise of Political Consultants,* 7, 287.

28. Martin P. Wattenberg, *The Decline of American Political Parties 1952–1980* (Cambridge: Harvard Univ. Press, 1984), 101–102.

29. See Kelley, *Professional Public Relations,* 216.

30. See Elizabeth Drew, *Politics and Money* (New York: Macmillan, 1983), chapters 5, 8; Larry Sabato, "Parties, PACs and Independent Groups," in Thomas E. Mann and Norman J. Ornstein, eds., *The American Elections of 1982* (Washington: American Enterprise Institute, 1983), 72–82; Gary C. Jacobson and Samuel Kernell, "Strategy and Choice in the 1982 Congressional Elections," *P.S.* XV (Summer 1982), 423–430; and articles in the *New York Times* dated 4 May 1982, p. A28, and 22 September 1983, p. B10.

31. Quoted in Drew, *Politics and Money,* 55; from "How Reaganites Push Reluctant Republicans To Back Tax-Rise Bill," the *Wall Street Journal,* 18 August 1982, p. 1.

32. Sabato, *Rise of Political Consultants,* 51–52.

33. See Nimmo, *Political Persuaders,* 194–195; Agranoff, *New Style,* 27–36; David Lee Rosenbloom, *The Election Men* (New York: Quadrangle Books, 1973), 166–167; and Sabato, *Rise of Political Consultants,* 7.

34. See Sabato, *Rise of Political Consultants,* 7, 311–312.

35. Quoted in Jeff Greenfield, *The Real Campaign* (New York: Summit Books, 1982), 142.

36. Lynda Lee Kaid and Keith R. Sanders, "Political Television Commercials," *Communication Research* V (January 1978), 57–70.

37. Quoted in "Ford and Carter Ad Consultants Call Short TV Commercials Best," the *New York Times,* 11 September 1976, p. 47.

38. Quoted in "Ford and Carter Ad Consultants," p. 47.

39. Quoted in "Baker's TV Drive Stresses Voters Can 'Trust' Him," the *New York Times,* 21 February 1980, p. B10.

40. Quoted in "Debate Will Focus on Noneconomic Matters," the *New York Times,* 5 October 1982, p. A24.

41. Quoted in Sabato, *Rise of Political Consultants,* 145.

42. Patrick H. Caddell, "Initial Working Paper on Political Strategy" (10 December 1976), 37. I am indebted to my colleague Everett Ladd for making it available to me.

43. Quoted in Rosenbloom, *Election Men,* 130.

44. Napolitan, *Election Game,* 130.

45. Quoted in, respectively, McGinniss, *Selling of the President,* 118, and Sabato, *Rise of Political Consultants,* 26.

46. Sabato, *Rise of Political Consultants,* 6.

47. For other examples, see Sabato, *Rise of Political Consultants,* 23.

48. See Sabato, *Rise of Political Consultants,* 149.

49. Quoted in Blumenthal, *Permanent Campaign,* 323.

50. Rosenbloom, *Election Men,* 163–168.

51. Senator Everett McKinley Dirksen of Illinois, quoted in Sabato, *Rise of Political Consultants,* 274.

52. California House Speaker Jesse Unruh, quoted in George Thayer, *Who Shakes the Money Tree?* (New York: Simon & Schuster, 1973), 208.

53. See Edward W. Chester, *Radio, Television and American Politics* (New York: Sheed and Ward, 1969).

54. Philip Norton, *The British Polity* (New York: Longman, 1984), 81.

55. Herbert E. Alexander, *Financing the 1980 Election* (Lexington, Mass.: Lexington Books, 1983), 103.

56. Herbert E. Alexander, *Financing Politics* (Washington: Congressional Quarterly Press, 1976), 26–34.

57. Alexander, *Financing the 1980 Election,* 117; and computations from data from Common Cause and the Federal Election Commission listed in the Appendices of Mann and Ornstein, eds., *American Elections of 1982.*

58. See G. William Domhoff, *Fat Cats and Democrats* (Englewood Cliffs, N.J.: Prentice Hall, 1972); David Nichols, *Financing Elections* (New York: New Viewpoints, 1974), chapter 5; Ronald Brownstein, "Republicans and Democrats Troop to Wall Street for Money and Support," *National Journal,* 4 February 1984, 210–214; and Alexander, *Financing the 1980 Election,* p. 234.

59. Mann and Ornstein, eds., *American Elections of 1982,* 189–191; Alexander, *Financing the 1980 Election,* 123, 129; and *Federal Election Commission Record,* October 1985, 7.

60. Alexander, *Financing Politics,* 20.

61. Alexander, *Financing the 1980 Election,* 193; Mann and Ornstein, eds., *American Elections of 1982,* 156–158; and Federal Election Commission, "FEC Reports on Financial Activity 1983–1984: Interim Report No. 1," dated March 1984.

62. See the Appendices in Mann and Ornstein, eds., *American Elections of 1982.*

63. Thayer, *Who Shakes the Money Tree?,* 110–111.

64. Jimmy Breslin, *How the Good Guys Finally Won* (New York: Ballantine Books, 1975), 16–22; and J. Anthony Lukas, *Nightmare* (New York: Viking Press, 1976), 127n.

65. Breslin, *How the Good Guys Finally Won*, 26–27.

66. Thayer, *Who Shakes the Money Tree?*, 157.

67. Thayer, *Who Shakes the Money Tree?*, 111, 115–116, 138–139; Breslin, *How the Good Guys Finally Won*, 16–22; and Lukas, *Nightmare*, 136–137.

68. Quoted in Thayer, *Who Shakes the Money Tree?*, p. 150

69. 424 U.S. 1 (1976).

70. Drew, *Politics and Money*, 12–13, 126–129.

71. Drew, *Politics and Money*, 16. See also 14–16, 104.

72. Drew, *Politics and Money*, 115–116.

73. Drew, *Politics and Money*, 17, 111.

74. *Congressional Quarterly Weekly Report*, 22 June 1985, 1215.

75. These and other data for 1984 are from the Federal Election Commission.

76. Alexander, *Financing the 1980 Election*, 299, 348.

77. Kim Quaile Hill, "Taxpayer Support for the Presidential Election Campaign Fund," *Social Science Quarterly* LXII (December 1981), 767–771.

78. Drew, *Politics and Money*, 14–17, 106, 142.

79. Sabato, "Parties, PACs, and Independent Groups," 99; and *Federal Election Commission Record*, October 1985, 5, 7.

80. Drew, *Politics and Money*, 134–145.

81. Quoted in Gary C. Jacobson, "Money in the 1980 and 1982 Congressional Elections," in Michael J. Malbin, ed., *Money and Politics in the United States* (Washington, D.C. and Chatham, N.J.: American Enterprise Institute and Chatham House Publishers, 1984), 54.

82. Sabato, *Rise of Political Consultants*, 283.

83. "Burford Joins Conservative Bid to Discredit Ferraro," the *New York Times*, 17 August 1984, p. A11.

84. Quoted in "Senators Weigh 'Cures' for the PAC 'Addiction,' " the *New York Times*, 3 February 1983, p. B6. For similar comments by defenders of the current system, see Michael Malbin, "The Problem of PAC-Journalism," *Public Opinion*, December/January 1983, 16; and Robert J. Samuelson, "The Campaign Reform Failure," *The New Republic*, 5 September 1983, 34–35.

85. Drew, *Politics and Money*, 38–52.

86. Representative Henry Reuss of Wisconsin, quoted in Drew, *Politics and Money*, 96.

87. Drew, *Politics and Money*, 120–124.

88. Quoted in Michael J. Malbin, "Looking Back at the Future of Campaign Finance Reform," in Malbin, ed., *Money and Politics*, 247.

89. Malbin, "Looking Back," notes 24–25.

90. Murray Edelman, *The Symbolic Uses of Politics* (Urbana, Ill.: Univ. of Illinois Press, 1964), 171.

91. Federal Election Commission press release dated 19 May 1985; Gary C. Jacobson, *Money in Congressional Elections* (New Haven: Yale Univ. Press, 1980), 76 and 194; and Alexander, *Financing the 1980 Election*, 127.

92. Respectively, William J. Crotty and Gary C. Jacobson, *American Parties in Decline* (Boston: Little, Brown, 1980), 67; Austin Ranney, *Channels of Power* (New York: Basic Books, 1983), 181; and Michael J. Robinson, "Television and American Politics: 1956–1976," *The Public Interest*, Summer 1977, 21.

93. Robinson, "Television and American Politics," 21. For a devastating critique from a fellow conservative, see George F. Will, "The Not-So-Mighty Tube," *Newsweek*, 8 August 1977, 84.

94. See, for example, Edith Efron, *The News Twisters* (Los Angeles: Nash Publishing, 1971); Kevin P. Phillips, *Mediacracy* (Garden City, N.Y.: Doubleday, 1975); and numerous publications of the American Enterprise Institute.

95. John W. C. Johnstone, Edward J. Slawski, and William W. Bowman, *The News People* (Urbana, Ill.: Univ. of Illinois Press, 1976), 92–93; MORI Research, Inc., *Journalists*

and Readers: Bridging the Credibility Gap (San Francisco: Associated Press Managing Editors Association, 1985), 45–46; Edward Jay Epstein, News from Nowhere (New York: Random House, 1973), 211, 222, 226; Stephen Hess, The Washington Reporters (Washington: The Brookings Institution, 1981), 87; S. Robert Lichter and Stanley Rothman, "Media and Business Elites," Public Opinion, October/November 1981, 43; and "Campaign Notes," the Washington Post, 11 April 1980, p. A3.

96. Quoted in Epstein, News from Nowhere, 214.

97. Quoted in Herbert J. Gans, Deciding What's News (New York: Random House, 1979), 197–198.

98. Epstein, News from Nowhere, chapter 7; and Gans, Deciding What's News, 68–69, 203–206, 211.

99. Edwin Diamond, "New Wrinkles on the Permanent Press," Public Opinion, April/May 1984, 4.

100. Editor and Publisher, 3 November 1984, 12.

101. "Ethics of Murdoch Papers Under Scrutiny as He Prepares to Buy London Times," the New York Times, 12 February 1981, p. B9.

102. For an example of this fallacy, see Michael Robinson, Maura Clancey, and Lisa Grand, "With Friends Like These . . ." Public Opinion, June/July 1983, 2–3, 53–54.

103. C. Richard Hofstetter, Bias in the News (Columbus: Ohio State Univ. Press, 1976), 187. See also Michael J. Robinson and Margaret A. Sheehan, Over the Wire and On TV (New York: Russell Sage Foundation, 1983), and Epstein, News from Nowhere, 234–236.

104. Michael J. Robinson, "The Media in Campaign '84," Public Opinion, February/March 1985, 48.

105. MORI Research, Journalists and Readers: Bridging the Credibility Gap, 28; and William Schneider and I. A. Lewis, "Views on the News," Public Opinion, August/September 1985, 11.

106. Patterson and McClure, The Unseeing Eye, 63–68; Thomas E. Patterson, The Mass Media Election (New York: Praeger Publishers, 1980), 78–79, 88; John P. Robinson, "Perceived Media Bias and the 1968 Vote," Journalism Quarterly XLIX (Summer 1972), 239–246; and John P. Robinson, "The Press as King-Maker," Journalism Quarterly LI (Winter 1974), 587–594, 606.

107. CBS News press release dated 7 October 1984. See also Sidney Kraus, ed., The Great Debates: Background, Perspective, Effects (Bloomington: Indiana Univ. Press, 1962); and Sidney Kraus, ed., The Great Debates: Carter vs. Ford, 1976 (Bloomington: Indiana Univ. Press, 1979).

108. See Robinson and Sheehan, Over the Wire, 81, 84, 88, 121–128; and Greenfield, The Real Campaign, 15–16.

109. Ranney, Channels of Power, 156–157; Doris A. Graber, Mass Media and American Politics (Washington: Congressional Quarterly Press, 1980), 35–36; and Ben H. Bagdikian, The Media Monopoly (Boston: Beacon Press, 1983), 4, 20–28, 121, 179, 205.

110. Epstein, News from Nowhere, 33–34; Joe Foote and Tony Rimmer, "The Ritual of Convention Coverage in 1980," in William C. Adams, ed., Television Coverage of the 1980 Presidential Campaign (Norwood, N.J.: Ablex Publishing Corp., 1983), 81–83; Gans, Deciding What's News, 176–179; and Robinson and Sheehan, Over the Wire, 221.

111. See Bagdikian, Media Monopoly; Epstein, News from Nowhere; Hofstetter, Bias in the News, 188; David L. Paletz and Robert M. Entman, Media Power Politics (New York: The Free Press, 1981), 10–13; and Robinson and Sheehan, Over the Wire, 220, 239.

112. Quoted in "Getting the Message," the New York Times, 8 September 1984, p. 5.

113. See Hofstetter, Bias in the News, 39; Patterson and McClure, The Unseeing Eye, 82–83; and Ranney, Channels of Power, 46.

114. See Epstein, News from Nowhere, 31–32, 102, 105–111, 127, 129, 133–151; Gans, Deciding What's News, 143–144, 215–216; Hess, Washington Reporters, 167; Robert C. Sahr, "Energy as a Non-Issue in 1980 Coverage," in Adams, ed., Television Coverage,

117–140; Bagdikian, *Media Monopoly,* 138; and "Network Documentaries an Endangered Species," the *New York Times,* 5 December 1985, p. C30.

115. Epstein, *News from Nowhere,* 38–39, 154–164, 172–180, 195–196; Gans, *Deciding What's News,* 157–160; and Patterson and McClure, *The Unseeing Eye,* 27–30, 88–90.

116. The *New York Times,* 6 February 1984, p. C17.

117. Paletz and Entman, *Media Power Politics,* 238; and Wattenberg, *Decline of American Political Parties,* 93. See also Peter Clarke and Susan H. Evans, *Covering Campaigns* (Stanford, Cal.: Stanford Univ. Press, 1983), 109; and Greenfield, *The Real Campaign,* 30–31.

118. 31 August 1984, p. A12.

119. Quoted in Sahr, "Energy as a Non-Issue," 135.

120. Quoted in Clarke and Evans, *Covering Campaigns,* 103.

121. Clarke and Evans, *Covering Campaigns,* 45; Graber, *Mass Media,* 169, 170, 173; Hofstetter, *Bias in the News,* 37, 96; Patterson, *Mass Media Election,* 40, 136–137, Patterson and McClure, *The Unseeing Eye,* 34, 36–40; Robinson and Sheehan, *Over the Wire,* 146; and William Crotty, *American Parties in Decline,* 2nd ed. (Boston: Little, Brown, 1984), 87.

122. Gans, *Deciding What's News,* 68–69, 203–206; Hofstetter, *Bias in the News,* 61; and Wattenberg, *Decline of American Political Parties,* 93–97. See also Ranney, *Channels of Power,* 52–54.

123. Clarke and Evans, *Covering Campaigns,* 41–42, 68, 71; Graber, *Mass Media,* 169; Robinson and Sheehan, *Over the Wire,* 57; Hess, *Washington Reporters,* 166; and Wattenberg, *Decline of American Political Parties,* 93–94.

124. Quoted in "Networks at Odds Over Convention Coverage," the *New York Times,* 20 July 1984, p. C24.

125. Paul H. Weaver, quoted in Ranney, *Channels of Power,* 55.

126. Roone Arledge, quoted in William Greider, "Terms of Endearment," *Rolling Stone,* 20 December 1984, 126.

127. Quoted in Robinson and Sheehan, *Over the Wire,* 109.

128. See Crotty, *American Parties,* 87; Foote and Rimmer, "Ritual of Convention Coverage," 85–87; Paletz and Entman, *Media Power Politics,* 35; Patterson, *Mass Media Election,* 24, 40, 45; Patterson and McClure, *The Unseeing Eye,* 41; Robinson and Sheehan, *Over the Wire,* 149, 209; and Graber, *Mass Media,* 179–183.

129. For evidence about the latter, see Donald R. Matthews, "Winnowing," in James David Barber, ed., *Race for the Presidency* (Englewood Cliffs, N.J.: Prentice-Hall, Inc., 1978), 65.

130. Quoted in Greenfield, *The Real Campaign,* 39, 41.

131. *Newsweek,* 19 March 1984, 23; and "The Mondale Mystery," the *New York Times,* 11 March 1984, sec. 4, p. 20.

132. Lichter and Rothman, "Media and Business Elites," 44, 59; and Gans, *Deciding What's News,* 42–52. The elite institutions studied by Lichter and Rothman included the *New York Times,* the *Washington Post,* the *Wall Street Journal, Time, Newsweek, U.S. News and World Report,* CBS, NBC, ABC, and PBS.

133. Quoted in Epstein, *News from Nowhere,* 169.

134. Epstein, *News from Nowhere,* 64, 192; Bagdikian, *Media Monopoly,* 181–183; Gans, *Deciding What's News,* 255–256; Hofstetter, *Bias in the News,* 13, 44; and Robinson and Sheehan, *Over the Wire,* 54–56, 73.

135. Michael J. Robinson, "Public Affairs Television and the Growth of Political Malaise," *American Political Science Review* LXX (June 1976), 409–432.

9

Parties in Congress

One of the major figures in the United States Senate in the middle of the twentieth century was Hubert H. Humphrey of Minnesota. In 1965, as vice president, Humphrey described what he saw as the role of Congress in American politics:

> Through reasonable discussion, through taking into account the views of many, Congress amends and refines legislative proposals so that once a law is passed it reflects the collective judgment of a diverse people.... It is a place where national objectives are sought—where Presidential programs are reviewed—where great societies are endlessly debated and implemented.... This is the essence of politics: to translate the concerns and the creative responses of a vast citizenry into effective and humane laws.[1]

Here is the liberal capitalist view of legislatures, institutions that face the critical issues of the day, take into account the opinions of the citizenry, and hammer out solutions.

In this view, political parties play a special role. They are supposed to serve as the mechanism by which the voters' views on the issues are transmitted to the legislature through elections. Within the Congress, parties can organize the members into majority and minority coalitions, each presenting a response to the issues, and on a particular subject a majority is formed around one of those responses, or a compromise between them. In particular, the majority party in each house has the responsibility of forging legislation.

The evidence presented in the preceding two chapters should already make you skeptical of the public's knowledge of, and participation in, great legislative undertakings. This chapter will argue that, whatever the degree of popular participation, members of Congress are geared toward other goals than the resolution of great issues. Furthermore, this is symptomatic of some of the deeper problems of legislatures in capitalist systems.

CONGRESSIONAL ELECTIONS

If Congress is truly responsive to the public will, then elections to it should be contested on the basis of the great issues of the day. When there is a liberal tide of public opinion, conservative members of Congress should be voted out of office, and when the trend is to the right, liberals should be ejected; this is what liberal capitalist theory would seem to imply. On the contrary, the overwhelming body of evidence suggests that the greatest success rate for congressional candidates consistently occurs not among liberals or conservatives, or Democrats or Republicans (despite the fact that the Democrats have controlled the House of Representatives for more than three decades, and the Senate for most of that period). The real winners of congressional elections are *incumbents*, those who already hold the seats at stake.

Consider the following facts about the House of Representatives, some of which are demonstrated in Table 9.1:

- In recent decades, more than nine out of ten members of the House have run for reelection.
- Of those House members who ran, nine out of ten won.
- Moreover, about three out of four House incumbents who run win with more than 60 percent of the vote.

Now consider these facts about the Senate, some of which are also shown in Table 9.1:

- In recent decades, about 85 percent of senators have sought reelection.
- The overwhelming majority of those running win: more than three out of four since 1956, and nine out of ten in 1982 and 1984.
- Nearly half of the Senate incumbents who run win with more than 60 percent of the vote.[2]

It is extremely important to bear in mind that this is a fairly recent development in American history. The best long-term indicators come in the House, which has always been popularly elected; senators have been popularly elected only since 1913. Here are some relevant indicators of the trend:

- From 1791 through 1899, the average election returned 55 percent of the members of the House; since 1950, the average has been 85 percent.
- From 1820 through 1900, about two-thirds of the members of the House ran for reelection; since 1950, more than nine out of ten have.

Table 9.1. Fate of incumbents in congressional elections, 1952–1984.

I. House of Representatives

| Years | Percent who ran for reelection | Of those who ran: | | |
		Defeated in primary	Defeated in November	Won reelection
1952–1960	93.2 %	1.4 %	6.3 %	92.2 %
1962–1970	93.9	2.1	6.4	91.5
1972–1980	90.1	1.7	5.9	92.3
1982–1984	92.9	1.6	5.6	92.7

II. Senate

| Years | Percent who ran for reelection | Of those who ran: | | |
		Defeated in primary	Defeated in November	Won reelection
1952–1960	84.7 %	2.5 %	20.1 %	77.3 %
1962–1970	89.3	6.6	12.6	80.8
1972–1980	78.7	8.1	24.2	67.7
1982–1984	89.4	0.0	8.5	91.5

Source: John F. Bibby, Thomas E. Mann, and Norman J. Ornstein, *Vital Statistics on Congress, 1980* (Washington: American Enterprise Institute, 1980), 14–15; and my calculations from the 1980–1984 elections.

· During the nineteenth century, about 18 percent of those House members running for reelection lost; since 1950, only about 7 percent have lost.
· While trends in the Senate since 1913 have not been as consistent as those in the House, it is worth noting that the high rate of senatorial reelection in 1982 produced the smallest turnover in the Senate since 1811.[3]

I could go on for a long time with such examples, but the point should be clear by now. Members of Congress, especially members of the House, are finding it easier than ever before to win reelection. To the defenders of the system, this might be interpreted as a healthy sign: people are increasingly satisfied with the quality of representation they are getting in Congress, and therefore they are returning their members of Congress to office by increasing margins. This explanation would make far more sense than it does were it not for the fact that numerous public opinion surveys show that the public holds Congress as a whole in low esteem. As the political scientist Richard Fenno put it so well, "If, as Ralph Nader says, Congress is 'the broken branch,' how come we love our congressmen so much?"[4]

Part of the answer to the question which has become known as "Fenno's paradox" lies in some of the advantages that incumbents derive from the electoral environment, and part of the answer comes from the behavior of members of Congress in their official duties. I shall deal with them separately, although it should be apparent that these two sets of factors are really interrelated.

The electoral environment

When the party organizations become weak, candidates must raise their own money and buy their own media time. In a number of respects, congressional incumbents benefit from these facts of life far more than most of the candidates who challenge them for reelection. For one thing, members of Congress are regarded by journalists as newsmakers, and they are covered accordingly. In the 1978 congressional races, for example, incumbents appeared in 96 percent of the newspaper articles about the campaign; challengers appeared in only 60 percent. More than 90 percent of newspaper editorial endorsements backed the incumbent over the challenger. This is a major reason that incumbents are better known than challengers—in 1978 more than twice the number of people remembered seeing the House incumbent on television or in the print media than remembered seeing the challenger, and a less sizeable advantage was enjoyed by Senate incumbents. This was undoubtedly a major reason that the House began to allow its floor proceedings to be televised several years ago. Small wonder that incumbents' names are usually far more familiar to voters than challengers' names. In an age of weak partisanship, this exposure gives incumbents an edge when the voter goes into the voting booth and, not wanting to rely on a party label for guidance, looks for a familiar name. Indeed, a CBS News/*New York Times* survey in the fall of 1984 found that 59 percent of the voters were unable to formulate a favorable or an unfavorable opinion of their representative, but of the remaining 41 percent, the overwhelming majority evaluated the representative favorably. This may be a politician's dream: not a lot of people follow what a representative is doing, but those who do are happy with what they see.[5]

Even if incumbent members of Congress did not benefit from all the free publicity that their office provides, they would have a leg up on their challengers in their ability to buy advertising time. In 1984, for example, incumbents were able to raise more than twice as much money as their challengers were, and political action committees (PACs) gave more than four times as much to incumbents as to challengers. There is little question that in most cases, the PACs are trying to secure influence with powerful members of Congress who are in a position to do them some good. Among the top six recipients of PAC money in House elections in 1982 were three committee chairmen (of Ways and Means, Budget, and Public Works), and the minority leader. In some cases, these incumbents did not need the money, as their seats were safe; the contributions were solely for the purpose of securing influence, not electoral support. As the political scientist Gary Jacobson has argued, the free publicity alone gives the incumbent so vast an advantage that the challenger would have to *outspend* his or her opponent in order to compete on an equal footing. Indeed, in 1978 and 1980, the average House incumbent who lost was outspent by his or her challenger. However, it is especially difficult for challengers to raise campaign funds, because people expect them to lose. Anyone seeking to buy influence on Capitol Hill wants to spend money only on winners. So the challengers are caught in a vicious cycle: they are unlikely to win unless they raise money, but they can't raise money because potential contributors don't expect them to win.[6]

Official behavior

The political scientist David Mayhew has written that "whether they are safe or marginal, cautious or audacious, congressmen must constantly engage in activities related to reelection." Moreover, writes Mayhew, "the organization of Congress meets remarkably well the electoral needs of its members."[7] As one representative told Fenno, "I've been in office nearly two years and I'm still campaigning. I'm still trying to please everyone, still running."[8]

What are the "activities related to reelection," and how is Congress organized to cater to them? Undoubtedly the most important, and the one around which all the others revolve, is personal services for constituents, or "casework." This is analogous to the machine favors we encountered in chapter 6. On the congressional level, casework may involve everything from helping a constituent get a tardy Social Security check, to sending new parents a federal pamphlet on baby care, to helping someone plan a vacation trip to Washington, to running an internship program for college students, to having a constituent's flag flown up the Capitol flagpole. All of these services are individualized, helping at most a few people at a time and not dealing with the problems of large groups, as major legislation does; all of these services are uncontroversial; and all can be distributed on a non-partisan basis. As such, they are as attractive to members of Congress as the Christmas turkey and the bucket of coal were to machine politicians, for nobody gets angry at a politician for distributing them. Indeed, assiduous attention to constituents has become the congressional norm, and the worst thing a member can do is to "lose touch with his or her district." As Speaker Thomas ("Tip") O'Neill was fond of saying, "All politics is local." A number of studies have concluded that casework can indeed help a member of Congress get reelected, especially by persuading the members of the opposition party that a representative is really all right despite his or her party.[9] Like machine favors, casework induces the voters to think that the purpose of politics is the pursuit of personal favors rather than the consideration of more serious matters such as broad issues or the functioning of the entire system.

In recent years, members of Congress have done everything they can to increase their ability to handle casework. Helping constitutents requires personnel, and in the quarter century from 1957 to 1981 senators and representatives more than tripled the size of their personal staffs, at taxpayer expense. (Their challengers, of course, do not have this advantage and must pay their staffs or rely on volunteers.) If the increased staff were used primarily to work on legislation, Humphrey's vision of Congress working on the issues of the day would be a realistic one. But the new staff, disproportionately situated in offices back in the member's district, busies itself primarily with casework. Even in Washington, more staff time is spent on casework than on legislation.[10]

Providing favors for constituents requires contacting them, and so the members of Congress provide themselves with free postage for official business and mass mailings. This privilege, which is, of course, denied to their electoral opponents, is called the "frank." In the mid-1950s, members of Congress sent out about 40 million pieces of franked mail per year; by the late 1970s, that figure was 400 million. Members who won their last election by narrow margins sent out nearly three times as much mail as those who held safe seats, and eight of the ten biggest per capita users of free mailing in the summer of 1985 were running for reelection the following year. Along with free postage, members of Congress receive office equipment, from word processing machines to computerized information services to the use of television and radio studios right in the Capitol. All of these are money-saving ways to keep track of casework and develop a favorable image with constituents. "Unsafe" members—those who won their seats by narrow margins—are especially likely to use computers. Finally, members of Congress have been increasing their travel allowances; from 1970 to 1976, they more than doubled the number of free trips back home.[11] In the words of one Representative,

> I came home every weekend. That's how I got reelected. The two previous congressmen moved their families to Washington and became congressmen. . . . Both were defeated after one term.[12]

This may be one of the primary reasons for the fact that the incumbency advantage has increased in the twentieth century. Much casework arises from the consequences of the growth of the federal bureaucracy; before there was a Social Security system, for example, there were no constituents worried about late Social Security checks. With the New Deal came new opportunities for members of Congress to serve constituents by being a link to the bureaucracy, or by explaining the system to the people back home. With increased federal grant programs in the 1960s came more ways for members to funnel aid to their districts.[13]

What could possibly be wrong with this increasing attention to the needs of constituents? The answer depends on how much one expects members of Congress to work on great issues, and dramatize them for the public. As one political scientist has put it, "As the federal role has expanded, congressmen have shifted emphasis from the controversial to the noncontroversial, from the programmatic to the nonprogrammatic." Another writes, "Clearly, the time that House members devote to constituent affairs reduces the attention they are able to give legislative business. In fact, a majority of House members see constituency work as interfering with their legislative responsibilities." Says one member of the House, "The frank and the technology together have turned most Congressional offices into full-time public-relations firms rather than offices that spend at least part of each day thinking seriously about serious issues." This is evidenced by the increasing unwillingness of members of Congress to serve on committees that deal with controversial subjects, such as Judiciary (which handles all constitutional amendments, including such hot potatoes as abortion, busing and the Equal Rights Amendment) and Education and Labor. A legislative body whose members shrink from controversy, fearing that they might alienate some voters, is scarcely worthy of the name. It must be acknowledged, however, that the public seems perfectly happy with this perversion of the legislative function. Surveys of attitudes toward members of the House of Representatives conducted in 1968 and 1977 found that respondents were far more likely to cite personal qualities and constituency service than policies, and policy positions were far more negatively regarded than personal qualities and constituency service. When a CBS News/*New York Times* survey asked respondents in 1982 whether they were more likely to vote for a congressional candidate who was more interested in casework or one who was more interested in major legislation, it found that casework was favored by a margin of 54 to 36 percent.[14] And the media sometimes encourage such behavior. When the representative from Hartford, Connecticut, died in 1981, his local newspaper began its editorial tribute as follows:

> A young professional man received a letter from U.S. Rep. William R. Cotter earlier this month wishing him well in his new job. The mother of a sick child was pleasantly surprised when she received a letter of sympathy and encouragement from Mr. Cotter, who apparently had read about the family's misfortune in a local newspaper. That was the essence of Bill Cotter, who died on Tuesday. . . . He prided himself in running a superb service-oriented staff in Washington and Hartford.[15]

In short, members of Congress keep getting reelected because they have turned Congress into a gigantic reelection machine, at some cost to its role as the developer of public policy. The significance of this is twofold. First, Congress becomes decreasingly likely to be interested in adopting public policies that might depart from the status quo. Policy is controversial, and change-oriented policy that much more so. Why endanger one's chances for reelection in this way? The second point is that, like the old machines, Congress socializes citizens into believing that the main role of their legislator is to provide individualized services rather than policies that affect entire classes of people. In this way it contributes to the depoliticization of the American citizenry, promoting the sense that politics is about self-interest rather than broader concerns.

THE CONGRESSIONAL POWER STRUCTURE

We might wonder whether, in its internal workings, Congress is led by effective political parties that raise great issues and dramatize their issue differences for the public. Here again, the answer is no, and the reasons tell us a great deal about popular government in a capitalist framework.

Choosing party leaders

Each party in each house of Congress has a hierarchical leadership structure that culminates in one person. The Senate has a majority leader and a minority leader, one for each party, and so does the House, but for the majority party in the House, the real leader is the Speaker. There are also assistant leaders of each party in each house, called "whips," and various assistant whips, regional whips, and heads of other party bodies. But real leadership within each party lies with the majority and minority leaders and the Speaker, all of whom are elected by their fellow party members in their house.

If Congress were primarily concerned with the issues of the day, then party leaders would be selected for their opinions on those issues and their ability to articulate those opinions and lead the party to carry them out. However, this is hardly the case. In 1962, for example, the Democrats in the House had a battle for majority leader between a certified liberal and supporter of the policies of the Kennedy Administration, Richard Bolling of Missouri, and a much less issue-oriented and more conservative Oklahoman, Carl Albert. Bolling attempted to win the post by stressing his allegiance to the principles of the national party, but he did so poorly against Albert that he withdrew from the campaign before the vote. In 1970, Senator Edward Kennedy of Massachusetts, whose very name epitomizes the national Democratic party, was deposed from the position of majority whip by Robert Byrd of West Virginia, a conservative who had fought vigorously against major civil rights legislation. In 1976, Byrd moved up to the post of majority leader despite the desire of Hubert Humphrey of Minnesota, another living symbol of the national party, to win that office. In 1976, there was a four-way fight for House majority leader, won by Jim Wright of Texas, easily the most conservative of the lot. On the Republican side, in 1969 and 1970 Senator Howard Baker of Tennessee, a conservative Republican, was twice defeated for the position of minority leader by Hugh Scott of Pennsylvania, a much less typical and more liberal Republican. And so on.[16]

My point is not that people who fit the party's national issue stance are automatically barred from leadership. After all, Baker did eventually become leader of the Senate Republicans, as did the equally conservative Robert Dole of Kansas, and Speaker Tip O'Neill was the most traditional of New Deal Democrats. But the cases cited above, and others, indicate that issue positions are hardly determinative of election to party leadership. In many cases, members of Congress want someone with whom they can get along, who has done them favors, and who has worked his or her way through the ranks. Such factors produce leaders who are often minimally interested in promoting particular issues. Even if they were, they would soon find that the need to mollify all wings of the party would put a crimp in their programmatic aspirations.

Other power centers

Once a person becomes a party leader, he—no woman has ever been considered seriously for a top party position in Congress—faces many constraints on his power. Some involve his relatively weak formal powers. Unlike leaders of some legislative bodies in other nations, he cannot discipline his members by depriving them of renomination by the party. Some party systems allow the leader to move members from one district to another, as though a recalcitrant Republican could be sent to Hawaii or a maverick Democrat to Utah; congressional leaders have no such power. Some legislative leaders, in state legislatures as well as abroad, have wide discretion as to who will chair various committees; congressional leaders must generally defer to the seniority system and give the chair to the member of the majority party who has served on the committee the longest. There have been a few exceptions in recent years, and I shall discuss them below.

If party leaders had complete control over who joins which committee, then they could maintain control over the functioning of those bodies. However, for the most part, the leaders are bound to the seniority system, which gives preference to legislators not on the basis of personal qualifications or, more important for our purposes, willingness to pursue party policy, but how long the legislator has served in the house. This is a pleasing system to most members, for it rids them of the controversies surrounding a more subjective choice. There may be a battle over who is a better Republican, Senator *A* or Senator *B*, or who is more qualified to serve on the Appropriations Committee, but there is no difference of opinion over who has been a senator longer. As one newly elected Republican senator said in 1981, "There's a great deal to be said for any set of objective rules. When it was over, nobody was mad at anybody else."[17] While this may keep the level of conflict down, it deprives party leaders of one of the most important decisions such leaders can make, who serves on which committee, and it is a prime reason for the uncoordinated nature of Congress.

Perhaps the most important constraint on the power of the congressional party leader is the committee structure. Unlike some legislative bodies, Congress organizes its committees by subject matter rather than by randomly assigning bills to various committees, the members of which are assumed to be generalists and capable of dealing with any subject. Congressional committees, dealing with such specialties as foreign affairs, agriculture, and the judiciary, are further divided into subcommittees which are even narrower in focus: African affairs, tobacco and peanuts, and civil rights. Every since a revolt in 1910 deprived the Speaker of his most autocratic powers, committees of the House have been very powerful, and subcommittees increasingly so; the same trend has been noted in the Senate. As the political scientist Arthur Maass has put it, "committees tend inevitably to lead Congress away from a concern for broad policy and general administrative performance . . . tend inevitably to challenge the President for control of the bureaus [in the executive branch] . . . [and] tend inevitably to challenge the whole House for control of the legislature's business."[18] In short, the committee system and the assignment process fragment Congress (and the executive branch) and render it less able to mount a sustained challenge to existing political relationships. Party leaders have a hard time coordinating policy-making.

In recent years, policy has devolved further to the subcommittees. In the two decades from 1955 to 1975, the number of Senate subcommittees shot up from 88 to 140, and House subcommittes rose from 83 to 151. Since then, the figures have dropped, especially in the Senate, and perhaps more important than the numbers are the effects of the so-called "subcommittee bill of rights" and other rules adopted by the House Democrats in the early 1970s. These include provisions to enable more representatives to become subcommittee chairs, allow committees to elect subcommittee chairs, guarantee subcommittee chairs the right to manage legislation reported out of their subcommittees, and provide staff for subcommittees.[19]

These trends further fragment Congress, for several reasons. One is that subcommittees have long been notorious for being targets of interest-group influence. Narrowly based groups such as tobacco growers have a small number (twelve in the House, in this example) of legislators who concentrate on their subject and who would be worth lobbying. Other members of Congress often defer to the views of that small number of legislators. Moreover, there is typically a bureaucratic agency that handles the same subject, and therefore a cozy three-way relationship can develop among interest group, subcommittee, and executive bureau.

How does this process work? The key actor here is the interest group, for it is the only element in the relationship that is not accountable directly or indirectly to the electorate. The interest group provides favors for the members of the subcommittee, but it is usually not what a cynical public suspects. As the vice president for governmental affairs at a large corporation has said,

> To a large extent, the three B's—booze, bribes, and broads—have disappeared. Not altogether, you understand. But today a good lobbyist must have the ability to draw up factual information—a lot of it—in a short period of time for people on [Capitol] hill who want it.[20]

The "information" may involve a draft of a speech for a sympathetic member of Congress, or suggested legislative language. Moreover, if out-and-out bribery is infrequent, there are more subtle inducements, such as campaign contributions and endorsements that urge constituents who belong to the interest group to support the member's reelection effort. In return, of course, the legislator supports the interest group's position.

Information is also the primary service that the interest group can provide for the bureaucratic agency. Moreover, the lobbyists can use their clout on the agency's behalf when communicating with members of Congress or, in some cases, with the president. In return, the agency will administer the law in the manner that the interest group desires. The third leg of this relationship is the tie between the congressional committee and the executive agency. The committee has power over the agency's legislative mandate—its powers, the size of its workforce, and its budget; the agency, on the other hand, has the ability to administer the laws on a day-to-day basis.

Often presidents and congressional leaders have little control over these relationships, which have been called "iron triangles," "unholy trinities," and "subgovernments."[21] Their effect is to help keep policy-making in Congress fragmented.

There are other ways in which the proliferation of subcommittees fragments the legislative process. Although Congress has never been tempted to alter the capitalist system in a fundamental way, there are times when it does seek to pass coherent legislation in a complex area of public policy. Such was the situation in energy policy in the late 1970s, when the fragmented nature of Congress rendered such legislation extremely difficult to coordinate, especially given the many subcommittees that had jurisdiction over part of the subject, their overlapping concerns, and the many interest groups involved. Further fragmenting is caused by the tendency of members of Congress to build personal coalitions to enhance their power. Perhaps the most notorious was Henry Waxman, a California Democrat who raised $40,000 for his colleagues during the 1978 elections and was then elected, over a more senior Democrat, to the chair of the Commerce Committee's Health and Environment Subcommittee.[22]

Finally, the vacuum that weak parties leave in Congress has been partially filled by other groups, notably caucuses of members united by ideological considerations (such as the liberal Democratic Study Group in the House), personal traits (caucuses for blacks and women in the House), regional common ground (southern or "frost belt" caucuses) or economic concerns (steel-producing districts). These provide not only another set of power bases with which party leaders must contend, but also, sometimes, a challenge to their authority.[23]

In such a setting, what does a party leader do in order to build a winning coalition? In the 1950s, Senate majority leader Lyndon Johnson adopted a strategy of building personal alliances around each issue, not with fellow Democrats alone, but with any senators he could persuade with an elaborate network of favors. The result was often legislation that was watered down and compromised away, and a process that did not present striking differences between the parties on issues. In 1957, for example, Johnson got a rather ineffectual civil rights bill passed due to a deal between Southerners who opposed the bill and Westerners who wanted a major water project. The Southerners voted for the water project, the Westerners supported an amendment that crippled the civil rights bill, and the Southerners agreed not to filibuster against the then-enfeebled civil rights bill. More recently, Democratic party leaders in the House have tried to woo members with individualized favors, in much the same way that members of Congress woo their constituents. This includes providing information, making campaign visits to members' districts, and offering choice committee assignments (when the seniority system permits). In energy and other areas, Speaker Tip O'Neill used special task forces as a way to coordinate activity while drawing in as many representatives as possible. In the long run, however, such techniques only cater to, and perpetuate, the fragmented nature of Congress.[24]

All in all, recent decades have witnessed the traditionally weak congressional parties becoming even weaker, and Congress becoming that much more difficult to coordinate. Members of Congress have become more and more like individual capitalist entrepreneurs, building their personal networks in order to secure their reelection at the expense of the policy-making role of the larger institution. Table 3.5 in chapter 3 shows that members are voting with their parties less frequently than they used to, and so far the evidence in this chapter is consistent with that trend. However, a complete picture must include the fact that the Speaker of the House did receive some new powers in the 1970s, notably increased control over who gets on the powerful Rules Committee (which decides on procedures for considering legislation) and the ability to name members of some other committees. In the early 1970s, House Democrats obtained the power to vote on who should be committee and subcommittee chairs, giving themselves the ability to break the seniority rule in favor of other considerations. In 1975, that power was exercised when three senior members were deposed from their committee chairs and two others from subcommittee chairs. Two years later, another subcommittee chair was ousted, and in 1979 three others. The criteria seemed to be that the legislators in question were mostly too conservative for their peers, and some ran their committees or subcommittees in too arbitrary a manner. There was an immediate effect on other conservative chairs, who began to vote in a more liberal direction.[25]

If these events were in keeping with a broader trend toward making members of Congress more accountable to their party, then very different conclusions could be drawn about the future of congressional parties. However, it may be that those who voted to depose the senior chairs were at least as concerned about having their toes stepped on by arbitrary committee autocrats as about whether those chairs were liberal enough for the Democratic party. In any case, these incidents stand out as exceptions to a general pattern of increasing fragmentation and individualism in Congress. This makes it far less likely than before that should it ever want to, Congress could mount an effective challenge to the socioeconomic order of corporate capitalism.

THE DECLINE OF CONGRESS

One of the major themes of congressional scholars in the twentieth century has been how much power Congress as a whole has lost to the executive branch. In the middle 1960s, the political scientist Samuel Huntington spoke for most when he wrote:

> Insulation [from the rest of the political system] has made Congress unwilling to initiate laws. Dispersion [of power within Congress] has made Congress unable to aggregate individual bills into a coherent legislative program. Constituent service and administrative overseeing have eaten into the time and energy which congressmen give legislative matters. Congress is thus left in its legislative dilemma where the assertion of power is almost equivalent to the obstruction of action.[26]

This twentieth century image of Congress is in direct contrast to its role in the nineteenth, when powerful legislators like Daniel Webster, Henry Clay, and John Calhoun debated the issues of the day and forged policies around them—Hubert Humphrey's ideal. In contrast, the great legislative strides of the twentieth century are nearly always the product of the executive branch, with Congress making only marginal adjustments.[27]

In the 1970s, after the rise of the so-called "imperial presidency,"[28] Congress attempted in numerous ways to reassert its role as a check on the executive branch. For example:

- With the help of the Supreme Court and its own Budget and Impoundment Control Act of 1974, it forbade the president from "impounding" funds, that is, refusing to spend money that it had appropriated;
- In the same act, it established a more integrated budgetary process, including a new Budget committee in each house and a Congressional Budget Office, in order to give Congress overall scrutiny of the president's budget;
- With the War Powers Act of 1973, it required the president to

report to Congress and seek its approval when committing combat troops abroad for any length of time;

- It developed a device called the "legislative veto" which enabled it to reject administrative regulations; and
- Most spectacularly, by threatening him with impeachment, it drove Richard Nixon out of office.[29]

After more than a decade of these practices, we can begin to evaluate their effectiveness in restoring Congress to its former glory. It seems fair to conclude that most of these developments have done little or nothing to change the supine posture of Congress when dealing with the executive branch. For example:

- The supposedly more integrated budgetary process did not prevent Ronald Reagan from manipulating the procedures to get the budget he wanted in 1981 or from gaining budget-cutting powers from the Gramm-Rudman Act of 1985;[30]
- The War Powers Act did not prevent Gerald Ford from using the military in the Mayaguez affair, Jimmy Carter from trying to rescue the hostages in Tehran by force, or Ronald Reagan from using troops in Lebanon and Grenada;[31]
- The legislative veto was itself vetoed by the Supreme Court in 1983;[32] and
- The expulsion of Richard Nixon did not confer any powers on Congress that it did not already have in the Constitution, and one presidential impeachment attempt per century is hardly a sign of congressional spunk. Indeed, the real significance of the Watergate affair may be how much presidential malfeasance must go on before Congress will bestir itself to act.

After the reforms of the 1970s, it is difficult to see any reason to change the assessment of one representative in 1973 that "we have seen congressional powers eroded and weakened over the years."[33] In fact, this long-term trend may provide one of the underlying reasons for congressional preoccupation with the reelection motive. In the nineteenth century, when Congress really did legislate, members would get caught on the wrong side of an issue and be thrown out of office by the voters, regardless of how hard they might have tried to hold their seat. As noted above, the percentage of House members defeated then was nearly three times what is has been since 1950. No longer do we see massive party shifts in the House of the proportions of 1874, when the Republicans lost ninety-six seats; 1890, when they lost eighty-five; 1894, when the Democrats lost 116; or 1932, when the Republicans lost 101. In recent decades, it has been easier to downplay the legislative function since Congress is not at the center of the policy-making process, and so other functions, such as constituent services, can be emphasized. This helps members get reelected;

in effect, the very decline in power of Congress as a whole has enabled its members to get reelected more easily, as they become less and less involved with *politics,* the framing of issues. Needless to say, this is a crude generalization; there are plenty of former members of Congress even today who were caught on the wrong side of a controversial issue. But this explanation may account for some of the change over time.

The final question of this chapter is, *why* has Congress lost the legislative momentum in the twentieth century? This question is usually answered in terms of "the rise of the modern presidency," but that is only a way of rephrasing the question: *why* has presidential power grown? Historians tend to date the rise in presidential power from the beginning of the twentieth century, the time when the rise of large corporations led to a massive reorientation of American party politics. That period also saw America's emergence as a military power, intervening in Latin America, China, and the Philippines. This suggests a connection between corporate capitalism and legislative decline. However, we would be wrong to see that decline as a purely American phenomenon, for most major capitalist nations have undergone the same trend.

In all the capitalist nations, there have been crises that have led to calls for the intervention of government. The massive depressions in the 1890s and the 1930s were the immediate cause of political transformations with the one in the 1930s leading to the watered-down version of the welfare state known as the New Deal. The decline, during the past couple of decades, in the performance of American capitalism, measured in such terms as corporate profits, unemployment, and inflation, has been on a long-term decline. The same is true in many other advanced capitalist nations. Such developments have led to cries for government policies to redress these problems. Some leaders, like Ronald Reagan, have looked to cuts in taxes, social programs, and regulation; others, including moderates in both parties, want an "industrial policy" in which an element of planning will be introduced to guide economic change; and some liberals have called for wage and price controls. The common element in all these programs is the need for some overall coordination of public policy, and it is clear, especially in recent years, that Congress is not the place to look for such coordination. Nor are legislatures in general.

The reasons for this have been established throughout this chapter. Members of Congress are too preoccupied with their own reelection either to devote the time it would take to analyze and try to solve these problems, or to advocate controversial solutions. Moreover, the very structure of Congress, with its emphasis on individual prerogatives, is poorly suited for coordinated action. Finally, Congress is too easily influenced by wellheeled private interest groups to be able to adopt policies that would seriously harm any of them. When Congress does enact policies of change, as it did in 1981, the initiative is invariably with the president, and before long the legislature reverts to its role as defender of the status quo—as it did in 1982. While Reagan won 82 percent of the congressional votes on which he took a stand in 1981, that figure dropped to 72, 67 and 66 percent in the following three years.[34]

Congress, then, perpetuates the corporate capitalist system in a variety of ways. With their emphasis on individualized benefits, members of Congress help to socialize the American people away from politics. With its internal lack of centralization, Congress is incapable of serving as an engine of social change. Its fragmentation also provides access for interest groups, which usually stand for the status quo. The only problem for the system is that this very ineffectiveness makes Congress a poor tool for coordinating *any* integrated policies, even those that would maintain the existing order by adapting to changes in the political, social and economic environment. Congress is becoming increasingly irrelevant to politics, and any action needed by either the defenders or the critics of the system requires the executive branch.

Given the weakness of political parties, this conclusion should not be surprising. Parties are supposedly the link between the mass of people and the government, and party weakness makes that linkage fairly meaningless. In similar terms, Congress is traditionally thought of, in James Madison's description of the House of Representatives, as "that branch of the federal government which ought to be dependent on the people alone."[35] This is because the House was the only part of that government directly elected by the people (a distinction shared by the Senate since 1913), and elections to it are more frequent than for any other part of the federal government. If the popular institution of party is weak, it stands to reason that the popular institution of Congress should be as well. In short, modern corporate capitalism needs the coordinating energies of government to preserve the socio-economic system, and leaving this task to popular institutions such as parties or legislatures would not only be inefficient, but potentially dangerous as well. What if the people, through parties and legislators, should choose policies which deliberately or inadvertently undermine the system? Instead, there is an increasing reliance on the institutions that are both more efficient and more insulated from electoral concerns, notably those of the executive branch. This does not mean that there has been a conspiracy to destroy the power of Congress, only that other power centers have not been concerned enough about the decline of congressional effectiveness to take the steps that would be necessary to reverse it. In the final analysis, capitalism is deemed too precious to be left to the mercy of democracy.

Further Reading

Congress is perhaps the institution of government that has been studied the most by American political scientists, and so the literature on it is massive. A fine collection of essays is *Congress Reconsidered,* 2nd ed. edited by Lawrence C. Dodd and Bruce I. Oppenheimer (Washington: Congressional Quarterly Press, 1981).

David R. Mayhew's *Congress: The Electoral Connection* (New Haven: Yale Univ. Press, 1974) has probably done more to impress upon scholars the role of the reelection motive than any other single work, and among the many good studies of congressional elections is Thomas E. Mann, *Unsafe At Any Margin* (Washington: American Enterprise Institute, 1978). Studies of leadership include Rowland Evans and Robert Novak, *Lyndon B. Johnson* (New York: New American Library, 1966), chapters 4–8, and Barbara Sinclair, *Majority Leadership in the U.S. House* (Baltimore: The Johns Hopkins Univ. Press, 1983).

Congress has always had its academic defenders, and vigorous defenses in recent years have included James L. Sundquist, *The Decline and Resurgence of Congress* (Washington: The Brookings Institution, 1981), and Arthur Maass, *Congress and the Common Good* (New York: Basic Books, 1983). A radical view, but one that differs sharply from mine, can be found in Philip Brenner, *The Limits and Possibilities of Congress* (New York: St. Martin's Press, 1983).

Notes

1. *Congressional Record,* 7 June 1965, 12763. Part of this quotation appears in Arthur Maass, *Congress and the Common Good* (New York: Basic Books, 1983), 11.

2. Sources of data are Norman J. Ornstein, Thomas E. Mann, Michael J. Malbin, and John F. Bibby, *Vital Statistics on Congress, 1982* (Washington: American Enterprise Institute, 1982), 46–48; Albert D. Cover and David R. Mayhew, "Congressional Dynamics and the Decline of Competitive Congressional Elections," in Lawrence C. Dodd and Bruce I. Oppenheimer, eds., *Congress Reconsidered,* 2nd edition (Washington: Congressional Quarterly Press, 1981), 63–64 and my updates of both sources through 1984.

3. Besides those cited in the preceding note, the sources are Nelson W. Polsby, "The Institutionalization of the U.S. House of Representatives," *American Political Science Review* LXII (March 1968), 146; Samuel Kernell, "Toward Understanding 19th Century Congressional Careers," *American Journal of Political Science* XXI (November 1977), 684; John R. Hibbing, *Choosing to Leave* (Washington: University Press of America, 1982), 102; and John R. Alford and John R. Hibbing, "Incumbency Advantage in the Senate and in Congress" (unpublished paper).

4. Fenno's essay with this title appears in Norman Ornstein, ed., *Congress in Change* (New York: Praeger Publishers, 1975), 277–287.

5. Peter Clarke and Susan H. Evans, *Covering Campaigns* (Stanford, Calif.: Stanford Univ. Press, 1983), 43, 74; Thomas Mann and Raymond Wolfinger, "Candidates and Parties in Congressional Elections," *American Political Science Review* LXXIV (September 1980), 627; Gary C. Jacobson, *Money in Congressional Elections* (New Haven: Yale Univ. Press, 1980), 17; and CBS News press release dated 6 October 1984.

6. Federal Election Commission press release dated 16 May 1985; William Crotty, *American Parties in Decline,* 2nd ed. (Boston: Little, Brown, 1984), 135, 137; Jacobson, *Money in Congressional Elections,* 76, 194; and Ornstein *et. al.,* Vital Statistics, 64–65.

7. David R. Mayhew, *Congress: The Electoral Connection* (New Haven: Yale Univ. Press, 1974), 49, 81.

8. Quoted in Richard F. Fenno, Jr., *Home Style* (Boston: Little, Brown, 1978), 180.

9. Morris P. Fiorina, "Some Problems in Assessing the Effects of Resource Allocation in Congressional Elections," *American Journal of Political Science* XXV (August 1981), 543–567; Diana Evans Yiannakis, "The Grateful Electorate," *American Journal of Political Science* XXV (August 1981), 568–580; Albert D. Cover and Bruce S. Brumberg, "Baby Books

and Ballots," *American Political Science Review* LXXVI (June 1982), 347–359; and Bruce E. Cain, John A. Ferejohn, and Morris P. Fiorina, "The Constituency Basis of the Personal Vote for U.S. House of Representatives and British Members of Parliament," *American Political Science Review* LXXVIII (March 1984), 110–125. For a contrary view, see John R. Johannes and John C. McAdams, "The Congressional Incumbency Effect," *American Journal of Political Science* XXV (August 1981), 512–542. Whether or not casework is effective in attracting votes, most members of Congress *think* it is, and act accordingly.

10. Ornstein *et al., Vital Statistics,* 110, 112; and Steven H. Schiff and Steven S. Smith, "Generational Change and the Allocation of Staff in the U.S. Congress," *Legislative Studies Quarterly* VIII (August 1983), 464. On staff in general, see Michael J. Malbin, *Unelected Representatives* (New York: Basic Books, 1980).

11. Ornstein *et al., Vital Statistics,* 140; Albert D. Cover, "Contacting Congressional Constituents," *American Journal of Political Science* XXIV (February 1980), 129; *The New York Times,* 15 December 1985, sec. 4, p. 4; Stephen E. Frantzich, "Computerized Information Technology in the U.S. House of Representatives," *Legislative Studies Quarterly* IV (May 1979), 262–263, 271; Austin Ranney, *Channels of Power* (New York: Basic Books, 1983), 117–118; and Glenn R. Parker, "Cycles in Congressional District Attention," *Journal of Politics* XLII (May 1980), 543.

12. Quoted in Fenno, *Home Style,* 40.

13. See also Morris P. Fiorina, *Congress: Keystone of the Washington Establishment* (New Haven: Yale Univ. Press, 1977), and, for an early example, Robert A. Caro, *The Years of Lyndon Johnson: The Path to Power* (New York: Alfred A. Knopf, 1982), chapter 14.

14. Morris P. Fiorina, "The Case of the Vanishing Marginals," *American Political Science Review* LXXI (March 1977), 181; Glenn R. Parker, "Sources of Change in Congressional District Attentiveness," *American Journal of Political Science* XXIV (February 1980), 123; Representative Patricia Schroeder, Democrat of Colorado, quoted in David Burnham, "Congress' Computer Subsidy," *The New York Times Magazine,* 2 November 1980, 98; Bruce A. Ray, "Committee Attractiveness in the U.S. House, 1963–1981," *American Journal of Political Science* XXVI (August 1982), 609–613; Lynette P. Perkins, "Member Recruitment to a Mixed Goal Committee," *Journal of Politics* XLIII (May 1981), 348–364; Glenn R. Parker and Roger H. Davidson, "Why Do Americans Love Their Congressmen So Much More Than Their Congress?" *Legislative Studies Quarterly* IV (February 1979), 53–61; and CBS News press release dated October 1982, 7.

15. "The End of a Political Era," *Hartford Courant,* 10 September 1981, p. A26.

16. See Nelson W. Polsby, "Two Strategies of Influence," in Robert L. Peabody and Nelson W. Polsby, eds., *New Perspectives on the House of Representatives,* 2nd ed. (Chicago: Rand McNally, 1969), 325–358; and Robert L. Peabody, *Leadership in Congress* (Boston: Little, Brown, 1976), 391–441.

17. Senator Slade Gorton, Republican of Washington, quoted in Martin Tolchin, "Congress Plays Party Games by Committee," the *New York Times,* 25 January 1981, sec. 4, p. 5.

18. Maass, *Congress and the Common Good,* 41–42.

19. Ornstein *et al., Vital Statistics,* 98–99; and Steven H. Haeberle, "The Institutionalization of the Subcommittee in the United States House of Representatives," *Journal of Politics* XL (November 1978), 1054–1065.

20. Quoted in Kay Lehman Schlozman and John T. Tierney, "More of the Same: Pressure Group Activity in a Decade of Change," *Journal of Politics* XLV (May 1983), 365.

21. These relationships are discussed further in Henry S. Kariel, *The Decline of American Pluralism* (Stanford, Calif.: Stanford Univ. Press, 1961); Grant McConnell, *Private Power and American Democracy* (New York: Alfred A. Knopf, 1966); and Theodore J. Lowi, *The End of Liberalism* (New York: W. W. Norton, 1969). See also chapter 4 of this book.

22. Bruce I. Oppenheimer, "Policy Effects of U.S. House Reform," *Legislative Studies Quarterly* V (February 1980), 5–30; and Elizabeth Drew, *Politics and Money* (New York: Macmillan, 1983), 70.

23. See Arthur G. Stevens, Jr., Arthur H. Miller, and Thomas E. Mann, "Mobilization of Liberal Strength in the House, 1955–1970," *American Political Science Review* LXVIII (June 1974), 667–681; and Arthur G. Stevens, Jr., Daniel P. Mulhollan, and Paul S. Rundquist, "U.S. Congressional Structure and Representation," *Legislative Studies Quarterly* VI (August 1981), 415–437.

24. Rowland Evans and Robert Novak, *Lyndon B. Johnson* (New York: New American Library, 1966), chapters 4–8; Louis P. Westefield, "Majority Party Leadership and the Committee System in the House of Representatives," *American Political Science Review* LXVIII (December 1974), 1593–1604; Barbara Sinclair, "The Speaker's Task Force in the Post-Reform House of Representatives," *American Political Science Review* LXXV (June 1981), 397–410; and Barbara Sinclair, "Majority Party Leadership Strategies for Coping with the New U.S. House," *Legislative Studies Quarterly* VI (August 1981), 391–414.

25. Sara Brandes Cook and John R. Hibbing, "Congressional Reform and Party Discipline," *British Journal of Political Science* XV (January 1985), 73–92.

26. Samuel P. Huntington, "Congressional Responses to the Twentieth Century," in David B. Truman, eds. *The Congress and America's Future* (Englewood Cliffs, N.J.: Prentice-Hall, 1965), 26.

27. For a contrary (and minority) viewpoint, see Ronald C. Moe and Steven C. Teel, "Congress as Policy-Maker," *Political Science Quarterly* LXXXV (September 1970), 443–470.

28. See Arthur M. Schlesinger, Jr., *The Imperial Presidency* (Boston: Houghton Mifflin, 1973).

29. For a fairly optimistic review of these developments, see James L. Sundquist, *The Decline and Resurgence of Congress* (Washington: The Brookings Institution, 1981).

30. See Lance T. LeLoup, "After the Blitz: Reagan and the U.S. Congressional Budget Process," *Legislative Studies Quarterly* VII (August 1982), 321–339; and Theodore J. Lowi, *The Personal President* (Ithaca, N.Y.: Cornell Univ. Press, 1985), 185–188.

31. See Lowi, *The Personal President*, pp. 183–185.

32. Immigration and Naturalization Service v. Chadha, 103 S. Ct. 2764 (1983).

33. Representative Joe Evins, Democrat of Tennessee, quoted in Sundquist, *Decline and Resurgence*, 5. A good overview of the reforms is Philip Brenner's *The Limits and Possibilities of Congress* (New York: St. Martin's Press, 1983), chapter 6.

34. *Congressional Quarterly Weekly Report*, 27 October 1984, 2802. For a general discussion of these themes by radical authors, see David A. Gold, Clarence Y. H. Lo, and Erik Olin Wright, "Recent Developments in Marxist Theories of the Capitalist State, Part 2", *Monthly Review* XXVII (November 1975), 50; C. B. Macpherson, *The Life and Times of Liberal Democracy* (New York: Oxford Univ. Press, 1977) 67–69; Ernest Mandel, *Late Capitalism*, trans. Joris DeBres (London: Verso Editions, 1978), 482, 489–490; Nicos Poulantzas, *Political Power and Social Classes*, trans. Timothy O'Hagan (London: New Left Books, 1973), 315; Nicos Poulantzas, *State, Power, Socialism*, trans. Patrick Camiller (London: New Left Books, 1978), 221–228, 238; Goran Therborn, *What Does the Ruling Class Do When It Rules?* (London: New Left Books, 1978), 88–89; and Alan Wolfe, *The Limits of Legitimacy* (New York: The Free Press, 1977), 184.

35. *Federalist* number 52, p. 326 in the edition by Clinton Rossiter (New York: New American Library, 1961).

10

Presidential Elections

In 1788, Alexander Hamilton defended the system outlined in the Constitution for choosing the president by arguing that "this process of election affords a moral certainty that the office of President will seldom fall to the lot of any man who is not in an eminent degree endowed with the requisite qualifications." He went on to deny that "talents for low intrigue, and the little arts of popularity," or what we would call demagoguery, would ever reach the highest executive office in the land.[1]

To a generation that has known Richard Nixon, among other questionable chief executives, Hamilton's "moral certainty" may seem rather naive. Much of this book has already placed in doubt the ability of the American electoral process to produce the wisest and most farsighted leadership for *any* high office. Candidates who stage media campaigns backed by lavish contributions face voters who have been socialized away from serious political concerns; who would expect such a system to produce the best executive talent?

The concern of this chapter is not with elections in general, but rather with the unique process by which Americans select their president. As with any other partisan office, choosing a president is a two-stage affair in which first the parties nominate their candidates, and then the electorate as a whole decides between them. Unlike that for any other office, however, the nominating process is extremely complex because states vary widely in the way in which they choose delegates to the national party conventions; unique, too, is the final election, which involves not a direct vote by the electorate, but an "electoral college" whose choice can be (but rarely is) different from that of the plurality of voters. We shall examine each of these two processes in turn. Since much of the postnomination phase is similar to other elections as described above in chapters 7 and 8, the bulk of this chapter will address the nominating stage. This examination will show that that process has been dominated in recent decades by the kind of progressivism described in chapter 6, and has provided an arena for middle-class activists.

FROM SMOKE-FILLED ROOMS TO WIDE-OPEN RACES

The Democratic and Republican parties nominate their presidential and vice presidential candidates at national conventions held during the summer of presidential election years. Ever since the 1920s, the party of the incumbent president has held its convention later than the other party's. Each state, and various nonstate areas such as the District of Columbia and Puerto Rico, send a predetermined number of delegates to the convention. In the case of states, the number of delegates is determined by a formula based partly on that state's population and partly on how well the party is doing there.

Each state can determine, within national party rules, how its delegates to the national convention are to be chosen. In recent years, most delegates have been chosen in *primaries* in which all of the voters who identify with a party go to the polls and choose from among the various presidential hopefuls. In the Democratic contest in 1984, for example, twenty-three states used primaries, including most of the states with large populations; 61 percent of the delegates came from the primary states. The other twenty-seven states used *caucuses,* meetings open to party members; 37 percent of the delegates came from those states.

In recent years, conventions have been conducted over a four-day period. The keynote address, a highly partisan speech, is delivered on Monday night, usually by a well-known party orator; for example, New York's Governor Mario Cuomo was the keynote speaker at the 1984 Democratic convention. On Monday convention business is also attended to, including electing officers, adopting the rules, and deciding which delegates have the proper credentials. All of these matters can lead to battles between candidates, like the fight at the 1980 Democratic convention over whether the rules should allow delegates to vote for any candidate, even if they had pledged to vote for someone else. This rule was favored by Massachusetts Senator Edward Kennedy and opposed by President Jimmy Carter, and when the Carter forces won the fight, Kennedy dropped out of the race.

Tuesday night is usually spent adopting the *platform,* a lengthy statement of the party's stands on issues, and disputes may arise over its planks. This can also be a forum for fighting among candidates. On Wednesday night, the names of the various presidential contenders are placed in nomination with lengthy speeches by their supporters, and finally the balloting produces a winner. Thursday night features a similar process for the vice presidential nomination, nearly always someone hand-picked by the presidential nominee. The convention ends with acceptance speeches by first the vice presidential and then the presidential nominee.

How do candidates win presidential nominations at national party conventions? This is a complicated question to answer, as the process has changed fundamentally over the years. Consider these famous conventions of the distant past:

- In 1860, the Republican party convened in Chicago to nominate its presidential candidate. Twelve men representing the pivotal states of Illinois, Indiana, New Jersey, and Pennsylvania assembled in a room to see if they could unite against the leading candidate, the controversial Senator William Seward of New York. After four hours of negotiating, a poll was taken, and former Representative Abraham Lincoln of Illinois came in first. All of the states involved agreed to cast their votes for Lincoln, and no later than the second ballot. When Pennsylvania held out for the position of secretary of the treasury for its "favorite son," Simon Cameron, Lincoln's campaign managers promised to get every Illinois delegate to urge Lincoln to appoint Cameron to the job and to let Cameron's campaign manager speak to Lincoln personally. Although Seward was ahead of Lincoln on the first ballot, the rail-splitter nearly caught up on the second and was nominated on the third. When Lincoln won the presidency later that year, Simon Cameron was appointed secretary of war.[2]
- Baltimore was the scene of the Democratic national convention in 1912, and by the tenth ballot House Speaker James "Champ" Clark had won a majority of votes. Unfortunately for Clark, the Democrats at that time required that the nominee receive not just a majority but two-thirds of the votes, which Clark did not have, and on the forty-third ballot the nomination was won by Governor Woodrow Wilson of New Jersey. According to a leading authority on that era, Wilson's victory was made possible by a series of deals made between his managers and the leaders of various state delegations. The price of securing Indiana's votes was to make its governor, Thomas Marshall, the vice presidential nominee.[3]
- The Republicans returned to Chicago in 1920, and there were several candidates who had sizable blocs of votes. However, none of them was nominated; instead, the convention followed the scenario outlined earlier to reporters by the campaign manager for one of the less prominent candidates, Warren G. Harding of Ohio:

> I don't expect Senator Harding to be nominated on the first, second, or third ballot, but I think about eleven minutes after two o'clock on Friday morning of the convention, when fifteen or twenty men, bleary-eyed and perspiring profusely from the heat, are sitting around a table some one of them will say: "Who will we nominate?" At that decisive time the friends of Senator Harding can suggest him and can afford to abide by the result. I don't know but what I might suggest him myself.

In the words of another Harding crony, "In plain vernacular, you are to be nominated by fifteen or twenty bosses." And that is exactly what happened on the tenth ballot.[4]

· The 1932 Democratic convention was held in Chicago, and the "front-runner" was Governor Franklin D. Roosevelt of New York. Although Roosevelt had a majority of the votes on the first two ballots, the Democrats' two-thirds rule threatened to send him the way of Champ Clark in 1912. Through such go-betweens as the powerful publisher William Randolph Hearst, who feared the nomination of some of Roosevelt's rivals more than he loved Roosevelt, and Joseph P. Kennedy, a Roosevelt ally and Hearst business partner, a deal was worked out: Speaker John Nance Garner would release his Texas and California delegates to vote for Roosevelt, and Garner would receive the vice presidential nomination. The California delegates entrusted all their votes to a three-person committee which chose Roosevelt, and he and Garner were nominated.[5]

Now consider these more recent conventions and how they were decided:

· In 1964 the Republicans convened in San Francisco. Arizona Senator Barry Goldwater's right-wing appeal had netted him most of the delegates through primaries in which he was unopposed and through caucuses and state conventions in which his followers seized control from traditional party elites. The only fully contested primary which Goldwater had won, California, drove his major competitor, New York's Governor Nelson Rockefeller, out of the race. By the time the convention opened, Goldwater's only serious opponent was a late entrant, Pennsylvania's Governor William Scranton. The Goldwater forces completely controlled the convention, easily turning back a more liberal substitute to the civil rights plank in the platform and shouting down Rockefeller when he addressed the convention. The Arizonan secured an easy first-ballot victory.[6]

· Emerging from a hard-fought series of primaries, the Democrats assembled in Miami Beach in 1972. Running in opposition to the continuing war in Southeast Asia and with unusually liberal policy positions, South Dakota's Senator George McGovern had won a series of primaries and driven most of his serious rivals from the race. Only Senator Henry Jackson of Washington and Governor George Wallace of Alabama remained with sizable blocs of delegates, and they were beaten in a test vote on whether McGovern should be allowed to claim all of California's delegates because he had won that state's "winner-take-all" primary. Once the South Dakotan had won that vote, and therefore all of California's delegates, it was clear that he would cruise to an easy first-ballot victory.[7]

· Kansas City was the site of the 1976 Republican national convention, a battle between incumbent President Gerald Ford and former Governor Ronald Reagan of California, who claimed that Ford was insufficiently conservative. The delegate hunt had given Ford a slight edge which Reagan hoped to overcome by announcing his choice of Pennsylvania's Senator Richard Schweiker as his running mate. The first vote of the convention was an attempt to change the rules and force Ford to announce *his* vice presidential choice, but the Ford forces beat back the challenge. Ford, who was nominated with only fifty-seven votes more than he needed to win, let the Reagan forces write the platform and consulted Reagan himself on the vice presidential nomination.[8]

· In 1984 the Democrats met in San Francisco after a sometimes close race between former Vice President Walter Mondale and Senator Gary Hart of Colorado, with Chicago civil rights leader Jesse Jackson winning a significant bloc of delegates. By the time of the convention, Hart and Jackson had adjusted to the inevitability of the Mondale nomination, and there was not even any mystery over the vice presidential nomination because of Mondale's earlier selection of Representative Geraldine Ferraro of New York. Several contests over the platform did not mar the harmonious mood, and the convention was used to spotlight party orators who included New York's Governor Mario Cuomo and Senator Edward Kennedy of Massachusetts as well as the various candidates.

If we compare the conventions of the distant past with those of the recent past, we can see several dramatic differences. Perhaps most important is the changing role of party leaders. Long ago many key delegations were controlled by a small number of party leaders, who could move delegates around like pawns from one candidate to another. Nominations would be decided by negotiations among the leaders over such matters as high-level appointments, including the vice presidency. In order to manipulate the situation most effectively, these state and local party leaders could tie up conventions for long periods of time by "freezing" their delegates behind secondary or minor candidates called "favorite sons." All of this is in keeping with the picture drawn in chapter 6 of powerful party leaders controlling the political activities of their underlings by the shrewd use of patronage.

Today party "leaders" lead precious little. A Goldwater or McGovern can ride to victory over the opposition of the party establishment. A Ford or Mondale backed by party elites can win, but must do so the hard way— by winning delegates. Each man came close to losing the nomination to a maverick of the Goldwater-McGovern stripe. No longer pawns, delegates go to the convention uncontrolled by anyone or anything other than their own preference for a candidate. When asked if he could tell his supporters to switch to another candidate, Arizona's Representative Morris Udall said in 1976, "If I gathered them together in a room and said, 'Dear friends, we're now going for so-and-so', they would be throwing things at me."[9] In 1984, despite the almost total lack of support for Gary Hart by party elites, the Coloradan won nearly as many votes in the primaries as Walter Mondale did. In 1976 nearly every Republican governor endorsed Gerald Ford, but nearly half the delegates were Ronald Reagan's.

As a consequence of these developments, conventions no longer determine nominations. Instead, nominations are decided in the delegate-selection process. Candidates arrive at conventions with enough votes to secure first-ballot nominations, and therefore old-style bargaining never has a chance to occur. (The most recent convention to take longer than one ballot to name a president was in 1952.) The Federal Election Campaign Act denies matching funds to candidates who do poorly in a series of primaries, and so they drop out of the race early, like John Glenn and Alan Cranston in 1984. Other candidates try to trip the front-runner with votes on the platform, rules, or delegate credentials, but they never succeed. As a *New York Times* reporter has put is, delegates "come to the convention simply to be unwrapped and counted." Or as a Republican politician said in 1980, "You could have these conventions by mail."[10]

If we can summarize these changes in a couple of phrases, candidates used to be supplicants, seeking the good will of party leaders; today, candidates (like the members of Congress we encountered in the previous chapter) are like capitalist entrepreneurs, each building his or her personal coalition and competing against all others in a struggle for the favors of an impersonal mass, the party activists.[11]

How has this change affected the kinds of people who are nominated? In the distant past, party leaders were looking first for a winner, or at least someone who would run well at the top of the ticket. Another important criterion was the nominee's reliability, the willingness to cooperate with the bosses over patronage and other concerns. Finally, they wanted someone who was "available," or, in the special meaning of this word, who fit everyone's image of what a president looked like. As political scientist Clinton Rossiter wrote in the 1950s:

> He ought not to be: from a state smaller than Kentucky, divorced, a bachelor, a Catholic, a former Catholic, a corporation president, a twice-defeated candidate for the Presidency, an intellectual, even if blooded in the political wars, a professional soldier, a professional politician, conspicuously rich.
>
> He almost certainly cannot be: a Southerner . . ., of Polish, Italian, or Slavic stock, a union official, an ordained minister.
>
> He cannot be, according to unwritten law: a Negro, a Jew, an Oriental, a woman, an atheist, a freak.[12]

There were also stereotypical sources of nominees, notably governors of large states; former governors occupied the White House for all except eighteen of the sixty-eight years from 1877 to 1945.

Today, while it would be wrong to claim that all of the old prejudices have died, clearly a number have. No longer are Roman Catholics handicapped in the race; Goldwater and McGovern were from states "smaller than Kentucky"; in 1980, Ronald Reagan broke the anti-divorce taboo; and Jimmy Carter buried the southern jinx. Other serious candidates who violated old taboos have included bachelor Jerry Brown, Polish-American Edmund Muskie, and black minister Jesse Jackson. Times have changed also with respect to the offices that nominees hold; while *former* governors Carter and Reagan have won nominations, no sitting governor has been nominated since 1952. From what kinds of offices do nominees come?

Perhaps the key to answering this question is to remember that no longer do nominations go to reluctant candidates. In 1952 the Republicans chose Dwight Eisenhower, who did not even announce his party affiliation until early that year, and the Democrats selected Adlai Stevenson, who had never expressed interest in the nomination. In recent years, nominees have been those who have fought hard for the nomination, for they have been unable to rely on party leaders' handing it to them. Nominees McGovern, Carter, Ford, and Mondale each publicly announced his candidacy more than a year before the opening of the national convention, and each had been working for the nomination even earlier. Early announcements are due in part to the Federal Election Campaign Act, described in chapter 8. A candidate can neither raise money nor receive federal matching funds without formally registering his or her candidacy with the Federal Election Commission. As a result, those who hold time-consuming jobs (besides the presidency itself), such as congressional leaders and incumbent governors, are impeded in their quest for the White House. Senate Majority Leader Howard Baker, who began to wonder in 1980 "if one has to be unemployed to run for President," left the Senate in 1984 in order to run for president in 1988.[13] Indeed, everyone who has been elected president since the mid-1960s has been out of a job at the time he was first elected.

So powerful is the outdated image of how conventions used to be conducted that many scholars, journalists and politicians assume that the nominating process is unchanged. Anticipating his presidential bid for 1984, Senator Alan Cranston of California decided to try to appeal to "key Democratic leaders" rather than campaign among the masses; columnists Mary McGrory and David Broder argued that New York's governor Mario Cuomo would compel his delegation to vote for whomever he supported; some New York Democrats wanted to make Cuomo or Senator Daniel Patrick Moynihan the state's "favorite son" in order to keep votes away from the major contenders; and columnist James Kilpatrick foresaw the convention turning to "dark horse" Edward Kennedy.[14] Of course, Cranston's strategy failed abysmally; Cuomo was able to lead a

Mondale delegation to the national convention only because Walter Mondale won the New York primary, and not because of Cuomo's muscle; there were no "favorite sons" (or daughters) in the presidential race; and there was no chance that an unannounced candidate like Kennedy would be tapped. In an earlier era, all of these hunches would have been plausible; today, they are anachronistic.

CAUSES AND CONSEQUENCES

Why did the presidential nominating process change so dramatically? Some attribute the transformation primarily to the changes in the rules that were described in chapter 6. They argue that some of the new rules have made it more difficult for party leaders to maintain their old control over the process. For example, rules that mandate adequate representation of women, young people and racial minority groups, as well as proportional representation of all candidates' supporters, limit the degree to which party leaders can control who goes to the convention. A similar argument contends that the dramatic growth in the number of primaries has had the same effect. Primaries selected barely more than a third of the delegates in 1968, but by 1980 they chose three-quarters. (Since 1980 they have declined, but not nearly to the levels of the 1960s.) It has been argued that primaries take delegate selection out of the hands of party leaders and give it to the party masses.[15]

My view is different. The decline in the power of party leaders at national conventions is part of the general pattern of party decline that we have seen throughout this book, and the trend began long before the Democrats began to rewrite the rules or primaries began to proliferate. The Goldwater nomination preceded these more recent developments, as did the nominations of Wendell Willkie (by the Republicans in 1940), Dwight Eisenhower (Republican, 1952) and John Kennedy (Democrat, 1960), all of whom had to engage in guerrilla operations like Goldwater's to work against or around party leaders who opposed their candidacies. Moreover, just as the new rules did not create the new system, newer rules have failed to restore leaders to their prior positions of power. While the Democrats successfully brought many party leaders back to the 1984 convention, their presence did not prevent insurgents Hart and Jackson from securing more than 40 percent of the delegates. The new style of national convention is a result of longstanding changes in American parties, and not the consequence of changes in the formal rules. Increasing the number of party "leaders" at the convention is like bringing back knights in armor in an age of gunpowder.[16]

In this decentralized nominating system, what factors help candidates get nominated? In contrast to an earlier age, we can see several particularly important kinds of appeals:

- While controversial politicians like William Seward were usually excluded from nominations in a bygone age, candidates with *ideological appeals* have done much better more recently. Goldwater, McGovern and Reagan won their parties' nominations, and Eugene McCarthy and Robert Kennedy (Democrats in 1968), George Wallace (Democrat in 1972), Edward Kennedy (Democrat in 1980), Jesse Jackson (Democrat in 1984), as well as Reagan in 1976, ran relatively strong races. Party leaders can no longer stand between an ideologue and the nomination. Indeed, the low turnout in primaries, along with the tendency of ideologically-minded voters to show up at the polls in disproportionate numbers (see chapter 6), often give ideological candidacies an advantage.
- As the primaries become the vehicle for winning the most delegates, campaign consultants encourage candidates to run flashy media campaigns based on *personality*. Surely a large part of the appeal of Dwight Eisenhower, all of the Kennedys, Jimmy Carter, and Gary Hart has been a personal attractiveness that cuts across ideological categories. Such personal appeals can overcome the opposition of party leaders rather easily these days, especially in primaries and also elevate journalists to an unprecedentedly prominent role in campaigns. Candidates consequently gear their strategy to what the media will play up.[17]
- Candidates have been able to build effective campaigns by appealing to specific *constituencies* within each party. As the more diverse party, the Democrats have seen more of this tactic than the Republicans, with much of organized labor's backing of Henry Jackson in the 1970s and Walter Mondale in 1984, Jimmy Carter's ties with the National Education Association (teachers' union) in 1980, and Jesse Jackson's appeal to blacks in 1984. And of course there was the support for Geraldine Ferraro's nomination by Democratic feminists. Both parties' national conventions are now marked by caucuses of women, blacks, young people, labor union memers, and other groups.
- At a time when nominations are determined by large numbers of party activists, it helps to have a *recognized face*. George McGovern and Jimmy Carter were able to win nominations after coming virtually out of nowhere, but most candidates would prefer to start out well known. This gives an advantage to vice presidents (Nixon, Humphrey, Mondale, Bush), who never used to be considered seriously for the White House, but whose familiar faces give them an edge today; to defeated vice presidential candidates (Henry Cabot Lodge, Jr., Edmund Muskie, Sargent Shriver, Robert Dole, and Mondale), who obtain enough exposure to mount campaigns later on; and to United States senators, who are covered by the national media.
- *Incumbents* continue to enjoy special advantages in nominating

races; the most recent incumbent whose name was rejected by his party's national convention was Chester Arthur in 1884. In his nominating battle against Edward Kennedy in 1980, Jimmy Carter expedited federal grants to key states, directed grants to others, had the government produce a mass-distributed poster showing all the women he had appointed to high office, held prestigious White House briefings for wavering delegates, and even gave federal employees a four-day Christmas weekend holiday. Ronald Reagan had no Republican opposition in 1984, but two adjacent front-page stories in the *New York Times* in September of that year show how an incumbent president can attract media attention by announcing policies: one story began, "President Reagan, in a decision to help the American steel industry, today ordered actions that the White House said would reduce steel imports;" the other began, "President Reagan today announced a program of Federal loan guarantees, temporary interest subsidies and other steps to ease pressure on debt-ridden farmers."[18] At national conventions, incumbents have several built-in advantages stemming from their control of the national party committee, which decides on the convention sites and dates, officers, and committee chairs. The platform, the rules, and even such matters as the allocation of guest passes are usually controlled by the White House.[19]

With all these advantages, the real surprise is that some incumbents have done worse in their nomination fights than we might expect. Harry Truman in 1952 and Lyndon Johnson in 1968 each dropped out of the race after a disappointing showing in the New Hampshire primary, and Gerald Ford in 1976 and Jimmy Carter in 1980 would have surely been denied the nomination had their foes run better (in Ford's case, only slightly better) in the delegate selection contests. Presidents are yet another type of party leader with less power over the party than they used to have, although they still have enormous advantages over their rivals.

In the transition from candidates as supplicants to candidates as entrepreneurs, has the American political system gained or lost? From the perspective of this book, problems with the mechanics of the process of presidential selection are trivial compared with those posed by corporate capitalism. Angry debates over party platforms, or whether a national primary makes more sense than the limited number of delegate selection primaries that now exist, seem inconsequential when compared to the more fundamental matters under discussion here. With this in mind, I present a few limited observations of the consequences of the changes presented in this chapter:

- One step forward is the decline of many of the irrational taboos of the past, when party leaders nearly always kept Roman Catholics,

Southerners, candidates from small states and others from the nomination. That there are other ridiculous taboos still in place, against women, nonwhites, non-Christians, and others, was illustrated by the absurdly self-congratulatory hullabaloo by the Democrats when Geraldine Ferraro was nominated for the vice presidency. After all, (1) the vice presidency is a virtually powerless office, (2) a number of nations, including Great Britain, Yugoslavia, India, and Israel, have given women their most powerful offices, and (3) the Democrats chose a woman only when they faced almost no chance of victory.

- The proliferation of primaries, while no panacea, has provided access to larger numbers of voters than were involved when party leaders ran conventions. This might help to politicize more people in the future.
- The greater tendency to nominate ideologues will produce more issue contrasts between nominees and can dramatize serious issue concerns for the voters. However, as noted below, the use of "issues" in such campaigns seldom goes beyond sloganeering.

The foregoing advantages of the new system must be weighed against the following drawbacks:

- If the old system discriminated against some population groups, the new system tends to screen out sitting governors and congressional party leaders. These are two groups with, respectively, administrative and Washington leadership experience who, in a more rational process, would be prime contenders.
- As I argued in chapter 6, primaries have been characterized by low turnout, and have become the arena for middle-class and upper-middle-class activists. Even Jesse Jackson's appeal in 1984 did not seriously modify this generalization, as data presented in that chapter show. Primaries are hardly a mechanism for giving the broad mass of people a voice in politics. Some have even argued that the bosses, with their emphasis on balanced tickets and candidates who could win, produced more representative candidates than primaries do.
- The political scientist Aaron Wildavsky has criticized the idea of a national primary as favoring only "wealthy athletes."[20] To the extent that the proliferation of primaries has produced the next-worst thing, more funds and energy are required for nomination than used to be. Some argue, not very plausibly, that a rugged and expensive primary campaign is good preparation for the White House; it is questionable how well the lame Franklin Roosevelt would have done under current norms, or how the ability to raise a large treasury correlates with wise leadership.

- The entrepreneurial system encourages an "every candidate for him or herself" mentality in which each candidate seeks advantage by tearing down his or her opponents, as when George Bush called Ronald Reagan's policies "voodoo economics" in 1980 or when Gary Hart called Walter Mondale "a spokesman from the past" in 1984. Speaking of the likelihood that Mondale would get the endorsement of the AFL-CIO, John Glenn's pollster told reporters in 1983 that "if he gets it, we want it to smell bad."[21] Not only do such attacks play into the hands of the other party—nothing George Bush has ever said has been so often quoted as "voodoo economics"—but they create disunity within one's own party and give whoever is elected president an "us-against-the-world" mentality instead of the confidence that party members will work together as a team. This problem can, of course, arise with any nominating system, but ours seems to encourage it.
- Another problem with frenetic, dog-eat-dog presidential preconvention campaigning is that candidates spend all their time plotting strategy and media tactics, rather than addressing major issues. Walter Mondale decided not to seek the Democratic presidential nomination in 1976, commenting that "I kept getting suggestions that I needed to buy different clothes and go to speech instructors and spend two days in Hollywood with a videotape machine. I hated that."[22] Said John Anderson in 1980, "The problem in a campaign is that you get no time to sit down and think. . . . Instead, the candidates tend to engage in a lot of frenetic activity that adds up to zilch."[23] In 1972 George McGovern proposed a system of welfare reform that was so poorly thought out that it became a campaign liability; the wonder was that he attempted some serious policy discussion in the midst of a campaign. The norm, rather, is superficial "debates" in which candidates vie to come up with a flashy comment, like Mondale's use of "Where's the beef?" in 1984 to question the seriousness of Hart's call for "new ideas." And, as argued in chapter 8, the media are not eager to play up issues anyway. Contrast this with parliamentary systems in which "shadow cabinets," or members of the opposition party who have been assigned to follow particular issues, study and propose policies for years prior to the election.

The result of all these problems is that the nominating process has contributed to the increasing weakening of party ties, making parties less and less a potential vehicle for social change and more and more an empty vessel in which shallow campaigns can be waged for the support of middle-class activists. Like so much of American politics, the process has become an exercise in superficiality, a diversion from serious political concerns. As such, this system fits very well the political needs of corporate capitalism.

THE ELECTORAL COLLEGE AND ITS CONSEQUENCES

In order to reach the White House the nominees must win in the electoral college. This is an institution that is understood by few Americans, and numerous public opinion surveys show a large majority preferring a system of direct popular election, the way in which all other elective offices are chosen. However, no attempt to abolish the electoral college has ever gotten very far, partly because the public is usually apathetic about the issue and partly because certain states and interests perceive that they benefit from the college's existence. Who benefits is a question to be considered as soon as the college itself is described.

Why the framers of the Constitution decided to choose presidents by means of an electoral college is a long story, but it is sufficient to understand that this procedure was a compromise among various proposals, from direct popular vote to election of the president by Congress.[24] As described in chapter 5, the election of 1800 demonstrated that the original process had to be changed in order to accommodate the rise of political parties, and so the Twelfth Amendment produced the outline for the system still in place today.

The first thing to bear in mind is that the president and vice president are chosen not by popular vote, but by people called "electors," who are chosen solely for that purpose. Each state is entitled to as many electors as it has senators and representatives in Congress, so that the minimum number for each state is three (since every state has two senators and at least one representative). Since there are 100 senators, 435 representatives, and three electors for the District of Columbia (under the terms of the Twenty-third Amendment), today there are 538 electors.

On election day, the voters go to the polls to vote for slates of presidential *electors* pledged to, say, Ronald Reagan or Walter Mondale. Most voters may think that they are voting directly for Reagan or Mondale, but they are not. The almost universal practice is for each state and the District of Columbia to give all its electors to whichever ticket wins the most votes, even if there are more than two candidates and the winning slate of electors nets less than a majority of the total vote cast.[25] The reason for this is to make the state a bigger prize in the presidential election than it would be if its electors were divided among the candidates. A candidate is more likely to spend a lot of campaign time in a state if he or she can win all its electors, than if those electors are to be split up and no candidate ends up with much of an advantage.

On the first Monday after the second Wednesday in December, the winning electors assemble in their state capitals and cast their ballots, which are sent to Washington. Since the electors themselves are usually party stalwarts, nearly all of them can be counted on to vote as expected, as all of them did in 1980 and 1984. However, in each of the previous three elections, one elector voted for someone other than the candidate on the ballot. This is not illegal, and fortunately no such "faithless elector" has ever changed the outcome of an election.

On January 6, and January 7 if the sixth is a Sunday, the outgoing vice president counts the ballots before a joint session of the newly elected Congress. The votes of a majority of electors—270 out of 538—are needed to choose a new president and vice president. If nobody wins such a majority, the House of Representatives makes a presidential selection from among the top three vote-getters; each state delegaton casts one vote, and the votes of twenty-six out of fifty state delegations are needed in order to win. The Senate selects a vice president from the top two vote-getters. These contingency procedures have not been necessary since 1824.[26]

In summary, then, each state casts all of its electoral votes for the candidate who obtains the greatest number of popular votes in that state, and the winner of the election is whoever can win 270 out of 538 electoral votes.

Who benefits from the existence of the electoral college? Who would gain if presidential elections were decided by direct popular vote? At first glance, small states seem to benefit from the electoral college, since even the least-populated state is guaranteed three electoral votes. Voters in the nine most populous states cast more than half the popular vote in 1984, but those states had less than 45 percent of the electoral votes; voters in the fourteen smallest "states" (including the District of Columbia) cast 5 percent of the popular vote, but had 9 percent of the electoral votes.

The story does not end there, however. Because of the "winner-take-all" practice of allocating electors within each state, the large states have a tremendous advantage. Even though, say, Alaska has more electoral votes than its population entitles it to, and California has fewer, California's prize of forty-seven electoral votes vastly outweighs Alaska's total of three. A shift of forty-seven votes would have kept five twentieth century presidents—Wilson, Truman, Kennedy, Nixon, and Carter—from an electoral vote majority, but a shift of three votes would not have changed any outcome in the past hundred years. In the words of two political scientists who studied this effect in the 1970s, "On a per-capita basis, voters in California are 2.92 times as attractive campaign targets as voters in Washington, D.C." Moreover, the scholars found that candidates had allocated their campaign schedules accordingly, spending proportionately more time in the states with the most electoral votes.[27]

Why should Americans tolerate a system that is biased toward populous states? For many years, it was argued that Congress had a conservative bias, because (1) rural, conservative states were overrepresented in Congress (especially the Senate), compared to their share of the population; (2) unfair state legislatures gave conservative, rural areas within each state too many seats in the U.S. House of Representatives; and (3) at a time when both houses were almost always controlled by the Democrats, the seniority system put conservative southern Democrats in the chair of most of the important committees. With Congress tilted rightward, it was argued, the presidency should have a leftward slant.[28] Therefore the large, liberal states should have their counterweight in the electoral college.

This argument is outdated in nearly every particular. First, it is unclear that large states are liberal any more. In the most recent close presidential election, that of 1976, four of the nine largest states voted Republican. (On the other hand, small states continue to be mostly Republican.) Second, since the 1960s the Supreme Court has forbidden state legislatures from grossly favoring particular areas when drawing congressional district lines. Finally, the rise of Republicanism in the South and the devolution of power within Congress have resulted in a decline in the power of southern Democratic members of Congress. In 1961, for example, 60 percent of the committee chairs in the House of Representatives were held by southern and border-state Democrats; in 1985 only 39 percent were. Even where Southerners have held on to committee chairs, trends such as the rise of subcommittees have diminished the power of those chairs. There is no longer any *political* excuse for a system of presidential selection that is biased toward large states.

One other argument has been raised by many defenders of the electoral college is that it reduces the chances for disputed elections. This is because it exaggerates the winner's percentage. With 59 percent of the popular vote in 1984, Reagan won nearly 98 percent of the electoral vote. Narrower victories result in less exaggeration: With 50 percent of the popular vote in 1976, Jimmy Carter netted 55 percent of the electoral vote. The electoral college is thereby supposed to "legitimize" narrow victories.

The problem with this argument is that the electoral college allows for the possibility that the candidate who wins the most popular votes will run second in electoral votes and therefore lose the election. This has happened in American history, but not more recently than in 1888. However, it is always a possibility when the popular vote is close. In 1976, a shift of 3,687 votes in Hawaii and 5,559 votes in Ohio from Jimmy Carter to Gerald Ford would have given Ford a majority in the electoral college, although Carter would still have had many more popular votes. Such an outcome would hardly have "legitimized" the election in the eyes of those who voted for Carter.

In reality, the perceptions of both large-state and small-state members of Congress that they benefit from the electoral college, combined with public apathy, will probably preserve the system until it results in the kind of outcome discussed in the previous paragraph.

PARTISAN AND IDEOLOGICAL ADVANTAGES

In the outcomes of presidential elections in the past several decades, two phenomena are evident: the greater incidence of landslides, and the frequency of Republican victories. How can these be explained?

If we define a landslide as winning a share of the popular vote at least as great as Reagan's 59 percent in 1984, then there have been five landslides since 1824, when reasonably accurate popular vote statistics were first assembled. They occurred in 1920, 1936, 1964, 1972, and 1984; notice the increasing incidence in recent years. If, on the other hand, we define a landslide as winning nine out of ten *electoral* votes, then there have been six landslides since 1824. They occurred in 1864, 1936, 1964, 1972, 1980, and 1984. Again, notice that recently they have been occurring more often. If we change the definition of a landslide to eight out of ten electoral votes, there were two landslides before 1928, and starting in 1928, eleven out of fifteen elections have been landslides.

Why are landslides occurring with greater frequency? Perhaps the decline in partisanship can provide an answer. In an earlier age, no matter how popular a candidate was, and no matter how many factors favored him over his opponent, large numbers of voters still had strong ties to the opposing party. If the winner's popularity was like a tidal wave, then the other party's voters represented a breakwater that limited its impact. Today, when far fewer voters have strong partisan attachments, there are fewer barriers against the tidal wave and more voters are carried along in its wake. In 1956, Eisenhower won 57 percent of the popular vote, and according to the Gallup poll he won 15 percent of the votes of Democrats; in 1984, winning 59 percent of the popular vote, Reagan carried 21 percent of Democrats. In the twenty-eight years from Eisenhower's landslide to Reagan's, Democrats became more susceptible to abandoning their party's nominee. This is also illustrated by the uniform nature of landslides: in 1984, for example, Reagan's vote percentages in the states ranged from nearly 50 percent in Minnesota to 75 percent in Utah; the very uniformity of the vote suggests that the barriers against Reagan's appeal were less systematically distributed across the population than in earlier elections. Winning by a similar popular vote margin in 1920, Warren Harding received a high of 78 percent in North Dakota and a low of less than 4 percent in South Carolina. The voters of South Carolina were going to stay Democratic no matter how popular the Republican candidate was.

We can now turn to the Republican advantage. After Reagan's forty-nine-state victory in 1984, many commentators began to point out that the Republican party has won a surprising number of presidential elections in recent decades, given its status as the minority party with relatively few adherents (as shown in Table 3.3 in chapter 3). Of the ten elections since the end of World War II, there have been six Republican victories, five by large margins, and four Democratic successes, only one a landslide. Democrats won only one of the five elections from 1968 through 1984. The political scientist Philip Converse once estimated that from 1952 to 1960, without short-term effects of candidates and issues, Democratic presidential nominees could expect to win 54 percent of the vote.[29] It is striking that only once since 1945 has any Democrat, Lyndon Johnson, reached that percentage.

There are some explanations for recent presidential election outcomes that help only a little in understanding why the Democrats have fared so poorly. For example, Republicans turn out to vote more than Democrats do; Republican voters are usually more loyal to their candidates than Democrats are; and Independents usually vote for the Republican nominee far more than for the Democrat. Moreover, a decreasingly partisan electorate is more likely to give the minority party an even break. All these generalizations are true, but they are only ways of rephrasing the Republican advantage.

Just how large that advantage is can be seen in Map 10.1, which is based on the number of times each state went Republican in the five elections from 1968 through 1984. Twenty-three states with 202 electoral votes, including California, Illinois and New Jersey, went Republican every time; this gives the Republicans a base of three-fourths of the electoral votes they need to win. Only one entity, the District of Columbia, with three votes, was equally loyal to the Democrats. In addition to the twenty-three normally Republican states, there are thirteen others that have voted Republican four out of five times in the period, and they have 152 electoral votes; this expands the usually Republican base to 354 electoral votes, or eighty-four more than are needed to win.

Another way to see where the political balance of power lies is to look at the "swing" states. Delaware, Missouri, and North Carolina were the only states that voted for the winner in every election from 1960 through 1984. There were three close elections in that period: John Kennedy's victory in 1960, Richard Nixon's in 1968, and Jimmy Carter's in 1976. Those three states plus South Carolina were the only ones to vote for the winner in each of those three close races. In addition, as Table 10.1 shows, the South was the only region to support the winner in each of those elections. Clearly, the "swing" region is the South and border states. Each victorious ticket in those three close contests had a southern or border-state candidate,[30] and each of the losing tickets lacked such regional representation. Since southern and border-state voters are known to be relatively conservative, the tendency of American politics to lean to the right is reinforced.

Even so, it should be noted that this apparent Republican and conservative electoral slant may not be as solid as it looks. Four of the six Republican victories were led by two unusually attractive candidates, Dwight Eisenhower and Ronald Reagan. Commentators who wondered after the 1984 election if the Democrats could remain electorally competitive ignored (1) the Democrats' continuing advantage in party identification (see Table 3.3); (2) the large majority of governors, state legislators and U.S. Representatives who were Democrats, demonstrating that the party was still very strong in most respects; and (3) the fact that the three

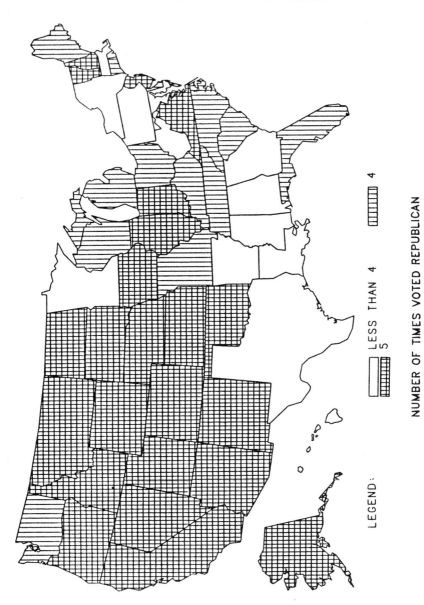

LEGEND:

LESS THAN 4

5

4

NUMBER OF TIMES VOTED REPUBLICAN

Figure 10.1 How States Voted, 1968—1984 Presidential Elections

SAS/GRAPH

Table 10.1 Electoral votes cast by region in the three close presidential elections since 1960.

	Northeast	Southeast	Midwest	Far West	Nation
1960					
Kennedy (D)	92%	59%	44%	12%	56%
Nixon (R)	8	31	55	88	41
Byrd	0	10	1	0	3
Total	100	100	100	100	100
1968					
Nixon (R)	18	48	80	86	56
Humphrey (D)	82	18	20	14	36
Wallace	0	34	0	0	9
Total	100	100	100	100	100
1976					
Carter (D)	74	91	38	4	55
Ford (R)	26	9	62	95	45
Reagan	0	0	0	1	*
Total	100	100	100	100	100

* Less than .5 percent.

Note: Percentages do not all sum to 100 due to rounding.

largest presidential landslides from 1945 through 1980, those of 1956, 1964 and 1972, were all followed by the winning party's loss of the White House four years later. In fact, on every conceivable measure, the Democrats were stronger in 1964 than the Republicans were in 1984, but this did not prevent the Republicans from making major gains in Congress in 1966 and recapturing the presidency in 1968. It would be foolish to assume that the Democrats will necessarily win the 1988 election, but it would be equally foolish to assume that they are doomed to lose.

In fact, even the striking picture shown in Map 10.1 should be modified by considering how close many of those Republican victories were in each state. Map 10.2 looks at the same five elections in terms of the *percentage* of the popular vote that the Republicans received, and averages it over the five elections. Thirty states, with a massive 400 electoral votes, fall neither in the solidly Republican nor the solidly Democratic category. The Republican advantage shown in Figure 10.1 shrinks to a cluster of sparsely populated states, mostly in the West.

On the other hand, it *is* anomalous that the Democratic party has not done better in presidential elections. Political parties in advanced capitalist nations are caught between policies that try to maintain corporate profit-

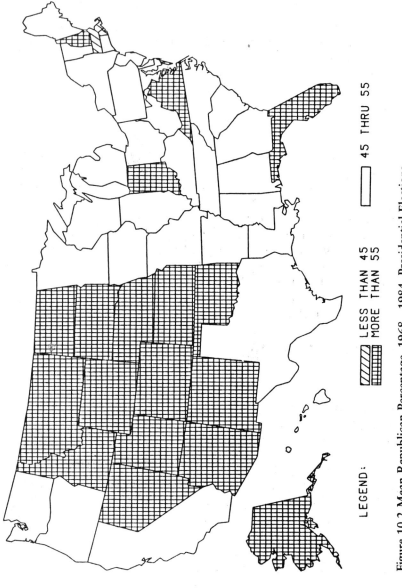

LEGEND:

LESS THAN 45
MORE THAN 55

45 THRU 55

Figure 10.2 Mean Republican Percentage, 1968—1984, Presidential Elections
SAS/GRAPH

ability, and those that try to keep the lower classes at least minimally satisfied. Democrats have tied themselves into knots trying to do both, and succeeding at neither. Republicans have in recent years adopted a posture of favoring policies that cater to corporate profits over those that buy off the working class and the poor, and in the short run the gambit has worked. Their posture has worked first, because it appeals to the dominant American ideology ("traditional values") so well; second, because it plays into the greed of the middle and upper-middle classes (including the "yuppies") who turn out to vote at a far higher rate than the lower classes; and third, because after the indecisiveness of the Carter years, the Republicans have in Reagan a president who looks as though he knows what he wants.

In the long run, the Republicans are playing a dangerous game. The 1982 elections destroyed Reagan's working majority in the House of Representatives and made the Senate more resistant to his policies. Even in the Republican year of 1984 the Democrats inched closer to regaining control of the Senate. Future economic problems may do greater damage to Republican fortunes. More important than the impact on the Republican party is the potential damage to the legitimacy of the political system, as the disadvantaged classes begin to mobilize against the corporate threat. The horn of plenty promised by Reaganomics may turn out instead to be Pandora's box.

PROCESS AND RESULT

To return to Hamilton's concern, does the current electoral process produce presidents of the "requisite qualifications," free of the "talents for low intrigue"? The nominating process seems to favor those who can best appeal to middle-class activists in primaries and caucuses, a skill which may or may not produce capable presidents. In several respects, the system seems to make presidential success more difficult. It discriminates against incumbent governors and congressional party leaders; it encourages candidates to attack other candidates within the party; and it reduces the role of the party to an empty shell in which any skillful campaigner can win the nomination. All of these factors make it more difficult for the new president to unite his party behind his programs. Even more serious is the fact that parties have become decreasingly likely to be instruments of social change.

What impact does the electoral college have on the kind of president who is produced? In order to win the presidency, candidates are well advised to concentrate a disproportionate amount of resources on states with large populations. No longer is this a formula for liberal presidencies, as Nixon and Reagan administrations have demonstrated. It is unlikely that the electoral college produces presidents any different in nature from those a direct popular vote would produce. Most assuredly, it does not protect the White House from candidates of "low intrigue."

Further Reading

For changes in the nominating process over time, see my *Selecting the President: The Nominating Process in Transition* (Philadelphia: Univ. of Pennsylvania Press, 1985). A lively debate over the wisdom of the reforms of the nominating process has produced a large literature; see the "Further Reading" section of chapter 6 for some of it.

For a defense of the existence of the electoral college, see Wallace S. Sayre and Judith H. Parris, *Voting for President* (Washington: The Brookings Institution, 1970); Neal R. Peirce and Lawrence D. Longley's *The People's President*, rev. ed. (New Haven: Yale Univ. Press, 1981) argues for its abolition. Trivia buffs will be amused by Walter Berns, ed., *After the People Vote* (Washington and London: American Enterprise Institute, 1983).

Notes

1. *Federalist* number 68, in the Clinton Rossiter edition (New York: New American Library, 1961), 414.

2. Willard L. King, *Lincoln's Manager, David Davis* (Cambridge: Harvard Univ. Press, 1960), 139–141.

3. George E. Mowry, "Election of 1912," in Arthur M. Schlesinger, Jr., ed., *History of American Presidential Elections,* (New York: Chelsea House, 1971), III: 2151.

4. Both quotations from Francis Russell, *The Shadow of Blooming Grove* (New York: McGraw-Hill, 1968), 341–342.

5. Richard Oulahan, *The Man Who* (New York: Dial Press, 1971), 114–121.

6. See Robert D. Novak, *The Agony of the G.O.P. 1964* (New York: Macmillan, 1965).

7. See Theodore H. White, *The Making of the President 1972* (New York: Atheneum Publishers, 1973).

8. See Jules Witcover, *Marathon* (New York: Viking Penguin, 1977).

9. Transcript of "CBS News Special Report, Campaign '76: The New York and Wisconsin Primaries," broadcast 6 April 1976, 8.

10. Max Frankel, "Ho Hum, Another Last Hurrah," *The New York Times Magazine,* 11 July 1976, 10; and "Gauging the Delegate Count as the Nominations Approach," *The New York Times,* 17 May 1980, p. 10.

11. The term "entrepreneurial" to describe the American nominating process was used by Hugh Heclo in "Presidential and Prime Ministerial Selection," in Donald R. Matthews, ed., *Perspectives on Presidential Selection* (Washington: The Brookings Institution, 1973), 19–48.

12. Clinton Rossiter, *The American Presidency,* 2nd ed. (New York: Harcourt, Brace & World, 1960), 201–202.

13. "Baker Says Campaign Survived Iowa," the *New York Times,* 27 January 1980, sec. 1, p. 16.

14. "Senator Cranston Ponders Bid for Presidency," the *New York Times,* 17 January

1982, sec. 1, p. 28; Mary McGrory, "Cuomo Wants a Say in the Democrats' Choice of a Candidate," the *Washington Post*, 14 April 1983, p. A3; David Broder, "Democrats Who Can't Stay Neutral," the *Washington Post,* 25 September 1983, p. C7; "Cuomo Considered as a 'Favorite Son'," the *New York Times,* 7 February 1983, p. A1; and James J. Kilpatrick, "Don't Count Kennedy Out," The *Hartford* (Conn.) *Courant,* 11 December 1982, p. A20.

15. Among those making such arguments are William Crotty, *Party Reform,* (New York: Longman, 1983), and Nelson W. Polsby, *Consequences of Party Reform* (New York: Oxford Univ. Press, 1983).

16. See my *Selecting the President: The Nominating Process in Transition* (Philadelphia: Univ. of Pennsylvania Press, 1985).

17. See F. Christopher Arterton, *Media Politics* (Lexington, Mass.: Lexington Books, 1984).

18. The *New York Times,* 19 September 1984, p. 1. On Carter's use of incumbency, see David S. Broder, "Jimmy Carter's 'Good News' Strategy," the *Washington Post,* 6 April 1980, p. E7; "As Long As Carter's Up He'll Get You a Grant," the *New York Times,* 21 April 1980, p. A19; Elizabeth Drew, "1980: The President," the *New Yorker,* 14 April 1980, 121–169; Terence Smith, "The Selling of the President," the *New York Times Magazine,* 24 February 1980, 24; and "White House Visits: New Campaign Tool," the *New York Times,* 13 March 1980, p. A21.

19. See my "The Gavels of August: Presidents and National Party Conventions," in Robert Harmel, ed., *Presidents and Their Parties* (New York: Praeger Publishers, 1984), 96–121.

20. In Nelson W. Polsby and Aaron Wildavsky, *Presidential Elections,* 6th ed. (New York: Charles Scribner's Sons, 1984), 225.

21. "Mondale's Machine, A Textbook Case," the *New York Times,* 26 September 1983, p. B8; Hart is quoted in "Hart Denounces Politics of Past," the *New York Times,* 27 January 1984, p. A14.

22. Quoted in "Mondale, and Why He Was Unable to Do The 'Required,' " the *New York Times,* 1 December 1974, sec. 4, p. 5.

23. Quoted in Tony Schwartz, "The Anderson Principle," the *New York Times Magazine,* 17 February 1980, 50.

24. See Neal R. Peirce and Lawrence D. Longley, *The People's President,* rev. ed. (New Haven: Yale Univ. Press, 1981), chapter 2.

25. The exception in recent years has been Maine, where each congressional district chooses one elector, and two are elected statewide.

26. For more details on the electoral college and related procedures, see *Congressional Quarterly's Guide to U.S. Elections* (Washington: Congressional Quarterly, Inc., 1975), 201–215.

27. Steven J. Brams and Morton D. Davis, "The 3/2's Rule in Presidential Campaigning," *American Political Science Review* LXVIII (March 1974), 113–134. The quotation is on 134.

28. Clinton Rossiter used to characterize this argument as "one good gerrymander deserves another."

29. Philip E. Converse, "The Concept of a Normal Vote," in Angus Campbell *et al., Elections and the Political Order* (New York: John Wiley & Sons, 1966), 27.

30. They were Lyndon Johnson of Texas in 1960, Spiro Agnew of Maryland in 1968, and Jimmy Carter of Georgia in 1976.

11

Parties and the Presidency

Corporate capitalism is in trouble. Over the past forty years, inflation and unemployment have been rising while corporate profits and other measures of economic health have been on the decline. Beleaguered corporations and owners of small businesses have turned to government for help, but government is increasingly unable to coordinate economic policies to rescue the private sector. As we saw in chapter 9, Congress, with its internal fragmentation and obsession with reelection, is ill equipped to do the job. The presidency looms as the ony institution in American politics capable of initiating comprehensive social and economic policy, as it did during the Great Depression, the middle 1960s, and the first year of the Reagan administration.[1]

Ever since the New Deal, the president has been held responsible for economic progress. The Emergency Banking Act of 1933 empowered him to close member banks in a crisis, the Securities and Exchange Act of 1934 gave him emergency powers to shut down the securities exchanges, and the Employment Act of 1946 was most explicit in directing the president "to foster and promote free competitive enterprise, to avoid economic fluctuations or to diminish the effects thereof, and to maintain employment, production, and purchasing power."[2] Substantial majorities of the American people expected Jimmy Carter in 1977 and Ronald Reagan in 1981 to reduce unemployment and the cost of government and to increase the efficiency of government: Reagan was expected to cut inflation as well.[3]

Does the American political system enable the president to deliver on these great expectations? It has often been remarked that in comparison with other chief executives around the world, the presidency is a remarkably weak institution. This may seem surprising in light of all the hoopla about "imperial presidents" and the very real power that control over nuclear arms affords. As this chapter will demonstrate, however, within the American political system presidents are limited in their sway over even their fellow partisans in the legislature, and over the executive branch of which they have only nominal control. This weakness results in one of two unsatisfactory alternatives. Either the president does not deliver, and seems weak—as the *New York Times* wrote in 1982, "The stench of failure hangs over Ronald Reagan's White House"[4]—or, like Richard Nixon, he breaks the law in order to overcome the frustrations of the limits on his power. John Kennedy's closest aide boasted of the president's ignoring the law, and a Nixon speechwriter claimed that "the worst thing a President can do is to be so paralyzed by propriety that he shrinks from bending the rules when the nation's security requires it."[5]

It has long been argued that effective presidential leadership requires strong party leadership.[6] Ever since George Washington left office, presidents have identified with a party, and the presidents regarded as great leaders have been those who could mobilize their parties behind them. Some historians have even argued that a contributing factor to Abraham Lincoln's successful prosecution of the Civil War was the fact that, unlike Jefferson Davis, he had a party with which to coordinate Congress and state governors.[7] Every twentieth century president who saw a major legislative program pass—Woodrow Wilson, Franklin Roosevelt, Lyndon Johnson, and (for one year) Ronald Reagan—enjoyed the strong support of his party in Congress.

As American parties become weaker and weaker, the president may be deprived of one of his most effective tools. Has this occurred? If it has, what does a president do to compensate? Are those efforts likely to be successful? These are the concerns of this chapter.

OPPORTUNITIES AND LIMITATIONS

There are several ways in which the job of the president involves his party. He is nominated by his party en route to the White House, he deals with its national committee, he must secure the cooperation of his fellow partisans in Congress, and he appoints people from his party to the executive branch. What is the state of each of these relationships?

Getting nominated

In order to reach the White House, a politician must be nominated by his or her party and appeal to fellow partisans in the delegate selection process. This would seem to guarantee that all presidents will be strongly socialized toward partisanship. However, chapter 10 demonstrated that the nominating process is oriented away from party cohesion. In order to advance their own cause, candidates attack each other, and there is a bias against party leaders in Congress and among incumbent state governors.

In recent years, presidents have come from states which lack strong party organization. Since 1964, everyone elected to the office has come from either California (Nixon, Reagan) or the South (Johnson, Carter). California has long been governed by party-weakening election laws dating from the progressive era, and when Johnson and Carter were growing up, the Democrats were so dominant in the South that they did not bother to build a strong organization. Nowhere in Jimmy Carter's campaign autobiography, for example, does he give any reason for considering himself a Democrat.[8] Perhaps candidates from weak-party states have learned how to campaign most effectively in primaries. In any case, they have been more successful in being elected to the White House than their competitors from strong-party states like Michigan (Ford) and Minnesota (Humphrey, Mondale).

Leading the National Committee

In 1947 Congress passed the Taft-Hartley Act, which was intended to roll back many of the gains that the labor movement had made during the New Deal. In the course of deciding whether to veto it, Harry Truman polled all the members of the Democratic National Committee to solicit their opinions. In 1979 Jimmy Carter conferred with 130 Americans at Camp David to analyze the condition of American society and government. Not one of them was a member of the Democratic National Committee.[9]

These two events illustrate the declining relationship between presidents and their national party committees. The president normally controls the national committee; as former Democratic National Chairman Robert Strauss once said, "If you're Democratic party chairman when a Democrat is president, you're a Goddamn clerk."[10] It is easy to imagine how a strong national committee can serve a president's interests, by providing campaign support to members of his party, by circulating party propaganda on his behalf, by conveying party opinion to him, by coordinating patronage, by establishing a link with members of Congress of his party, and by providing liaison with interest groups. Instead, as Thomas Cronin has written, "Most presidents of late have mistreated their national party committees."[11]

There are several reasons why presidents shy away from a close relationship with their parties. Every president tries to woo people from outside his party, and especially when that party is the minority party, he does not want to appear too partisan because that would antagonize many voters. When others of his party are running against his quest for nomination to another term, his national committee must act as though it is neutral in the intraparty battle. Even when he is the obvious nominee, the campaign finance laws require a campaign organization separate from the party.[12]

Perhaps the real reason that presidents and national committees often do not get along is that the president wants the committee to do only what is best for him, and the committee often believes that it must take into account the interests of the entire party. In 1966, when Richard Nixon was planning his presidential campaign, he toured the country campaigning for Republican congressional candidates. When he asked the Republican National Chairman, Ray Bliss, to help defray his expenses, Bliss refused, partly to avoid complaints from other Republicans with an eye on the White House. The relationship between the two men suffered beyond repair, and Nixon got rid of Bliss soon after he became president in 1969. In 1978, Ronald Reagan tried to convince Republican National Chairman William Brock to spend $50,000 trying to defeat the Panama Canal Treaty. Brock, knowing that the party was divided on the issue, refused, and Reagan replaced Brock when he was elected in 1980. The Panama Canal Treaty debate also saw the Democratic National Committee refuse to pass a resolution supporting Jimmy Carter's endorsement of the treaty.[13]

What do presidents do when they want to reduce the independence of the national committee? Every recent president has simply given party functions such as patronage and campaign planning to the White House staff. Presidents also send trusted allies to keep an eye on the national committee, as Lyndon Johnson did with Clifton Carter. Johnson's paranoia about the Democratic National Committee's being a cabal to promote Robert Kennedy's presidential ambitions finally grew out of hand, and he ordered wholesale cuts in the committee's staff, budget, and operations. Nixon's chief of staff sent his colleagues a memorandum telling them that they could ignore the Republican National Committee. After ten weeks in office, Jimmy Carter was censured by the Democratic National Committee for ignoring the party on patronage matters, and it was more than a year later that he first met with national committee members. Reagan's first Republican National Chairman, Richard Richards, complained that "every clerk in the White House thinks he can do my job better than I can—and they don't even know what it is."[14]

This kind of relationship seems to have worked to the detriment of the national committee, but as Harold Bass has pointed out, "It may have isolated and alienated this source of traditional support from the president, leaving him more vulnerable than in the past to the tides of fortune." In Johnson's case, destroying the effectiveness of the Democratic National Committee probably contributed to the Democrats' losses in congressional elections in 1966, and the Republican capture of the White House in 1968; as one Democratic campaign aide in 1968 put it, "We had no money. We had no organization. We were fifteen points behind in the polls. We did have a media plan, but we didn't have the money to go with it." The result was a new Republican administration that cut back on many of the programs that had been most important to Johnson.[15]

Perhaps this is the real lesson. A president may believe that his interests are best served by destroying alternative power bases in his party, but if he wants to institutionalize his political legacy, there may be no better way than to build his party. This was the course of Abraham Lincoln and Franklin Roosevelt.

Working with Congress

When American political parties are effective, there is probably no greater good that they can do for a president than to solidify his relations with his party in Congress. Unquestionably there is still a sizable degree of party loyalty, reflected in the fact that in recent decades, members of the president's party in Congress supported him about two-thirds of the time, while members of the other party backed him less than half the time. When Carter took office, Speaker of the House Tip O'Neill, said, "We loved to send Jerry Ford's vetoes back to him. But we have a Democratic President now, and who needs that?" When Reagan became president four years later, his Senate majority leader, Howard Baker, said, "I intend to try to help Ronald Reagan [carry out] the commitments he made during the campaign."[16] This is partly due to old-fashioned party loyalty, and partly to self-interest: if the president fails, he might pull the entire party down with him, as Carter did in 1980. What can a president do to encourage the cooperation of representatives and senators of his party?

One method has been to rely on his popularity, expressed both in the election returns and in ongoing public opinion surveys. Several scholars have shown that members of Congress are especially likely to vote for the programs of a president who ran well in their districts, or who is getting favorable ratings in the Gallup poll. In particular, consider a president who ran better in a state or a congressional district than the member of Congress did. He is likely to tell that member that the constituents love the president and want his programs to be supported. As a White House aide told a journalist in 1981, "Some Democrats are getting the picture that by going with Reagan they are doing the popular thing." If the member belongs to the president's party, was elected narrowly, and ran far behind the president, then the president is likely to argue that his popularity helped pull the member into office on his "coattails." This means that the member is indebted to the president, and should pay off that debt by voting the president's way.[17]

Another avenue of presidential influence is to provide favors for members of Congress. He can give them patronage by accepting their recommendations for high federal appointments; swing the clout of the White House behind their legislative proposals, as Reagan did with New York Representative Jack Kemp's and Delaware Senator William Roth's tax cut bill in 1981; meet with or write letters to member's constituents; inform members of new federal projects in their districts so that the legislators can announce them; steer discretionary spending projects to their districts; campaign for their reelection and appear at fund-raising affairs; and provide personal favors such as tickets to the president's box at the Kennedy Performing Arts Center or a ride on Air Force One. The White House staff has long included an Office of Congressional Relations, institutionalized in the Kennedy and Johnson administrations, which coordinates such efforts and keeps track of the president's legislative program. In 1961, Kennedy had approximately 2,500 personal contacts with members of Congress. Under Reagan, a Political Affairs Office was established for this purpose.[18]

Along with the carrots, the president has some sticks. He can deny the above resources to members of his party who do not vote his way often enough to suit him. In chapter 8, I recounted how Reagan staffers wooed Republican legislators in 1982 by promising lavish campaign funds. The other side of the coin was shown in 1985, when a White House staffer said, "If the Senator doesn't support us on the MX [missile] and he wants a fund-raiser in the next three or four months, he's not going to get a fund-raiser." Said Reagan's chief spokesman, "There are 22 Republicans up [for re-election], and our rule is we're going to take care of our friends first." The assistant majority leader of the Senate, Alan Simpson of Wyoming, added about some of his colleagues, "We have to slap them along the head with a piece of stove wood." This brought to mind the boast of a White House aide in 1982 about a Republican senator from Iowa, "We just beat his brains out. That's all. We just took [Roger] Jepsen and beat his brains out." The image of their senator's being bludgeoned into voting Reagan's way did not sit well with some Iowa voters, and Jepsen was defeated for reelection in 1984.[19]

The ultimate threat a president can make is to work to have a member of Congress defeated for reelection. This is seldom attempted, particularly since Franklin Roosevelt took sides in several Democratic primaries in 1938, only to see most of the anti-New Deal incumbents win. In 1970, Vice President Spiro Agnew, representing the Nixon administration, sided with a third-party candidate for the United States Senate in New York in order to defeat incumbent Republican Charles Goodell, considered too liberal by the Nixonites. The gambit was successful, but no president has made a similar effort since then.[20]

This inventory may look impressive, but every president is frustrated by his inability to get more from his party in Congress than he does. In his memoirs, Jimmy Carter wrote:

> Some of the Democratic leaders promised me full support in implementing my general platform, but as we began to discuss the hard details, the support often evaporated. I had to seek votes wherever they could be found. . . . I learned the hard way that there was no party loyalty or discipline when a complicated or controversial issue was at stake—none. Each legislator had to be wooed individually. It was every member for himself, and the devil take the hindmost.[21]

A number of circumstances discourage a close relationship between a president and his party in Congress. Since the presidential nominating process discriminates against congressional party leaders, people who are elected president are mostly ex-legislators who were not part of the congressional establishment (Kennedy, Nixon) or Washington outsiders (Eisenhower, Carter, Reagan). Congressional insiders have gotten to the

White House only after the death or resignation of their predecessors (Truman, Johnson, Ford). Most presidents, then, get to the office without a close working relationship with their party's congressional leaders. Indeed, they often win nominations by defeating some of those very leaders and by running against the Washington establishment.

Perhaps the most serious problem for presidents is that members of Congress do not need most of the amenities that presidents can give them. Such congressional perquisites as staff, computers, and trips home have increased substantially over the years, enhancing the ability to secure reelection. Reelectability means that few, if any, members are likely to be impressed with the president's claims of being able to help them win another term.[22]

For example, let us consider the question of coattails more carefully. The coattail phenomenon occurs when enough voters cast their ballots for everyone on the president's party's ticket, providing the margin of victory for the member of Congress. This means that (1) the member of Congress of the president's party won by a small margin; and (2) the president ran substantially ahead of the member of Congress. Let us assume, therefore, that if the member won by less than 55 percent, and the president ran at least 5 percent better than the member, then presidential coattails made the crucial difference.

By this standard, coattails have been short indeed. First, as I show in Table 11.1, a sizable number of presidents win the White House by small margins; Kennedy in 1960, Nixon in 1968, Carter in 1976, and Reagan in 1980 won by no more than 51 percent. This means that there were few districts in which they ran up large margins of victory. Even Johnson in 1964, Nixon in 1972, and Reagan in 1984 did not have long coattails, because few members of Congress win narrowly. Even in three of the largest presidential landslides in history, coattails were limited to less than a tenth of each house of Congress.

Table 11.1 During the presidential elections from 1960 through 1984, how many members of Congress of the President's party were elected with less than 55 percent of the vote while running at least 5 percent behind the president?

Year	President and popular vote percentage	Senators	Reps.	Opposition party's gain in House, two years later
1960	Kennedy (49.7)	0	2	1
1964	Johnson (61.1)	4	41	47
1968	Nixon (43.4)	0	6	12
1972	Nixon (60.7)	7	29	49
1976	Carter (50.1)	0	6	15
1980	Reagan (50.7)	4	13	26
1984	Reagan (58.8)	2	25	

The foregoing was not simply an academic exercise, for members of Congress are hardheaded about such matters. Speaker Tip O'Neill said of Jimmy Carter, "Seventy-five percent of the members up here got more votes than he did." (And that was an understatement.) Another Democratic representative noted, "Most members ran in their districts ahead of Jimmy Carter, and Jimmy Carter didn't help them." This may be the reason for Carter's disappointments, expressed in his remarks quoted earlier.[23]

Even if a president has coattails, he loses the advantage two years later when all representatives are up for reelection. Table 11.1 points out that two years after a presidential election the president's party usually loses more seats in the House than it had gained in the presidential election year. Any representatives who owe their seats to the president's coattails will be especially vulnerable. A majority of the coattail Democrats carried in by Johnson in 1964 lost their seats in 1966, and about half of the Nixon class of 1972 were ousted in 1974. With the single exception of 1934, every off-year congressional election since the Civil War has seen a loss of House seats by the president's party.

Besides the lack of a coattail advantage, a major handicap for presidents is their reliance on public opinion surveys as a measurement of popularity. It is well known that over a president's term in office, his Gallup poll ratings decline. This means that just as high ratings gain him support in Congress, slipping ratings decrease that support. A Carter aide said, "When you go up to [Capitol] Hill and the latest polls show Carter isn't doing well, then there isn't much reason for a member to go along with him." Added a Reaganite several years later, "Congress is no longer dictated by a fear that Ronald Reagan can go to the country" and appeal to public opinion over television.[24]

Finally, presidents tend to shy away from tying themselves too closely to their party's congressional campaigns. Republican chief executives are especially unlikely to do this since they do not want to be saddled with too close an association with a minority party. During the Watergate hearings in 1973, a Republican senator heard from a Nixon aide about White House policy toward aiding Republican candidates for Congress during Nixon's reelection campaign in 1972:

Sen. Weicker: Let me be very clear on this point, in the instance of certain Republican candidates in the South, support was withheld from them because their Democratic opponents had supported the President on the war, would that be a fair paraphrase?

Mr. Strachan: Yes, that is my understanding.

Sen. Weicker: And now also apparently there is another category of Republican from whom support was withheld and that was a category that the choice was made on the basis since the President enjoyed labor support it would be offensive to go ahead and finance the Republican candidacy against the Democrat, is that correct?

Mr. Strachan: Yes. . . .

Sen. Weicker: In other words, in effect, if I am not mistaken is that we have Republicans doing in Republicans here, is that correct?[25]

Similarly, in 1981 Reagan told Democratic conservatives in Congress that he "could not in good conscience campaign against any of you Democrats who have helped me." In 1984 he spent precious campaign time in Minnesota, trying for a fifty-state sweep, rather than helping out beleaguered Republican candidates elsewhere. As Theodore Lowi has put it, "The Republican approach [in 1984] was *partisan* without being *party*."[26]

Finally, presidents threaten recalcitrant members of their party sparingly. First, as Franklin Roosevelt learned, a president may not be able to get rid of members of Congress he dislikes. Second, the price may be to lose the seat to a member of the opposition.

Perhaps the real verdict on presidential influence is the argument of political scientist George Edwards, who has pointed out that all the factors that help a president the most—his electoral margin, the number of his party's seats in Congress, and his popularity—are ultimately beyond his control, while those that he controls, such as the carrots and sticks, are least effective over the long run. "His burdens are great," concludes Edwards, "and his assets are few."[27]

Managing the bureaucracy

According to the Constitution, the president's main responsibility is to exercise "executive power." He appoints (subject to senatorial confirmation), oversees, and fires the top administrators of the federal government. This would seem to give him enormous powers to direct the vast federal bureaucracy. The authority to appoint officials also provides him with a resource that can be immensely helpful in cementing his relations with his party's patronage.

As every president in modern times has learned, his powers have definite limits, and all recent presidents have expressed frustration with the bureaucracy. Franklin Roosevelt compared dealing with the Navy Department to punching a feather bed; Harry Truman said that his successor, Dwight Eisenhower, would be frustrated to find the executive branch unlike the army, where (according to Truman) orders are swiftly and faithfully executed; John Kennedy regarded the State Department as a bunch of inanely grinning paper-shufflers who could be replaced by a staff of thirty; Richard Nixon saw the whole bureaucracy as an enclave of liberal Democrats committed to protecting programs that Nixon wanted to eliminate; and Jimmy Carter said that the bureaucracy was even harder to manage than he had expected, and the most pervasive problem his cabinet brought to him.[28]

Nixon's suspicions about the partisan and ideological proclivities of high-ranking federal civil servants were partially confirmed in a survey by two political scientists, but if liberal bias were the main problem, then Roosevelt, Truman, Kennedy, and Carter should have had no difficulties.[29] Instead, we must look for more systemic sources of frustration for all presidents, regardless of party or ideology.

First, the president can name only about 650 out of the two or three million federal civilian employees. Granted, those are the highest policy-making positions, but the execution of policy is left in the hands of millions of people protected by the civil service system. As noted above in chapter 5, there has been a gradual tendency over the years for a president to appoint nonpoliticians to high executive positions, further reducing the party-building potential of the partonage power. Moreover, a preference for "experts" instead of politicians might reduce a president's sway over the bureaucracy, as experts often have more faith in their own views than in the president's political goals.[30]

In addition, the federal bureaucracy suffers from various problems of disorganization, including insufficient staff in key positions, fragmentation, and parochialism—some of the same characteristics that make Congress so ineffective as a policy-making body. Parochialism is a special problem, as various departments and agencies become advocates of the clients they serve. The Agriculture Department promotes the interests of wealthy farmers, the Treasury Department serves bankers, and the Education Department was envisioned as an advocate for educational institutions and teachers' unions. Bureaucratic agencies are one point of the "iron triangles" noted in chapter 9, in which interest groups and congressional subcommittees share power with agencies which evade control by the president as they form alliances with the other power centers. Nixon's top domestic policy aide said of high presidential appointees: "We only see them at the annual White House Christmas party; they go off and marry the natives."[31]

In recent years, presidents have tried to gain control over the bureaucracy by concentrating power in the White House staff. Since such concentration was considered one of the excesses of the Nixon years, each of his successors has vowed instead to keep power in the cabinet. Nevertheless, each president has ended up with a powerful staff, usually headed by one extremely powerful aide—Nixon's H. R. Haldeman and then Alexander Haig, Carter's Hamilton Jordan, Reagan's James Baker and then Donald Regan. Had Nixon not been engulfed by the Watergate revelations, he would have tried to concentrate even the cabinet into three "super-secretaries" and send White House staffers into various departments to keep an eye on the bureaucracy. In his second term Reagan did the same by assigning to two cabinet officers supervision over all of domestic policy. In foreign policy, we have seen the president's national security adviser rivaling and even (under Nixon and Carter) eclipsing the secretary of state. All in all, the picture presented is one of enormous presidential frustration with what is constitutionally the least controversial of presidential powers.[32]

We have seen a selection process that orients a president away from cooperation with the rest of his party; a relationship between the president and his party's national committee that veers between hostility and manipulation; limited presidential control over the factors that most effectively govern his dealing with his fellow partisans in Congress; and great frustrations in every president's attempts to control the bureaucracy. This is not to paint a totally bleak picture of presidential powers, for every president has been able to accomplish a great many of his policy goals. However, success in the White House is contingent on the effective marshalling of political resources, and parties that are weak deprive presidents of one such resource.

THE PRESIDENT AS ECONOMIC SAVIOR

As noted earlier, the ineffectuality of Congress makes the presidency the institution most responsible for the coordination of economic policy. With the institutional weakness just discussed, demands on the president to "solve" economic problems may often go unmet. In this role, the president's degree of power depends upon the nature of the policy in question. There are several, listed here in order of greatest presidential weakness to those of greatest strength:

· In dealing directly with the *private sector,* the President is weakest of all, as is appropriate in a capitalist system. Presidents who seek to convince corporations not to raise prices or labor unions not to seek higher wages, must rely on persuasion or "jawboning." The most dramatic attempts to exert leverage on corporations only dramatize the limits of presidential power. When Harry Truman seized the steel mills in 1952 during the Korean War, the Supreme Court ruled that he was acting unconstitutionally.[33] When several major steel corporations raised prices in 1962, John Kennedy threatened investigations and various changes in policy. The Inland Steel Company then announced that it would not raise prices, so the others backed down. Although Kennedy got what he wanted, the political scientist Grant McConnell concluded that "there was almost no power to deal with the crisis at the president's disposal save persuasion and appeal to public opinion."[34]
· In the area of *fiscal policy,* or taxes and spending, the president enjoys the resources of the Treasury Department and the Office of Management and Budget, but he shares power with Congress, and Congress is susceptible to pressure from constituents and interest

groups. All of the resources and limitations outlined above come into play here.

· The same goes for the scope of *social welfare programs,* the economic consequences of which increase the size of the public budget and give lower-class people some spending money. The president shares power in this area with Congress.

· *Regulation of the economy* is a mixed area. Some regulatory agencies, like the Food and Drug Administration and the Occupational Safety and Health Administration, reside squarely in the executive branch and are relatively susceptible to presidential influence and the president's power to appoint top officials. Of course, as with the rest of the bureaucracy, his control is far from absolute; recall the "iron triangles" mentioned earlier. Other regulatory bodies, like the Federal Communications Commission and the Federal Trade Commission, are more independent. Some of their commissioners are holdovers from previous administrations, but as vacancies arise, the president can nominate new members who are subject to senatorial approval.

· *Monetary policy,* or the amount of money in the economy, is determined in a manner similar to the independent regulatory agencies. The key agency is the board of governors of the Federal Reserve System, whose members are presidential appointees but who are independent of presidential command. Presidents normally try to "jawbone" the governors but have no direct control. During the Nixon adminstration, a presidential assistant tried to put pressure on the board's chairman, Arthur Burns, by floating rumors that Nixon would try to expand the size of the board (in order to add friendlier governors) and that Burns had sought a sizable pay raise. The pressure was unsuccessful and Nixon had to disassociate himself from it publicly.[35]

· Surprisingly, the president has the greatest power when it comes to the most fundamental decisions, *the structure of economic relations.* In 1970 Congress gave Richard Nixon the power to impose temporary wage and price controls, and, in the face of rising inflation and international economic problems in 1971, he exercised that power and also allowed the dollar to fluctuate in relation to other currencies for the first time since World War II. These decisions were made at a secret meeting between Nixon and a small circle of advisers, and they reflected the recognition by other sectors of government and the economy that only the president can take swift, coordinated action to rescue the economy.[36]

However, it must be underscored that even vigorous presidential action reflects the weaknesses of the political system. The hunger for decisiveness—don't just stand there, do something—leads presidents to promulgate poorly thought-out policies that often fail to achieve their stated goals in the long run. The journalist David Broder wrote of Lyndon Johnson's major legislative successes:

> So long as any President thinks he has only an occasional chance to move on the national agenda, the likelihood is he will over-react—as Johnson did—when that opportunity comes along. . . . There is also a risk of "overkill," of hasty, ill-considered, profligate action when leaders try to seize the few moments for initiative they are granted.[37]

When Nixon decided to let the dollar fluctuate, he told his staff, "We cannot know fully what effect it will have."[38] When Reagan's staff produced the economic projections that underlay his tax and spending proposals in 1981, his budget director called the figures "one part error, one part haste, one part conscious contrivance." In the House of Representatives, the final budget was so sloppily constructed that the pages were unnumbered and various scribbles appeared in the margins. Reagan's closest ally in the Senate, Paul Laxalt of Nevada, later admitted, "If there had been a secret ballot in the Senate, there wouldn't have been more than twelve votes for the tax cut."[39] Thus are major economic decisions made in the bastion of capitalism.

In a sense, it should not be surprising that economic policy is so haphazard. Every president in recent years has tried to balance the needs of the corporate sector—the accumulation of profits—with the needs of the masses of the people—social programs that legitimize the system. It is a delicate balancing act that usually errs in one direction or the other, due in part to the weaknesses of the office and also because the needs of each sector are too great to accommodate those of the other. We expect magic of presidents, and presidents have begun to behave with the razzle-dazzle of stage magicians.

FILLING THE VOID: GOVERNING BY IMAGERY

What does a president do when he must try to fulfill the many expectations the public has of him, but lacks the institutional means with which to resolve fundamental economic contradictions? Since parties were seen as a link between the president and "the people," at least since Andrew Jackson's day, the decay of party leads presidents to try to forge a more direct link to the masses. Every president since Eisenhower has sought to govern in this way, which political scientists have come to call the "plebiscitary presidency"—presidents behaving as though their only constituency is the voting public, and not any intermediary institution such as a party. We have, in Lowi's words, "a virtual cult of personality revolving around the White House."[40]

For many years, observers have known that one of a president's political strengths has been his popularity, and some of the studies cited earlier found a direct link between his standing in the polls and his success with Congress.[41] In recent years, presidents have sought to nurture their public standing by the kinds of public relations gimmickry described in chapter 8. How have they sought to do so?

Packaging the President

To a remarkable extent, the White House staff has been oriented toward tending the president's public image. "A congressional staff assistant who has evaluated White House organizations in the postwar period estimates that 85 percent of those working in the White House, including those in policy-making and service roles, are involved directly in public relations activities." Presidential behavior has reflected this. Since 1953 there has been a sharp rise in the number of presidential addresses, the amount of travel by presidents, and the number of presidential public appearances. The public has responded in kind: Eisenhower received 800,000 letters per year compared to 5 million for Reagan in 1981.[42]

While much was made of the public relations gimmickry of Richard Nixon and Jimmy Carter, it has been said that no president has been more reliant on advertising and imagery than Ronald Reagan.[43] One out of four presidential aides listed in the *U.S. Government Manual* for 1984 had some kind of public relations function in his or her title. In his first term, Reagan's Assistant for Communications saw him more than anyone except his three top aides. In 1984 one of those aides took over those communications functions. The Reagan White House included a press office, a public affairs office, a media relations office, a speechwriting staff of fifteen, and an office of travel specialists. In 1985 the director of communications was regarded as the second most important person on Reagan's staff.[44]

Presidents and pollsters

Modern survey research was developed in the 1930s, and every president since Franklin Roosevelt has consulted the polls and used pollsters as advisers. They seem to think that following public opinion is essential to their popularity, and that pollsters can help them figure out how to keep that popularity up. Like all the other trends under discussion, this one has intensified in recent years. Patrick Caddell became so important an adviser to Jimmy Carter that he had an office in the White House. But no president has integrated survey analysts into White House operations the way Ronald Reagan has. His campaign pollster, Richard Wirthlin, was made director of planning during the 1980–1981 transition, and another pollster, Richard Beal, was appointed chief of the Office of Planning and Evaluation and helped write Reagan's State of the Union Address in 1982. During Reagan's first term, Beal reported to one of the top three presidential aides, and Wirthlin presented his findings directly to Reagan himself. In 1982 slippage in Reagan's support among Roman Catholics induced him to fly to Chicago and endorse tax credits for tuition to parochial schools. The polls also persuaded the White House staff not to emphasize too strongly the divisive "social issues" like tuition tax credits, prayer in schools, and outlawing abortion.[45]

It is ironic that as presidents become more entwined with pollsters, their standing in the polls gets lower and lower. With the exception of Harry Truman, every president before 1969 had generally higher approval ratings in the Gallup poll than the presidents since 1969, despite the pollsters and the increasing presidential concern with public relations. Indeed, the decline in presidential popularity has become steeper in recent years. Either the pollsters do not give very good advice, or the obstacles to presidential effectiveness are so great that even more sophisticated survey analysis does not help.[46]

Public liaison

Another way to deal with the public is to build relationships with interest groups. With the decline of parties, congressional leadership, and the cabinet, the White House staff has increasingly taken on this role, with the goal of forging direct and unmediated ties between the president and segments of the public. Gerald Ford was the first president to establish an Office of Public Liaison, which in the Carter adminstration dealt with more than 800 groups. Under Reagan the office played an important role in maintaining good relations with right-wing organizations, and was divided into functional categories such as business, labor, women, Jews, blacks, and Hispanics. The first director of the office, Elizabeth Dole, went on to join the cabinet.[47]

The Presidency and journalists

When all the president's attempts at manipulation of public opinion fail, he typically responds not by blaming his own policies, nor by acknowledging that the task of running a healthy corporate capitalist economy is probably insuperable. The most common response in recent decades takes two forms. The first is to blame his imagery, and assume that a primary reason that the public is not entranced by his wonderful programs is that they have not been well packaged. Thus whenever Reagan is asked why black Americans are opposed to him, he has replied that they misperceive his policies as unfavorable to blacks. The second response is to blame the news media for treating him unfairly and adding to public misperceptions; during the recession of 1982 Reagan accused the press of exaggerating unemployment with stories about laid-off workers in "South Succotash." White House dissatisfaction with the treatment of presidents by journalists is nothing new; it began with George Washington. In the current age of weak parties, however, as presidents see public opinion as their main resource, they are even more obsessed than before with how their image comes across on the printed page and over the airwaves.[48]

It is ironic that presidents are dismayed by their press coverage, because that treatment is generally quite copious and favorable. In 1975 and 1977, for example, more than half the lead stories in *Time* and *Newsweek* dealt with presidential activities, and a study of the *New York Times, Time,* and CBS News from the Eisenhower administration through the Carter years concluded that most stories about the president were favorable to him.[49] Sam Donaldson, the White House correspondent for ABC News, has said, "I have to argue *not* to be on 'World News Tonight' some nights, because I don't think I have a story."[50] Presidents seem to be bothered that news reports do not begin, "The president, who combines the dignity of George Washington with the humility of Abraham Lincoln, made another historic breakthrough today when he announced that . . ." Most reporting, while not quite that laudatory, would satisfy any reasonable expectations of favorable treatment.

In the words of one critic, the White House press corps is "a kind of *Pravda* of the Potomac, a conduit for White House utterances and official image-mongering intended to sell Reaganomics." This is not an uncommon view. One of Lyndon Johnson's press secretaries has written, "All presidents seek to manage the news and all are successful to a degree;" a high-ranking aide to Gerald Ford has said, "We are trying to make [the press] use what we want them to use, not what they want. That is what we are trying to do, and it often works." The newspaper reporter Peter Lisagor once said, "Anyone who says they're not being manipulated is lying to you," and Sam Donaldson adds, "I get used by the White House every time they trot out a story and I put it on the air."[51]

There are many ways that a president can try to manipulate the press, and they go well beyond the purview of a textbook on political parties and elections. For the moment it is worth repeating the finding of chapter 8 that nearly all journalists share the dominant values of the American culture, and do not wish to appear unpatriotic or "enter the dens of millions of American homes as troublemaking bastards."[52]

Playing the diplomatic card

At a time when presidents are increasingly preoccupied with public relations, foreign policy beckons as a way to enhance their image. So much of it is dramatic and colorful, from trips to exotic lands abroad to tours of military installations with all their trappings of power. There has been a sharp rise in presidential travel abroad since 1945. When Nixon returned from China and the Soviet Union in separate trips in 1972, his arrivals in Washington were carefully timed for nine or nine-thirty in the evening, in order to assure the widest possible television audience. A foreign service officer working on Nixon's 1973 meeting with the French president Georges Pompidou recalled, "All they cared about was how things would look on television . . . who would stand where, what the background would be, and the furniture." Twelve years later, a Portuguese official said of Reagan's trip to that country, "Everything was TV. That's what they cared about. What the TV was going to do."[53]

Second, foreign policy generally does more than domestic policy for a president's popularity. Theodore Lowi has demonstrated that traditionally foreign policy crises are followed by a rise in presidential popularity, while after domestic crises a decline in popularity occurs.[54] Presidents seem to know this and react accordingly, traveling abroad when their poll ratings decline, and drawing on the symbolism of bipartisanship in foreign policy to rally support for their policies.

Ordinarily, fewer Americans follow foreign policy than domestic policy, and so a third reason for presidents' preference for foreign policy is that they see it as more manipulable. The Reagan administration has viewed Central American policy largely as a problem in public relations. In 1981, a White House aide spoke of a plan to "low-key the issue" in order not to let it hurt Reagan's domestic priorities. Pollster Richard Beal, also on Reagan's staff, said, "What was wrong with El Salvador was the packaging of the activity, in terms of policy and presentation to the public. It wasn't well staged or sequenced." Conversely, in 1985 a "senior State Department official" said that the administration would "hype this issue as much as we can;" thus Reagan and Secretary of State George Shultz characterized Nicaragua as a communist satellite, and the antigovernment forces as the moral equivalent of the United States' "founding fathers." Foreign policy, like most other aspects of the Presidency, is now seen as a media production.[55]

CONSEQUENCES OF PRESIDENTIAL IMAGERY

All the conditions are in place for a vicious circle. The public has high expectations of presidents, but the decline of party and the policy dilemmas of corporate capitalism make presidents unable to fulfill those hopes. Numerous political observers of various persuasions have pointed out how this process feeds on itself.

At the heart of this syndrome is a cynical view of both the political process and the public itself. The White House is claimed by men skilled in the arts of campaigning, who have no clear idea of the uses to which power will be put should they reach their goal. Most are like Gary Hart, calling for "new ideas" without clarifying what those ideas are. Ronald Reagan is somewhat of an exception here, for unlike most of his predecessors he had a firm ideological vision when elected (though it was a conglomeration of shallow claims and tunnel vision). As a result, presidential rhetoric is inflated in order to overcome the very serious limitations of presidential power. In Lowi's formulation, both problems and solutions are "oversold," so that even moderate accomplishments are disappointing when measured against inflated promises. Most striking is that it does not work: presidential popularity is increasingly fragile, and an overreliance on media gimmickry further isolates the president from others in his party.[56]

There are equally serious effects on the public, whom recent presidents and their advisers view as "a mass of fluid voters who can be appeased by appearances, occasional drama, and clever rhetoric." More sophisticated than these strategies allow, much of the public becomes cynical, and so presidents must exaggerate their rhetoric further in order to attract attention—which further increases the cynicism. Others, fascinated with the glitter, become bored with serious political concerns, believing that electing a hero will solve all problems. They become distracted both from their own needs ("Reagan makes us feel good about ourselves") and from the realities of power. Even many who dissent from existing policies often share this fascination with personality, and make the president a diabolical figure whose replacement is a primary priority. A better understanding of the situation would occur if more attention were directed to the impersonal aspects of the system.[57]

As a consequence, the president himself becomes a product to be merchandised, a soulless commodity. The most penetrating analysis of Richard Nixon states:

> He is the least "authentic" man alive, the late mover, tester of responses, submissive to "the discipline of consent." A survivor. There is one Nixon only, though there seem to be new ones all the time—he will try to be what people want.[58]

Of Jimmy Carter it has been said, "He had a keener sense of media power than of what he wanted to do after mastering it." When asked, "What does the guy stand for?" Carter's media adviser in 1976 said, "Come on. Be serious. He stands for getting elected to the White House." No wonder he seemed so inconsistent as president.[59]

If corporate capitalism is in trouble, the presidency is an increasingly ineffective means of rescuing it. A political system without strong parties elevates men without identities to administer an economy without a soul. In 120 years, the nation has gone from the Great Emancipator to the Great Communicator, although exactly what Reagan is trying to communicate is becoming harder and harder to discern.

Further Reading

The first book-length collection of essays on presidents and political parties is Robert Harmel, ed., *Presidents and Their Parties* (New York: Praeger Publishers, 1984). Two traditional liberal arguments for a strong-party presidency are Charles

M. Hardin, *Presidential Power and Accountability* (Chicago: Univ. of Chicago Press, 1974), and James MacGregor Burns, *The Power to Lead* (New York: Simon & Schuster, 1984). Michael Baruch Grossman and Martha Joynt Kumar's *Portraying the President* (Baltimore: The Johns Hopkins Univ. Press, 1981) is a thorough review of the elements of the plebiscitary presidency, and Theodore J. Lowi discusses the implications of such a presidency in his *The Personal President* (Ithaca, N.Y.: Cornell Univ. Press, 1985). For a fine collection of essays on the presidency in general, see Thomas E. Cronin, ed., *Rethinking the Presidency* (Boston: Little, Brown, 1982), especially those essays by Bruce Miroff and by Alan Wolfe.

On presidential attempts to rescue the economy, see Edward R. Tufte, *Political Control of the Economy* (Princeton, N.J.: Princeton Univ. Press, 1978); Robert M. Collins, *The Business Response to Keynes, 1929–1964* (New York: Columbia Univ. Press, 1981); and Kim McQuaid, *Big Business and Presidential Power* (New York: William Morrow, 1982).

Notes

1. See Alan Wolfe, "Presidential Power and the Crisis of Modernization," in Thomas E. Cronin, ed., *Rethinking the Presidency* (Boston: Little, Brown, 1982), 139–152.

2. Quoted in Clinton Rossiter, *The American Presidency,* 2nd ed. (New York: New American Library, 1960), 33–34.

3. "Early Expectations," *Public Opinion,* February-March 1981, 39.

4. "The Failing Presidency," the *New York Times,* 9 January 1982, sec. 4, p. 22.

5. Theodore C. Sorensen, *Kennedy* (New York: Bantam Books, 1966), 388; and Raymond K. Price, "10 Years Out, but Not Down," the *New York Times,* 9 August 1984, p. A23.

6. See, for example, Charles M. Hardin, *Presidential Power and Accountability* (Chicago: Univ. of Chicago Press, 1974), and James MacGregor Burns, *The Power to Lead* (New York: Simon & Schuster, 1984).

7. David M. Potter, "Jefferson Davis and the Political Factors in Confederate Defeat," in David Donald, ed., *Why the North Won the Civil War* (New York: Collier Books, 1962), 111–112; and Eric L. McKitrick, "Party Politics and the Union and Confederate War Efforts," in William Nisbet Chambers and Walter Dean Burnham, eds., *The American Party Systems* (New York: Oxford Univ. Press, 1967), 117–151.

8. Jimmy Carter, *Why Not the Best?* (Nashville, Tenn.: Boardman Press, 1975).

9. Godfrey Hodgson, *All Things To All Men* (London: Penguin Books, 1984), 150–151. Truman vetoed the Taft-Hartley Act, but Congress overrode his veto.

10. Quoted in Joseph A. Califano, Jr., *A Presidential Nation* (New York: W. W. Norton, 1975), 153.

11. Thomas E. Cronin, "The Presidency and the Parties," in Gerald M. Pomper, ed., *Party Renewal in America* (New York: Praeger Publishers, 1980), 178–179.

12. Cronin, "The Presidency and the Parties," 180; and Harold Bass, "The President and the National Party Organization," in Robert Harmel, ed., *Presidents and Their Parties* (New York: Praeger Publishers, 1984), 65–66.

13. Jules Witcover, *The Resurrection of Richard Nixon* (New York: G. P. Putnam's Sons, 1970), 168–169; Rowland Evans, Jr., and Robert D. Novak, *Nixon in the White House* (New York: Vintage Books, 1972), 30–33, 70–74; "Working Profile: Bill Brock," the *New York Times,* 17 March 1982, p. A20; and "Carter Asks Democratic Leaders To Help Him on Panama Treaties," the *New York Times,* 8 October 1977, p. 24.

14. Quoted in Harmel, ed., *Presidents and Their Parties,* 91. See also Bass, "The President and the National Party Organization," 68–69, 77; Roger G. Brown, "The Presidency and the Political Parties," in Michael Nelson, ed., *The Presidency and the Political System* (Washington: Congressional Quarterly Press, 1984), 318–320; David S. Broder, *The Party's Over* (New York: Harper & Row, 1971), 62–63; Evans and Novak, *Nixon in the White House,* 74; "National Committee Scolds Carter For Bypassing State Party Chiefs," the *New York Times,* 2 April 1977, p. 12; and Roger G. Brown, "Presidents as Midterm Campaigners," in Harmel, ed., *Presidents and Their Parties,* p. 133.

15. Bass, "The President and the National Party Organization," 85; Broder, *The Party's Over,* 63–64; and Lewis Chester, Godfrey Hodgson, and Bruce Page, *An American Melodrama* (New York: Viking Press, 1969), 632.

16. Quoted in George C. Edwards III, "Presidential Party Leadership in Congress," in Harmel, ed., *Presidents and Their Parties,* 185, 187. See also Edwards, *Presidential Influence in Congress* (San Francisco: W. H. Freeman, 1980), 61–62.

17. See J. Vincent Buck, "Presidential Coattails and Congressional Loyalty," *Midwest Journal of Political Science* XVI (August 1972), 460–472; George C. Edwards III, "Presidential Influence in the House," *American Political Science Review* LXX (March 1976), 101–113; Edwards, "Presidential Influence in the Senate," *American Politics Quarterly* V (October 1977), 481–500; Edwards, "Presidential Electoral Performance as a Source of Presidential Power," *American Journal of Political Science* XXII (February 1978), 152–168; Kathryn Newcomer Harmon and Marsha L. Brauen, "Joint Electoral Outcomes as Cues for Congressional Support of U.S. Presidents," *Legislative Studies Quarterly* IV (May 1979), 281–299; Edwards, *Presidential Influence in Congress,* p. 109; Jeffrey E. Cohen, "The Impact of the Modern Presidency on Presidential Success in the U.S. Congress," *Legislative Studies Quarterly* VII (November 1982), 515–532; Richard Fleischer and Jon R. Bond, "Assessing Presidential Support in the House," *Journal of Politics* XLV (August 1983), 745–758; and Samuel Kernell, "The Presidency and the People," in Nelson, ed., *The Presidency and the Political System,* 253.

18. See John F. Manley, "Presidential Power and White House Lobbying," *Political Science Quarterly* XCIII (Summer 1978), 255–275; Brown, "Presidents as Midterm Campaigners," 140–144; and Edwards, "Presidential Party Leadership in Congress," 191–193.

19. Edwards, "Presidential Party Leadership in Congress," 194; and "22 G.O.P. Senators Pressed to Back Reagan Programs," the *New York Times,* 15 March 1985, pp. A1, B6.

20. See my "Purging the GOP," *The Nation,* 18 January 1971, 71–74; and Sidney M. Milkis, "Presidents and Party Purges," in Harmel, ed., *Presidents and Their Parties,* 151–175.

21. Jimmy Carter, *Keeping Faith* (New York: Bantam Books, 1982), 69, 80.

22. See Herbert M. Kritzer and Robert B. Eubank, "Presidential Coattails Revisited," *American Journal of Political Science* XXIII (August 1979), 615–626; Cronin, "The Presidency and the Parties," 184–185; Edwards, *Presidential Influence in Congress,* 70–78, 81; and Randall L. Calvert and John A. Ferejohn, "Coattail Voting in Recent Presidential Elections," *American Political Science Review* LXXVII (June 1983), 407–419.

23. Quotations from Elizabeth Drew in *The New Yorker,* 28 February 1977, 86.

24. Quoted in Kernell, "The Presidency and the People," 246–247, 253.

25. *Presidential Campaign Activites of 1972: Hearings Before the Select Committee on Presidential Campaign Activities of the United States Senate: Watergate and Related Activities: Book 6* (Washington: Government Printing Office, 1973), 2483–2484. The dialogue is between Senator Lowell P. Weicker, Jr., Republican of Connecticut, and Gordon Strachan, former staff assistant to the White House chief of staff.

26. "The GOP and the Boll Weevils," *Newsweek,* 29 June 1981, 17; Gary C. Jacobson, "Congress," in Michael Nelson, ed., *The Elections of 1984* (Washington: Congressional Quarterly Press, 1985), 222–224; and Theodore J. Lowi, *The Personal President* (Ithaca, N.Y.: Cornell Univ. Press, 1985), 78. The emphasis is Lowi's.

27. Edwards, *Presidential Influence in Congress,* 205. See also 81, 109, 202.

28. Richard E. Neustadt, *Presidential Power* (New York: Signet Books, 1964), 50, 22; Arthur M. Schlesinger, Jr., *A Thousand Days* (Boston: Houghton Mifflin, 1965), 406–413; Richard Nixon, *RN* (New York: Grosset & Dunlap, 1978), 761, 769; George C. Edwards III, *The Public Presidency* (New York: St. Martin's Press, 1983), 204; "Self-Assured Carter Is Buoyant Despite Bruises and Frustrations," the *New York Times,* 23 October 1977, sec. 1, p. 36; and "Carter Describes Major Worries," the *New York Times,* 30 July 1978, sec. 1, p. 14.

29. Joel D. Aberbach and Bert A. Rockman, "Clashing Beliefs Within the Executive Branch," *American Political Science Review* LXX (June 1976), 456–468.

30. George C. Edwards III and Stephen J. Wayne, *Presidential Leadership* (N.Y.: St. Martin's Press, 1985), 368. See also Cronin, "The Presidency and the Parties," 180, 186–187; and Gary R. Orren, "The Changing Styles of American Party Politics," in Joel L. Fleishman, ed., *The Future of American Political Parties* (Englewood Cliffs, N.J.: Prentice-Hall, 1982), 41.

31. Quoted in Richard P. Nathan, *The Plot That Failed* (New York: John Wiley & Sons, 1975), 40. See also Edwards, *The Public Presidency,* 204–205.

32. For Nixon's plans, see Nathan, *The Plot That Failed;* on Reagan, see "Reagan Revamping Cabinet Councils; 2 Key Aides Named," the *New York Times,* 12 April 1985, pp. A1, A15.

33. Youngstown Sheet & Tube Company v. Sawyer, 343 U.S. 579 (1952).

34. Grant McConnell, *Steel and the Presidency, 1962* (New York: W. W. Norton, 1963), 103.

35. William Safire, *Before the Fall* (New York: Belmont Tower Books, 1975), 491–496.

36. Safire, *Before the Fall,* 509–528; and Kim McQuaid, *Big Business and Presidential Power* (New York: William Morrow, 1982), 268–283.

37. Broder, *The Party's Over,* 58.

38. Safire, *Before the Fall,* 511.

39. Laurence I. Barrett, *Gambling with History* (Garden City, N.Y.: Doubleday, 1983), 142, 163; and Steven R. Weisman, "Reaganomics and the President's Men," the *New York Times Magazine,* 24 October 1982, 28. See also William Greider, "The Education of David Stockman," *The Atlantic,* December 1981, 46–47.

40. Lowi, *The Personal President,* xi.

41. See also Neustadt, *Presidential Power,* especially chapter 5.

42. Michael Baruch Grossman and Martha Joynt Kumar, *Portraying the President* (Baltimore: The Johns Hopkins Univ. Press, 1981), 83; Kernell, "The Presidency and the People," 242, 244–245; and Michael J. Robinson and Margaret A. Sheehan, *Over the Wire and On TV* (New York: Russell Sage Foundation, 1983), 266.

43. See, for example, Sidney Blumenthal, "Marketing the President," the *New York Times Magazine,* 13 September 1981, 43; and Edwards, *The Public Presidency,* 17.

44. See Blumenthal, "Marketing the President," 110; Dick Kirschten, "Communications Reshuffling Intended To Help Reagan Do What He Does Best," *National Journal,* 28 January 1984, 153–154; *The United States Government Manual 1984/1985* (Washington: Government Printing Office, 1984), 78–81; and "Buchanan Assumes A Powerful Position In the White House," the *New York Times,* 11 April 1985, A1, A25.

45. In general, see Seymour Sudman, "The Presidents and the Polls," *Public Opinion Quarterly* XLVI (Fall 1982), 301–310. See also Edward R. Tufte, *Political Control of the Economy* (Princeton, N.J.: Princeton Univ. Press, 1978), footnote p. 47; and Blumenthal, "Marketing the President," 43, 110, 118.

46. See Edwards, *The Public Presidency,* 222; and Kernell, "The Presidency and the People," 236, 255.

47. On the public liaison role in general, see Martha Joynt Kumar and Michael Baruch Grossman, "The Presidency and Interest Groups," in Nelson, ed., *The Presidency and the Political System,* 282–312. See also Cronin, "The Presidency and the Parties," 182; Dick

Kirschten, "Tending to Fences," *National Journal*, 18 April 1981, 657; and "Inside Washington," *National Journal*, 31 December 1983, 2659.

48. See Grossman and Kumar, *Portraying the President*, 302. For a history of the relationship between the presidency and the press, see Richard L. Rubin, *Press, Party, and Presidency* (New York: W. W. Norton, 1981), chapters 2–6.

49. Bruce Miroff, "Monopolizing the Public Space," in Cronin, ed., *Rethinking the Presidency*, 221; and Grossman and Kumar, *Portraying the President*, chapter 10.

50. Quoted in Robinson and Sheehan, *Over the Wire*, 191.

51. C. T. Hanson, "Gunsmoke and Sleeping Dogs," *Columbia Journalism Review*, May/June 1983, 27; George Reedy, "There They Go Again," *Columbia Journalism Review*, May/June 1983, 35; Grossman and Kumar, *Portraying the President*, 182, 227; and Robinson and Sheehan, *Over the Wire*, 183.

52. David L. Paletz and Robert M. Entman, *Media Power Politics* (New York: The Free Press, 1981), 60–61. For an account of various presidential techniques of media manipulation, see Grossman and Kumar, *Portraying the President*.

53. Kernell, "The Presidency and the People," 244; David Wise, *The Politics of Lying* (New York: Random House, 1973), 259; Grossman and Kumar, *Portraying the President*, 236; and "A Reporter's Notebook," *The New York Times*, 10 May 1985, p. A10.

54. Theodore J. Lowi, *The Politics of Disorder* (New York: Basic Books, 1971), 93–94. See also his *The Personal President*, 161–173.

55. Blumenthal, "Marketing the President," 112; and "White House Rejects Indirect Assistance To Nicaragua Rebels," the *New York Times*, 13 March 1985, p. A7.

56. Sidney Blumenthal, *The Permanent Campaign*, rev. ed. (New York: Simon & Schuster, 1982), 24; Wolfe, "Presidential Power," 149; Theodore J. Lowi, *The End of Liberalism* (New York: W. W. Norton, 1969), 174–186; James W. Ceaser *et al.*, "The Rise of the Rhetorical Presidency," *Presidential Studies Quarterly* XI (Spring 1981), 160–161; Austin Ranney, *Channels of Power* (New York: Basic Books, 1983), 140; Kernell, "The Presidency and the People," 236; and Orren, "Changing Styles," 41.

57. Blumenthal, *Permanent Campaign*, 24; Paletz and Entman, *Media Power Politics*, 77; and Miroff, "Monopolizing the Public Space," 224–225, 229.

58. Garry Wills, *Nixon Agonistes* (Boston: Houghton Mifflin, 1970), 406.

59. Blumenthal, *Permanent Campaign*, 325, 63.

12

Democrats and Republicans: What's the Difference?

To many foreign observers, and even to many Americans, one of the most confusing aspects of American politics is the lack of apparent difference between the major parties. In chapter 3 I pointed out that there is less ideological distance between the Democrats and the Republicans than there is between major parties in other industrialized capitalist states. Both parties advocate corporate capitalism (despite some farfetched conservative rhetoric about liberal Democrats being socialists), both accept the values of liberal capitalism and the decentralized American state that fits those values, and both espouse the premise of the cold war that the United States should compete with the Soviets for the allegiance of the rest of the world, militarily if necessary. It is easy to infer from this that there is, in the words of third-party candidate George Wallace in 1968, "not a dime's worth of difference" between the Democrats and the Republicans.

If I have conveyed that notion in some parts of this book, then this chapter is an opportunity to correct the misimpression. Within the bounds of a shared commitment to liberal capitalist values and corporate capitalist reality there are indeed interparty differences. They are not as fundamental as the differences between parties in other nations, but they are real nonetheless. Perhaps the most fruitful way to think of them is as quarrels within a family, or as some commentators have put it, between two factions of one capitalist "party."[1] By studying these differences, we can learn much about the political needs of capitalism.

How can we tell whether there are real differences between the parties, and what those differences are? There are many ways to find out, and I shall explore several of them empirically. The questions I shall answer are (1) Does the public perceive differences between the parties? (2) Do rank-and-file Democrats and rank-and-file Republicans differ from each other demographically or ideologically? (3) Do the parties have different allies among interest groups? (4) Do the parties' platforms and campaign stands differ from each other? (5) Do Democrats in Congress

258

vote differently from congressional Republicans? And finally, (6) Do the parties produce different economic policies?

Before proceeding, it is necessary to define the standard ideological categories used in analyzing American politics. The term "liberal" is used to denote those who are more favorable to the use of government, and especially of the federal government, to promulgate social programs and the kinds of economic regulation opposed by business. Relatively speaking, liberals want social programs to promote greater equality among the classes, among the races, between the sexes, and among similar social categories. They tend to emphasize civil rights and civil liberties more than conservatives do. In recent years, liberals tend toward a foreign policy that emphasizes diplomacy and human rights and is less oriented toward high Pentagon budgets and military action abroad, although this is a very crude generalization. "Conservatives" are those who want to keep the government, especially in Washington, out of the areas of social policy and the kinds of economic regulation opposed by business. They are relatively unconcerned with equalitarianism, civil rights, and civil liberties, and some are inclined to use governmental power to enforce moral values such as banning pornography and abortion and promoting school prayer. Conservatives usually favor high Pentagon budgets and are often more inclined than liberals to use military power abroad. These concepts will be used throughout this chapter to ascertain whether the parties differ.

PERCEPTIONS OF DIFFERENCES

Do the American people discern any significant differences between the major parties? The answer to this in itself does not prove whether there are any real differences; perhaps the public thinks there are real differences when there are none, or maybe the people fail to see that there are such differences in reality. Nevertheless, this is a good starting point, for it may guide us to what the differences are.

Over the years the Center for Political Studies of the University of Michigan (CPS) has been asking its nationwide samples whether they think there are any "important differences" between the parties. From 1952 until 1976, about half the population saw such differences. In 1980 the proportion rose to 58 percent, and in 1984, 63 percent said that there were important differences between the parties, while 30 percent disagreed and 8 percent simply did not know. The political scientist Gerald Pomper found that from 1956 to 1972 there was a substantial rise in the proportion of Americans who thought that there were differences between the parties on a range of domestic issues, and there was increasing agreement that it was the Democrats who took the more liberal position. Pomper attributed this to the increasing differences between the parties' presidential candidates, which recalls the "conditionality hypothesis" discussed in chapter 7.[2]

Fortunately for purposes of analysis, when the CPS asks if there are any important differences between the parties, it goes on to ask those who say yes what those differences are. In 1984 the interviewers recorded up to three responses per individual, and the results were striking. Virtually everyone—98 percent—who was able to state at least one important difference cited class differences. Within this category, the most frequent references were to the Democrats being the party of the working people or the Republicans being the party of the wealthy or of big business. I have also included in this category references to social programs associated with class interests, such as Social Security and welfare. Although I have been asserting that the Democrats do not serve the real interests of the working class, a sizable majority of Americans believed that there were significant class differences between the parties.

In addition, a majority of those who cited differences also saw the parties as having distinctive ideologies; particularly, they saw the Democrats as more liberal or the Republicans as more conservative. More than a quarter of the respondents said that there were differences on foreign policy, particularly on national defense, and the same proportion said that there were differences on fiscal policy and the management of government, especially on the size of the national debt. But clearly the major interparty differences cited in 1984 were on social class and ideology.

The CPS also asks respondents if there is anything they like about the Democratic party, anything they dislike about it, anything they like about the Republican party, and anything they dislike about it. In 1984, the interviewers recorded up to five responses per respondent for each of these four questions. By examining the results, we can see each party's strong points and weak points. Table 12.1 has the results, and once again references to social class predominate. Nearly everyone who had something positive to say about the Democratic party included a reference to its association with the average or working people, and four out of five of those who made negative references to the Republican party cited its association with the privileged classes.

As noted in chapter 5, these images are nothing new. The Republican alliance with big business began in the 1890s, while the Democrats' association with the labor movement dates back to the 1930s. Indeed, Richard Trilling's exhaustive analysis of the survey question under review covering the years 1952 through 1972 concluded that "the Democratic Party is liked because it is seen as the party of the common person and because it is perceived as having helped people in the Depression. The Republican image suffers from the perceived association of the Republicans with the Depression and with business and the upper class." The most frequent pro-Democratic response in each year that Trilling examined was that "it promotes good times for average people," and the most common anti-

Table 12.1. What people responded when asked what they liked or disliked about the major parties in 1984.

	Pro-Democratic	Anti-Democratic	Pro-Republican	Anti-Republican
Social class	94	37	26	81
Ideology	7	17	20	8
Management of government	5	30	21	18
Foreign policy	12	20	31	24
Management of the economy	10	4	15	7

Note: Read this table as follows: 94 percent of the people who said something positive about the Democrats said something about social class; 37 percent of the people who made a negative reference to the Democrats said something about social class.
Source: National survey, University of Michigan Center for Political Studies

Republican comment in each year was that "it causes bad times for average people and stands for business interests."[3] In 1984, such perceptions were an asset to the Mondale campaign, and became known as the "fairness issue."

If the most common perception of interparty differences strongly favors the Democrats, then how can Republicans win presidential elections? The rest of Table 12.1 provides a substantial part of the answer. References to ideology favor the Republicans, as there are far more anti-Democratic and pro-Republican responses in this category than pro-Democratic or anti-Republican comments. The Republicans are seen as more faithful to the traditional American values of capitalism, limited government, and militancy in foreign policy. The fact that "conservative" is a far more popular term among Americans today than "liberal," even among people who believe in much of the liberal agenda,[4] surely helps the Republicans. The Republicans are also seen as better managers of government, largely on the grounds of greater efficiency and more businesslike direction. On foreign policy, pro-Republican responses outnumber anti-Republican comments, and the reverse is true of the Democrats. Since references to national defense were frequent, the American people were apparently satisfied with the jingoistic policies of the Republican administration. All of these Republican advantages on ideology, government management, and foreign policy, reports Trilling, were common in the period from 1952 to 1972 as well.[5]

The only anomaly in Table 12.1 is on management of the economy; each party's "pro" responses outnumber its "con" responses. Since few people perceived an economic crisis in 1984, respondents were not thinking along these lines, but within this category the Republicans were seen as better on controlling inflation, the Democrats on providing jobs.

All in all, then, it appears that a majority of Americans do perceive that there are important differences between the parties, and that each party has its strong points. The Democrats are seen as more receptive to the needs of the common people, while the Republicans are seen as ideologically preferable and better managers of government and foreign policy.

DIFFERENCES BETWEEN THE RANK AND FILE

"As a general rule," wrote the humorist Robert Benchley, "Republicans are more blonde than Democrats."[6] Are there in fact any such obvious differences in how Democrats and Republicans look, or how they think?

Demographic differences

First we will examine, in Table 12.2, how the parties differ in the social background of their members. However, instead of showing, for example, what proportion of Democrats belong to group X, I am showing the proportion of group X that belongs to the Democratic party. This is because the former method can be misleading. If group X is only a small proportion of the American people, than it will be a small proportion of both parties, and any difference in the attractiveness of each party to group X will be minimized. For example, blacks comprise only 19 percent of the Democratic party, but 65 percent of blacks are Democrats; the latter figure is a dramatic illustration of the appeal the Democrats have for blacks, while the 19 percent figure is largely due to the fact that blacks are a distinct minority of the total population.

Table 12.2 shows that the Democratic party is especially attractive to blacks, Catholics, Jews, Southerners, women, and the lower socioeconomic classes. Republicans attract white Protestants, Midwesterners, and the higher socioeconomic classes. Both parties are more effective at attracting older voters than younger voters, who are most likely to call themselves independents.

It has long been a remarkable feature of American political parties that, unlike parties in other competitive capitalist regimes, they have more effectively divided the population along sectional, racial and religious lines than along class lines.[7] The extent to which American parties' coalitions are based on section, race and religion can be determined by a simple comparison: in 1984, more than half of all Republicans were northern white Protestants, while only one-fourth of Democrats were northern white Protestants.[8] In chapter 5 I argued that Franklin D. Roosevelt's New Deal introduced an unprecedented degree of social class to American party alignments. According to James Sundquist, Roosevelt's successor Harry Truman was the last Democratic presidential contender to use explicit

Table 12.2. Party identification of various social groups, 1984. (Percentages sum horizontally to 100.)

	Democrat	Republican	Independent
All	38	28	35
Men	33	28	39
Women	41	27	32
White Protestants	30	38	32
White Catholics	42	22	36
Jews	43	17	41
All Whites	34	31	35
Blacks	65	4	31
Northeast	37	26	37
Southeast	44	21	35
Midwest	31	34	35
Far West	37	32	31
Age 17–29	32	24	44
Age 30–39	33	29	38
Age 40–49	39	28	32
Age 50–69	45	26	29
Age 70 and Over	40	36	24
Middle-Class Identifiers	33	34	33
Working-Class Identifiers	42	22	36
Family Income:			
Under $11,000 (bottom 25%)	46	18	36
$11,000–34,999 (middle 50%)	36	28	36
$35,000 and Over (top 25%)	32	34	34
Education:			
Less Than 12 Years	46	22	32
12 Years	37	25	38
Some College	35	31	34
College Graduate	29	38	32
Graduate School	36	27	37

Note: Some rows do not sum to 100 due to rounding off.
Sources: National survey, University of Michigan Center for Political Studies, and (for Jewish sample) Los Angeles Times exit poll results provided by Everett Ladd

class appeals. As a consequence, the upper classes have tended to divide their loyalties between the parties, and the Democratic party like the Republican, has since become a middle-class party.[9]

I have maintained that even in the heyday of the New Deal, when class differences between the parties were at their apex, the Democrats were unable to represent the real interests of the working class, bound as that party was to corporate capitalism. Since then, the Democrats have been even less oriented to working-class demands, as the relatively conservative Carter administration demonstrated. There are indeed real social differences between the parties, but less along the crucial dimension of social class than along other lines. Although the public is most likely to see interparty differences in class terms, other demographic differences are at least as important in distinguishing the parties' mass bases from each other.

Ideological differences

Over the years, survey analysts have found significant differences between Democrats and Republicans on many specific issues. As the political scientist Benjamin Page put it, Democrats are likely to favor "an active federal government, helping citizens with jobs, education, medical care, and the like; Republicans have wanted less government spending and lower taxes."[10] In other words, Democrats tend to be liberal, Republicans conservative. This was borne out in the 1984 University of Michigan survey, when about four times as many self-described liberals identified with the Democrats as with the Republicans, and more than twice as many self-labelled conservatives identified with the Republicans as with the Democrats.

More particularly, Democrats and Republicans have often been most likely to disagree on the class-oriented issues that stem from the New Deal, such as those cited in Page's quotation. In contrast, foreign policy issues seem least likely to divide the parties. In addition, numerous scholars have found an increase in interparty differences from the 1950s to the 1960s, which again brings to mind the "conditionality hypothesis" introduced above in Chapter 7. There is, however, some difference of opinion among scholars as to whether the increase in interparty differences is concentrated among the highly educated.[11] Many researchers have found that interparty differences are especially striking among party elites such as national convention delegates.[12]

All in all, then, the issue differences between the parties' rank and file seem to confirm the picture presented earlier in parts of this chapter of class taking precedence over other concerns.

INTEREST GROUP SUPPORT

The political scientist Theodore Lowi has addressed the question posed by this chapter's title as follows:

The most important difference between liberals and conservatives, Republicans and Democrats—however they define themselves—is to be found in the interest groups they identify with. Congressmen are guided in their votes, Presidents in their programs, and administrators in their discretion by whatever organized interests they have taken for themselves as the most legitimate; and that is the measure of the legitimacy of demands.[13]

Benjamin Page suggests that big business groups are more likely than labor organizations to support Republicans, with labor more apt to donate to Democrats. However, Page notes, some business sectors are particularly attracted to the Democrats: "merchandising, construction and building materials, hard and soft drinks, publishing, advertising, and entertainment."[14]

We can test these assertions by looking at the contributions to the campaigns of the members of Congress who were serving in 1985. In chapter 4, I pointed out that a sizable majority of members received more money from business than from labor; Table 12.3 breaks these contribu-

Table 12.3. Members of Congress serving in 1985, and whether they received more contributions to their most recent campaign from business or labor political action committees.

	All	Reps.	Dems.	Democrats Non-South	South
A) Senators					
More from business	74%	98%	47%	32%	85%
More from labor	25	2	51	65	15
Accepted no contributions	1	0	2	3	0
Total	100	100	100	100	100
Number of members	100	53	47	34	13
B) Representatives					
More from business	63%	99%	37%	20%	75%
More from labor	37	1	63	80	25
Accepted no contributions	*	1	0	0	0
Total	100	101	100	100	100
Number of members	434	182	252	176	76

Note: Percentages do not always sum to 100 due to rounding. Data were missing for one representative.

* Less than .5 percent.

Source: Michael Barone and Grant Ujifusa, *The Almanac of American Politics 1984* (Washington: National Journal, 1983); and Barone and Ujifusa, *The Almanac of American Politics 1986* (Washington: National Journal, 1985).

tions down between Democrats and Republicans. Nearly every Republican in both houses received more donations from business than from labor, while Democrats in both houses were divided. We can see striking sectional differences between southern and nonsouthern Democrats.[15] Most southern Democrats were backed more by business than by labor, while most northern Democrats received more from labor than from business. Interparty differences on this important variable are reduced by the presence in the Democratic party of a sizable conservative wing concentrated in the Southeast.

Again there appears to be a significant difference between the parties on a class-related dimension. Here, however, we can for the first time see the difference-blurring effect of the heterogeneity of the Democratic party, whose southern members are in this instance closer to the Republicans than to their fellow partisans outside the South.

PLATFORMS AND CAMPAIGNS

By common impression, party platforms and candidates' speeches are lists of empty rhetoric and meaningless promises that are ignored as soon as candidates are elected. Some of the more infamous examples are Franklin Roosevelt's promise to balance the budget, Lyndon Johnson's pledge not to send American "boys" to do the job Asian "boys" should do, Richard Nixon's statements about restoring respect for the law, and Ronald Reagan's assurances about low budget deficits. Are these isolated examples, or do the parties routinely fail to offer the electorate meaningful guides about the future during campaigns?

Platforms

No scholar has examined party platforms more closely than Gerald Pomper, who has analyzed both parties' documents sentence by sentence from 1944 through 1976.[16] Among the questions he asked were: are platforms filled with empty rhetoric, or do they contain specific policy-oriented information for the voter? Do the parties differ in their pledges? Are the pledges carried out?

What did Pomper discover? The following is a breakdown of sentences from the average platform from the period he examined, grouped into categories with examples of mine taken from both parties' platforms in 1984:[17]

1. *Rhetoric.* These statements, totally useless to the reader who is trying to figure out what the party wants to do, comprised about 17 percent of the average platform.

"From freedom comes opportunity; from opportunity comes growth; from growth comes progress." (Republicans)

"Our party is built on a profound belief in America and Americans." (Democrats)

2. *General evaluations of the past.* Vague assertions about the past four years comprised another 12 percent of platforms.

"The Republican Administration has turned its back on basic industries and their communities." (Democrats)

"We brought about a new beginning." (Republicans)

3. *Specific policy statements about the past.* These more explicit remarks presumably help the voter tell what kinds of policies are likely to be maintained or changed, and they comprised 19 percent of platforms.

"With the Economic Recovery Tax Act of 1981, we carried out the first phase of tax reduction and reform by cutting marginal tax rates by 25 percent." (Republicans)

"While thousands of toxic waste sites already exist, and more and more are being created constantly, the Reagan Administration is cleaning them up at a rate of only 1.5 per year." (Democrats)

4. *Pledges for the future.* These are presumably the most helpful kinds of statements in a platform for a voter, and they comprised about 52 percent of all the sentences in an average platform. However Pomper points out that future pledges can be general or specific. Here is a general statement, followed by a specific policy pledge, from each party's 1984 platform:

"For the economy, the Democratic Party is committed to economic growth, prosperity, and jobs." (Democrats)

"We will cap the effect of the Reagan tax cuts for wealthy Americans and enhance the progressivity of our personal income tax code, limiting the benefits of the third year of the Reagan tax cuts to the level of those with incomes of less than $60,000." (Democrats)

"We will therefore continue to return control of the economy to the people." (Republicans)

"For families, we will restore the value of personal exemptions, raising it to a minimum of $2,000 and indexing to prevent further erosion." (Republicans)

Pomper concluded that roughly half of platform statements can help the voter reach a rational decision, but perhaps a better indication of the usefulness of platforms is that when he wanted to see if pledges were being carried out, Pomper found that fewer than a third of platform sentences were specific enough to test.[18] Whether this figure is higher or lower than expected is up to you to assess.

On what issues did the parties make their specific pledges for the future? In the platforms drafted from 1968 to 1976, Pomper found that the specific pledges tended to be aimed toward particular constituencies, in the areas of labor, natural resources, social welfare, and agriculture. More to the point of this chapter, the parties differed in the issues they stressed. Democrats were more likely to discuss labor and social welfare, while Republicans concentrated more on military policy and government management.[19] It is clear from earlier sections of this chapter that each party stresses its areas of strength, with Democrats emphasizing class-related issues and Republicans concentrating on others. This is confirmed by an analysis of platforms from 1960 through 1980 by Alan Monroe, who concluded that Democrats' pledges were most popular in the areas of social welfare and natural resources, while Republican pledges were closest to public opinion in the areas of civil rights and government management.[20]

Do party platforms differ? Pomper found that there were three times as many bipartisan pledges—those in which both parties took the same position—as conflicting pledges. The latter were most likely to occur on issues related to labor, followed by social welfare, economic policy, and natural resources. The area of least conflict between the parties' platforms was civil rights, followed by government management and military policy.[21] Again, class-related issues seem disproportionately to differentiate the parties. Benjamin Ginsberg concluded from an analysis of all platforms from 1844 through 1968 that interparty differences were greatest during periods of realignment, which confirms an argument presented in chapter 5.[22] Finally, Pomper reports that about two-thirds of platform pledges are carried out, a ratio which rises to three-quarters for the party that controls the White House. However, in recent years the proportion of pledges fulfilled has dropped, perhaps suggesting the problems of policy management during times of difficulty for corporate captialism.[23]

Pomper concludes that a party's platform is important "not as an inspired gospel to which politicians resort for policy guidance. It is important becasue it summarizes, crystallizes, and presents to the voters the character of the party coalition."[24]

Campaigns

Whatever platforms say, there is a well-known phenomenon of political campaigns in which both parties' nominees begin to converge to the point on the policy spectrum where they think most voters are.[25] Benjamin Page has concluded from an intensive examination of candidates' speeches that even the nominees who were perceived as extremists—Barry Goldwater in 1964 and George McGovern in 1972—moved closer to the center of the spectrum as their campaigns wore on, and McGovern was not all that far from the center to begin with.[26]

This process was clear in Walter Mondale's 1984 campaign. Nervous about being considered "big spenders," the Democrats adopted a cautious platform, and Mondale assured business groups that the tax increase he was proposing would be used only to reduce the deficit, not for new social programs.[27] On foreign and military policy, Mondale endorsed a quarantine of Nicaragua and further increases in spending on the military; as one critic put it, "the only significant difference between Republicans and Democrats over intervention in Central America is the speed and the amount of guilt with which they would approve it."[28] Viewers of the Reagan-Mondale foreign policy debate were treated to an amusing spectacle as each candidate raced toward the center and ended up past each other, with Reagan proposing the sharing of military information with the Soviets as a gesture toward peace and Mondale denouncing the idea as irresponsible.

The convergence of candidates during campaigns is one of the primary reasons why American parties often seem to offer little choice to the electorate.

CONGRESSIONAL VOTING

Chapter 9 discussed the decline of the power of party leaders in Congress but left unexamined whether the members of Congress vote differently from each other, the subject to which we now turn. Part of the answer was given in Table 3.5, which showed that on the votes that pit a majority of Democrats against a majority of Republicans, the average member voted with his or her party about three-fourths of the time.

These are crude figures. They lump together very important votes with insignificant votes, and if a major piece of legislation required many votes during a session, the partisan configuration on that one issue will have a disproportionate effect on the voting statistics for that session. We turn instead to a consideration of the most important issues in a session, as determined by two ideological organizations. Americans for Democratic Action (ADA) is a liberal group that selects a handful of what it considers the most important votes in each session of Congress, and rates each member of Congress on those votes. Someone who voted the ADA way on every vote gets a rating of 100, and someone who opposed ADA on every vote (or was absent) is rated zero. Americans for Constitutional Action (ACA) is a conservative organization that does the same thing, except that members of Congress who get high ADA ratings are likely to get low ACA ratings, and vice versa.

For the congressional session of 1984, I have combined the ADA and ACA ratings for each member. Since the groups represent the opposite ends of the American political spectrum, the most appropriate way to combine them would be to subtract one of the scores from 100 and then average it with the other. Mathematically, the new "ADA/ACA Score" can be represented by:

$$[ADA + (100 - ACA)]/2$$

The higher the ADA/ACA Score, the more liberal the senator or representative. Just as the data in chapter 3 could be criticized, so can these ideological ratings. They deal with only a handful of votes for each session, and they ignore other kinds of congressional activity such as chairing a committee or being especially effective on a certain issue. Moreover, these groups have sometimes been accused of choosing the votes carefully in order to make certain members of Congress look good or others look bad.[29] However, I shall use these scores because they cover only the most important votes and are a widely cited measure of the ideological proclivity of members of Congress. Furthermore, there is evidence that ideology determines an overwhelming proportion of the voting variation in Congress over the years.[30]

In Table 12.4 I have divided each house of Congress into three roughly equal groups based on their ADA/ACA Scores. In each house the great majority of Republicans are located in the most conservative third of the spectrum and the Democrats are clustered in the liberal third. Southern Democrats occupy a centrist position and their northern counterparts are heavily concentrated at the liberal end.

In the exceptions to these generalizations, we can see some of the geographic divisions within the parties. Most of the Republicans found in

Table 12.4. ADA/ACA Scores of members of Congress, 1984. Each house is divided into three approximately equal parts based on the score, and the table shows the number of members in each third.

	All	Reps.	Dems.	Democrats Non-South	South
A) Senators					
0–19 (conservative)	33	33	0	0	0
20–63 (moderate)	34	19	15	5	10
64–100 (liberal)	33	3	30	27	3
Total	100	55	45	32	13
B) Representatives					
0–26 (conservative)	144	124	20	2	18
26.5–74.5 (moderate)	145	41	104	49	55
75–100 (liberal)	143	2	141	131	10
Total	432	167	265	182	83

Note: Data are missing for three representatives due to vacancies or to the fact that the Speaker ordinarily does not vote.

the liberal third of the Congress in 1984 were from New England. The most conservative Democrats outside the South were from the border states and the Great Plains. Within the South, the most liberal members were from the so-called rim or peripheral southern states, Arkansas, Florida, Kentucky, Tennessee, and Texas, rather than the Deep South.

We can get a better picture of the geographic configuration within each party from Table 12.5, which shows the mean ADA/ACA score for each party in each section of the country. In both houses, Southern Democrats stand out as their party's most conservative group by far, and the Northeastern and Far Western Democrats are the most liberal. Northeastern Republicans are that party's most liberal group in both houses, with Southerners and Far Westerners most conservative. We will consider the implications of the patterns in chapter 13, but for the moment the bottom-row figures in both parts of the table are noteworthy. They indicate that differences between the congressional parties are lowest in the Northeast and the Southeast. Northeastern members of Congress are relatively liberal, regardless of what party they belong to, and southeastern members are quite conservative. In the Far West the interparty differences are greatest.

On what issues are the congressional parties most likely to differ? Edward Schneier's study of the House from 1948 through 1964 concluded that class-oriented issues such as monetary and fiscal policy, health and welfare, housing, education, and labor were among the most divisive issues, and foreign policy (including foreign aid) produced much smaller differences between the parties. Wayne Shannon's analysis of the House from 1959 through 1962 reached similar conclusions, although Shannon found fewer interparty differences on civil rights than Schneier did. In 1984 William Schneider found greater interparty differences on economic issues than on social issues and foreign policy, with social issues producing the smallest interparty differences.[31]

Now that I have established that on major issues of ideological signifi-

Table 12.5. Mean ADA/ACA scores, 1984, by party and section.

	All	Northeast	Southeast	Midwest	Far West
A) Senators					
Democrats	72	86	52	70	82
Republicans	22	44	8	24	16
Difference	50	42	44	46	66
B) Representatives					
Democrats	70	80	48	76	86
Republicans	19	37	13	18	11
Difference	51	43	35	58	75

cance the congressional parties vote dissimilarly, we should consider the paradoxical fact that this occurs despite the weakness of party leadership in Congress. The evidence of chapter 9 suggests that party leadership is not strong enough by itself to compel Democrats and Republicans to unite against each other. What then is the glue that binds the congressional parties?

One factor is the different kinds of constituencies that each party represents. In most parts of the country, Republicans represent upper-class districts and suburban or rural areas, both of which tend to be conservative. Democratic districts tend to be urban and lower-class, and hence liberal. These are of course crude generalzations, but they are partly borne out by the exceptions to these rules. Some of the most liberal Republicans are those who represent urban areas, like the "silk-stocking" House district in Manhattan that has produced ultra-liberal Republicans like John Lindsay and, currently, William Green. Some of the most conservative Democrats outside the South are from rural districts, like Samuel Stratton from upstate New York. By and large, Democrats and Republicans vote differently because for the most part they represent different kinds of districts.

There is another reason why the congressional parties differ: they tend to attract different kinds of members. In most parts of the country, a politically ambitious liberal will join the Democratic party, just as a politically ambitious conservative will become a Republican. If they are elected to Congress, they will vote differently from each other, not because the party leaders forced them to, but because their own ideological beliefs led them to do so. We might say that there is a self-selected recruitment process going on, and it explains much of the difference between the Congressional parties.[32]

We are left to conclude that the parties indeed differ in their congressional voting patterns, especially on class-related issues, despite relatively weak party lcadershp.

ECONOMIC POLICY

Even if the parties differ in their mass bases, their interest group allies, their campaign pledges, and their voting patterns in Congress, the skeptical reader might say that the proof is in the pudding, and wonder whether the parties really do produce different policies. This can be a vast and far-ranging subject, and so I shall limit it by discussing just a few major economic policies: the size of the budget for social services and the management of inflation and unemployment. There are several reasons to concentrate on these policies: they have society-wide impact; they can each be measured quantitatively and therefore give us a more precise picture of trends than other areas can; and they are related to the course of corporate capitalism and consequently to the major themes of this book.

We might expect from the earlier findings of this chapter that the parties will indeed handle these policies differently. On the other hand, it may be that, as Richard Rose has written, "much of a party's record in office will be stamped upon it by forces outside its control."[33] Which is more accurate?

Social spending

Numerous studies have concluded that those capitalist nations that have been most often governed by parties at the left end of the spectrum have increased the public budget the most, especially in the area of social services such as health, welfare, education, housing, and so forth.[34] Moreover, some studies have concluded that capitalist nations governed by parties of the left have a more equal distribution of income that those governed by parties of the right;[35] if this is true, it may be a consequence of the more generous social programs.

Within the United States, have the Democrats and Republicans produced different levels of social spending? The problem for analysis is that the budget is determined by an interplay of the president with Congress. When they have been controlled by different parties, as has been the case for twenty-four of the forty-two years from 1947 through 1988, it becomes difficult to single out the impact of each party. Another problem is that some social spending is determined by laws of eligibility established years earlier. The most conspicuous examples are Social Security and Medicare, whose steep increases in spending are due in large part to the aging of the American population and cost-of-living increases. A fiscally tight-fisted president and Congress might see the budget for those two programs skyrocket because of factors beyond their control. Therefore our examination of trends in social spending will omit the costs of those two programs.

Table 12.6 show the spending by the federal government on human services, minus Social Security and Medicare, in every presidential election year since the end of World War II. By expressing each amount in 1967 dollars, this table controls for the effects of inflation. To some extent, we can see evidence of the effects of partisanship, with all of the large increases occurring in the years of undivided Democratic control of Congress from 1955 through 1980. Two of the smallest increases occurred when the Democrats lost control of at least one house, in the early 1950s and the 1980s. On the other hand, two of the declines in social spending occurred when the Democrats controlled both the White House and Congress, during the Truman and Carter administrations.

Perhaps the greatest anomalies are seen when we consider the party of the president. The greatest human services spending increase occurred during a Republican's (Nixon's) first term, the greatest decline during a Democrat's (Truman's) second. Indeed, the clearest picture comes when we ignore the parties on the left side of the table and just concentrate on

Table 12.6. Federal spending on human resources, minus Social Security and Medicare, in millions of 1967 dollars.

Year	Party of President, Prior 4 Years	Party controlling Congress, Prior 4 Years	Amount	Percent Change
1948	Democratic	Mixed	12,913	
1952	Democratic	Democratic	12,179	− 5.7%
1956	Republican	Mixed	12,982	+ 6.6
1960	Republican	Democratic	16,440	+26.6
1964	Democratic	Democratic	20,101	+22.3
1968	Democratic	Democratic	29,766	+48.1
1972	Republican	Democratic	47,545	+59.7
1976	Republican	Democratic	66,781	+40.5
1980	Democratic	Democratic	65,938	− 1.3
1984	Republican	Mixed	63,132*	− 4.3*

* Estimate

Source: Historical Tables: Budget of the United States Government, Fiscal Year 1986 (Washington: Government Printing Office, 1985), Tables 3.1 and 3.2

the last column. Social spending shot up higher and higher until its peak in the early 1970s, and since then it has been declining at an increasing rate. While it would be foolhardy to ignore, for example, the role of Reagan and the Republican Senate in the early 1980s, we should not forget the similar role played by Carter and the Democratic Congress in the late 1970s. To a great extent, we are observing long-term trends that seem to have a momentum apart from short-term partisan fluctuations.

Spending may be the most important way to measure a government's commitment to social services, but it is only one. Enforcement of civil rights laws and labor legislation may not cost the government much compared with other programs, but they too can be an important part of a liberal agenda.

Unemployment and inflation

Social services normally have a relatively clear class orientation, supposedly to help the lower classes. Dealing with unemployment and inflation, on the other hand, seems less clearly focussed in class terms. Economists discuss the so-called Phillips curve, in which unemployment rises as inflation falls, and vice versa. Actually, over the long run both have risen, as I shall demonstrate later, but in the short run the relationship often holds. When a choice must be made, whose interests are affected, and how? It is often alleged that everyone suffers equally from both, but further consideration suggests that there are class interests involved in each.

To the working class the greatest economic catastrophe that can occur is rising unemployment, because those at the bottom of the social scale are first to be laid off. Given a choice between seeing prices rise and losing one's job, most people have little problem making a decision. To the managers of businesses, high unemployment has some serious consequences, including fewer customers with spending money. However, this is offset in the minds of many business executives by the fact that organized labor becomes less demanding when workers fear losing their jobs. Indeed, many unions are willing to give back gains previously won at the bargaining table when faced with a choice between doing that or watching the company lay off workers. In addition, executives whose businesses and banks have debtors fear high inflation because it reduces the value of the money that those debtors will pay them back.

In any case, there is plenty of evidence from public opinion surveys that lower-class people are far more likely than their upper-class counterparts to fear unemployment more than inflation and to vote their class interests in times of high unemployment.[36] In 1980, the most recent presidential election in which there was a great deal of public concern about the economy, the *New York Times*/CBS News survey gave respondents a list of eight issues and asked them to check off one or two that were important in deciding how they voted. Table 12.7 shows how different income groups responded to the issues of "jobs and unemployment" and "inflation and economy." The lower the income category, the more the people cited the former and the less they cited the latter.

Given the concentration of upper-class individuals and corporate interests in the Republican party and lower-class individuals and labor interests in the Democratic party, it is not surprising that the parties' mass bases differ on the choice between unemployment and inflation. Survey data from 1976 bear this out.[37] In 1980, on the question in Table 12.7, Republicans cited inflation as an important issue twice as often as unemployment, while Democrats designated each about as often as the other. In 1982 the same survey asked people if they were more likely to vote for a

Table 12.7. Selected responses to the question, "Which issues were most important in deciding how you voted today?" on Election Day, 1980.

Family income	Jobs and unemployment	Inflation and economy
Under $10,000	29%	23%
$10,000–15,000	28	32
$15,000–25,000	24	37
$25,000–50,000	22	40
Over $50,000	13	42

Note: Read this table as follows: 29 percent of the lowest income group cited "jobs and unemployment," while 23 percent of the same group cited "inflation and economy" as an important issues.

Source: New York Times/CBS News exit poll

representative who wanted to keep inflation down, or one who sought to reduce unemployment. Those who intended to vote Republican chose inflation-fighters by a margin of 50 to 37 percent, while Democratic-leaners preferred unemployment-reducers by 65 to 23.[38]

Edward Tufte has demonstrated that party elites have behaved similarly. In 1976, the Republican platform laid far greater stress on inflation than on unemployment, while the Democratic emphasis was the reverse. Tufte's analysis of the Economic Reports of the Presidents and the Annual Reports of the Council of Economic Advisers from 1962 through 1977 revealed that the party of the president was more important than actual economic conditions in determing the relative emphasis those documents put on unemployment or inflation. He concluded that unless one of the problems was unusually severe, Democratic presidents wil generally try to get unemployment down, while Republicans in the White House will stress the control of inflation.[39]

What has been the record of the presidents on unemployment and inflation? Because presidents have major resources to manage macroeconomic policy, as noted in chapter 11, we need not pay as much attention to the party that controls Congress as we did in Table 12.6. In Table 12.8 we can see the average levels of unemployment and inflation during the administration of every president since Harry Truman.[40] The most obvious trend in the table is that over the long run both unemployment and inflation have been rising, regardless of who was president. This is part of the increasing difficulty of managing a corporate capitalist economy.

Table 12.8. Mean level of unemployment and inflation, 1949–1984, by party of the president.

Years	Presidents and Party	Unemployment	Inflation
1949–52	Truman (Democrat)	4.4%	2.5%
1953–60	Eisenhower (Republican)	4.9	1.4
1961–68	Kennedy, Johnson (Democrats)	4.8	2.0
1969–76	Nixon, Ford (Republicans)	5.7	6.4
1977–80	Carter (Democrat)	6.4	9.8
1981–84	Reagan (Republican)	8.5	5.9

Sources: *Historical Statistics of the United States,* (Washington: Government Printing Office, 1975), I:127, 210
Monthly Labor Review CVIII (March 1985), 73, and (April 1985), 67
Statistical Abstract of the United States 1985 (Washington: Government Printing Office, 1984), 467

However, our immediate concern with Table 12.8 is with the short-term fluctuations. We shall observe the change in each index over the previous administration's level, because each administration could only work with the levels of unemployment and inflation that it inherited.[41] It is clear that in nearly every instance, Democrats were better at holding down unemployment and Republicans more successful at combating inflation. Under Republicans Eisenhower and Reagan, unemployment rose over their predecessors' levels while inflation fell; under the Democratic Kennedy and Johnson administrations, unemployment held steady while inflation rose. Jimmy Carter's Democratic administration saw increases in both phenomena, but, as expected, inflation rose more than unemployment did. The only exception in the table was the Republican era of Nixon and Ford, when inflation shot up more than unemployment. This was probably due the inflation caused by the war in Southeast Asia and the oil exporters' embargo.

It appears that the levels of unemployment and inflation really are affected by the party of the president, while the level of social spending is much less influenced by the party in control in the White House and Congress.

THE SIGNIFICANCE OF PARTY DIFFERENCES

We have discovered that large numbers of Americans perceive differences, especially on social class, between the parties; the masses of partisans differ ideologically, especially on class-related issues, although other demographic cleavages seem to divide them more than class does; outside the South, the parties attract business and labor allies at widely diverging rates; members of Congress from different parties vote differently, especially on class-related issues; and the parties seem to produce different levels of unemployment and inflation. On the other hand, most of their platform pledges do not offer a choice to the public, although those that do offer a choice tend to concern class-related issues; and parties seem less influential than long-term trends in determining the level of social spending.

In general, then, there are quite a few real differences between the parties within the context of liberal capitalism. Throughout this chapter I have been setting aside the broad context in which both parties operate, and this tends to obscure their similarities. Let us now recall that they are both parties of liberal capitalist values and corporate capitalist reality. Even when they disagree, it is often over the best way to promote capitalism. For example, some of the liberal Democrats who were most ardent in arguing for a larger federal government at the time of the Kennedy administration claimed that a bigger government could more effectively compete with the Soviets in the cold war.[42]

The best way to think of the differences between the parties is to bear in mind the concepts of accumulation and legitimacy.[43] Captialism requires that business firms accumulate sufficient funds for investment, and over time the government is called upon more and more to augment the resources of the private economy, whether through its own investment (for example, in transportation facilities), its policies (tax breaks and restrictions on imports), its contracts (the military establishment), and sometimes out-and-out financial aid (Lockheed Aircraft, Chrysler). At the same time the government must keep the rest of the population satisfied that the system is legitimate, that Uncle Sam does not spell his name with a dollar sign and that everyone gets an even break from the American system. In particular, the lower classes must be kept from the kind of despair that can lead to revolution. Therefore government must persuade people to accept the dominant American values and provide social services for those in need. Accumulation for those on top, legitimacy for those on the bottom.

To a great extent, the major American political parties have differed on which of these two imperatives they choose to emphasize. Since the late 1800s the Republicans have diligently sought to provide for the needs of business. The Reagan administration's policies exemplify this: tax breaks for the upper classes, reductions in many social programs, a tolerant eye toward corporate mergers and anti-labor practices, and a foreign policy that both lines the pockets of military contractors and seeks to repress foreign regimes and revolutionary movements that are unsympathetic to American investment abroad. None of this has been out of keeping with Republican policy for many decades. On the other hand, the demand for legitimacy has limited some of Reagan's excesses to a greater degree than if he had totally free rein.

The Democrats, on the other hand, have since the 1930s laid greater emphasis on legitimizing social programs than the Republicans have. They are "the party of the bigger Band-Aid."[44] Although Table 12.6 showed that the rate of increase in spending on such programs seems independent of which party is in power, there is no question that Democratic administrations, notably those of Franklin Roosevelt and Lyndon Johnson, were responsible for creating those programs. At the same time the dominance of liberal capitalist values and the needs of accumulation keep the Democrats from producing an all-out welfare state of the sort found in Western Europe. Democrats continue to restrain their liberal tendencies by wooing the confidence of business and supporting modified versions of the Republican foreign policy, as Mondale did in 1984. In the case of Jimmy Carter, this produced an administration that did not seem to be able to decide what its priorities were. A Republican administration, such as that of Ronald Reagan, which comes down foursquare on the side of accumulation, looks far more decisive.

In this context it is interesting that the parties are seen by so many people in class terms. This has been a recurring theme of this chapter. While parties in much of the rest of the capitalist world present to the voters genuine ideological and class differences, with some representing socialism and the working classes and others speaking for capitalism and the upper classes, American parties offer only a pale imitation. Even so, these muted differences have become the basis of whatever distinctions exist between the Democrats and Republicans. This shade of difference helps to justify the existence of the party system in the eyes of those voters who still take it seriously.

If corporate capitalism is to survive, the needs of both accumulation and legitimacy must be met, providing a role for both parties. If such a role did not exist, the system would have to create it. Conservatives are especially unlikely to understand this. When they rant and rave about liberals being insufficiently patriotic or insufficiently devoted to capitalism, they show their failure to understand that by helping to legitimize American politics, liberals help ensure the the survival of the system that conservatives hold so dear.

Further Reading

Major studies of the differences between partisans and the public's perceptions of interparty differences include Gerald M. Pomper, *Voters' Choice* (New York: Dodd, Mead, 1975), 166–185, and Richard J. Trilling, *Party Image and Electoral Behavior* (New York: John Wiley & Sons, 1976). Useful analyses of platforms and campaigns include Gerald M. Pomper with Susan S. Lederman, *Elections in America*, 2nd ed. (New York: Longman, 1980), 128–178; and Benjamin I. Page, *Choices and Echoes in Presidential Elections* (Chicago: Univ. of Chicago Press, 1978). A classic account of voting patterns in Congress is Edward V. Schneier, Jr.'s revised edition of Julius Turner, *Party and Constituency* (Baltimore: The Johns Hopkins Univ. Press, 1970). Finally, no study of American party differences on economic policy would be complete without Edward R. Tufte, *Political Control of the Economy* (Princeton, N.J.: Princeton Univ. Press, 1978).

The student who is particularly interested in the partisan impact on economic policy should consult some of the cross-national studies that have been produced in recent years, notably the collection in Francis G. Castles, ed., *The Impact of Parties* (Beverly Hills: Sage Publications, 1982).

Notes

1. See, for example, Ferdinand Lundberg, *The Rich and the Super-Rich* (New York: Lyle Stuart, 1968), 41.

2. Gerald M. Pomper, *Voter's Choice* (New York: Dodd, Mead, 1975), 170–173, 177–178. For a criticism of Pomper's method see Michael Margolis, "From Confusion to Confusion," *American Political Science Review* LXXII (March 1977), 31–43; see also the exchange between Pomper and Margolis in the same *Review* LXXII (December 1977), 1596–1597.

3. Richard J. Trilling, *Party Image and Electoral Behavior* (New York: John Wiley & Sons, 1976), 74–78.

4. See, for example, Lloyd A. Free and Hadley Cantril, *The Political Beliefs of Americans* (New York: Simon & Schuster, 1968), 41–50; and " 'Conservatives' Share 'Liberal' View," the *New York Times*, 22 January 1978, sec. 1, pp. 1, 30.

5. Trilling, *Party Image*, 63–68.

6. Robert Benchley, "Political Parties and Their Growth," in his *20,000 Leagues Under the Sea or David Copperfield* (Garden City, N.Y.: Blue Ribbon Books, 1946), 4.

7. See Robert R. Alford, *Party and Society* (Chicago: Rand-McNally, 1965); and Ivor Crewe, "Electoral Participation," in David Butler, Howard R. Penniman, and Austin Ranney, eds., *Democracy at the Polls* (Washington and London: American Enterprise Institute, 1981), 255.

8. See also Everett Carll Ladd, Jr., *Where Have All the Voters Gone?* (New York: W. W. Norton, 1978), 9.

9. James L. Sundquist, *Politics and Policy* (Washington: The Brookings Institution, 1968), 387; and Sundquist, *Dynamics of the Party System* (Washington: The Brookings Institution, 1973), 216–217. For confirmation of Sundquist's argument about the mass base of the parties, see Everett Carll Ladd, Jr., with Charles D. Hadley, *Transformations of the American Party System* (New York: W. W. Norton, 1975), 226–259.

10. Benjamin I. Page, *Choices and Echoes in Presidential Elections* (Chicago: Univ. of Chicago Press, 1978), 63.

11. See, for example, Everett Carll Ladd, Jr., and Charles D. Hadley, *Political Parties and Political Issues* (Beverly Hills: Sage Publications, 1973); Pomper, *Voters' Choice*, 167–170, 173–178; and Page, *Choices and Echoes*, 66–68, 100.

12. The first proof of this was offered by Herbert McClosky, Paul J. Hoffmann, and Rosemary O'Hara, "Issue Conflict and Consensus Among Party Leaders and Followers," *American Political Science Review* LIV (June 1960), 406–427. Their findings have often been corroborated; a recent example can be found in the *New York Times*, 24 August 1984, p. A10.

13. Theodore J. Lowi, *The End of Liberalism* (New York: W. W. Norton, 1969), 72; his emphasis.

14. Page, *Choices and Echoes*, 63.

15. In this chapter, Southerners will be defined as those who live in any of the eleven former Confederate states or in Kentucky.

16. Gerald M. Pomper with Susan S. Lederman, *Elections in America*, 2nd ed. (New York: Longman, 1980), 128–178.

17. Pomper, *Elections in America*, 134–135, 140–143. The 1984 platforms can be found in the *Congressional Quarterly Almanac, 1984* (Washington: Congressional Quarterly, 1985), 41-B to 62-B, and 73-B to 106-B. These sentences are from 41-B, 42-B, 73-B, 74-B, and 78-B.

18. Pomper, *Elections in America*, 150–151, 158.

19. Pomper, *Elections in America*, 140–143, 146.

20. Alan D. Monroe, "American Party Platforms and Public Opinion," *American Journal of Political Science* XXVII (February 1983), 35.

21. Pomper, *Elections in America*, 169.

22. Benjamin Ginsberg, "Critical Elections and the Substance of Party Conflict," *Midwest Journal of Political Science* XVI (November 1972), 603–625; and Ginsberg, "Elections and Public Policy," *American Political Science Review* LXX (March 1976), 41–49. See also Walter Dean Burnham, *Critical Elections and the Mainsprings of American Politics* (New York: W. W. Norton, 1970), 6–7.

23. Pomper, *Elections in America*, 169. See also Monroe, "American Party Platforms," 36–38.

24. Pomper, *Elections in America*, 173.

25. The classic explanation of this is Anthony Downs, *An Economic Theory of Democracy* (New York: Harper & Row, 1957), chapter 8.

26. Page, *Choices and Echoes,* 91–98, 118–142.

27. See the *New York Times* articles dated 8 July 1984, sec. 4, p. 4; 22 July 1984, sec. 1, p. 20; 31 August 1984, p. A12; and 11 September 1984, p. A24.

28. Alan Tonelson, "Mondale's G.O.P. Latin Policy," the *New York Times,* 24 August 1984, p. A25; see also news articles in that paper dated 12 September 1984, p. B9; 18 September 1984, p. A1; and 20 September 1984, p. B20.

29. See for example Arlen J. Large, "Rating Your Congressman," *Wall Street Journal,* 26 January 1968, p. 10.

30. See Keith T. Poole and R. Steven Daniels, "Ideology, Party, and Voting in the U.S. Congress, 1959–1980," *American Political Science Review* LXXIX (June 1985), 373–399.

31. Edward V. Schneier, Jr.'s revised edition of Julius Turner, *Party and Constituency* (Baltimore: The Johns Hopkins Univ. Press, 1970), 103–104; W. Wayne Shannon, *Party, Constituency and Congressional Voting* (Baton Rouge: Louisiana State Univ. Press, 1968), 94; and William Schneider, "Politics of the '80s Widens the Gap Between the Two Parties in Congress," *National Journal,* 1 June 1985, 1268–1282.

32. See also Helmut Norpoth, "Explaining Party Cohesion in Congress," *American Political Science Review* LXX (December 1976), 1156–1171.

33. Richard Rose, *Do Parties Make a Difference?* (Chatham, N.J.: Chatham House Publishers, 1980), 141.

34. See Christopher Hewitt, "The Effect of Political Democracy and Social Democracy on Equality in Industrial Societies," *American Sociological Review* XLII (June 1977), 450–464; David R. Cameron, "The Expansion of the Public Economy," *American Political Science Review* LXXII (December 1978), 1243–1261; Edward R. Tufte, *Political Control of the Economy* (Princeton, N.J.: Princeton Univ. Press, 1978), 97–98; Valerie Bunce, "Changing Leaders and Changing Policies," *American Journal of Political Science* XXIV (August 1980), 390; Bunce, *Do New Leaders Make a Difference?* (Princeton, N.J.: Princeton Univ. Press, 1981), 85; and Francis G. Castles, "The Impact of Parties on Public Expenditure," in Francis G. Castles, ed., *The Impact of Parties* (Beverly Hills: Sage Publications, 1982), 21–96. Cameron concluded that parties are important but that a nation's degree of involvement in international trade is even more important as a determinant of its public spending.

35. E. S. Kirschen *et al., Economic Policy in Our Time* (Amsterdam: North-Holland Publishing, 1964); Hewitt, "Effect of Political Democracy;" Robert W. Jackman, "Socialist Parties and Income Inequality in Western Industrial Societies," *Journal of Politics* XLII (February 1980), 135–149; David R. Cameron, "Political, Public Policy, and Economic Inequality," (unpublished, March 1981); and J. Corina M. van Arnhem and Geurt J. Schotsman, "Do Parties Affect the Distribution of Incomes?" in Castles, ed., *The Impact of Parties,* 283–364.

36. Tufte, *Political Control,* 84–85; Douglas A. Hibbs, Jr., "The Mass Public and Macroeconomic Performance," *American Journal of Political Science* XXIII (November 1979), 715; and M. Stephen Weatherford, "Economic Conditions and Electoral Outcomes," *American Journal of Political Science* XXII (November 1978), 917–938.

37. Tufte, *Public Control,* 76–77.

38. *New York Times*/CBS News press release dated October 1982, 7.

39. Tufte, *Political Control,* 72–75, 78–83, 101–103. Douglas A. Hibbs, Jr., in "Political Parties and Macroeconomic Policy," *American Political Science Review* LXXI (December 1977), 1467–1487, concluded that capitalist nations that are governed by parties of the left are better at controlling unemployment and worse at stemming inflation than those governed by parties of the right. His methodology has been criticized by James L. Payne in the same *Review* LXXIII (March 1979), 181–185, and Hibbs's response is on 185–190. Manfred G. Schmidt, in "The Role of the Parties in Shaping Macroeconomic Policy," in Castles, ed., *Impact of Parties,* 97–176, found no relationship between parties and unemployment or inflation.

40. I have not included Truman's first term, as inflation was unusually high due to the relaxation of the price controls imposed during World War II.

41. Economic policies take time to go into effect, and you may wonder why I did not incorporate a time lag into Table 12.8. When a two-year time lag was added, the results of the table remained the same.

42. See, for example, John Kenneth Galbraith, *The Affluent Society* (Boston: Houghton Mifflin, 1958), 161–180, especially 178; and Seymour E. Harris, *The Economics of the Political Parties* (New York: Macmillan, 1962), 342–344, 348–349.

43. See, for example, James O'Connor, *The Fiscal Crisis of the State* (New York: St. Martin's Press, 1973), and Claus Offe, "Advanced Capitalism and the Welfare State," *Politics and Society* II (Summer 1972), 479–488.

44. I am indebted to my colleague Wayne Shannon for this formulation.

13

What Will be the Future of American Party Politics?

As we approach the end of this excursion into the American party system, it is natural to wonder where the political system is heading. In this endeavor, I am not concerned with which party will win the next election or who the next presidential nominees will be. Far more important than such questions are the long-term structural changes in American society and politics, and what the consequences will be for party development. In a sense this is the sequel to chapter 5, which looked at past developments in the American party system in the context of broader socioeconomic changes. Now we shall apply similar questions to the very recent past and the present, hoping to infer from this investigation some guideposts to the future.

Looming over this chapter will be two questions that have been raised by social commentators again and again through the years: has the United States undergone a partisan realignment, and is the United States moving to the right? These subjects seem to have a special bite in this "age of Reagan," and we shall explore them in a number of ways. Again, keep in mind that we are less concerned with short-term fluctuations than with ways in which the political system may be *structured* toward increasing Republicanism or conservatism, regardless of the results of a particular election or the fate of a particular administration.

REALIGNMENT OR DEALIGNMENT?

Much has been written in the past several years about the so-called "Reagan revolution," and whether it means long-term fundamental changes in American politics and public policy. Has the Reagan administration inaugurated a new era in American history, establishing a framework within which future administrations must work, or will Ronald Reagan be remembered as a president who was popular but, in the long run, no more significant than any other?

To political parties specialists, the question boils down to one of realignment. In chapter 5 I discussed realignments, those periodic eras of instability in which the parties and voters shift to new partisan allegiances around new issues and new political institutions, engendering new political eras. Ever since the 1950s, when scholars began to analyze realignments systematically, politicians, pundits, and professors have been counting down until the next realignment. Every time the Republican party enjoys a victory—when Richard Nixon was elected president in 1968, when he was reelected in a landslide in 1972, when the Republicans recaptured the White House and Senate in 1980, and when Reagan was overwhelmingly reelected in 1984—some see signs of that long-awaited new era of Republican dominance. They see the Republicans winning unprecedentedly high proportions of such traditionally Democratic constituencies as white Southerners, blue-collar workers, and Roman Catholics, thereby carving out a majority of the electorate.[1]

Has Ronald Reagan demonstrated the success of that strategy, and will his party hold on to those constituencies long after he leaves office? Table 3.3 in chapter 3 showed that the Republican proportion of the electorate in 1984 was higher than it had been in more than twenty years, and other surveys in 1984 put the Republicans nearly neck-and-neck with the Democrats. Even more troubling to the Democrats is the fact that a *New York Times*/CBS News poll in the fall of 1984 found that "53 percent of persons 18–29 years of age either clearly identified with the GOP or leaned to it, compared to just 37 percent for the Democrats."[2] If new voters are becoming Republican, this could mean continuing Republican growth over the foreseeable future. These facts, combined with the Republican advantage in the past five presidential elections shown in chapter 10, has led some political scientists to write of a "Republican presidential majority."[3]

As suggestive as such trends are, other facts have thrown cold water on them. Perhaps the most important is that the decline of parties makes realignments less likely. But there are specific indicators of Republican weakness that call into question the whole idea of realignment. First, those Republican presidential victories were by narrow margins in most states. Second, for all those trends cited earlier, most surveys indicate that the American people are still more likely to describe themselves as Democrats than as Republicans. Third, Democrats still hold substantial edges in the House of Representatives, governorships, and state legislatures. After Franklin Roosevelt's reelection in 1936, the Democrats claimed three-fourths of the members of Congress and state governors and two-thirds of state legislators; after Reagan's reelection in 1984, the Republicans held only a narrow majority in the Senate and were considerably outnumbered in the House of Representatives and on the state level; indeed, on that day the electorate reduced the Republican majority in the Senate by two seats. This is why political scientists shrewdly write of a Republican *presidential* majority.

Of course, optimistic Republicans could still argue that the real gains that their party has made in recent years will soon be translated into a more sweeping realignment. However, there is reason for skepticism. William Adams has shown that the level of Reagan's popularity during his first term was closely correlated with the unemployment rate; the higher the latter, the lower the former.[4] This means that all of the recent trends toward Republicanism could turn around with a downturn in the economy. Perhaps the most fragile reed on which Republican hopes rest is the Republicanism of many young voters. Being new to the electoral process, their allegiances are not set in concrete and can be reversed by reverses in the economy or other events. A good object lesson was the situation in 1964, when the Democrats, by nearly every conceivable measure, were far better off than the Republicans are today; two years later they suffered large losses in Congress and among the governorships, and two years after that they lost the White House.

But I have saved the most important factor for last. Most realignment theorists have acknowledged the significance of the rise in independence. Thirteen years after predicting an "emerging Republican majority," the conservative author Kevin Phillips concluded that "our current volatility suggests a process of *de-alignment.*"[5] Coincident with his suggestion of possible realignment, the political scientist Walter Dean Burnham presented a model of "the onward march of party decomposition."[6] In assessing the state of party politics after the 1984 election, the political scientist Everett Ladd wrote not only of a Republican presidential majority but also of *simultaneous* "dealignment" and a "two-tier electoral system" in which voters vote Republican for the White House and Democratic for lower offices, one of the most obvious signs of the decline of party.[7]

Although Burnham and Ladd have tried to argue that some elements of realignment and some of party decline have been occurring simultaneously, there is a fundamental contradiction between these two phenomena. If we think of parties as competing churches, it is as though one church were trying to convert all the members of a nearby church, and the latter congregation decided to become atheists instead. In a sense, the voters are turning to political atheism—independence—rather than to a firm commitment to either party.

Throughout this book, but especially in chapter 4, I have discussed some of the consequences of this decline of partisanship, and there will be more discussion of it later in this chapter. Party decline is to a substantial extent the result of changes in the condition of corporate capitalism. As low economic growth continues to plague the United States and the rest of the capitalist world, corporations turn more and more to the state to help protect them with policies ranging from lower taxes to rising arms contracts to direct subsidies to higher tariffs. This in turn puts a premium on those political institutions, notably the administrative branch of the state, that can coordinate policies while remaining relatively immune from the fluctuations of public opinion. It also means that those institutions that are less centralized and more fickle, notably legislatures and parties, can contribute far less to the survival of corporate capitalism. Therefore there is no strong incentive for powerful segments of society to reverse their decline.[8] This may be the most important reason not to expect a resurgence of political parties to their previous position of strength.

For proponents of a Reaganite "revolution," this has clear strategic implications. Previous political "revolutions" in the United States were spearheaded by popular forces, and this was demonstrated by the fact that the more frequently elected Congress went over to the new majority before the presidency did. The Republican presidential victory of 1860 was foreshadowed by the Democrats' loss of the House of Representatives in 1854; the Republicans captured Congress in 1894 before winning the presidency in 1896; and the Democrats won control of Congress in 1930 and then won the White House in 1932. However, for Reagan the pattern changed, with only the Senate changing hands, and only at the same time as Reagan's presidential victory. This suggests that Reaganism did not come to power as the result of a growing popular tide, as occurred in realignments in the past. At no time did the Republicans win control of the House or the partisan allegiances of the American people. This, in addition to the weakening of party and Congress, meant that for his "revolution" to have a lasting impact, Reagan would have to rely on factors other than the traditional ones of party and legislature. I shall concentrate on two sets of factors, the first being long-term structural changes that benefit the conservative side of the American political spectrum, and the second being deliberate political action that is concentrated on the less popular institutions of American national government.

A STRUCTURALLY RIGHTWARD TIDE

When people ask if the United States is moving to the right, they usually think of narrowly defined political indicators like the electoral fortunes of the Republican party, how many Americans call themselves conservatives, and opinions on public policy. The Republicans have indeed been enjoying more victories in recent years than previously, and more Americans call themselves conservatives than used to. However, on many issues, particularly "social" issues like abortion and desegregation, as well as spending on education and the military, public opinion has been moving in a more liberal direction lately.

My purpose now is to argue that a nation can move rightward or leftward even if these narrowly political indicators are moving at cross-purposes or if they reverse direction. More fundamental are changes in the economy and social structure that in the long run can strengthen or weaken the various political forces that determine the nation's future. In the United States today the most important of these *structural* changes serve to bolster conservative forces and undercut liberal movements. These trends long predated the "Reagan revolution." Even if the Republican party suffers a string of defeats, even if the public begins to see itself as more and more liberal, and even if public opinion moves consistently leftward, there will be great constraints on the ability of liberals to control the American agenda. What are these structural trends?

Economic changes

At the root of many of the changes are far-reaching shifts in the world economy, whose origins and details are far beyond the scope of this book. For the moment it is sufficient to note that, in contrast to the two decades after the end of the World War II, when the United States dominated much of the world's economy, declining productivity and a worsening balance of trade have combined with the problems of corporate capitalism to cause increasing economic problems at home. This has led directly or indirectly to a number of long-term economic transformations that help conservatives.

With corporate profits on a long-term decline, large corporations are seeking to reduce risk by combining with each other. Scarcely a month goes by without news of one behemoth threatening to engulf and devour another. As a consequence, the percentage of manufacturing assets controlled by the two hundred largest corporations rose from 48 percent in 1950 to 61 percent in 1982.[9] This has brought about a greater concentration of wealth, and therefore a greater conglomeration of political power: in Chapter 4 the uses of that power were demonstrated. In the labor-relations sphere, too, business has been getting the upper hand, and corporations have been increasingly prone to violate labor law and to hire consultants to instruct them how to fight the growth of unions. These trends, combined with higher unemployment, have induced labor unions to reduce bargaining demands and even give back some earlier gains. All of this long predated the Reagan administration and its anti-union policies.[10]

As business has been consolidating its power, the labor movement is on the decline. The figures are stark: one-third of the nonagricultural work force was unionized in 1956, but by 1980 only one-fourth was. To some extent this decline was due to the shrinking social base of organized labor. Blue-collar workers comprised about 40 percent of the American workforce through much of the first half of the twentieth century, but their number dropped to 32 percent of the workforce by 1980.[11] Moreover, partly as a result of anti-union drives by businesses in recent years, unions have been losing a majority of collective bargaining elections, and the workplaces that they have been able to organize are much smaller than those organized in the past.[12]

With a shrinking percentage of the workforce wearing blue collars, unions look to other occupations for members. In recent years there has been an increase in the proportion of service workers in the economy. However, many are already unionized, and others are exceedingly difficult to organize. A case in point is one of the fastest-growing occupations, fast-food workers. The Bureau of Labor Statistics expects a 50 percent increase in the size of this group through the 1980s.[13] These are low-skill, low-paid workers who seem ideal candidates for unionization. However, most of them are young people with rapid job turnover and little interest in the long-term prospects of fast-food workers.

But the occupation group that has been growing the most—it is now a majority of American workers—is white-collar workers. The labor movement has been trying to organize as much of this group as it can. In 1955, for example, 13 percent of union members were white-collar; in 1978, 19 percent were. When employee associations are included with unions, about one out of four members wear white collars.[14] Many white-collar union members are teachers and other government employees; in 1980, government employees were twice as likely to belong to unions as workers in the private sector.[15] The implications of such a shift in the base of unions are unclear. The sociologist Daniel Bell has suggested that white-collar workers will make unions less class-oriented, less concerned with bread-and-butter issues of wages and fringe benefits and more oriented to "problems of production and the character of work."[16] The economist James O'Connor argues conversely that service-oriented professionals like teachers and social workers might try to use their unions as vehicles for social change, particularly to alter the priorities of government budgets.[17] So far the impact of such attempts has been meager. Perhaps a better indication of the political role of organized labor was the AFL-CIO's role in the 1984 presidential campaign, when though helping Walter Mondale win the Democratic nomination, the union was seen by many voters as a liability. The very fact that labor found it necessary to fight for its favorite in the Democratic primaries shows how much power it has lost; in the 1940s and 1950s, the AFL-CIO never felt it necessary to flex its muscles because any Democrat with a shot at the presidency knew that he had to appease the labor federation.

The consolidation of corporate power and the decline of the power of the labor movement cannot but push the nation's politics to the right.

Geographic shifts

When the dust from the 1980 census had settled, eleven states had gained seats in the House of Representatives and, therefore, votes in the electoral college. The big winners were Florida (four seats), Texas (three), and California (two). In addition, Arizona, Colorado, Nevada, New Mexico, Oregon, Tennessee, Utah, and Washington each gained a seat. The big loser in this reshuffle was New York, which lost five seats; Illinois, Ohio and Pennsylvania lost two each. Moreover, Indiana, Massachusetts, Michigan, Missouri, New Jersey, and South Dakota lost one apiece.

You perhaps noticed that the losers and gainers were distributed not randomly but geographically. Each of the gainers was in the Far West or Southeast. While some have called this part of the nation the Sun Belt, the list of gainers includes states as far north as Oregon and Washington, and so I prefer the less colorful designation of the "South and West." By the same token, each of the losers was in the Northeast or Midwest. This is not a fluke, for it reflects long-term demographic changes. At the height of the New Deal, the Northeast and Midwest controlled 65 percent of the House of Representatives; today, they have 52 percent of the seats. Nor will the trend end with the 1980 census; a congressional agency projects that thirty-eight more seats will shift to the South and West by the end of the century, reducing the Northeast/Midwest total to 43 percent.[18]

This trend can be easily linked to the economic shift described above, notably the transformation of the American economy from the manufacturing sector concentrated in the "rust belt" cities of the Northeast and Midwest to the service sector and high-technology firms, many of which are located elsewhere in the nation. In this context the arms buildup under Reagan is especially sgnificant, with so much of the space and military industries located in such places as California, Texas and Florida.

What are the political consequences of this? Our main concern here is with partisanship, and by nearly any measure the states that have been gaining the most in population are those that are voting more and more Republican. First let's look at presidential elections. At the height of the Democratic ascendancy, Franklin Roosevelt won reelection in 1936 by carrying all but two states. In 1984 Ronald Reagan won reelection with all but one state and the District of Columbia. We can compare in each state both how much better Reagan did than Roosevelt's Republican opponent, and the percentage increase in population of that state from 1940 to 1980. There are statistically more sophisticated ways to make the same point, but this method has the advantage of being easy to understand even if you have not studied statistics.[19] Map 13.1 shows that most of the states whose populations rose at a greater rate than the media also experienced a higher-than-median Republican gain, and all of those states were in the South and West. Similarly, most states with a *lower*-than-average population gain had lower-than-average gains in Republicanism. All but Kentucky were in the Northeast and Midwest.

Congressional elections show the same trend, in Table 13.1. Here the base-line will be the senators and representatives who served with Roosevelt in 1937, and they will be compared with the strongest Republican congressional showings during the Reagan administration, the Senate in 1983 and the House in 1981. In both houses, the greatest Republican gains were in the fastest-growing third of the states, the smallest Republican increases in the slowest-growing third. Again, the South and West saw the largest Republican increases.

Of course, we can overgeneralize about Republicanism and conserva-

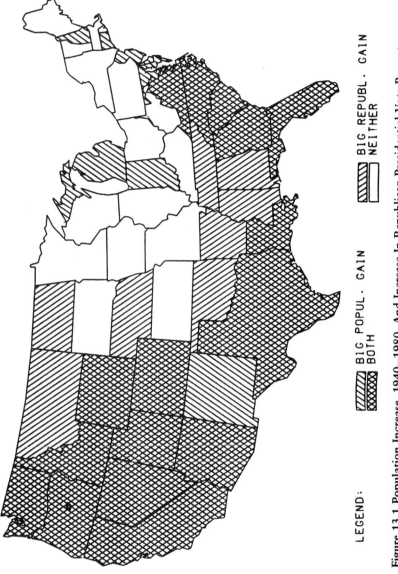

LEGEND:

BIG POPUL. GAIN
BOTH

BIG REPUBL. GAIN
NEITHER

Figure 13.1 Population Increase, 1940–1980, And Increase In Republican Presidential Vote Percentage, 1936–1984 SAS/GRAPH

Table 13.1. Changes in the Republican representation in Congress from the height of the New Deal to Reagan's first term, by section and by the percentage of population growth from 1940 to 1980.

I. Senate

	1937	1983	Change
Northeast	33%	46%	+ 13%
Southeast	0	46	+ 46
Midwest	19	58	+ 39
Far West	18	69	+ 51
Fastest-growing third*	16	72	+ 56
Middle-growing third	13	47	+ 34
Slowest-growing third	25	47	+ 22

II. House of Representatives

	1937	1981	Change
Northeast	33%	42%	+ 9%
Southeast	3	37	+ 34
Midwest	24	50	+ 26
Far West	12	49	+ 37
Fastest-growing third*	7	41	+ 34
Middle-growing third	18	47	+ 29
Slowest-growing third	29	44	+ 15

Note: *Alaska and Hawaii are excluded from the lower part of each half of the table. Figures in the table indicate the percentage of Republicans among that group of states' members of Congress.

tism in the South and West. The South is still predominantly Democratic at most levels of government. Moreover, there is no simple correlation between the South and West and conservatism, or the Northeast and Midwest and liberalism. One of the leaders of Republican conservatives, Representative Jack Kemp, represents the suburbs of Buffalo, New York, and some of the most prominent liberal Democrats—Colorado Senator Gary Hart, California Senator Alan Cranston, Arizona Representative Morris Udall—represent some of the fastest-growing parts of the Southwest. But these important exceptions do not nullify the general rule that Republican gains have been greatest where the population has been growing fastest.

By 1984, both parties were trying to capture these fast-growing parts of the nation by appealing to people in "high tech" industries. Reagan made a point of campaigning where computer industries were located, and his "tax reform" proposals of 1985 seemed to give special benefits to that sector of the economy.[20] Gary Hart represented a newer breed of what critics call the "Atari Democrats" and others call "neoliberals." Most analysts of neoliberalism agree that it includes resistance to organized labor, which is concentrated in older industries such as steel and automobiles. Governor Richard Lamm of Colorado lamented that at the 1984 Democratic national convention, the party leaders did not confront organized labor, and Representative Richard Gephardt of Missouri has commented that "many on our side of the equation think that labor wants to go back to 1940 or 1950 and starve out all the high-tech industries and throw billions of dollars into re-creating the 1950s."[21] But as one observer has asked, "Who will look after the rights and needs of American workers, if not their unions?"[22]

To the extent that the nation is perceived as moving to its more conservative locales, and to the extent that older unionized industries are seen as on the way out, politicians will be encouraged to move to the right and ignore labor unions which are one of the few major liberal forces in the nation. These are structural changes that help promote a politics of conservatism.

Social tendencies

It has become commonplace to observe that the egoism of the American people has been taking more pronounced forms in recent decades. The liberalization of sexual mores, the use of psychedelic drugs, greater marital instability, and the resort to psychological fads aimed at personal "liberation" are among the trends that allegedly constitute a "culture of narcissism."[23] There is nothing necessarily inconsistent about such trends and the development of a social consciousness, but the pervasive individualism and egoism of American society lead too many to concentrate on the gratification of the self rather than concern for others. "Looking out for number one" and "What's in it for me?" are watchwords of a society that is losing the ability to share love and community. The political equivalent of these slogans is "Are you better off than you were four years ago?" implying that all we seek in a candidate is someone whose policies will line our pockets. To this extent, the new egoism plays right into the hands of politicians who want us to forget about social responsibility.

This trend dovetails with another that has been widely noticed by political analysts, the sharp rise in people's distrust of government. Table 13.2 shows the dramatic figures, indicating that distrust of government reached a peak in the 1970s; while this feeling has declined since then, Americans are still far less trustful of government than they were two or three decades ago. While some lament this trend as a sign of the alienation of the American people,[24] we might interpret it as an indication of the growing sophistication of the population. For example, a theme of this book is that the proposition that the government is "run by a few big

Table 13.2. Trends in distrust of government, 1958–1984.

A) "Would you say the government is pretty much run by a few big interests looking out for themselves or that it is run for the benefit of all people?"

Percentage saying "A few big interests":
1964: 29%	1980: 70%	1984: 55%

B) "How much of the time do you think you can trust the government in Washington to do what is right—just about always, most of the time, or only some of the time?"

Percentage saying 'Some" or 'None" of the time:
1958: 23%	1980: 73%	1984: 54%

C) "Do you think that people in the government waste a lot of money we pay in taxes, waste some of it, or don't waste very much of it?"

Percentage saying "A lot of money":
1958: 43%	1980: 78%	1984: 65%

Note: Question A was asked for the first time in 1964.
Sources: Warren E. Miller, Arthur H. Miller, and Edward J. Schneider, *American National Election Studies Data Sourcebook 1952–1978* (Cambridge: Harvard University Press, 1980), 257–258; and the 1980 and 1984 surveys of the Center for Political Studies of the University of Michigan

interests looking out for themselves" is not as far from reality as conventional wisdom would have it, and if the masses are increasingly prone to that perception, then they should be complimented for their growing perspicacity. However, instead of organizing to change that situation, most people adopt a cheap cynicism about politics and turn to other matters. One consequence is the decline in voter turnout.

Again, the American parties help to perpetuate the system, by depriving the disaffected citizenry of alternatives to cynicism. A vigorous party system would include parties that provide constructive alternatives to the status quo; instead, Americans too frequently respond to the failings of the political system by dropping out. This turning inward is fully consistent with the egoistic impulse of American culture. As egoism increases and parties decline, the system faces less and less challenge.

Political trends

Several of the most important political developments discussed in this book also benefit conservatives. The decline in voter turnout outlined in chapter 7 is concentrated among the lower classes, depriving liberals of a significant part of their traditional constituency. The decline of parties weakens one of the greatest potential institutional props for lower-class interests, as discussed in chapter 4. In each case, the trend only exacerbates a long-standing feature of American politics: the gap in participation between rich and poor, and the failure of parties to differ substantially in ideological and class terms.

Another political trend to describe takes us back to the subject of realignment. Some authors use realignment to describe a situation in which the minority party becomes the majority party; indeed, this was how I used the term earlier in this chapter when I argued that there is no certainty that the Republicans will soon be the majority party. But this may be too strict a definition. Read literally, the word realignment simply means a change in the alignment, and such a change need not mean that the old majority party becomes the new minority party; it could be a fundamentally altered majority party. Or, there may be no clear majority party. I believe that this was the case throughout much of the nineteenth century, when Democrats and Whigs competed nationally on a more or less equal footing and Democrats and Republicans contested a series of remarkably close presidential elections from 1876 through 1888. If we forget about which party is ahead, we might find some important changes in the alignment of various social groups.

Indeed, as Table 13.3 shows, we do find such changes over the past third of a century. In constructing this table I sought an indicator of partisanship that had been asked in public opinion surveys over a long period of time, and one that would minimize the effects of the rise in independents. For want of a better measure, I chose to examine how people identified their partisanship, and excluded those who, even after the interviewer probed their feelings for some preference for one party or the other, steadfastly claimed to be independents. Therefore the figures in the table represent the people who either claimed a party identification (Democratic or Republican) or said they were independents who "leaned" toward one of the major parties. In each year, they represented at least 85 percent of the American people. Of those people, the table shows what percentage were Democrats.

In the first part of the table, we can see that the percentage of blacks who were Democrats rose dramatically from the 70 percent range to the 87-to-97 percent range, beginning in 1964. In most years a clear majority of whites identified themselves as Democrats, although in 1984 whites divided evenly between the parties. The net effect of an increased Democratic affiliation for blacks and a relatively constant party allegiance for whites has been a major increase in the differences between the races, shown in the third line of Table 13.3.

If the races are growing farther apart in their partisan affiliations, what is happening to geographic section as a correlate of white partisanship? The high level of support for the Democrats among white Southerners in the 1950s and early 1960s resulted in major differences between the sections, but beginning in 1968 white Southerners began to draw away

Table 13.3. Percent Democratic of all those who expressed a party preference, either by calling themselves Democrats or Republicans or by calling themselves independents who "leaned" toward a party, 1952 to 1984.

	1952	1956	1960	1964	1968	1972	1976	1980	1984
Blacks	79%	74%	70%	91%	97%	87%	95%	91%	89%
Whites	61	56	57	64	58	57	55	57	50
Difference	18	18	13	27	39	30	40	34	39
Southern whites	81˙	74	74	74	68	63	63	61	55
Non-southern whites	54	49	50	60	55	54	51	55	49
Difference	27	25	24	14	13	9	12	6	6
All below this line are non-Southern whites:									
Class self-identification:									
Working class	65	57	58	72	62	60	60	62	55
Middle class	39	38	36	50	48	48	43	49	43
Difference	26	19	22	22	14	12	17	13	12
Population of place of residence:									
50,000 plus	62	57	56	65	61	58	55	66	51
Under 50,000	50	44	46	58	52	53	49	51	47
Difference	12	13	10	7	9	5	6	15	4
Roman Catholic	72	69	79	76	72	69	67	67	58
Protestant	43	37	35	51	44	43	41	45	39
Difference	29	32	44	25	28	26	26	22	19

Source: National surveys, University of Michigan Center for Political Studies

from that party. The net effect is that just as the races have been *diverging* in their partisanship, among whites the sections have been *converging*.[25]

Convergence is also the picture in the lower parts of the table, which in order to set aside the effects of race and section look only at non-Southern whites. Partisan divisions between the classes, urban and rural dwellers, and the major religions have been shrinking.[26] In short, the American party system seems to be polarized more around race than around any other major social dimension. Table 13.3 shows that in 1952, religion, section and class produced the largest cleavages in partisanship; by 1984, racial cleavages were far and away the most pronounced. As the races diverge, various groups of whites converge.

Why has the American electorate undergone these changes? Chapter 5 indicated that during the New Deal blacks became attracted to the Democratic party in large numbers, due in part to the Roosevelt administration's working-class-oriented policies and in part to gestures of racial liberalism on the part of some prominent New Dealers. However, many blacks retained their traditional Republican allegiance, and this internal division gave blacks a newfound political status as a "swing group" in many northern states. From the 1940s through 1960, both parties tried to woo black voters with the rhetoric of civil rights. During the same period, and partly for that reason, white Southerners were beginning to deviate from Democratic voting in presidential elections, most notably in their support of Strom Thurmond's third-party candidacy in 1948 and in the capture of several southern states by Republicans Eisenhower and Nixon from 1952 to 1960. This put both major parties through the gyrations of trying to appeal both to blacks and to white Southerners. In 1960, for example, Democratic nominee John Kennedy chose a Southern running mate, Lyndon Johnson, but also wooed the black vote by telephoning Coretta King when her husband, Martin Luther King, Jr., was sentenced to hard labor in Georgia; Republican nominee Richard Nixon accepted a relatively liberal civil rights plank in the party platform but repudiated his running mate's promise to include a black in the cabinet.

After winning that election with the crucial support of black voters, Kennedy moved very cautiously on civil rights for most of his administration.[27] It was more than two years after taking office and only under the pressure of an increasingly militant black community and in response to violence (some by the police) perpetrated against black demonstrators in the South, that Kennedy mobilized his administration's full political resources in support of a meaningful civil rights bill. When he died several months later, his successor Lyndon Johnson made the bill a top priority and saw it passed in 1964.

As the national Democratic party was for the first time in its history embracing the cause of civil rights, the Republican party was for the first time in its history turning its back on the same cause. In an effort to take full advantage of the wedge that had been driven into the southern electorate by the Eisenhower and Nixon campaigns, the Republicans in 1964 nominated Senator Barry Goldwater, who had voted against the civil rights bill championed by Kennedy and Johnson. Since that time all Republican presidential nominees—Nixon, Ford, and Reagan—have expressed opposition to many of the goals of the civil rights movement, while their Democratic counterparts—Humphrey, McGovern, Carter, and Mondale—have been more supportive of those goals. This explains the clear break in black partisanship shown in Table 13.3. Similarly, the decline in the white southern attachment to the Democrats dates from the middle 1960s as well, notably in 1968 with George Wallace's third-party campaign that was based primarily on white racial fears. Only once since 1964 has a Democratic presidential nominee (Jimmy Carter) carried the South, and that was only because of the sizable black vote there.

In no national campaign since 1964 has civil rights been as salient an issue as it was then, but racial issues such as busing and affirmative action have persisted, and since then race has been lurking as a silent dimension behind many other issues. These issues have included "law and order" and welfare. Blacks were one of the very few voting groups whose backing of Reagan declined from 1980 to 1984, while his white support rose by about eleven percent over the same period.[28] This is only the most recent demonstration that the races now march to different drummers in American politics.

Given the relatively small numbers and small turnout of black Americans, and given the phenomenon of lower-class whites dropping out of the electorate, it is not surprising that the major parties aim their appeals at middle-class whites. Therefore their campaigns have an increasingly uniform impact on geographic, economic and religious subgroups of whites, as shown in Table 13.3. This is the essence of the realignment that the nation has been undergoing in the past couple of decades. Although it will not necessarily benefit the Republicans, as recent congressional and gubernatorial election results confirm, it is conservative because it occupies the electorate's mind with matters other than class. Those lower-class whites who participate in the political system are encouraged to respond to their racial fears rather than to ally with blacks of their social class. Therefore with most lower-class people simply out of politics, and the rest diverted from class concerns, upper-class interests continue to go unchallenged.

THE MOBILIZATION OF THE RIGHT

No conservative movement worthy of the name would be content to sit back and watch these trends slowly accrue to its benefit. Besides the obvious electoral efforts expended by conservative candidates and their supporters, there have been conscious efforts to change the framework of American politics in ways that will make it harder to revive the liberal agenda in the future. They include increasing business involvement in politics, which began long before the 1980 election, and efforts since that year by the Reagan administration to lock the agenda of the right into the political structure.

The corporate juggernaut

In chapter 4 I discussed how, as political parties decline, interest groups rise, and also how the American interest group process is weighted toward business and other conservative groups. In the 1970s and 1980s this advantage has increased. One critical journalist has written of

... a major ideological shift in Congress. Business has played a key role in this shift, using not just PAC contributions but increasingly sophisticated grass-roots lobbying mechanisms, the financing of a sympathetic intellectual community, and the expenditure of somewhere in the neighborhood of $1 billion annually on institutional advertising.[29]

Business people make no bones about this. Said one PAC manager, "We were set up because management had a strong belief that business has a right and obligation to change the direction of government"—an interesting twist on democratic theory.[30] The head of the Chase Manhattan Bank said in 1980, "We must take our message directly into American homes, to the people, to the ultimate deciders of our society's fate. We need nothing less than a major and sustained effort in the marketplace of ideas."[31] A survey of business elites found that they saw media elites as the "most influential group in America," and wanted to supplant them.[32]

There is more than impressionistic evidence that major business people have mobilized to make government even more sympathetic to their desires than it had been. A survey of corporate executives published in 1980 found heavy majorities favoring expressing their political views to the public, to employees, to stockholders, to customers, and to suppliers; with executives' resources, this propagandizing could be very effective. It also found that a majority of corporations surveyed had programs to propagandize employees, stockholders, retirees and/or customers, and that very few of them had had such programs before 1970. In chapter 4 I cited a study of Washington lobbyists that showed a dramatic increase in the extent to which corporations engaged in such activities. "Electoral politics, so to speak, has come out of the corporate closet and is now recognized as a legal and appropriate activity for business."[33]

Politicizing employees and others is one of the newer forms of corporate politicking; another is organizing such people in congressional districts for more effective grass-roots lobbying. This constituent pressure plays on the great desire of members of Congress to get reelected.[34] Perhaps the most novel forms of political influence are the attempts to bend the climate of public opinion into an even more probusiness direction. William Simon, a former secretary of the treasury, has urged businesses to "cease the mindless subsidizing of colleges and universities whose departments of economics, government, politics and history are hostile to capitalism and whose faculties will not hire scholars whose views are otherwise."[35] Simon conveniently neglected to name any American school that fits this description, probably because none exists. He continued by arguing that "business money must flow away from the media which serves as megaphones for aniticapitalist opinion;"[36] again, he failed to mention specifics.

Whatever the truth of Simon's flamboyant assertions about schools and media, business has taken action on both fronts. Millions of dollars have been poured into such conservative research firms as the American Enterprise Institute, the Heritage Foundation, and the Hoover Institution, which provide lavish platforms for appropriate scholars. To influence the media, businesses have engaged in issue advertising, to the tune of a billion dollars a year in the late 1970s. Such ads are designed to influence public opinion on major issues, and often appear on the editorial pages of major newspapers. Liberal and labor groups cannot match the resources poured into such research outfits and advertising campaigns.[37] Coordinating these many activities are the business networks such as the Business Roundtable, the Chamber of Commerce, the Business Council, and the Conference Board.[38]

It is important to realize the significance of these new patterns of mobilization. No longer do individual firms seek merely to acquire specific gains for their own industry, such as tax benefits or government contracts. This old style of lobbying still goes on, but the newer forms of influence include attempts to promote the interests of corporate capitalism across the board. One's employees, stockholders, and clients do not have to be convinced that the industry needs a new tax loophole, and the independent research firms that a corporation subsidizes are not going to be devoting most of their time advocating the corporation's narrow interests. Rather, the focus of these activities is to propagandize the public about how wonderful capitalism and especially large corporations are, and how even the mild forms of government regulation developed in the 1960s and 1970s are a threat to freedom, prosperity, and everything Americans hold dear. They also aim to strengthen the image of corporations during struggles with labor unions. At a time when the performance of corporate capitalism is weakening, there is a frantic attempt to improve its image.[39]

Since business began to mobilize in these new directions in the 1970s, the nation has experienced the most conservative Democratic president since Grover Cleveland, the most conservative Republican president since Calvin Coolidge, Republican party control of a house of Congress for more than two consecutive years for the first time since the 1920s, and a decline in federal human services spending. While it would be misleading to suggest that the business mobilization was the only, or even the principal, cause of those political developments, nobody can deny that it helped bring about those results.

Reaganizing American politics

As important as these kinds of business activism are, they have one limitation: should a new, more liberal era arise due to a shift of public opinion in a leftward direction and the election of liberal Democrats to the White House and the Congress, business and conservatives in general could find themselves on the defensive in the short run. To counter this possibility, the Reagan administration has been engaged in trying to establish policies and policymakers who will be immune to short-term electoral and legislative fluctuations. While the conservative agenda of the Reagan administration has been no secret,[40] it puts special emphasis on political processes that are relatively immune from popular forces. What are they?

One of the best–known consequences of national policy in the 1980s has been the unprecedented budget deficit stemming from the combination of tax cuts and increased spending on the military. While a full discussion of the economic and political consequences of the deficit would take us far afield, many have noted that one of the most important effects has been to discourage liberals from coming up with new social programs until the deficit is sharply reduced. I recounted in chapter 12 that in 1984 Walter Mondale promised that none of the revenue raised by his proposed tax cut would go to new spending programs. Another fiscal bulwark against liberals is a key feature of the 1981 tax cuts, the "indexing" of the federal income tax. This was a reaction to the phenomenon of inflation leading to wage and salary increases that matched the rise in the cost of living, placing many people in higher tax brackets even though, in constant dollars, they were not earning any more. Tax indexing meant that there would be no more automatic tax increases due to inflation, and its consequence was to limit the amount of money flowing into the federal treasury, which cut off resources for costly new programs if the economy expanded. Finally, the heavy-handed Congressional budget-cutting measures epitomized by the Gramm-Rudman-Hollings Act of 1985 were intended to achieve spending reductions automatically, without the input of popular forces.

High deficits and tax indexing mean that even if the American people were to demand new social programs, and elect a very liberal president and Congress, those officials would have a hard time increasing such spending. This is a prime example of what I mean by conservative reliance not on the shifting sands of party and legislative politics, but on factors beyond the reach of public opinion. For the foreseeable future the deficit and indexation will be a fiscal wall staring liberals in the face.

One structural consequence of Reagan's policies has been a shift of power within the American federal system. As Reagan was planning to reduce federal social programs in 1981, a Republican congressional leader quoted the president as saying that

> . . . it's far easier for people to come to Washington to get their social programs. It would be a hell of a lot tougher if we diffuse them, and send them out to the states. All their friends and connections are in Washington.[41]

In saying this, Reagan was echoing the insight of James Madison, who noted in the tenth *Federalist* that in smaller constituencies (like states) a small number of interests is more likely to be dominant.[42] By the beginning of the second Reagan administration, local political power had shifted to the county level, where public officials are more conservative than in the cities, which had received so much federal support during the Democratic heyday of the 1960s.[43] To redress the emphasis would require a liberal shift of titanic proportions. In addition, Reagan's 1985 proposal to eliminate the federal tax deduction for state and local taxes was a thinly disguised effort to make it harder for sub-federal governments to raise revenues, despite public opinion in those locales.

Earlier in this chapter I mentioned the Reagan policies that favor "high tech" industries. As "smokestack" industries continue to decline, so will the traditional sectors of the labor movement that have been a bulwark for economic liberalism in the United States.

No discussion of the less popular institutions of American government would be complete without including the judiciary. Much attention has been focused on the conservative tenor of the Reagan appointees to the federal bench. However, it is certainly not unusual for a president to appoint like-minded judges. More germane to my argument are two facts, the number of Reagan appointees to the lower federal courts and the age of these Reagan judges. On the first point, according to one scholar, "Reagan will accomplish what only Roosevelt and Eisenhower accomplished during the last half century—naming a majority of the lower federal judiciary in active service."[44] While Supreme Court appointments get most of the attention, lower court appointments are extremely important because those courts decide thousands of cases each year, with only a couple of hundred reaching the Supreme Court.

By and large the judges Reagan has appointed are younger. In his first term, the mean age of Reagan's appeals court appointees was less than the ages of those appointed by his predecessors, although the mean age of his district court appointees was about average.[45] However, there is more to the story: more than 11 percent of those appointees were under forty, compared with less than 5 percent of those named by Lyndon Johnson and Richard Nixon, and Reagan's second-term judicial appointees were even younger.[46] The intention is apparently to lock the federal judiciary into conservative legal interpretation for the foreseeable future. As one Republican senator said of a thirty-one-year-old nominee, "He will be making rulings when I'm dead."[47]

This has been a sample of the kinds of trends that constitute, in Walter Dean Burnham's words, "a *policy* realignment without *electoral* realignment."[48] Favoring certain industries, fostering fiscal policies that have implications for future social spending, promoting friendly levels of government, and locking allies into the judiciary are not new techniques of political power,[49] but in realignments of the past they would have accompanied and augmented power shifts in the voting population. However, major changes in the electorate that could enthrone the Republicans for a generation have not occurred. Therefore it is shrewd of the Reagan administration to put its faith in these less popular processes and institutions to maintain its issue agenda. Shrewd, and altogether typical of a phase of corporate capitalism in which democratic politics is underplayed.

IS THERE A WAY OUT?

This book has portrayed the system of parties and elections in the United States as a buttress for corporate capitalism. I have discussed a political system in which much power is concentrated in the corporate sector, and the public is anesthetized both by a party system that fails to offer the kinds of major ideological and class differences found elsewhere in the world, and by the mass media which concentrate on trivia. This system produces political leaders who lack the means to carry out public purposes effectively, and who too often turn away from serious issues and toward gimmickry that can ensure reelection, whether it be the favors provided by political machines, casework in Congress, or media manipulation in the White House. For the final time, I will stress that this is the result not of any conspiracy, but of people following their perceived self-interest in the incentive structure of a capitalist system. To make matters worse, those Americans who are sympathetic to social change too often devote their energies to a reformism that undercuts the effectiveness of political parties, damaging perhaps the only mechanism which can both represent those with few material resources and organize to carry out social change.

This is a rather grim picture. It ignores the potential for change that exists within all social systems, and particularly within capitalism. For example, I have argued that the capitalist system has been finding it increasingly difficult to maintain both the accumulation of profits and the perpetuation of legitimizing social programs. Ever since Karl Marx, radical authors have stressed the internal contradictions of capitalism, and many have predicted that these contradictions would lead to a socialist revolution and the demise of the capitalist order.[50]

Among the internal contradictions of capitalism that have been stressed by contemporary writers are (1) the contradiction between the political equalitarianism contained in democratic theory and the socioeconomic *in*equalitarianism that is part of capitalist practice; (2) the contradiction between the concentration of economic power in the private sector and the increase in the power of the state as it seeks to assist the private sector; (3) the contradiction between businesses' need for profits and the state's need for tax money in order to assist businesses; and (4) the contradiction between the free-market ideology and the political reality of the positive state, which leads to cynicism about the official ideology ("Get Chrysler off welfare").[51] While all of these contradictions create problems for American capitalism, in my opinion there is no reason to believe that they will bring it crashing down, especially in a socialist revolution. American capitalism has demonstrated remarkable resiliency in perpetuating itself, and there is little more evidence of socialist sympathies among the American people than there ever was. On the other hand, within broad constraints there is a variety of courses that the nation can take. The task of political activists is to take advantage of the stresses within capitalism to exert pressure on the political system to push it in a leftward direction.

The political system reacts not only to structural factors but to popular movements as well. By "reacts" I do not mean any simple and straightforward correlation between what the masses want and what the regime delivers, but certainly politicians do respond to what they perceive their constituents will let them get away with. For decades those on the left have hoped for an alliance among poor people, the labor movement, racial minority groups, segments of the educated middle class (including college professors and students), and issue activists such as feminists, environmentalists, consumerists, and other sympathizers. Such an alliance was helpful in pushing the New Deal as far leftward as it ever got.

A major question for activists is how to organize for change. Three options have been suggested. The first is to work within the Democratic party, which has both the advantage of utilizing a thriving concern that holds the promise of early victories and also the drawback of sharing the party with many who do not have similar goals. Indeed, the history of the party is full of stories of left-wing activists who eventually became more conservative themselves as they adapted to the norms of the party.[52] A second strategy is to work within a minor party. This has the advantage for activists of not risking being co-opted, but the drawback of suffering all the problems of third parties that were discussed in chapter 3. Finally, activists can work within nonparty issue movements such as those mentioned in the previous paragraph. This strategy implies that it is more effective to change public opinion at the grass roots than to elect someone to office who at best will be constrained by the rest of the political system, and at worst will fail to work for the movement's goals. However, critics argue that "grass-roots groups have often dissipated their energies by working at cross-purposes, and have failed to unite behind a common political agenda. Their power is diffused and lacks an institutional context."[53] Perhaps this is another way of saying that in the final analysis there is no substitute for a political party.

We are left with the fact that massive political transformations begin with miniscule, almost imperceptible changes that begin to mushroom when structural factors and political coalitions converge. Until that moment the work is hard and unrewarding, especially for Americans who are conditioned to expect instant gratification in all endeavors. The first step is for people to understand what is going on, to realize how they are being manipulated by the social system to accept political passivity and, therefore, exploitation. Toward that task of understanding, this book has been devoted.

Further Reading

Among the perceptive accounts of recent political developments in the United States are Walter Dean Burnham, *The Current Crisis in American Politics* (New York: Oxford Univ. Press, 1982) and Thomas Byrne Edsall, *The New Politics of Inequality* (New York: W. W. Norton, 1984). Thomas Ferguson and Joel Rogers's edited volume about 1980, *The Hidden Election* (New York: Random House, 1981), includes some useful essays, notably their own and Burnham's.

The reader who wishes to follow developments in radical political thought should consult the academic journals *Politics and Society* and *New Political Science*. More popular journals which provide a variety of perspectives of leftist thought and are informative about current developments include *Dissent, In These Times, The Nation,* and *The Progressive.* They demonstrate how little of the "news that's fit to print" appears in the mainstream news media.

Notes

1. For early arguments of this sort, see M. Stanton Evans, *The Future of Conservatism* (New York: Holt, Rinehart & Winston, 1968); Kevin P. Phillips, *The Emerging Republican Majority* (New Rochelle, N.Y.: Arlington House, 1969); and Walter Dean Burnham, *Critical Elections and the Mainsprings of American Politics* (New York: W. W. Norton, 1970), chapter 6.

2. Everett Carll Ladd, "On Mandates, Realignments, and the 1984 Presidential Election," *Political Science Quarterly* C (Spring 1985), 19. Ladd presents more general survey results on the following page.

3. The term is Ladd's, in "On Mandates," 17. See also Walter Dean Burnham, "The 1984 Election and the Future of American Politics," in Ellis Sandoz and Cecil V. Crabb, Jr., eds., *Election 84* (New York: New American Library, 1985), 230, 246; and J. Merrill Shanks and Warren E. Miller, "Policy Direction and Performance Evaluation," unpublished paper presented to the 1985 annual meeting of the American Political Science Association, 20.

4. William C. Adams, "Recent Fables About Ronald Reagan," *Public Opinion,* October/November 1984, 9.

5. Kevin P. Phillips, *Post-Conservative America* (New York: Random House, 1982), 222; emphasis his.

6. Burnham, *Critical Elections,* chapter 7.

7. Ladd, "On Mandates," 22–24.

8. See, for example, the San Francisco Bay Area Kapitalistate Group, "Political Parties and Capitalist Development," *Kapitalistate* VI (1977), 7–38; and the essays in Claus Offe, *Contradictions of the Welfare State,* edited by John Keane (London: Hutchinson, 1984).

9. *Statistical Abstract of the United States 1982–83* (Washington: Government Printing Office, 1982), 535, and *Statistical Abstract of the United States 1984* (Washington: Government Printing Office, 1983), 538.

10. See, for example, Thomas Byrne Edsall, *The New Politics of Inequality* (New York: W. W. Norton, 1984), 141–178.

11. *Historical Statistics of the United States,* (Washington: Government Printing Office, 1975), I: 127, 139, 176–177; and *Statistical Abstract of the United States 1985* (Washington: Government Printing Office, 1984), 400, 424.

12. Edsall, *New Politics of Inequality,* 153–154.

13. The *New York Times,* 18 September 1983, sec. 1, p. 28.

14. *Statistical Abstract of the United States 1984*, 439.

15. Andrew Hacker, ed., *U/S: A Statistical Portrait of the American People* (New York: Viking Press, 1983), 138.

16. Daniel Bell, *The Coming of Post-Industrial Society* (New York: Basic Books, 1973), 164.

17. James O'Connor, *The Fiscal Crisis of the State* (New York: St. Martin's Press, 1973), 236–256.

18. *Congressional Quarterly Weekly Report*, 15 October 1983, 2153.

19. For the 1936 election returns, see *Congressional Quarterly's Guide to U.S. Elections* (Washington: Congressional Quarterly, 1975), 290. For the 1984 returns, see *Congresional Quarterly Weekly Report*, 13 April 1985, 688. For state populations, see the *Statistical Abstract of the United States 1985* (Washington: Government Printing Office, 1984), 12.

20. See for example "New Threat to Smokestack America," the *New York Times*, 26 May 1985, sec. 3, pp. 1, 7; and Robert B. Reich, "Reagan's Hidden 'Industrial Policy,'" the *New York Times*, 4 August 1985, sec. 3, p. 3.

21. Lamm is quoted in Richard Reeves, "Whose Party Is It, Anyway?" the *New York Times Magazine*, 5 August 1984, p. 14; Gephardt is quoted in Randall Rothenberg, *The Neoliberals* (New York: Simon & Schuster, 1984), 91. See also Edsall, *New Politics of Inequality*, 23–66.

22. Rothenberg, *The Neoliberals*, 246.

23. See Christopher Lasch, *The Culture of Narcissism* (New York: W. W. Norton, 1978), and Robert N. Bellah *et al.*, *Habits of the Heart* (Berkeley: Univ. of California Press, 1985).

24. See, for example, Seymour Martin Lipset and William Schneider, *The Confidence Gap* (New York: The Free Press, 1983).

25. This is consistent with Richard J. Trilling's discovery that the races are polarizing and northern and southern whites have been converging in terms of the perceptions of the parties; see his *Party Image and Electoral Behavior* (New York: John Wiley & Sons, 1976), 95–148.

26. Trilling has found that there has been a decline in class polarization around the parties' images. See *Party Image and Electoral Behavior*, 149–173.

27. See Richard M. Scammon, "How the Negroes Voted," *The New Republic*, 21 November 1960, 8–9, and Bruce Miroff, *Pragmatic Illusions* (New York: David McKay, 1976), 223–270. For a more sympathetic treatment of the Kennedy civil rights record than Miroff's see Carl M. Brauer, *John F. Kennedy and the Second Reconstruction* (New York: Columbia Univ. Press, 1977).

28. See the *New York Times/CBS* News survey data in Michael Nelson, ed., *The Elections of 1984* (Washington: Congressional Quarterly, 1985), 290; the only other group whose backing for Reagan dropped were Jews. On the role of race as a hidden issues in 1972, see Samuel Lubell, *The Future While It Happened* (New York: W. W. Norton, 1973), 13, 66, and 146; and "The 'Secret' Key Issue," the *New York Times*, 6 November 1972, p. 47.

29. Edsall, *New Politics of Inequality*, 139.

30. Quoted in Larry J. Sabato, *PAC Power* (New York: W. W. Norton, 1984), 30.

31. Quoted in Michael Useem, *The Inner Circle* (New York: Oxford Univ. Press, 1984), 87.

32. Stanley Rothman and S. Robert Lichter, "Media and Business Elites," *The Public Interest* 69 (Fall 1982), 118.

33. Edwin M. Epstein, "Business and Labor under the Federal Election Campaign Act of 1971," in Michael J. Malbin, ed., *Parties, Interest Groups, and Campaign Finance Laws* (Washington: American Enterprise Institute, 1980), 146. See David G. Moore, *Politics and the Corporate Chief Executive* (New York: The Conference Board, 1980), 3, 47; and Kay Lehman Schlozman and John T. Tierney, "More of the Same: Pressure Group Activity in a Decade of Change," *Journal of Politics* XLV (May 1983), 361.

34. See chapter 9, above, and Edsall, *New Politics of Inequality*, 109–112, 115–116.

35. William E. Simon, *A Time for Truth* (New York: Reader's Digest Press, 1978), 231.

36. Simon, *Time for Truth*, 232–233.

37. Edsall *New Politics of Inequality*, 116–120.

38. Edsall, *New Politics of Inequality*, 120–128; and Useem, *The Inner Circle*, p. 73.

39. See Edsall, *New Politics of Inequality*, 109–110; and Useem, *The Inner Circle*.

40. A particularly perceptive dicussion is Martin Shefter and Benjamin Ginsberg's "Institutionalizing the Reagan Regime," an unpublished paper presented to the 1985 annual meeting of the American Political Science Association. However, Shefter and Ginsberg do not share my emphasis on the relatively nonpopular political institutions.

41. Quoted by Representative Silvio Conte of Massachusetts, ranking Republican on the House Appropriations Committee, in Steven V. Roberts, "Budget Ax Becomes a Tool of Social Change," the *New York Times*, 21 June 1981, sec. 4, p. 4.

42. See also Grant McConnell, *Private Power and American Democracy* (New York: Alfred A. Knopf, 1966).

43. See 'Counties Gain Power as Federal Influence Wanes," the *New York Times*, 10 November 1985, 1, 34.

44. Sheldon Goldman, "Reaganizing the Judiciary," *Judicature* LXVIII (April–May 1985), 314.

45. Goldman, "Reaganizing the Judiciary," 319, 325.

46. Graeme Browning, "Reagan Molds the Federal Court in His Own Image," *ABA Journal*, August 1985, 61. Note also that Reagan's Supreme Court appointees, Sandra Day O'Connor and Antonin Scalia, were two of the youngest justices since the Civil War.

47. Senator Phil Gramm of Texas, quoted in Browning, "Reagan Molds the Federal Court," 61.

48. Burnham, "The 1984 Election," 250; his emphasis.

49. For a New Deal comparison, see Sidney M. Milkis, "Franklin D. Roosevelt and the Transcendence of Partisan Politics," *Political Science Quarterly* C (Fall 1985), 479–504.

50. For an early treatment of the subject by Marx, see his "Wage Labour and Capital," reprinted in *Karl Marx and Friedrich Engels: Selected Works in Three Volumes* (Moscow: Progress Publishers, 1969), I: 150–175.

51. Among the works that stress such contradictions are O'Connor, *The Fiscal Crisis of the State;* Claus Offe and Volker Ronge, "Theses on the Theory of the State," *New German Critique* VI (Fall 1975), 144–147; and Alan Wolfe, *The Limits of Legitimacy* (New York: The Free Press, 1977).

52. A recent example of the problem is California legislator Tom Hayden. See Dan Walters, "Tom Hayden's Political Prison," *Wall Street Journal*, 16 July 1985, p. 32; and Joan Walsh, "The 'New, Improved' Campaign for Economic Democracy," *In These Times*, 21 August–3 September 1985, 6, 10.

53. John Atlas, Peter Dreier and John Stephens, "Progressive Politics in 1984," *The Nation*, 23–30 July 1983, 82.

Index